Anglo-German relations during the Labour governments 1964–70

MANCHESTER
1824

Manchester University Press

For Elsa, Nick and Tina

Anglo-German relations during the Labour governments 1964–70

NATO strategy, *détente* and European integration

Terry Macintyre

Manchester University Press

Manchester and New York

distributed exclusively in the USA by Palgrave

Published by Manchester University Press
Oxford Road, Manchester M13 9NR, UK
and Room 400, 175 Fifth Avenue, New York, NY 10010, USA
www.manchesteruniversitypress.co.uk

Distributed exclusively in the USA by
Palgrave, 175 Fifth Avenue, New York,
NY 10010, USA

Distributed exclusively in Canada by
UBC Press, University of British Columbia, 2029 West Mall,
Vancouver, BC, Canada V6T 1Z2

British Library Cataloguing-in-Publication Data
A catalogue record for this book is available from the British Library

Library of Congress Cataloging-in-Publication Data applied for

ISBN   978 0 7190 7600 8   *hardback*

First published 2007

16 15 14 13 12 11 10 09 08 07   10 9 8 7 6 5 4 3 2 1

Typeset by R. J. Footring Ltd, Derby
Printed in Great Britain
by Biddles Ltd, King's Lynn

Contents

Preface

The idea for research into the area of Anglo-German relations developed as a result of my experiences as a former member of the Royal Air Force stationed in Germany and, more recently, from an interest in international politics that was stimulated during my studies as an undergraduate at Royal Holloway, University of London. In many ways, the complexity of the relationship between Britain and Germany during the period since 1945 still exists, but what I have tried to do here is to introduce new thinking on the period between 1964 and 1970, to bring out why, in my view, the understanding between the two governments was closer than seems to have been previously assumed. As I make clear in the Introduction, both governments had an interest in developing and maintaining a stronger bilateral relationship at the time, not only for reasons connected with European integration but also for reasons to do with NATO strategy, conventional and nuclear, East–West relations and *détente*. It is through the use and interpretation of primary and supporting secondary material, British and German, in these main areas, that I hope the book makes a different, useful and valid contribution to the study of international relations during an important period of British history.

I have deliberately refrained from any further analysis of the actions and competency of Britain's leading politicians of the day, particularly those of Harold Wilson, on the basis that this is a quite separate debate. The focus instead is on the relationship between the two governments at the time and on policy outcomes rather than personalities. Also, detailed economic comparisons have not been made to any great extent, because the relative performance of the two economies is a matter of fact and is not in dispute.

Acknowledgements

The completion of every academic book depends to a greater or lesser extent on the advice, help and support of others. That is certainly true in this case. The most striking thing about the experience of producing this book was how willing and helpful people were to facilitate my research, and to assist in establishing my views on Anglo-German relations during the 1960s. My thanks should really go far and wide but, in the interests of brevity, I will mention a representative sample here.

The starting point must be Professor Matthew Jones, who, as the academic supervisor of my doctoral thesis, provided the encouragement and expertise that led to its successful completion. I am also grateful to Professor John Young for his comments on the manuscript. I would make specific mention of the contribution made by Sir Roger Jackling, Sir Michael Palliser, Sir Andrew Stark, Sir Oliver Wright and Mr John Adam Watson, who consented to be interviewed and who helped explain aspects of British foreign policy during the period in question. I would like to thank staff at The National Archives (Public Record Office), the German Historical Institute, the Churchill Archives Centre, the Royal United Services Institute and the Royal College of Defence Studies. I was warmly received and generously helped at the Politisches Archiv des Auswärtigen Amts in Berlin, at the Bundesarchiv in Koblenz and at the Stadtarchiv in Höxter; and my thanks are extended to all those involved.

Finally, my thanks go to the staff at Manchester University Press who guided me through the intricacies of preparing this book.

Key events, October 1964 to June 1970

Date	Event
1964	
16 October	First Chinese atomic weapon test
16 October	Election of Harold Wilson's first Labour government, with a majority of five
17 October	Wilson and economic ministers rule out devaluation
26 October	Labour government announces measures to restore economic stability, including a surcharge on imports
21–22 November	Defence conference and meetings at Chequers
7–9 December	Wilson, ministers and officials hold talks in Washington
1965	
21 January	Patrick Gordon Walker, British Foreign Secretary, defeated in Leyton by-election
22 January	Michael Stewart appointed British Foreign Secretary
6–9 March	Wilson visits Berlin and holds talks in Bonn
1 April	Wilson meets French President Charles de Gaulle and Prime Minister Georges Pompidou in Paris
18–28 May	Queen Elizabeth II makes state visit to the Federal Republic of Germany
17–25 June	Commonwealth Prime Ministers' conference in London
20 July	Agreement between Britain and Germany on off-set payments
19 September	Federal German elections; Ludwig Erhard remains Chancellor

1966

7 March	De Gaulle advises US President Lyndon B. Johnson of French withdrawal from NATO's military organisation
25 March	German Peace Note issued
31 March	Wilson's Labour government re-elected, with a majority of ninety-seven
23–25 May	Erhard holds talks in London
10 August	George Brown appointed British Foreign Secretary
11 October	President Johnson announces trilateral talks between the United States, Britain and Germany to report on NATO force levels, including offset payments
29 November	CDU/SPD 'Grand Coalition' under Kurt Georg Kiesinger replaces the Erhard government
30 November	Britain removes import surcharge
13 December	Kiesinger's policy statement stressing importance of French–German understanding and German support for Britain's entry into the EEC
14–16 December	NATO Council initiates Harmel study

1967

16 February	Wilson and Brown visit Bonn for talks about a possible British application for membership of the EEC
6–7 April	First meeting of the NATO Nuclear Planning Group
27–28 April	Agreement in trilateral talks on offset payments to Britain
9 May	NATO adopts ministerial guidance for the new strategy of flexible response
10 May	Formal application by Britain for membership of the EEC
23–25 October	Kiesinger holds talks in London
18 November	Devaluation of sterling
27 November	De Gaulle's press conference at which he expresses opposition to Britain's entry into the EEC
12 December	NATO Defence Planning Committee adopts new strategic concept of flexible response
13–14 December	NATO ministers agree Harmel study report
18–19 December	EEC Council of Ministers decides not to proceed with Britain's application for membership

1968

16 March	Michael Stewart appointed British Foreign Secretary
28 March	Agreement between Britain and Germany on off-set payments
1 July	Britain signs the Non-Proliferation Treaty
21 August	Warsaw Pact forces invade Czechoslovakia
27 November	Britain ratifies the Non-Proliferation Treaty

1969

4 February	Meeting in Paris between de Gaulle and Nicholas Soames, British Ambassador (the so-called Soames affair)
11–13 February	Wilson holds talks in Bonn
24 February	Newly elected US President Richard Nixon visits London for talks with Wilson
28 April	De Gaulle resigns as President of France
22 July	Agreement between Britain and Germany on off-set payments
28 September	Federal German elections
21 October	Willy Brandt appointed Federal German Chancellor in an SPD/FDP coalition
28 November	Federal German Republic signs the Non-Proliferation Treaty
1 December	At an EEC summit in the Hague, Brandt expresses strong support for Britain's application for membership

1970

2–4 March	Brandt holds talks in London
19 March	Meeting between Brandt and Willi Stoph, East German Chairman of Ministers, in Erfurt, East Germany
21 May	Follow-up meeting between Brandt and Stoph in Kassel, West Germany
17 June	Election defeat of Wilson's second Labour government
30 June	Negotiations open for British membership of the EEC

Abbreviations

AAPD	*Akten zur Auswärtigen Politik der Bundesrepublik Deutschland*
ACDA	Arms Control and Disarmament Agency
ADM	atomic demolition munition
AFTA	Atlantic Free Trade Area
ANF	Atlantic Nuclear Force
BA	Bundesarchiv
BAOR	British Army of the Rhine
CDS	Chief of the Defence Staff
CDU	Christlich Demokratische Union (Christian Democratic Union)
CND	Campaign for Nuclear Disarmament
CSU	Christlich Soziale Union (Christian Social Union)
DBPO	*Documents on British Policy Overseas*
DDR	Deutsche Demokratische Republik (German Democratic Republic)
DOP	Defence Overseas Policy (Committee)
ECSC	European Coal and Steel Community
EEC	European Economic Community
EFTA	European Free Trade Association
ENDC	Eighteen Nation Disarmament Conference
EURATOM	European Atomic Energy Community
FAZ	*Frankfurter Allgemeine Zeitung*
FDP	Freie Demokratische Partei (Free Democratic Party)
FRG	Federal Republic of Germany
FRUS	*Foreign Relations of the United States*
FTA	free trade area
GATT	General Agreement on Tariffs and Trade
GDP	gross domestic product
HMG	Her Majesty's government
IAEA	International Atomic Energy Agency

IMF	International Monetary Fund
KSA	*Kölner Stadt Anzeiger*
MC	Military Committee (NATO document series)
MLF	multilateral force
MOD	Ministry of Defence
MP	Member of Parliament
MRBM	medium-range ballistic missiles
NATO	North Atlantic Treaty Organisation
NPD	Nationaldemokratische Partei Deutschlands (National Party)
NPG	Nuclear Planning Group
NPT	Non-Proliferation Treaty
OECD	Organisation for European Co-operation and Development
OPD	Overseas Policy and Defence (Committee)
PAAA	Politisches Archiv des Auswärtigen Amts
PM	Prime Minister
PRO	Public Record Office
RUSI	Royal United Services Institute
SAC	Strategic Air Command
SACEUR	Supreme Allied Commander Europe
SHAPE	Supreme Headquarters Allied Powers Europe
SPD	Sozialdemokratische Partei Deutschlands (Social Democratic Party of Germany)
TNA	The National Archives
UK	United Kingdom of Great Britain and Northern Ireland
UN	United Nations
WEU	Western European Union

Introduction

For students of contemporary history, study of the conduct of British foreign policy between 1964 and 1970 offers a fascinating and rewarding insight into developments that would have a profound impact upon the future of Britain and its place in the world. As Michael Palliser, the influential Private Secretary to the British Prime Minister, Harold Wilson, was to put it in a note of 1967: 'To say that Foreign Policy is in transition is perhaps a platitude; it is certainly a truism. We are in an immensely stimulating but also exceedingly delicate and difficult period in our history.'[1] What Palliser had in mind in referring to a transition was the intention of the British government to withdraw its armed forces from east of Suez, and henceforth to concentrate Britain's defence priorities on Europe, and to seek once again membership of the European Economic Community (EEC). Whilst Britain's relationship with the United States would continue to be important and the United States' involvement in the North Atlantic Treaty Organisation (NATO) would remain central to Britain's security strategy, Europe would ultimately provide the means whereby Britain would exercise influence on the world stage. Palliser went on to summarise the situation as follows:

> we cannot afford to reach the position where the Americans have discarded us as a useful world ally before we have managed to join the Community ... it does mean that there are very strong reasons, in terms of major British interests, why we should keep the maximum pressure consistent with avoiding the direct 'non' and thereby to begin the process (which will, I believe, flow inevitably from our entry) of translating Western Europe into a force for world rather than simply continental influence.[2]

This book will argue, and will draw from British and German official records to demonstrate, that central to Britain's strategy towards

Europe developed by the Labour governments between 1964 and
1970 was a close relationship with Germany.[3]

In his excellent study of the foreign policy process in Britain, which
includes the development of bilateral relationships, in many fields,
between Britain and Germany since the Second World War, as well
as showing with convincing clarity the depth and extent of economic,
cultural and intergovernmental links that underpinned Anglo-German
relations during the 1960s, William Wallace touches on a theme that
continues to find a place in other scholarly works. He suggests that:

> British relations with Germany are heavily overlaid with historical
> memories and associations. World War II and the adverse image of
> Germans and Germany which it re-established and sharpened in
> British public opinion still retained a certain force twenty-five years
> later.[4]

In this context, it would be optimistic to assume that the British
public in the 1960s would have as passively received as did the British
public during 2006 the findings of a study, carried out by researchers
at University College London, which showed that most of our DNA is
German and that English is a German language that retains nothing
of the Celtic past, so that, in effect, the English are German.[5] There
is no doubt that for many adults living in Britain in the aftermath
of the Second World War, Germany and indeed the German people
evoked painful and bitter memories.[6] These feelings were epitomised,
at one level, by the claims of the son of a former wartime Royal Air
Force Bomber Command navigator who said that his father 'would
never have anything German in the house'[7] and, at another, by the
assertion made by Sabine Lee regarding Harold Macmillan:

> [he] had ambivalent feelings about the country with greatest
> responsibility for the outbreak of both World Wars. Germany was
> associated with militarism, manifested across Europe especially in
> its Prussian image. The strength of Macmillan's feelings about war
> and his recollections of the First World War in particular, made a
> certain reserve *vis-à-vis* Germany almost inevitable.[8]

In an authoritative assessment of Macmillan's feelings about
Germany, Peter Hennessy also underlines the fact that he 'never
forgave the Germans for the Great War' and that he 'simply could
not stand the Germans'.[9] Nevertheless, Macmillan was himself well
aware of the need to guard against anti-German feelings and to lead
public opinion in that regard. As he expressed it in his memoirs:

> apart from the papers which specialise in working-up anti-German
> feeling … there is I think genuine apprehension … we must

persuade the British people that isolation [as opposed to involvement in Europe] was the least practical of all courses. We could not
prevent German recovery. We could only try to secure that her new
power ... should be used for the common good.[10]

Despite Germany's integration into the Atlantic Alliance and
European institutions as a democratic state on a Western European
model, it is clear that mixed perceptions about the country continued
to linger in Britain, not least in the minds of those members of the
political elite who had experienced the Second World War and its
immediate aftermath. That this was clearly true in 1965, during the
early months of the Labour government, was demonstrated when
Michael Stewart, the Foreign Secretary, suggested to his Cabinet
colleagues that 'two world wars and the horrors of Nazism have left
such a bitterness that we cannot be sure that Anglo-German reconciliation will last unless we for our part work to make it do so'.[11] As
recently as 1990 also, leading British politicians could be found
associated with decidedly unflattering comments about Germany, in
Margaret Thatcher's case in connection with familiar but nonetheless critical remarks about the German character and in the case of
Nicholas Ridley, her Secretary of State for Trade and Industry, through
startlingly frank and, from his viewpoint, politically fatal assertions
concerning the danger behind Germany's commitment to further
European integration.[12] In his account of the so-called 'Chequers
affair', one of the participants suggested that the tone of what had
been said in the incidents involving Thatcher and Ridley reflected in
part 'age and personal experience, and no doubt it [was] easier for
someone of my [that is, the participant's] generation born after the
war, to come to like and admire present-day Germany, and to make
friendships unburdened by the past'.[13] Whilst this was as unquestion-
ably true during the years of the Labour governments between 1964
and 1970 as it was in 1990, the existence of a latent antipathy in
Britain towards Germany is one of the factors that must be taken into
account in any scholarly account of the period. Whilst there is evidence
that such feelings were resented by the Germans, and to some extent
reciprocated, what will become clear in the course of this particular
appraisal is that neither the British nor the German government was
prepared to allow such emotions to affect their relationship.[14]

In this regard, it is clear that, in seeking better relations with
Germany, Harold Wilson and his ministers moved broadly in step
with public opinion, which, by the mid-1960s, had evidently adopted
more favourable attitudes towards the Germans. For example, in
October 1964, shortly after the general election, *The Times* saw
'nothing unusual about the evident determination of the Labour
leaders to improve relations with Germany'[15] and in June 1965 the

same newspaper referred to the 'several years of careful tending of Anglo-German relations by both Governments and by many official or private bodies ... (which had brought home to countless people) ... the realisation that Anglo-German relations had now reached the level where they ought to be'.[16] By 1967, in a Gallup opinion poll on 'Attitudes and Prejudices', 71% of those asked said they had an attitude towards the Germans that varied between 'fairly' and 'very good'.[17] Therefore, it will be argued that, against a background where there were indications that public opinion was in favour of improved relations with Germany, the approach of Wilson and his ministers was to foster in a positive manner areas of shared interests and to seek practical bilateral agreements and understandings.

A review of the historiography covering Anglo-German relations primarily before but also during the period of the Labour governments from 1964 to 1970 reveals a lack of consensus. For example, Wallace suggests that: 'Differences of opinion, often deeply felt ... made for an uneasy relationship through much of the 60s. It was only in 1968–9 that underlying suspicions on both sides were dispelled, with the British decision to withdraw from East of Suez'.[18] Klaus Larres and Anne Deighton develop a similar theme. Larres describes the relationship between London and Bonn as one between 'uneasy allies' and argues that 'it was only in the 1970s when the UK was under great pressure from its increasing economic problems, that London began to view the British–German relationship as a partnership between equals' and that it was 'only when Britain became a member of the then European Economic Community (EEC) ... [that] the bilateral ... relationship gradually intensified'.[19] In a general overview of British–West German relations between 1945 and 1972, Deighton asserts that there was a relationship of common interests in the hard security field but different paths over integrative policies; she makes the point that the pattern of the relationship between the two countries has been uneven and asserts that 'if the years 1958–63 mark the lowest moment ... the period from 1967 to 1972 were years in which a shift and an easing of relations became possible'.[20] In his authoritative account, John Young surveys British policy towards Germany but limits his findings to the first half of the Labour governments of 1964–70. The focus of his work is on aspects of policy where the two governments had differences, which creates the impression that, during this period at least, relations were far from good.[21]

Until the publication of her most recent work on Anglo-German relations,[22] Lee's research concentrated on the period before the Wilson governments. In her earlier works, Lee brought substance to the reasons why, during the 1950s and early 1960s, the complex relationship between the German Chancellor, Konrad Adenauer, and the British Prime Minister, Harold Macmillan, degenerated into one of mistrust and dislike. She argues that it was only after 1961, when Macmillan adopted a more low-key approach to East–West questions, in conjunction with an increase in the Atlanticist influence in Bonn, relations between Britain and Germany were able 'to resume a better quality ... [although] it was not until both Adenauer and Macmillan had left the scene as heads of government that any lasting improvement occurred'.[23] Now that she has completed further research, made possible by the thirty-year rule, Lee concludes in her later work that 'by 1967 developments in Germany (the Grand Coalition) and in Britain (the EEC membership application) coupled with the continuing lack of constructiveness on the part of de Gaulle had created an atmosphere which was much more likely to deepen Anglo-German understanding'.[24]

What seems to emerge from this historiography is that it was only at some stage towards the end of, or even after, the period of the Wilson governments that misunderstandings between Britain and Germany, which had developed during the Macmillan–Adenauer era, diminished to the extent that relations between the two countries stabilised, and that this improvement could be directly attributed to Britain's renewed interest in membership of the European Communities.

As will become clear in following chapters, there would certainly seem to be grounds for the claim about the effects that a reorientation of foreign policy which placed a higher priority on Europe had on British strategy from 1966 onwards. However, we are still left with a lack of consensus about the state of Anglo-German relations during the whole of the period of these Labour governments, and with differences of opinion about if, when and why these relations began to improve. This is an unsatisfactory situation, given the misunderstandings that had blighted the relationship before 1964 and, to some extent, adds to an impression of mutual antipathy between Britain and Germany that some observers believe still exists.[25] In this context, it is also true, as John Ramsden reveals in his recent work, that, like Joschka Fisher, a former German Foreign Secretary, he believes a people-to-people problem still exists between Britain and Germany, and that this contributes to latent sensitivities on the German side.[26] Whilst this problem has been aggravated by Britain's media, and the emphasis on the Second World War and negative perceptions of Germany in British popular culture, there is little to suggest that this particular problem, such as it was during the Labour governments of the 1960s, was allowed to have an adverse effect on intergovernmental relations. Rather, it is the contention here that, by an analysis of official documents covering the whole of the period from 1964 to 1970 made possible under the thirty-year rule – unavailable during the completion of many of the scholarly works that have previously dealt with the interaction of the foreign policies pursued by London and Bonn during this time – a clearer picture will emerge of the relationship between the two governments than has hitherto been possible. Both governments not only consistently stated that they were committed to good relations, but also, in private and at an official level, believed they existed. It will be argued here that it is reasonable to accept, notwithstanding the differences that became apparent, Anglo-German relations were good or better than much of the existing historiography has suggested.

All of this, of course, gives rise to the question as to why the period of the Labour governments and Anglo-German relations are so important. We have already discussed the fact that only with the release of official documents, German as well as British, is it possible to conduct authoritative research on the period from 1964 to 1970 as a whole, and to advance conclusions on key events that affected the two governments and their relationship. From the British perspective, the election in 1964 of a Labour government under Harold Wilson, after thirteen years of continuous Conservative rule, seemed to herald a new dawn in British politics. Labour's programme, as its election manifesto claimed, would feature 'a deliberate and massive effort to modernise the economy; to change its structure and to develop … the advanced technology and the new science-based industries with which [Britain's] future lies'.[27]

In terms of Britain's foreign policy, the manifesto referred to the changes that had been witnessed in recent years: 'the end of the colonial era, thawing of the Cold War and the new military role for Britain which these developments require'.[28] Labour's response to these challenges would be: firstly, to 'seek closer links with our European neighbours' whilst accepting that 'the first responsibility of a British Government is still to the Commonwealth';[29] secondly, to do everything possible to halt the spread of nuclear weapons and to 'resolve the differences at present dividing East and West';[30] and thirdly, to put Britain's defences 'on a sound basis to ensure that the nation gets value for money on its overseas expenditure', because Britain's previous insistence on maintaining an independent nuclear deterrent had been little more than a pretence and carried with it the 'grave dangers of encouraging the spread of nuclear weapons to countries not possessing them, including to Germany'. Labour also proposed 'renegotiation of the Nassau agreement'.[31] Although the manifesto referred to the still intractable problems dividing Germany and to Labour's insistence on guarantees for the freedom of West Berlin, its reference to preventing German access to nuclear weapons laid bare an attitude that would be a bone of contention between

London and Bonn, especially during the early Labour years. In fact, the question of the use and control of nuclear weapons, which was central to the proposals for a multilateral force (MLF) (see Chapter 2), and with it how best to involve the non-nuclear members of the Atlantic Alliance in decisions affecting their defence in a thermonuclear era, was one of the major legacies inherited by the Labour government that took office in 1964. The way that Wilson and his ministers tackled this legacy, and in so doing affected Britain's relations with Germany, was an important issue during the period.

Beside the question of nuclear defence, and the unwavering determination of Wilson and his ministers to deny the Germans access to the control of nuclear weapons, the crisis within NATO that was precipitated in 1966 by the French withdrawal from its military organisation threatened to undermine the cohesion of the Atlantic Alliance, and struck at the heart of the strategic interests of both Britain and Germany. That this crisis occurred when public opinion within Europe was questioning the whole basis of NATO, and looked instead for arms control agreements with the Soviet Union as a means of improving East–West relations, added to the pressure on Western governments to achieve a *détente* in Europe. Within Britain, problems with the economy caused by the weakness of sterling and chronic balance of payments difficulties that handicapped the Labour governments throughout the period up to 1970, even after devaluation in November 1967, meant that Britain was dependent upon the financial support of its allies – principally the United States and Germany. This was manifested in part in the protracted negotiations between London and Bonn over the 'offset agreements' to cover the exchange costs of the British Army of the Rhine (BAOR). Problems with the economy were the underlying reasons why, 'once Indonesia pulled back from confrontation in the summer of 1966, and the Americans had become more ambivalent about the price to be paid for maintaining the British role', policy makers were prepared to concede that Britain's historic 'east of Suez' defence commitments could no longer be maintained.[32]

As for Germany, the election in 1966 of the 'Grand Coalition' under Federal Chancellor Kurt Georg Kiesinger, and the appointment of Willy Brandt as Vice Chancellor and Federal Foreign Minister, brought a new dimension to the policy of *Ostpolitik* and with it a more flexible approach by Bonn to East–West relations and the question of German reunification.[33] Finally, the decision by Britain in 1967 to reopen negotiations with the Six over membership of the European Communities, and the intention to focus Britain's defence priorities on Europe, not only marked the most fundamental change in British strategy of the 1960s but also emphasised the need for stronger ties between Britain and its Western European partners, particularly Germany.

Thus, major developments affecting Western defence, East–West relations and Europe underscore the importance of the period between 1964 and 1970, and are the obvious policy areas within which answers about the state of Anglo-German relations at the time are to be found.

As to the importance of the relationship to the two governments, Wallace asserts that 'Anglo-German relations span the entire range of politically significant external affairs; and in almost every dimension of that relationship West Germany ranks as one of Britain's two or three most important partners'.[34] However, Wallace finds common ground with Larres when he argues that the experience of collaboration with American and European partners, in the institutionalised arrangements underpinning NATO and within the Eurogroup (that is, the grouping of European states within NATO, with Britain, Germany and the Netherlands at its core), had 'accustomed the British Government to conducting important aspects of its foreign relations through multilateral channels, and to using bilateral relations as a necessary means of preparing for and of supplementing institutionalised multilateral negotiations'.[35] Whilst it is perfectly reasonable to assert that Britain with its three circles of influence – the 'special relationship' with the United States, the links with Europe, and the Commonwealth – had long been accustomed to multilateral policy making, Wallace's point is a valid reminder that Anglo-German relations cannot be considered in isolation. Both countries placed the highest priority on maintaining the involvement of the United States in the defence of Western Europe, Germany remained committed to the Franco-German relationship as an essential element of its *Westpolitik*, and Bonn, like London, would come to accept that only through *détente* with the Soviet Union could appropriate arms control and political agreements be realised that would bring an end to the divisions within Europe.[36] Thus, the United States, France and the Soviet Union were key players in the complex web of issues that engaged both Britain and Germany in the conduct of foreign policy between 1964 and 1970, and their influence on policy outcomes is a factor that must be taken into account in assessing the relationship between London and Bonn.

In bilateral terms, there were clear continuities in Anglo-German relations in the post-war period, continuities that made the relationship important to both countries. Whilst it is beyond the scope of this book to go over ground already well trodden by other historians, even Macmillan and Adenauer, despite their mutual antipathy, recognised the value of the relationship between their countries. As Macmillan asserted, 'the countries of the West have, thank God for it, decided to rebuild their bridges with Germany ... we all have an interest, because the Germans are our Allies against the Communists'.[37] Similarly, when asked why so many German politicians, journalists and business people took Britain's side without asking seriously whether it helped Germany or not, Adenauer responded that 'perhaps it is above all because Britain has not yet been conquered. They respect Britain, consider it a strong friend and want to be allied with it.'[38] Thus, mutual concern about security, and with it recognition of the need for a strong Atlantic Alliance, were the principal factors motivating both countries to seek good relations, a feature that remained prominent during the period 1964–70. As Stewart informed the Cabinet in August 1965:

> France is threatening to break away from the present integrated structure of NATO which the rest of the Allies intend to preserve and if possible strengthen. In this situation, Germany's attitude is vital. In the last resort, NATO can and if necessary will exist without France; without Germany it could not.[39]

Stewart went on to spell out other 'compelling reasons of national interest for ... trying to work constructively with the Germans'. Important here was that, as the Americans had a strong interest in preserving a good understanding with the Germans, Britain's 'influence in Washington [was] bound to be affected to an important degree by [its] standing in Bonn'. Moreover, in terms of East–West relations and arms control, 'the position of the German Government [was] crucial in any moves towards an East/West *détente* in Europe because German territory [was] bound to be involved ... any British initiative in the realm of European security [was] unlikely to prosper unless it [had] the support of the Government in Bonn'. With regard to the EEC, 'the Federal Republic [had] always wanted Britain to be a part of political and economic Europe ... if we can secure German cooperation, our prospects of shaping Western Europe's economic and political future to the designs which suit us best [would] be greatly improved'.[40] Finally, Germany played a key role in the operation of international financial institutions.

Whilst the election of a Labour government in Britain caused initial uncertainty in Bonn about the future direction of British foreign policy, especially when such uncertainty was heightened by comments made by Wilson in November 1964 in the House of Commons that were interpreted in Bonn as being unhelpful to Anglo-German relations, there remained a wide measure of agreement between all political parties in Bonn on fundamental foreign policy issues.[41] These were set out in some detail by Frank Roberts, the British Ambassador in Bonn, in a brief prepared for Wilson's first visit to West Berlin and Bonn as Prime Minister, in March 1965. This brief described Germany's: commitment to reunification; dependence on the United States and the Western Alliance; determination to protect its position *vis-à-vis* Berlin and the Hallstein doctrine, under which the Federal Republic would not recognise any state which recognised East Germany; intention to play a full part in the movement towards European political and economic union (in which Germany hoped to see British participation); and wish to maintain a close relationship with France.[42] Against a background of these broad policy objectives, Britain's nuclear status in support of the United States, the commitment of a substantial British army, stationed on German territory, to the defence of the Federal Republic and West Berlin, the influence that Britain still retained by virtue of its status and power, and the possibility of a more wholehearted British commitment to European political and economic integration strongly support the assertion that good relations with Britain were also important to Germany.

The discussion in this book attempts to break new ground. It focuses on the whole of the period of the Labour governments between 1964 and 1970, and analyses in greater detail than has been done hitherto the bilateral relationship between the British and German governments, as it was affected by the main foreign policy issues and multilateral pressures at the time. In that sense, this book fills the gap that still seems to exist in the current historiography. Whilst the availability of official records at the Public Record Office (PRO) within The National Archives (TNA) has facilitated the research that supports the arguments made in this book, the use of official material at the German archives in Berlin and Koblenz,[43] together with published documents in the excellent *Akten zur Auswärtigen Politik der Bundesrepublik Deutschland* series, provides necessary balance to the discussion and an opportunity to consider the relationship from a German viewpoint. The research has also been enhanced by interview material from discussions with key advisers to Wilson and his ministers, and with a senior member of staff and the son of an Ambassador in the Bonn Embassy during the 1960s.[44] Much of the historiography on the economic, political and social policies of the Labour governments of 1964–70 has been critical, and it is evident that Wilson is increasingly perceived as one of Britain's least successful Prime Ministers since 1945.[45] On this last point, in a recent article published in a special supplement to *The Observer*, Dominic Sandbrook assessed the comparative performance of British Prime Ministers since 1945 and suggested that 'for the past few decades … Wilson's reputation has slipped further and further'.[46] However, Wilson is not the issue here. The purpose of this book is to explore aspects of foreign policy pursued by the Labour governments under Wilson that were intended to serve Britain's interests and, in so doing, to maintain good relations with Germany. There is no intention to argue for any revision to historical opinion on Wilson's record in office.

The book is structured around eight main chapters, each dealing with a particular issue that confronted the Wilson governments in relations with Germany between 1964 and 1970; some of these proved transitory (perhaps because satisfactorily resolved), whilst others endured. The first chapter sets the scene for what follows. It establishes the state of relations between Britain and Germany as the Labour government took office, as a yardstick against which to determine whether continuity or change marked the following six years. It also explores the domestic pressures – economic, party political and public opinion – that motivated actions by Wilson and his ministers, especially in the period immediately after October 1964. In this period, as the discussion will show, there were incidents that might have had a damaging and lasting effect upon the understanding between Britain and Germany, but both governments recognised that ultimately their interests were better served by a good relationship, and agreed to increase their bilateral contacts to ensure that the improvement in relations that had been fostered by the previous Conservative government was maintained. For Britain in particular, a major factor in its attitude towards Germany was the assessment that the support of the Federal Republic would be crucial to any new approach towards Europe.

Chapter 2 covers the exchanges between London, Bonn and Washington over the MLF proposal and the British alternative, of an Atlantic Nuclear Force (ANF). Wilson claimed that the ANF proposals were designed to 'kill off' the MLF concept, a claim that on the evidence seems justified, although it is clear that US President Lyndon B. Johnson's role was pivotal in the eventual outcome. In this context, whilst Britain and the United States were anxious to accommodate German demands for a greater say in the use by NATO of nuclear weapons, both governments agreed that this could not be at the expense of a non-proliferation agreement with the Soviet Union. Britain's underlying concern was to prevent any suggestion of German control of nuclear weapons; this objective was achieved by the creation of the Nuclear Planning Group (NPG), with German representation, as the solution to NATO's nuclear sharing problem. The outcome should be seen as a vindication of British policy and a success in terms of Anglo-German relations.

The negotiations between Britain and Germany leading to the series of offset agreements, under which Germany agreed to buy British exports, in the form of armaments and civilian purchases, to offset the deutschmark exchange costs incurred by the BAOR, forms the subject of the third chapter. Under pressure from a serious balance of payments problem, Britain demanded more support than Germany was prepared to give, and resorted to threats of troop withdrawals if its demands were not met. The dispute reached its peak in 1966, when the United States, under similar economic pressure, and concerned about the knock-on effect that British troop withdrawals might have, was drawn into the dispute. The trilateral deal that was struck in 1967 marked the decline of the dispute in importance, when Britain and Germany agreed subsequently that collaborative projects, such as the joint development of a multi-role combat aircraft, might shape future negotiations, and when Britain pledged its future to Europe. In reality, Britain's position on offset payments was based on bluff and deception, a fact that was well known to the Germans. The dispute was an irritant to both governments. However, despite the rhetoric, Britain and Germany did not fail to reach agreements on the payments and this supports the argument that their relationship was never seriously threatened.

Chapter 4 deals with the Harmel report and the involvement during 1967 of Britain and Germany in the reappraisal of NATO and its future tasks, proposed by Pierre Harmel, the Belgian Foreign Minister. That such a reappraisal was both necessary and urgent was evident after the French withdrawal from the military organisation of NATO and in the light of questioning by public opinion in NATO countries of the utility of the organisation. Whilst Britain initially had doubts about the outcome of such a study, the Foreign Office came to see in it the possibilities for stabilising the Alliance, steering it in a direction that might lead to an improved *détente* with the Soviet Union and attaching Germany more firmly to the West. For Germany, the exercise was regarded as an important opportunity to reinforce its own *Ostpolitik* and to ensure that the German problem was deemed by members of the Alliance as an essential ingredient of a settlement in Europe. An important consideration, in terms of Anglo-German relations, was that Britain and Germany co-operated closely as co-rapporteurs for one of the Harmel study working groups. This ensured their mutual understanding on an important aspect of Harmel, facilitated agreement on the eventual outcome of the study, and enabled Britain to create goodwill as it attempted to demonstrate its commitment to Europe.

The fifth chapter examines the background to the formal adoption by NATO in 1967 of the revised nuclear strategy of 'flexible response'. By the early 1960s, the security guarantee provided to NATO members by the United States had been undermined as the Soviet Union achieved nuclear parity and by the demand that its European allies strengthen their conventional forces assigned to NATO. For the

Germans in particular, either the consequences of a failure of deterrence or the prospect of a conventional battle fought on their territory was too serious to contemplate. Britain clearly understood German concerns and to some extent shared them, but believed that anything other than a minor incursion by Warsaw Pact forces across the German border would require a nuclear response by NATO. The agreement on the revised NATO strategy represented a compromise between these respective positions. Britain was a key player in the development of NATO strategy and, with Germany, was influential in developing guidance on the use of tactical nuclear weapons by the Alliance as part of flexible response. The evolution of NATO strategy affected the security of Britain, and even more so of Germany, and was another important factor in the relationship between the two countries.

Chapter 6 discusses Anglo-German relations in the context of the negotiations leading to the agreement reached between the United States, the Soviet Union and Britain, and ultimately by Germany, on the Nuclear Non-Proliferation Treaty (NPT). The negotiations were complex, in that they spilled over into other issues of concern to members of the Atlantic Alliance. Principally, these included the MLF/ANF project and whether moves within the Alliance (driven by the United States but involving Britain and Germany) to create opportunities for greater nuclear weapons sharing would prove acceptable to the Soviet Union. Then, once difficulties over the MLF/ANF project and its successor, the NPG, had been overcome, the question arose of whether two sets of proposals for the NPT could be made more palatable to Germany: the first was for inclusion in the NPT of clauses affecting the nuclear status of any future European state; and the second (one more contentious from the viewpoint of the European Communities) concerned the arrangements under the NPT for mandatory international safeguards (i.e. inspection of nuclear facilities). These multilateral negotiations were influenced by the changes of government in Bonn in 1966 and 1969, and the Soviet-inspired invasion of Czechoslovakia in 1968. They also occurred at a time when the British government was anxious to strengthen relations with Germany in support for Britain's commitment to Europe. Whilst Britain played essentially a supporting role to the United States during the negotiations, remaining determined to uphold the principle that Germany should be denied access to nuclear weapons, ministers and officials showed considerable understanding of Bonn's concerns and an evident intent not to undermine Anglo-German relations. An important consideration in this strategy was the impact that it might have on German support for Britain's application to join the EEC.

In Chapter 7, discussion centres on German *Ostpolitik* in its three phases and the reaction to it by the British government. Britain was a

firm advocate of moves designed to improve East–West relations, and
encouraged Germany away from the Hallstein doctrine, towards a
position that was based on an improved *détente* with the Soviet Union
and Warsaw Pact countries as the best means of achieving a settlement in Europe. Despite misgivings, which were deliberately not
made known to Bonn, Britain supported the German 'Peace Note'
initiative in May 1966, but became more openly enthusiastic with the
advent of the Grand Coalition in Bonn and the new shape of German
foreign policy towards Eastern Europe. The chapter includes detail of
a seemingly little-known British *Ostpolitik* initiative launched in 1966,
which proposed a 'Declaration on Europe' (in essence, a code of international conduct to which all nations of East and West Europe could
subscribe). Like the British reaction to the Peace Note, the Germans
were lukewarm about the Declaration, but it was an indication of the
state of relations at the time that neither country was prepared to
express outright opposition. Britain welcomed the appointment of
Brandt as Chancellor and supported his concept of *Ostpolitik*. British
ministers and officials had misgivings about where this phase might
lead and how it would affect Allied rights in Berlin, but these concerns
were never allowed to undermine a policy that advocated German
support for Britain's entry into the EEC and maintaining good relations with Bonn.

Chapter 8 discusses the events leading up to Britain's decision in
1967 to reapply for membership of the European Communities and
bilateral contacts with Germany after the application was rejected.
Wilson proved to be the key figure in establishing British policy
towards membership of the EEC, as he coaxed a divided Labour
government into supporting a second application. From the outset, in
October 1964, the advice from officials to ministers was that Britain's
future rested in Europe and that a close understanding with Germany
would facilitate Britain's entry to the EEC. The chapter argues that
although this strategy did not succeed, it did serve to demonstrate a
more convincing commitment to Europe and placed Britain in a position from which membership of the EEC could be negotiated once de
Gaulle had left the scene. Again, Britain's approach to Europe and
the strategy of a close relationship with Germany were key foreign
policy issues of the period.

Brandt, as German Foreign Minister, told a British audience in
1967 that 'common interests are a sound basis for good cooperation'.[47]
The picture that will emerge from the discussion in the chapters of
this book is indeed one of two governments sharing common interests and seemingly committed to deepening their understanding.
We challenge the claims in the existing historiography that the late
1960s mark some kind of a 'watershed' in Anglo-German relations,

after which the relationship improved considerably. Rather, this book argues that the relationship was strong, healthy and robust throughout the period, with both states working hard to overcome the differences that sometimes came between them.

Notes

1 Note to Prime Minister on 'British Foreign Policy' by Michael Palliser, 7 July 1967, PREM 13/326, The National Archives, Public Record Office (hereinafter PRO).
2 *Ibid.*
3 To be strictly accurate, the reference in the text should be to the Federal Republic of Germany or West Germany. By way of clarification, the reader should note that all references to Germany in the rest of the text should be taken as meaning West Germany; any reference to East Germany will be made in full.
4 William Wallace, *The Foreign Policy Process in Britain* (1975), p. 225. Sabine Lee asserts that 'Anglo-German relations have never had the special quality that has been attributed at times to Anglo-American or Franco-German relations'. Sabine Lee, 'Pragmatism Versus Principle? Macmillan and Germany', in Richard Aldous and Sabine Lee (eds), *Harold Macmillan: Aspects of a Political Life* (1999), p. 113. Klaus Larres makes the point that 'Throughout the twentieth century British–German relations have been of fundamental importance in shaping the course of European and world history. Often those relations were strained and hostile'. Klaus Larres (ed.), *Uneasy Allies: British–German Relations and European Integration since 1945* (Oxford, 2000), p. 1. Jonathan Wright suggests that 'Anglo-German relations since 1949 have been a curious mixture of harmony and tension'. Jonathan Wright, 'The Role of Britain in West German Foreign Policy since 1949', *German Politics*, 5, 1 (April 1996), p. 26.
5 Stuart Wavell, 'Apartheid in the UK? They're Having a Genetic Joke', *Sunday Times News Review*, 23 July 2006, p. 7.
6 Whilst the findings of opinion polls have to be approached with some care, a Gallup poll conducted in August 1945 in Britain revealed a mixed response to the question 'What are your feelings at the present time towards the German people?'. Whilst 21% of those asked indicated 'hatred' and 14% indicated 'dislike', it is significant that 25% expressed 'sympathy'. See George H. Gallup (ed.), *The Gallup International Public Opinion Polls: Great Britain 1937–1975: Volume 1 (1937–1964)* (New York, 1976), p. 117.
7 William Ivory, 'My Father the Hero', *Times Magazine*, 2 February 2002, pp. 51–52.
8 Sabine Lee, 'Pragmatism versus Principle?', p. 113. Macmillan's sensitivity about the Germans was confirmed by Michael Palliser, Private Secretary to Harold Wilson 1966–68, when relating the story of their arrival by car for Adenauer's funeral service: 'As we approached the Cathedral there was a guard of honour of the German army presenting arms ... Macmillan ... turned to me and said "Magnificent aren't they. They always scare me stiff"'. Interview material.
9 Peter Hennessy, *Having It So Good: Britain in the Fifties* (2006), p. 389.
10 Harold Macmillan, *Pointing the Way 1959–1961* (1972), p. 98.
11 Memorandum to the Cabinet by Michael Stewart, 'Policy Towards Germany', 5 August 1965, C (65) 119, CAB 129/122 (Pt 2), PRO.
12 Full accounts can be found in the following articles: Timothy Garton Ash,

'The Chequers Affair', *New York Review of Books*, 27 September 1990, p. 65; and Gordon A. Craig, 'Die Chequers Affäre von 1990: Beobachtungen zum Thema Presse und internationale Beziehungen', *Vierteljahreshefte für Zeitgeschichte*, 39 (1991), pp. 611–623. In brief, Ridley commented that 'the proposed European Monetary Union [was] a German racket designed to take over the whole of Europe'. Whilst Thatcher was not personally linked to criticisms of the Germans, a leaked and highly confidential memorandum of her meeting at Chequers suggested that 'less than flattering attributes of the Germans were mentioned'. See also Chapter 1, note 61.

13 Ash, 'The Chequers Affair', p. 65.

14 There is little doubt that the Germans resented what they believed were adverse feelings about them. As the head of the Chancery in Bonn put it, 'there have always been suspicions ... that a large section of the British public is anti-German ... there are also fears that the British Government is unsympathetic to German interests'. See Andrew Stark, head of Chancery, British Embassy, Bonn, to Bernard Ledwidge, head of Western Division at the Foreign Office, 19 January 1965, RG 1903/3, FO 371/183174, PRO. Lee argues that the 'Germans were equally prejudiced against the British, seeing them as a nation of shopkeepers whose main characteristics were jealousy and scepticism'. See Lee, 'Pragmatism Versus Principle?', p. 115; and telegram, German Embassy, London, to Foreign Office, Bonn, 22 March 1965, B31/285, Politisches Archiv des Auswärtigen Amts, Berlin (hereinafter PAAA Berlin).

15 'Labour's Positive Attitude Towards the Six', *The Times*, 23 October 1964, p. 10.

16 'Germany Awaits New Friendship Ideas', *The Times*, 17 June 1965, p. 9.

17 George H. Gallup (ed.), *The Gallup International Public Opinion Polls: Great Britain 1937–1975: Volume 2 (1965–1975)* (New York, 1976), p. 955. Although not directly related to attitudes about Germany, the validity of the assertion about the government moving broadly in step with public opinion can also be seen in the Gallup surveys taken on membership of the Common Market. Whereas in November 1964, at the start of Wilson's period in office, 44% of those asked favoured an attempt to join the EEC, by the time of Wilson's re-election in May 1966, 70% of those asked favoured joining. See Gallup, *Gallup International, Volumes 1 and 2*, for the movement in opinion about Britain's membership of the Common Market.

18 Wallace, *Foreign Policy*, p. 225.

19 Larres, *Uneasy Allies*, p. 1.

20 Anne Deighton, 'British–West German Relations, 1945–1972', in Klaus Larres (ed.), *Uneasy Allies: British–German Relations and European Integration since 1945* (Oxford, 2000), p. 41.

21 John W. Young, 'West Germany in the Foreign Policy of the Wilson Government, 1964–67', in Saki Dockrill (ed.), *Controversy and Compromise: Alliance Politics between Great Britain, Federal Republic of Germany, and the United States of America, 1945–1967* (Bodenheim, 1998), pp. 173–195.

22 Sabine Lee, *Victory in Europe: Britain and Germany since 1945* (Harlow, 2001).

23 Lee, 'Pragmatism Versus Principle', p. 128. See also Sabine Lee, 'Perception and Reality: Anglo-German Relations During the Berlin Crisis 1958–1959', *German History*, 13, 1 (1995), pp. 47–69. Other historians highlight the poor relationship between Adenauer and Macmillan. See for example A. J. Nicholls, *The Bonn Republic: West German Democracy, 1945–1990* (1997), p. 166. Macmillan's own feelings about his German opposite number are made quite clear in his memoirs; as examples, he refers to Adenauer as 'vain, suspicious and grasping'. See Macmillan, *Pointing the Way*, p. 64; and in the

context of a visit to Bonn at the German Chancellor's invitation to discuss Anglo-German relations he asserts that 'I am not looking forward to our visit to Bonn. Dr Adenauer has deceived me before'. *Ibid.*, p. 317.

24 Lee, *Victory in Europe*, p. 121.

25 A. J. Nicholls comprehensively described British attitudes towards Germany in *Fifty Years of Anglo-German Relations: 2000 Bithell Memorial Lecture* (2000). However, his comment that 'by the mid-1990s … united Germany had become a whipping boy for the nationalist British media' may tempt a casual reader to believe that press rantings are confined to Fleet Street. However, elements of the German press indulge in similar activities. Recent examples are 'The Island Where Nothing Works', *Stern*, May 2001; and 'The Last Queen – Britain Celebrates Its Fading Monarchy', *Der Spiegel*, May 2002.

26 John Ramsden, *Don't Mention the War: The British and the Germans since 1890* (2006), p. 417. See also 'For You British the War Has Never Ended, Says Fischer', *The Times*, 21 October 2004, p. 44.

27 F. W. S. Craig (ed.), *British General Election Manifestos 1959–1987* (Aldershot, 1990), p. 47.

28 *Ibid.*, p. 55.

29 *Ibid.*, p. 56.

30 *Ibid.*, p. 58.

31 *Ibid.*, p. 59. The Nassau agreement is discussed in Chapter 2.

32 Matthew Jones, 'A Decision Delayed: Britain's Withdrawal from South East Asia Reconsidered, 1961–1968', *English Historical Review*, 472 (June 2002), pp. 569–595.

33 Timothy Garton Ash reminds us that 'in the second half of the 1960s the policy initiated by the Grand Coalition was called the "new" *Ostpolitik*, but by the 1980s the adjective "new" had been silently absorbed into the noun. No serious analyst would deny that major elements of the thinking behind Brandt's "new" *Ostpolitik* were present already in the early to mid-1960s, and even in the late 1950s'. Timothy Garton Ash, *In Europe's Name: Germany and the Divided Continent* (1993), p. 36.

34 Wallace, *Foreign Policy*, p. 226.

35 *Ibid.*, p. 218.

36 The assertion about British and German attitudes towards *détente* is not meant to imply that, in the initial stages of the Wilson governments, Germany necessarily accepted that a lessening of tension in Europe and improved East–West relations were essential precursors to reunification. It is clear, however, that by the time the Grand Coalition was formed at the end of 1966, *Ostpolitik* was based on the assumption that a *détente* with the Soviet Union would have to be created before reunification could become a serious consideration.

37 Harold Macmillan, *At the End of the Day 1961–1963* (1973), p. 461.

38 Quoted in Wright, 'The Role of Britain', p. 34.

39 Memorandum to the Cabinet by Michael Stewart, 'Policy Towards Germany', 5 August 1965, C (65) 119, CAB 129/122 (Pt 2), PRO.

40 *Ibid.*

41 Karl Carstens, First Secretary of State at the German Foreign Office, reported that he had told Sir Frank Roberts, British ambassador in Bonn, that Wilson's reference to the Nassau agreement arousing Germany's nuclear appetite had not gone down well in Bonn. See Aufzeichnung des Staatssekretärs Carstens, 26 November 1964, *Akten zur Auswärtigen Politik der Bundesrepublik Deutschland* (hereinafter *AAPD*) *1964 II*, p. 1406.

42 Brief for Bonn talks by Sir Frank Roberts, March 1965, PMV (G) (65) 17, FO 371/182999, PRO.

43 PAAA Berlin, and the Bundesarchiv, Koblenz (hereinafter BA Koblenz).
44 Interviewed were: Sir Oliver Wright, Private Secretary to Harold Wilson, 1964–66, and Sir Michael Palliser, Private Secretary to Harold Wilson, 1966–68; Mr J. H. Adam Watson, Assistant Under-Secretary, Foreign Office, and British co-rapporteur for the Harmel study, 1967; Sir Andrew Stark, Head of Chancery, British Embassy, Bonn, 1964–68; Sir Roger Jackling, son of Sir Roger Jackling, British Ambassador, Bonn, 1968–72.
45 See for example Clive Ponting, *Breach of Promise: Labour in Power 1964–1970* (1989); Kenneth O. Morgan, 'The Labour Party's Record in Office: The Wilson Years 1964–70', *Contemporary Record*, 3, 4 (April 1990), pp. 22–25; David Marquand, *The Progressive Dilemma* (1991); Kevin Jeffreys, *The Labour Party since 1945* (1993); Christopher Hitchens, 'Say What You Will About Harold', *London Review of Books*, 2 December 1993, pp. 7–9; John W. Young, *The Labour Governments 1964–1970. Volume 2: International Policy* (Manchester, 2003); and Leo McKinstry, 'Which Decade Really Swung?', in 'Times Books' supplement to *The Times*, 5 August 2006, p. 10, in comment on Dominic Sandbrook, *White Heat: A History of Britain in the Swinging Sixties* (2006).
46 Dominic Sandbrook, 'Put Him in His Place', in 'The Blair Years 1997–2007', supplement to *The Observer*, 8 April 2007, p. 49.
47 Address by the German Federal Minister for Foreign Affairs in London, 12 April 1967, B31/307, PAAA Berlin.

Chapter 1

Anglo-German relations in 1964 – continuity or change?

The Labour government that came to power in October 1964 prom- ised the renewal of Britain. Labour's election manifesto provided little evidence, however, that the Party harboured any enthusiasm for the ideal of a united Europe, with Britain at its heart. Rather, it would be the nurturing of Britain's links with the Commonwealth that would form the bedrock of Labour's foreign policy.[1] For a more detailed exposition of Labour's foreign policy objectives, should it come to power, we would have to turn towards an article written by Patrick Gordon Walker, Labour's Foreign Secretary designate, some six months before the 1964 election.[2] However, even this source reveals neither any expectation of the fundamental reappraisal of Britain's place in the world that economic realities would force upon Harold Wilson and his ministers, nor any appreciation of the growing political and economic importance that the European Communities as an entity were rapidly assuming. In the event, the Labour govern- ment that assumed power was soon obliged not only to consider that its longer-term interests would best be served by a closer attachment to Europe but also to recognise that this objective required a close understanding with Germany.

This chapter helps to establish the context for the rest of the book by examining the state of relations between Britain and Germany at the time of the election of the Labour government. Providing such a context enables us to determine the extent of any change during the years up to 1970 and the Conservative election victory in that year. At first glance, there seem certainly to be grounds for assertions that things did change and that relations between Britain and Germany varied over the period, and that it was not until much later in the Wilson era that any improvement was achieved, after a low point that has been attributed in part as the consequence of the mutual dislike and misunderstandings of Harold Macmillan and Konrad Adenauer.[3]

However, when a detailed appraisal is made of the exchanges between the British and German governments in the months immediately before and after Wilson's election victory in October 1964, especially those covered in official documents, when account is taken of public opinion and allowance is made for the foreign policy and economic interests that drew London and Bonn closer together at the time, a somewhat different picture emerges. What becomes clear is that, notwithstanding signs of ill feeling deriving from the experiences of two World Wars, both governments not only were determined to maintain the good relations that had already developed since the departure of Adenauer and Macmillan but were anxious to agree institutionalised arrangements that would ensure that this state of affairs continued.

Relations before October 1964

If there were misgivings about the state of Anglo-German relations before Wilson secured election victory in October 1964, these were certainly not shared by the Foreign Office. In a briefing note on Anglo-German relations prepared for ministers during the previous February, the opening statement claimed, in an obvious reference to the difficulties of the Macmillan era, that 'relations between the Federal Republic of Germany and Britain [were] improving' and that 'the friendly tone of British press comment on it [the relationship] showed that there [was] now a better climate'. The briefing also made clear that 'West Germany [was] now one of our most important partners and it [was] very much in our interests to inject more warmth into Anglo-German relations'.[4] Despite this advice, there were obvious areas where political differences between the two governments could develop. For example, the Germans were concerned that the West would be tempted to make a deal over their heads with the Soviet Union that would lead to the permanent division of Germany and for this reason they tended to be more sceptical about the prospects for *détente* than Britain.[5] Moreover, the Germans sought reassurance that there was no possibility that suggestions of *de facto* recognition of the East German regime would become British government policy.[6] From Britain's point of view, the BAOR helped defend Germany and Europe as a whole, and it was only fair that the Germans should do more to share the burden of the exchange costs involved in keeping British troops stationed in the Federal Republic.

Nevertheless, despite these sensitivities, there were sound reasons why, by 1964, Britain needed a closer understanding with Germany. As the Foreign Office saw it, 'the closer our ties with Germany the more successful will be our efforts to develop a constructive common Western approach to international issues' and, even more pertinently for the future (and in support of the arguments in this book), 'friendly political relations between Britain and the Federal Republic ... [were] essential for the building of a prosperous and united Europe'.[7]

The Foreign Office was not alone in believing that the corner had turned in the relations between London and Bonn. By June 1964, Sir Frank Roberts, the British Ambassador in Bonn, was able to report to R. A. Butler, the Conservative Foreign Secretary, that it had become clear 'that there [was] no divergence of policy on major issues'. Roberts had taken up his appointment in Bonn during 1963, and was an experienced and widely respected representative of the British government.[8] The Germans in particular came to consider him as one of the most capable diplomats and best-informed German experts in the British foreign service.[9] Roberts also felt able to advise Butler that although much of the mutual uneasiness and suspicion that had marked relations had now disappeared, and whilst it would be tempting to explain this by the retirement of Adenauer, in reality 'the causes ... [were] more profound'. As Roberts saw it, the departure of Adenauer was a necessary precondition so that 'the forces which were working in favour of better relations could produce their full effect'.[10] The implication behind Roberts' remarks was that, whilst the opinions that ministers hold of one another can and do influence the dealings between governments, the relationship between states is governed primarily by the extent to which they share and work towards common policy objectives. Whilst Roberts could point to these and other factors, and especially to the forthcoming state visit to Germany by the Queen in May 1965, which he felt would mark the high point of Anglo-German relations since the war, as evidence that relations could be considered to be normal he flagged up interests that were fundamental to policy makers in Germany.[11] Not only was German foreign policy determined ultimately by the fact of German membership of the EEC, of which the Franco-German alliance had become a vital element, but the proposed MLF had become for the Germans the counterpart to the EEC, since it constituted the means whereby American security protection could be guaranteed, regardless of the way the Community developed. Whereas policy makers in London and Bonn clearly believed that relations between their countries had improved, the challenge in October 1964 for the incoming Labour government, if it wished to maintain this momentum, would be to articulate policies that were sensitive to German interests in these fields.

When he referred to the more profound causes that were working in favour of better relations between London and Bonn, Roberts suggested that the visit to Bonn by Butler in December 1963 and that by Ludwig Erhard, the German Chancellor, to London in January 1964 had revealed common policy interests, and that, once this had been appreciated, 'the uneasiness and suspicion which had characterised ... relations in the Adenauer era disappeared'.[12] However, there were other forces at work, which, in Britain's case in the difficult early days of Wilson's first government, motivated an even closer relationship with Germany. In economic terms, Germany had become a force to be reckoned with, whereas by October 1964 the British economy needed both time and help to regain its strength. As the Long Term Study Group in its report on British interests in Europe emphasised, 'even without reunification the Federal Republic will be economically the strongest country in Europe'.[13]

It is beyond the scope of this book to detail the reasons for the relative strengths of the British and German economies in 1964, but some brief comment is relevant to an understanding of the appeal to the incoming Labour administration of a closer relationship with Germany. Whilst both countries had prospered in the so-called 'golden age' (1950–73) of the international economy, with most of the developed world experiencing high growth rates, high employment and low inflation, fostered by the stability of an international monetary system that was rooted in the agreements reached at Bretton Woods in 1944, and by the reductions in trade restrictions implemented by international concessions negotiated through the General Agreement on Tariffs and Trade (GATT), Britain's major competitors, and Germany in particular, had performed significantly better. For example, between 1951 and 1963 the German economy expanded at an average rate of 7.1% per annum and over the period of the golden age economic growth in Germany averaged 5.9% compared with 3.0% in Britain.[14]

The reasons for what has been described as Britain's relative economic decline is the subject of an on-going debate between academics and political observers, but one contributory factor must be the impact of catch-up as war-torn economies made up ground on those, like Britain, less affected by the ravages of war. Giles Radice implies support for this line of reasoning when he points out that, 'during the 1950s and 1960s, the German growth rate was the fastest in Europe and living standards trebled'.[15] Fuelling this growth rate were the concepts of sound money and free markets, under which Germany's output would be stimulated and sustained by export-led demand. Moreover, foreign trade in goods became an important determinant of Germany's national income. By the mid-1950s trade accounted for about 20% of gross national product and this ratio continued to rise. To put these statistics into context, between 1950 and 1990 Germany's export share in world trade rose from 3.5% to 12.1%, with a peak of 12.9% in 1973. It is also relevant to the discussion that Germany's share of world imports consistently grew less than exports during the same period.[16] Although there is evidence to suggest that the Germans strongly supported industrial tariff reductions in Europe and those negotiated under GATT, and that Erhard in particular was a fanatical believer in the value of the free market economy and was known to prefer the wider economic possibilities offered by Britain's proposal for a European-wide free trade area (FTA), Germany's economic policy remained firmly based on a commitment to the EEC and an alliance with France.[17]

In Britain's case, however, where there was a more consistent attachment to Keynesian demand management, designed to smooth out economic fluctuations and to sustain full employment, whilst many economic pointers were positive – average rates of gross domestic product (GDP) in particular were higher than at any time since the mid-nineteenth century – there was considerable concern about persistent balance of payments problems.[18] As Sir Alec Cairncross, an economic adviser to Conservative and Labour governments during the 1960s, makes clear, 'the central problem of the decade [the 1960s] for the United Kingdom was the balance of payments. It had been a problem in the 1950s as other countries recovered and gained a larger share of world trade.'[19] In his account of how Britain's trading patterns developed from the 1940s onwards, Jim Tomlinson highlights the significance attached by the Labour Party to trade with the Commonwealth and how, even when the Commonwealth began its long decline in significance as a trading bloc, Labour's economic statements in the run-up to the 1964 general election still presented 'the weakening economic link with the Commonwealth as an undesirable and reversible consequence of Conservative policy'.[20] The obvious difficulties that the Labour government would face can be seen by the following facts. Whilst in 1950 nearly half Britain's exports and 38% of its imports went to and came from the sterling area (involving mainly members of the Commonwealth), by 1960 the rapid expansion in continental markets and the much greater competition in sterling area markets were already changing the flows of Britain's trade. Whereas exports to sterling area countries had declined to about 35% of the total, exports to the EEC and members of European Free Trade Association (EFTA) amounted to some 25%. This trend continued throughout the 1960s, so that by the time the Labour government took office in 1964, Western Europe had become the principal focus for Britain's trade.[21] The importance of Germany, as a principal economy within the EEC, was not solely as a trading partner. Rather, its importance to Britain should be seen by the strength of its economy as a whole, by the standing of its currency and in its position within the international economy. As Michael Stewart, the Foreign Secretary, reminded his Cabinet colleagues less than a year after the 1964 general election:

The German economy is so strong that the Federal Government has a part to play only second to the United States in deciding whether we obtain what we need from the international community ... the Germans will continue to be in a key position in deciding international policies on support for sterling, liquidity questions, and aid to developing countries. We need their support for our aims and we are most likely to obtain it if the general atmosphere of Anglo-German relations remains as good as it has recently been.[22]

For a government beset by balance of payments problems, as was the case with the Labour government elected in October 1964, and dependent upon financial support from international institutions, the message was clear: in economic terms, good relations with Germany would be in Britain's best interests.

In a letter sent to the Foreign Office on the day of the general election in Britain, Roberts reported the detail of a conversation with the Federal Chancellor. The British Ambassador was anxious that he had the latest thinking in Bonn on Anglo-German relations, so that he could brief whatever government emerged after the voting. Roberts would not have been surprised by the mixed message he was given. On the one hand, Erhard readily agreed with the Ambassador's assertion about 'the present happy state of Anglo-German relations ... which could be improved still further with the Queen's visit next year', but, on the other hand, whilst confirming that he would want co-operation with London to be as close and effective as possible even under a Labour government (see below), Erhard flagged up his doubts about 'the attitude towards European integration of a Labour administration'.[23] In this context, the British Labour Party was known to be split over the issue of Europe and Wilson was thought to be opposed to membership of the EEC. It was typical of Wilson's approach to politics and how he managed the diverse elements within his party that, although as Leader of the Opposition he had laid down strict conditions that would have to be satisfied before he would support British entry to the EEC, he still managed to 'hedge his bets to an extent that gave even the most ardent European grounds for hope that if things went well with the negotiations all might yet be all right on the night'.[24]

Although Britain had yet to decide on its future in Europe, a commitment to a united Europe through membership of the EEC was one of two central planks on which German foreign policy was based. In the opinion of German policy makers, the best means of overcoming the division of Germany, which was fundamental to the interests of the Federal Republic, would be through creating a united Europe. For the Germans, as one eminent historian cogently argues, 'the phrase "unifying Europe" was applied both to the process of integration inside the (West) European Community and to the larger enterprise of overcoming the division of Europe'.[25] In this context, Britain was also divided from Europe, in the sense that it remained excluded from the EEC, and it was Germany's objective that Britain should be economically and politically integrated with the rest of Western Europe that largely explains the positive attitude it consistently demonstrated towards British membership of the Communities throughout the period.

As well as the inevitable uncertainties that would exist with a change of administration in London, of which Wilson's attitude towards the EEC was but one, there was another potential area of difficulty with the election of a Labour government, which Erhard did not apparently mention to Roberts but which would have been clearly understood by both men. To say that there was no obvious affinity between the far left of the Labour Party in Britain and the right-wing governing Christlich Demokratische Union (Christian Democratic Union; CDU) in Bonn would be an understatement.[26] Some Labour Members of Parliament (MPs) associated the CDU with Germany's darker past. They opposed any arrangement with Germany where there was a suggestion of involvement by former members of the Nazi Party and they strongly resented the financial burden of maintaining the BAOR, as well as the perceived back-sliding by Bonn to contribute properly to such costs, at a time when the threat posed by the Soviet Union was felt to be low. Such sentiments were never far beneath the surface throughout the Wilson years, although they carried more force when the Labour government had to operate with such a narrow majority.[27] As late as 1969, for example, Georg Ferdinand Duckwitz, a State Secretary in the German Foreign Ministry, reported that Stewart had admitted both to pressure on the government from its left wing, which he and Wilson would have to take into account in their dealings with Germany, and that this element in the Party was 'traditionally anti-German'.[28] Whilst there is no suggestion that left-wing attitudes towards Germany materially affected ministerial decisions, the same is not necessarily true of ministerial posturing, particularly over the question of funding the BAOR.

One striking example of left-wing pressure, and the government's reaction to it, occurred shortly after the 1964 election. In an exchange of letters, the Reverend George MacLeod, representing the Iona Community on the Clydeside, sought a denial from the government to the claims of an East German publication, the *Democratic German Record*, that Herbert Blankenhorn would be appointed as German Ambassador in London despite having been a member of the Nazi Party, and having inspected the Warsaw ghetto in September 1941.[29] The British Embassy in Bonn confirmed the validity of the charge

of Nazi Party membership made against the Ambassador designate. Andrew Stark, head of the Chancery, then advised Bernard
Ledwidge, head of the Western Department at the Foreign Office,
that Blankenhorn had indeed been a member of the Nazi Party, a
fact he had never denied, but that he, like others in the German
foreign service, had been obliged to join it. However, there was
absolutely nothing in the allegation about his connection with the
action against Jews. Stark added that Blankenhorn had already
been 'checked out' by the Embassy and had been given a clean bill
of health. An all-party Bundestag committee had also investigated
Blankenhorn, following allegations by the *Frankfurter Rundschau* that
the Federal Foreign Ministry was strongly infiltrated by former
Nazis, but had concluded that his membership of the Nazi Party was
of a purely formal nature and that, on the contrary, Blankenhorn
belonged to the resistance group that had attempted to assassinate
Hitler on 20 July 1944. The committee had confirmed his suitability
for employment in the German foreign service.[30]

But the accusations against Blankenhorn went further. Stark also
referred to a letter received by the Embassy in December 1964, from
an unknown but suspected East German source, which alleged that
Blankenhorn had signed the Wannsee Protocol and that it was in
this connection that he had visited the Warsaw ghetto.[31] However,
as Stark could find no evidence that Blankenhorn had been at the
Wannsee Conference he attributed the letter to be 'part of the
generalised smear technique used by communist propaganda'.[32] In a
recent account of the Wannsee Conference, the eminent Holocaust
historian Mark Roseman does refer to 'follow-up meetings to
Wannsee that took place in March and in October 1942, involving
subordinates of the Wannsee participants'.[33] Whilst it is a possibility
that Blankenhorn could have had some connection with these meetings, Roseman's account fully supports Stark's assertion made in
1965 that Blankenhorn neither attended the Conference nor signed
the Protocol. As it was, the British Embassy in Bonn concluded that,
from all the reliable evidence, Blankenhorn's behaviour before 1945
had been beyond reproach.[34]

However, the matter of Blankenhorn's acceptability to the British
government did not end with these exchanges. In March 1965, Stewart
was obliged to provide a written answer to a parliamentary question
from Tom Driberg, a prominent left-wing Labour MP, defending the
decision to advise the Queen that Blankenhorn's appointment as
German Ambassador to Britain would be welcome, notwithstanding
his known connection with the Nazi Party.[35] Stewart was also aware
by this time that Blankenhorn had been obliged to make an official
trip to see the Russian front at Vitelsk and 'on the return journey had

been taken rapidly through the Warsaw ghetto but had not stopped there and had not been officially photographed'.[36] Driberg's question had clearly been motivated by a German Democratic Republic propaganda sheet which carried an article under the title 'Yet Another Nazi for London', which officials suggested to the Foreign Secretary 'stimulated ... letters of protest [from the Iona Community] ... the Beaverbrook press [had] been critical and so [had] the *Daily Worker*'.[37] A more balanced article about Blankenhorn that appeared in *The Times* in February 1965 highlighted the involvement of East German propaganda, pointed out that this had found little echo in Britain and concluded that it was 'hardly likely he would have been given this post had there been the least suspicion against him'.[38] In further exchanges in the House of Commons, Renée Short, another left-wing Labour MP, added to the challenge against Blankenhorn's appointment and suggested that his work in Washington before the war and his service in Switzerland later in the war would have given him ample opportunity to seek asylum if, as he had claimed, he had been so opposed to Nazi ideology.[39]

It is clear that the controversy surrounding Blankenhorn's appointment was minor, and as such has not previously been regarded as a significant landmark in the development of Anglo-German relations. But a closer examination of it is important for two reasons. Firstly, it was indicative of the latent feelings about Germany that still existed at the time within sections of British society, although this was hardly surprising, since it was still barely twenty years since the end of the Second World War and memories on both sides ran deep. Secondly, despite its trivialities, the incident was potentially serious. It contained all the ingredients that might have opened up old wounds and caused a damaging blow to relations between Britain and Germany at a time when both governments were intent on maintaining the improvement that had already begun under the previous British administration. Had Wilson wanted to make a point with the Germans, Blankenhorn's Nazi past would certainly have provided the opportunity to do so, even though to decline an ambassadorial nomination would have been an unusual and serious occurrence in both diplomatic and political terms.[40] The robust stance of Wilson, who when welcoming Blankenhorn to London specifically told the Ambassador that Anglo-German relations were in a particularly happy state,[41] and his ministers in resisting the challenge from the left wing of the Party, at a very delicate moment in the fortunes of the government, was symbolic of a determination not only to assert their authority but also to do nothing that would impede a fresh approach towards Europe and the friendship with Germany on which it would be based.

Press reaction in Germany to Labour's election victory revealed an understanding of the problems that the new government would face, but also concern over the direction that British foreign policy might take and the implications for Anglo-German relations. As Roberts put it:

> in general there is little enthusiasm for the result, all papers emphasising the narrowness of the Labour Party's majority and the inhibiting effect that this may well have on British policy both at home and abroad ... [and] some comment also expressed anxiety about the new Government's likely attitude towards Europe and the Federal Republic and about the possible influence of the 'Left Wing' of the Labour Party.

Roberts further reported that the *Kölner Stadt Anzeiger* (*KSA*) had suggested that doubts about the Labour government's position were justified, given its known opposition to the MLF, lack of enthusiasm towards Europe and suspicion of Germany, and that the *Frankfurter Allgemeine Zeitung* (*FAZ*) was sharply critical of Wilson, depicting him as 'a man who is in his political instincts a Germanophobe anti-European'.[42] Despite these unflattering comments about the new government, the *FAZ* correspondent suggested that the British Prime Minister was sufficient of a realist to recognise that a foreign policy shaped by prejudice would have little practical future, whilst the *KSA* observed that as long as the left wing of the Labour Party was kept in check there would not be unpleasant consequences for Anglo-German relations. As Roberts was later to confirm, 'the reaction of the Federal Government is correct and friendly. The Chancellor himself made it clear ... that he wanted existing good relations to be continued and developed regardless of party differences'.[43]

Relations after October 1964

There are certainly grounds for asserting, therefore, that by the time that the Labour government came to power relations between London and Bonn were already recovering from the misunderstandings of the past. Both governments seemed to believe that this was the case. Moreover, even though there were doubts in Germany about the future course of British foreign policy, expectations in Bonn at least of 'business as usual' appeared not to be misplaced. However, this positive assessment overlooked certain factors that would complicate dealings between London and Bonn. Firstly, it can be argued that Labour's long period in opposition had left it short of practical experience of government and that its initial moves in foreign policy matters would reveal, at the very least, some uncertainty. Secondly,

Labour's actions would be constrained both by the margin of its majority in the House of Commons, which would give its left wing greater influence than might otherwise have proved to be the case, and by its manifesto commitments, particularly those relating to nuclear strategy. Both these factors could be seen in play in a speech made by Wilson on 23 November 1964 during a defence debate in the House, which caused considerable misgivings in Bonn and seemingly threatened to undo the positive nature of the relations between Britain and Germany. In remarks criticising the Nassau agreement (on which, see Chapter 2), Wilson argued that not only had it 'set back ... for two years the world's hope of an anti-dissemination agreement to stop the spread of nuclear weapons' but it had 'stimulated nuclear appetites in other members of the Alliance including ... Germany'.[44] Whereas this was the sort of language that the left wing of the Parliamentary Labour Party would wish to hear, and Wilson would have been well aware of this, it was also entirely consistent with comment in Labour's election manifesto.[45]

However, whilst Labour Party manifesto statements on nuclear policy, particularly when in opposition, might be seen as little more than pandering to left-wing points of view, a statement by the Prime Minister in the House publicly warning of German nuclear aspirations was hardly likely to win friends and gain influence in Bonn. Although Wilson's comments were almost certainly designed for domestic consumption, they revealed not only a degree of insensitivity in terms of their likely impact on the Germans but also some *naïveté* in the conduct of international relations. The extent of their impact in Germany became evident within days, when Rainer Barzel, leader of the CDU in the German Bundestag, reacting to Wilson's speech, announced that his party 'could accept neither the political nor the military basis for the opinion of the British Government' and that 'they were worried and disturbed'.[46] As Karl Carstens, First Secretary of State at the German Foreign Ministry, was to put it to Roberts during an unscheduled meeting in Bonn, 'Wilson's comments about Nassau and their effect upon Germany's nuclear appetite would naturally not be received with enthusiasm'.[47]

Domestic politics apart, any hiccup in relations with Germany was certainly unwelcome to the British government. Indeed, the German Embassy in London drew attention to comment in *The Times* to the effect that there had already been a friendly exchange of telegrams between the British and German foreign ministers and that the Labour government had evidently decided to improve relations with Germany.[48] As evidence of this, and in a damage-limitation exercise, British ministers and diplomats moved to reassure their German counterparts that Wilson's statement in the House did not represent a change in policy. Although Wilson conceded to Gerhard Schröder, the German Foreign Minister, that his remarks may have caused offence, he made it clear that 'he had only spoken as he had to emphasise the need for a permanent American veto' on the use of nuclear weapons by the MLF and that within the next few days he would clarify the position of his government to Germany's satisfaction. In conciliatory terms, Wilson went on to detail how the new British proposal for an ANF also had as its aim the German objective of creating 'a credible and collective deterrent, in which every participant had the same rights but with no finger on the trigger'.[49] In comments made in the House a few days after his meeting with Schröder, Wilson referred to his remarks made on 31 January 1963 during the Commons debate on the Nassau agreement in which he had stated Labour's opposition for all time to any new finger on the nuclear trigger, without exception, but then reaffirmed a commitment to co-operation 'in finding the arrangements which best meet the legitimate interests of all members of the Alliance, while retaining existing safeguards on the use of nuclear weapons and preventing their further proliferation'. As an evident gesture to address German concerns, Wilson went on to commit his government to promoting 'increasing cooperation within the Alliance on the policy of the Western Powers in regard to nuclear weapons in any part of the world'.[50] Whilst there was no question of Britain supporting any proposal that would give Germany control of nuclear weapons, the language of co-operation and understanding of Germany's concern for its security then expressed by the British Prime Minister can be seen as a positive move designed to mend fences and ensure that relations between London and Bonn were restored to a sounder footing.

Nevertheless, British diplomats recognised that more should be done by the new administration if recent misunderstandings were to be avoided in future. As Roberts emphasised in a letter to Sir Harold Caccia, Permanent Under-Secretary at the Foreign Office, 'the record of de Gaulle's handling of Germany is an object lesson in what can be achieved by a few warm and friendly public remarks, however empty they may seem and however wide of the actual policies being pursued'. Moreover, in an obvious reference to Wilson's comments in the House of 23 November, Roberts made it clear that 'there is at present a most unfortunate tendency, which I have been attacking strongly in every quarter here, to interpret individual statements by British Ministers as revealing basic unfriendliness towards Germany'.[51] Roberts followed this letter with a further approach to Caccia in which he recalled how, when he had been in London in November 1964, ministers had emphasised the importance they attached to Anglo-German relations, which they regarded as second only to those with the United States, and their hopes of really close and confident dealings with their German opposite numbers. However, public statements by ministers had done little to reassure the Germans that this was indeed the case.

The remedy that the British Ambassador proposed was simple. As Roberts commented, 'in contrast to our American and French allies, we have in our relations with Germany, at least in recent years, consistently neglected the valuable weapon of personal messages between Heads of Government'.[52] The point made by Roberts clearly found its mark when, as tangible evidence of the British government's wish to put previous misunderstandings to one side and to maintain good relations with Germany, and as an indication of the weight placed by ministers on Roberts' advice, Wilson despatched a letter to Erhard following his visit to Germany in March 1965 and suggested that they should exchange personal messages from time to time. The suggestion motivated an immediate response from Erhard, who agreed with the suggestion and saw in it 'an ideal way to improve the trustworthy, friendly cooperation between [the] two Governments'.[53] Wilson's visit to Bonn resulted in a further initiative to consolidate relations between the two governments, which would be in addition to and separate from the already successful, and long-standing, facility afforded by way of the annual Königswinter Conferences.[54] At his suggestion, Erhard agreed that consultations between respective British and German ministers and their officials should be increased and put on a more formal basis. As a consequence, officials in Bonn were soon briefing the British Ambassador on the satisfaction of their ministers, including the Chancellor, with 'the happy developments and present state of Anglo-German relations', whilst in London their British counterparts began examining 'the question of positive action ... to strengthen Anglo-German relations'.[55]

If an improvement in Anglo-German relations was already underway by October 1964, as we have argued here, what can be said about the relationships between the political leaders of the two countries, and to what extent did this personal dimension affect the implementation of policy? This is an important and relevant question, given the personality differences that patently existed between Adenauer and Macmillan and what has been claimed about Anglo-German relations during their era. The picture that emerges after the early exchanges between the new British government and Bonn was of two governments anxious to ensure that the initial misunderstandings did no lasting damage to their future relations and ready to formalise procedures typical of those that would have been the norm between close allies and friends. However, official documents suggest that the warmth in the official relationship between London and Bonn that had been re-established by the beginning of 1965 did not necessarily extend to the personal level, particularly so between Wilson and his CDU counterparts, although, as we have already argued, this did not influence co-operation between the two governments. When forming the new Labour government, Wilson was careful to place the key ministries, including the Foreign Office, in the hands of former Gaitskellite supporters, so that the Cabinet had a distinct right-wing bias.[56] Nevertheless, the appointment of Gordon Walker, and subsequently that of Stewart, as Foreign Secretary was a clear indication that Wilson would maintain the tradition of a Prime Minister having a close involvement with foreign affairs. As one of his closest colleagues was to confirm, 'what is clear is that Harold himself is taking a predominant interest in foreign affairs' and that same colleague would subsequently emphasise that Wilson had 'completely dominated foreign affairs and defence, as well as all the main economic decisions'.[57] The right-wing bias of key British ministers meant that, by design or chance, the personalities involved would tend to have a more positive view of Anglo-German relations. This was clearly how it was seen in Bonn, when Roberts, in a despatch to the Foreign Office with further press comment about the new government, reported that 'the point is widely made that the Prime Minister ... has made sure that power rests firmly in the hands of the moderates' and that 'they represent a foreign policy of Western solidarity'.[58]

Wilson, on the other hand, as the article in the *FAZ* would tend to suggest, was believed by the Germans to be less than sympathetic towards and to harbour resentments about Germany, a belief that was never eradicated, notwithstanding Wilson's subsequent actions. One of his advisers, by way of support for this line of argument, suggested that Wilson was indifferent about the Germans.[59] That doubts continued to linger about Wilson's personal attitude towards Germany can be seen in a brief prepared by the German Foreign Ministry in 1966 for the visit to London by Erhard. Although the British Prime Minister's political skills and his pragmatism were acknowledged, reference was made to Wilson's 'resentment', which could be seen in:

> his various statements, especially those on the question of German rearmament and the potential use by Germany of atomic armaments ... and how during the recent election he did not reject the reservations about Germany still held by some of the British population, or the danger of a German finger on the nuclear trigger and the connection of this possibility with the Nazi past.[60]

It is certainly reasonable to assert, therefore, that Wilson personally could have been a Germanophobe as the *FAZ* had suggested. In this regard, of course, he was by no means unusual and would have shared such views with many of his generation, including members of his government, whose attitudes had been shaped by experience of the Second World War. As the German Ambassador admitted in an assessment of British impressions of Germany:

> most Britons have mixed feelings about the Germans ... negative clichées would have disappeared a long time ago if the Second World War had not confirmed them. After [the war] the Germans were looked upon by many British as authoritarian, intolerant, sentimental, superior and without humour.[61]

That prejudice existed within Wilson's Cabinet, and would continue to do so, was made clear by Richard Crossman, then his Secretary of State for Social Services and a confidant. Crossman, in response to a suggestion in 1968 that training facilities in Britain be made available to the German air force, told colleagues that 'nobody hates this more than I do but I am sixty, we are out of date. Nothing would appeal to the younger generation more than a dramatic action to set aside the old feud against the Germans.'[62] However, it is important to put such feelings into perspective. There is absolutely no indication from the official records, or from the opinions of some of those who worked with him at the time, that Wilson allowed either such resentment or prejudice that may have existed in his mind to influence his judgements about or the dealings of his government with Germany, even though, as events later showed, he was prone to make threats about the consequence of German actions that he considered ran counter to British interests. Such threats, however, were, and should be seen as, little more than political tactics designed to persuade the German government towards a particular course of action more favourable to Britain. Moreover, even though German ministers and officials had misgivings about some of Wilson's public pronouncements, they were satisfied that his official policy towards Germany proved the point that 'he [was] too much of a political realist to allow his political decisions to be influenced by resentment'.[63]

It is also relevant to the discussion to determine the extent to which ministerial attitudes towards Germany might have been shaped by public opinion. One important influence in this regard was the press. However, during the 1960s the picture that emerges about the attitude of the British press towards Germany is mixed. There is little doubt that throughout the post-war period elements of the press, and particularly the tabloids, have displayed a particularly negative mind-set about Germany and the German character. On the other hand, and this can be seen quite clearly during the period of the Labour governments, the majority of press reporting about Britain's relations with Germany was both measured and positive. One obvious example of this was *The Times* article on Blankenhorn's appointment as German Ambassador.[64] Another was an article in *The Guardian* in March 1965, which asserted the importance of Germany to the creation of 'the Europe idea' and the role for a Labour government in fulfilling this idea, notwithstanding 'conditioned British reflexes of hostility to Germany'.[65] Nevertheless, the effect on the public of press reporting about Germany during the 1960s is difficult to judge, particularly as memories of the war would still have been relatively fresh. However, a good indication can be formed from the sampling conducted in opinion polls either side of Labour's election victory in 1964. In a poll taken in March 1963, in response to the question 'As things are today, do you think that Britain and West Germany can or cannot cooperate closely?', 61% of those asked replied in the affirmative.[66] Similarly, in a poll taken in December 1967, in response to the question 'If you had to choose between France and Germany as the chief ally of this country, which would you choose?', 49% of those asked opted for Germany against 22% for France.[67]

Despite this broadly favourable picture, there is no doubt that, during the 1960s, there were mixed feelings in Britain about Germany as a growing economic and military power. Economically, the British public viewed Germany's status more with admiration than with envy. As a report by the German Embassy on British public opinion suggested, 'German support for sterling was widely welcomed ... and Germany's economic recovery since the war is much admired'.[68] In military terms also, as Stewart advised his Cabinet colleagues, 'the Germans ... are already contributing a good deal ... they are prosperous enough to contribute still more ... [they] already provide the largest national contingent in the conventional forces in Europe'.[69] Whilst Germany's increasing military strength had attracted little press comment, Gallup polls consistently revealed that the British public clearly opposed any suggestion that Germany should be armed with nuclear weapons. Just one month after the 1964 election, for example, some 53% of those asked indicated opposition to the MLF concept if it resulted in Germany having a share in the handling of nuclear weapons.[70]

Within the upper reaches of British society also, some elements had considerable forebodings about Germany's military strength, its latent right-wing nationalism and its potential for instability. During a debate in the House of Lords in November 1966 on the defence of Western Europe, several speakers identified these factors. In surprisingly forthright language, one of them, the Earl of Arran, said that 'British troops should be kept there in full strength, not only because of Russia but because of possible trouble within Germany itself ... Germany, and not Russia, [was Britain's] potential enemy....

A reunited Germany would be a great threat to world peace.'[71] Whilst a spokesman for the government quickly conceded that right-wing gains that had occurred in German state elections were a cause for concern, he regretted the use of extreme language and the fact that it would not add to Alliance cohesion. More seriously, however, he regarded the accusation that one of Britain's principal partners was a potential enemy as an insult.[72] To emphasise the government's position, and in a move designed to reassure Bonn, George Brown, then Foreign Secretary, in a statement during a foreign affairs debate in the House of Commons, 'stressed the stability of the German political system and the confidence of the British Government in its further democratic development'.[73] The incident reflected not only the concern in Britain about the rise of right-wing German extremism, as even featured in popular culture, but also was symptomatic of a small undercurrent of anti-German sentiment that continued to run through British society.[74] Nevertheless, it is important to put this into perspective. British opinion was predominantly and consistently sympathetic towards Germany and supportive of moves designed to enhance Anglo-German relations. Wilson and his ministers could develop their policies accordingly.

It is of some significance, but of no real surprise, that, right from the outset in 1964 as Labour took office, officials were stressing the importance of Europe (meaning both NATO and the EEC) to British strategy. As the Long Term Study Group stressed, 'The importance of Europe to our national survival means that we have a major political interest in the area; and in ensuring that Europe does not develop politically or economically in such a way as to inhibit our economic interests'.[75] Some months later, in equally forthright language, Stewart reminded his Cabinet colleagues that:

> German attitudes are important because the Federal German Government are bound to play a key role in developments in many spheres of vital interest to us ... there is too much at stake for our own future to allow feelings about the past to govern our approach to Anglo-German relations.[76]

On a similar note, *The Guardian* suggested that 'the hard driving force behind the European idea has always been the desire to harness German energies and power to a common purpose, so that the most powerful European state outside Russia would never again run wild'.[77] The thrust of this advice to Wilson and his ministerial team was clear: Britain's future was in Europe and a close relationship with Germany, in which prejudice and resentment would have no place, would help secure that objective and contain any latent extremism that might resurface in Germany.

In the aftermath of the 1964 election, Britain's trade continued the reorientation that was becoming evident before Labour took office, although the balance of payments crisis worsened. By this time also, Germany's importance as a trading partner was more clearly established, to the extent that Roberts, in his annual report on events in 1965, felt able to refer to an expansion of bilateral trade which 'reached about £500 million with British exports well up on 1964 and about in balance with German exports to us'. On more general economic relations, Britain's Ambassador went on to report that 'the Germans [had] worked well with us in WEU [Western European Union] and also with EFTA and over the Kennedy Round [of GATT]'.[78] In this context, the newly elected Labour government, like its Conservative predecessor, fully supported trade liberalisation through the GATT negotiations and saw in this a means of improving not only Britain's trade in general but also trade within the Commonwealth in particular. Despite the Labour government's commitment to strengthening economic ties with the Commonwealth, it quickly became apparent that this was an unsustainable policy. As Wilson was soon to discover at a Commonwealth conference held in May 1965, 'there was virtually no willingness to improve intra-Commonwealth trading arrangements'.[79] If there was any doubt on the matter before, the limitations of strengthening trade within the Commonwealth, or within EFTA, made a second application for membership of the EEC almost certain. As an example of the growing trading strength of the EEC at the time, during the ten years up to 1968 its share of the world's total exports had increased to just over 30%, against a decline to 7.3% for the United Kingdom, to 16% for the United States and to 14.9% for the EFTA.[80] Moreover, as one assessment made clear, in the four years up to 1969, Britain's position as a leading exporter to the Commonwealth had been badly shaken, and so had its position as a leading importer, whilst the EEC's trading performance had improved substantially in both cases.[81]

We have already emphasised that the greatest economic problem to confront ministers throughout the Labour years was Britain's relatively poor competitive position and its continuing balance of payments deficits. As Tomlinson points out, 'the whole period from 1964 to 1970 saw the government lurching from crisis to crisis as it grappled with short-term macro-economic problems, mostly arising from external problems'.[82] Although Wilson claimed that Britain was facing a deficit of £800 million on its overseas payments for the year 1964 (a figure that has been widely accepted), and a scarcely less daunting prospect for 1965, Tomlinson, in a recent account, convincingly demonstrates, with the benefit of revisions to contemporary official calculations, that 'on no measure did the deficit reach the £800 million commonly quoted at the time as the scale of the problem'. Whilst he does acknowledge that there was a balance of payments problem in 1964, and that this was the widespread perception that so undermined confidence in sterling and the ability of the government to restore the situation, Tomlinson goes on to cite other reasons for the international lack of confidence in Britain's ability to manage its economy in a way that would ensure the stability of sterling, namely: the rising trend in overseas government expenditure; the continued high level of foreign investment, which in the short run worsened the payments position; the government's commitment to the fixed exchange rate entered into at Bretton Woods; and the support for a continuation of the sterling area.[83] Seemingly the obvious solution to Britain's economic problems in 1964 was devaluation, but this was immediately ruled by Wilson and his key economic ministers on the grounds that Labour would be identified as the party of devaluation and that, more seriously, a devaluation of sterling would cause a breakdown of the international monetary system and lead to economic protectionism.[84] The strength of Wilson's arguments about devaluation and its likely effects was reinforced in March 1965, when, on Wilson's first visit to Germany as Prime Minister, Erhard told him that 'a healthy British economy and a strong pound sterling were of great importance to Germany'.[85] The implications behind this remark were twofold: that, in terms of international relations, more account had to be taken of the growing interdependence between states, which was an important fact of the global economy at the time; and that, more immediately, Britain could continue to expect German support for its currency. Such economic interdependence could be attributed to tariff reductions negotiated under GATT, the substantial increase in international trade and the growing flows of capital investment. Whilst the devaluation of sterling, when it occurred in 1967, did not have the dire consequences predicted by Wilson, for the reason that there was little in the way of an alternative, and the outcome had largely been expected, it is relevant to note that it can now be seen as part of the general realignment of currencies in Europe that occurred towards the end of the 1960s, as the Bretton Woods international monetary system, put under pressure by a weakening American dollar caused by the enormous cost of the Vietnam War and an increasing federal budget, began to collapse.

Little attention has been focused, hitherto, on the implications for Anglo-German relations of Britain's economic difficulties during the Wilson years, almost certainly because of the greater interest in the controversial decision by Wilson and his key ministers not to devalue and their reasoning at the time. Nevertheless, the decision left Britain economically dependent upon the support that would be provided for sterling by other countries, either directly or through the medium of the International Monetary Fund (IMF). Inevitably a price would be attached to this support, at least as far as Germany was concerned, in the form of a *quid pro quo*, a fact that was brought home to British officials within weeks of the Labour government taking office. During an informal meeting with the British Ambassador, Carstens drew attention to German support for the pound, declared that it was an act of solidarity because of the extent to which Germany could identify with British interests and expressed the hope that the British government would do the same for Germany.[86] The importance that Bonn attached to its help, and the wish to have this fact recognised, was implied by Wilson when he felt compelled to thank 'Erhard for German help for sterling in recent weeks' and to acknowledge that Britain 'greatly welcomed both the speed and the extent of German support of sterling at a difficult time'.[87]

The conclusion that can be drawn from these exchanges was that a direct link had been created between Britain's economic weakness and German goodwill. This was brought home to Wilson when, in the context of the discussions with Germany on the costs of stationing British troops there, Sir Burke Trend, the Cabinet Secretary, reminded the Prime Minister that Britain 'may need to enlist German political support for our next battle with the IMF'.[88] In essence, as Trend's minute to the Prime Minister implied, dependency on Germany's support would limit Britain's leverage on support costs. It was a point also well appreciated by the Federal Chancellor, who told Wilson during their meeting in March 1965 that:

> it would be even more unfortunate if ... the United Kingdom might henceforward be less willing to contribute to the defence of Germany, since this would appear to be incompatible with the spirit in which the Federal Government had recently tried to help the United Kingdom during the period of very heavy pressure on sterling.[89]

Thus, in the period after Labour assumed office, economic imperatives drew both countries into a closer relationship. This is not to imply that either country would be prepared to sacrifice essential economic interests at any cost but, in a Cold War era of uncertain international relations, the argument here is that both Britain and Germany recognised that closer co-operation would be to their advantage and acted accordingly.

Notwithstanding Britain's commitments in the Far East, derived largely from the confrontation with Indonesia and American pressure to retain a defence presence east of Suez, it is evident from recent accounts that, even before the announcement in 1967 of the intention to depart from South East Asia and the Persian Gulf, ministers 'were prepared to contemplate withdrawal and adjustment'.[90] As Denis Healey, the Defence Secretary, also later admitted when discussing the decision by the government, made on overriding grounds of national interest, to reduce the percentage of national wealth which Britain spent on defence, 'from the beginning [in 1964] it was clear that any cut in our commitments must come outside rather than inside the European theatre, since our interest in European security was, and [would] remain, irreducible' and that 'it was only when we brought Confrontation [with Indonesia] to a successful conclusion in the summer of 1966 that we were able to make detailed plans for the reduction of our commitments and capability in that area'.[91] That this withdrawal would become a reality and that Europe would become the focus of Britain's strategy must have been perfectly clear to Wilson and his ministers, contending as they were in 1964 with a worsening economic situation, and is a fundamental reason why a sound relationship with Germany was so important to Britain's interests.

We have already discussed how Wilson was seemingly a late convert to the European ideal, symbolised by the EEC and the movement towards greater political and economic unity. In this context, German doubts about both his personal commitment to Europe and the ability of Britain to counter the claims by French President Charles de Gaulle to the effect that, until its Commonwealth and world-wide commitments were reduced, Britain would not be a suitable candidate for membership of the EEC, were probably reinforced when, soon after taking office, Wilson proclaimed 'We are ... a world power and world influence or we are nothing'.[92] The question is, however, did Wilson really believe his own rhetoric? The answer is almost certainly in the affirmative, as some of his ministers and his Private Secretary at the time have since confirmed. Even by 1966, according to one minister, when an approach to determine whether negotiations for EEC membership would receive a favourable response was under active consideration, Wilson told the Labour Parliamentary Party that 'though he was prepared to withdraw and reduce the number of troops East of Suez he would never deny Britain the role of a world power'.[93] Nevertheless, Wilson's comments have to be considered in the context in which they were made. Whilst they almost certainly reflected a sincere regret that Britain's world standing was under threat, and may have been designed with electoral benefit in mind, Wilson was too astute a politician not to recognise the economic and political imperatives that made a scaling-down of commitments inevitable.

Even setting to one side Wilson's view of Britain's place in the world, the fact remains that in 1964, because of problems connected with Rhodesia and confrontation with Indonesia, as well as the difficulties caused by the management of an economy in decline, Britain's commitments beyond Europe meant that it had to afford a higher priority to those areas rather than to seeking a more active partnership with Germany. Similarly with Bonn, whilst Britain was and would remain an important ally, German interests would dictate that greater emphasis would have to be afforded to relations with the United States, France and, ultimately, with the Soviet Union. The United States, as Germany's most important ally, provided the ultimate guarantee of German security, a role that Britain could not and probably never would fulfil, whilst friendship with France, particularly after the signing of the Franco-German Élysée Treaty in 1963, became a consistent feature of German foreign policy; that treaty ended the history of enmity between the two countries, provided for consultation on all important questions of foreign policy, offered the prospect of leadership within the EEC and formed the bedrock of what might be termed Germany's *Westpolitik*. In addition, if progress was to be made towards political union and the removal of artificial barriers in Europe, and ultimately the reunification of Germany, such developments could be made only through and with the agreement of the Soviet Union, hence the importance of the Soviet Union to Germany strategy. The reality of priorities in foreign policy would have a bearing on Anglo-German relations throughout the Wilson years, a fact recognised by the Cabinet Office Planning Staff when, in 1969, officials advised Trend that 'the difficulty about our relations with Germany is that we rank no higher than fourth in her order of priorities: relations with the US, France and the USSR are more important to the Germans'.[94]

Nevertheless, notwithstanding orders of priority, the wish for a close and positive relationship existed on both sides. Despite suggestions to the contrary, the tone and intensity of official and personal exchanges reveal that, by early 1965, Britain and Germany believed their relationship to be strong, building on the positive signs that had developed once Macmillan and Adenauer had passed from the scene. As for Britain, Stewart's Cabinet memorandum of August 1965 put it this way: 'it is more and more through a close relationship of real confidence with Bonn as well as with Washington that we can work effectively towards our vital aims in foreign and even in domestic affairs'.[95] It is against this background that discussion can focus on an assessment of Anglo-German relations during the whole span of the Labour governments up to 1970, as both governments confronted a number of issues where differences of opinion and problems could have emerged.

Notes

1 Craig, *British General Election Manifestos*, pp. 43–60.
2 Patrick Gordon Walker, 'The Labour Party's Defense and Foreign Policy', *Foreign Affairs*, 42, 3 (April 1964), pp. 391–398.

3 See Introduction, note 23.
4 Briefing note for ministers on Anglo-German relations, February 1964, RG 1051/12, FO 371/177927, PRO. It is also relevant to this theme that at the 1964 Königswinter Conference, Edward Heath, then a minister in Sir Alec Douglas Home's Conservative government, described the 'Anglo German partnership as a basis for a new future for the Atlantic Community' and described 'Anglo German relations as being better than at any time in this century'. See letter from Andrew Stark, head of the Chancery, Bonn, to Paul Holmes, Western Department at the Foreign Office, 11 March 1965, RG 2232/17, FO 371/183187.
5 German fears dated back to at least 1955, when 'Adenauer ... thought that the Americans were getting ready to make a deal with Russia at the expense of their European allies'. See Marc Trachtenberg, *A Constructed Peace: The Making of the European Settlement, 1945–1963* (Chichester, 1999), p. 231.
6 Briefing note for ministers on Anglo-German relations, February 1964, RG 1051/12, FO 371/177927, PRO.
7 *Ibid.*
8 Roberts had a long and distinguished career. He came to prominence in 1946, as acting Ambassador in Moscow, through association with George Kennan, his American counterpart and the 'Long Telegram'. He served as Ambassador to Yugoslavia and Moscow before taking up his final appointment in 1963 as Ambassador in Bonn.
9 Aufzeichnung, 16 January 1967, B136/6187, BA Koblenz.
10 Despatch by Sir Frank Roberts to Mr R. A. Butler, 'Anglo-German Relations', 24 June 1964, RG 1051/33, FO 371/177927, PRO.
11 Roberts' views on the importance of the Queen's visit to Germany and West Berlin were echoed in an article published in an East-German-influenced journal. This described the visit as the high point in all the outward signs of a new understanding and, by implication of a better relationship, between London and Bonn. See Hans Walter Callenius, 'Die Deutschland-politik der britischen Labour-Regierung', *Deutsche Aussenpolitik*, 10, 2 (1965), pp. 1061–1072.
12 Despatch by Sir Frank Roberts to Mr R. A. Butler, 'Anglo-German Relations', 24 June 1964, RG 1051/33, FO 371/177927, PRO.
13 Report of the Long Term Study Group, Regional Study on Europe, 23 October 1964, CAB 148/10, PRO. The Long Term Study Group was set up as a sub-committee of the Defence Overseas Policy Committee and was asked to produce three papers: on Britain's responsibilities in the Far East, the Middle East and Europe.
14 See Dietrich Orlow, *A History of Modern Germany: 1871 to Present* (1995), p. 267; and Peter Howlett, 'The Golden Age 1955–1973', in Paul Johnson (ed.), *20th Century Britain: Economic, Social and Cultural Change* (1996), pp. 320–339.
15 Giles Radice, *The New Germans* (1995), p. 86.
16 Eric Owen Smith, *The German Economy* (Abingdon, 1994), pp. 499–500. Smith attributed Germany's export strength to the following factors: the significant increase in world trade due to the Bretton Woods pegged exchange rate agreement of 1944; successive GATT rounds after 1947, which led to world-wide tariff cuts, particularly for industrial products; lower transport costs and improved telecommunications; and the beginnings of European economic integration, which removed custom barriers within Europe.
17 Andrew Moravcsik, *The Choice for Europe: Social Purpose and State Power from Messina to Maastricht* (1998), p. 202: Foreign Office brief on Professor Dr Ludwig Erhard, January 1965, RG 1015/5, FO 371/182999, PRO.

18 For a recent assessment of Keynes' influence on German economic policy in the post-war period, see Johannes R. B. Ritterhausen, 'The Postwar West German Economic Transition from Ordoliberalism to Keynesianism', Institut für Wirtschaftspolitik an der Universität zu Köln discussion paper 2007/1 (January 2007), pp. 1–63. Available at www.iwp.uni-koeln.de/DE/Publikationen/dp/dp1_07.pdf (last accessed May 2007).

19 Sir Alec Cairncross, _Managing the British Economy in the 1960s: A Treasury Perspective_ (1996), p. 18. See also Peter Dewey, _War and Progress: Britain 1914–1945_ (1997), p. 331, Table 17.6, for the United Kingdom's real economic growth rates, 1856–1973.

20 Jim Tomlinson, _The Labour Governments 1964–1970. Volume 3: Economic Policy_, (Manchester, 2004), p. 22.

21 Cairncross, _Managing the British Economy_, p. 21.

22 Memorandum by Michael Stewart, 'Policy Towards Germany', 5 August 1965, C (65) 119, CAB 129/122 (Pt 2), PRO.

23 Letter from Roberts to Sir Harold Caccia, 16 October 1964, RG 1051/54, FO 371/177928, PRO.

24 Philip Ziegler, _Wilson: The Authorised Life of Lord Wilson of Rievaulx_ (1993), p. 141. This theme of Wilson's attitude towards the EEC is discussed in more detail in Chapter 8.

25 Ash, _In Europe's Name_, p. 24.

26 See Stefan Berger and Darren G. Lilleker, 'The British Labour Party and the German Democratic Republic During the Era of Non-recognition, 1949–1973', _Historical Journal_, 45, 2 (June 2002), pp. 433–458.

27 The final figures from the October 1964 general election were: Labour 317 seats; Conservatives 303 seats; and Liberals 9 seats. Therefore Labour had a majority of five seats over the other parties. Wilson also calculated the effect of the retiring Speaker, which reduced his majority by one seat. See Harold Wilson, _The Labour Government 1964–1970: A Personal Record_ (1971), p. 1.

28 Aufzeichnung des Staatssekretärs Duckwitz, 20 January 1969, _AAPD_ (1969), I, p. 96.

29 Letter from Very Reverend G. F. MacLeod, 5 January 1965, FO 371/183174, PRO. The Reverend MacLeod was the founder member of the Iona Community, an ecumenical Christian community, founded in 1938, committed to seeking ways of living the gospel of Jesus Christ in the world. In his letter he asked for guidance on what he was to say to communists on the Clydeside if Blankenhorn's appointment was accepted.

30 Although Stark's letter contains no evidence to support the claim that Blankenhorn had been part of the 20 July 1944 conspiracy against Hitler, it appears to have been accepted in the Foreign Office – and ultimately by the government. See Stark to Ledwidge, 19 January 1965, RG 1903/3, FO 371/183174, PRO, and Foreign Office brief for the Prime Minister, 10 May 1965, RG 1903/3, FO 371/183174, PRO.

31 The Protocol resulted from the Conference held on 20 January 1942 at Wannsee in Berlin to discuss the implementation of the 'Final Solution' for Europe's Jews. See Eberhard Jäckel, Peter Longerich and Julius Schoeps (eds), _Enzyklopädie des Holocaust. Volume 3_ (München, 1998), pp. 1516–1519.

32 Stark to Ledwidge, 19 January 1965, RG 1903/3, FO 371/183174, PRO, and Foreign Office brief for the Prime Minister, 10 May 1965, RG 1903/3, FO 371/183174, PRO.

33 Mark Roseman, _The Villa, the Lake, the Meeting: Wannsee and the Final Solution_ (2002), p. 100.

34 Stark to Ledwidge, 19 January 1965, RG 1903/3, FO 371/183174, PRO, and Foreign Office brief for the Prime Minister, 10 May 1965, RG 1903/3, FO 371/183174, PRO.
35 *Hansard*, House of Commons, 709 (29 March 1965), cols 178–179. The answer was in response to a question by Driberg, which asked 'In view of Herr Blankenhorn's former support of Hitler and the ideologies and policies of the Nazi Party, why it was decided not to advise the West German Government that he would be *persona non grata* as West German Ambassador in London'. Dislike of the CDU was not necessarily confined to left-wing elements of the Labour Party. As Sir Michael Palliser, Wilson's Private Secretary, suggested in interview, 'The Labour party did not like the CDU'.
36 Telegram, Roberts to the Foreign Office, 29 March 1965, RG 1903/12, FO 371/183174, PRO.
37 'Background to the Parliamentary Question by Mr Tom Driberg', 29 March 1965, RG 1903/10, FO 371/183174, PRO.
38 'Herr Blankenhorn as London Envoy', *The Times*, 19 February 1965, p. 10.
39 For details of the exchanges between George Thomson, Minister of State at the Foreign Office, and Renée Short in the House of Commons, see RG 1903/19, FO 371/183174, PRO.
40 A rejection of Blankenhorn's appointment on grounds of his membership of the Nazi Party would also have created a potentially embarrassing precedent for dealings with Kurt Georg Kiesinger, the future German Chancellor, who had been an active member of the Nazi Party. See Lothar Kettenacker, *Germany since 1945* (Oxford, 1997), p. 136.
41 Meeting between Wilson and Blankenhorn, 5 April 1965, RG 1903/21, FO 371/183174, PRO.
42 Telegram number 1013, Sir Frank Roberts to Foreign Office, 17 October 1964, RG 1051/51, FO 371/177928, PRO.
43 Telegram number 1030, Sir Frank Roberts to Foreign Office, 23 October 1964, RG 1051/51, FO 371/177928, PRO.
44 *Hansard*, House of Commons, 702 (23 November 1964), col. 936.
45 Craig, *British General Election Manifestos*, p. 59. The manifesto proposed renegotiation of the Nassau agreement and stated that 'Britain's insistence on … nuclear pretence carries with it grave dangers of encouraging the spread of nuclear weapons to countries not possessing them, including Germany'.
46 Aufzeichnung des Staatssekretärs Carstens, 26 November 1964, *AAPD* (1964), II, p. 1406, fn 2. See also Introduction, note 41.
47 *Ibid*.
48 'Britische Presse über Labour-Außenpolitik', Telegram Number 1074, German Embassy to Foreign Ministry, 23 October 1964, B31/272, PAAA Berlin.
49 Gespräch des Bundesministers Schröder mit Premierminister Wilson, 11 December 1964, *AAPD* (1964), II, p. 1511.
50 *Hansard*, House of Commons, 704 (16 December 1964), cols 432–434.
51 Letter from Roberts to Caccia, 16 January 1965, RG 1051/14, FO 371/183042, PRO.
52 Letter from Roberts to Caccia, 29 January 1965, RG 1051/14, FO 371/183042, PRO.
53 Letter from Erhard to Wilson, 19 March 1965, PREM 13/329, PRO.
54 Meetings of the Deutsch-Englishe Gesellschaft had been held annually since 1948 at Königswinter, near Bonn, hence the name Königswinter Conference. Representatives of the main political parties in Britain and Germany as well as academics and journalists attended such meetings. For the first meeting

after the election in October 1964, Wilson asked Walter Padley, Minister of State at the Foreign Office, to attend and make a speech. See 'Preliminary List of British Participants for Conference in April 1965', RG 2232/1, FO 371/183187, PRO.

55 Letter from Ledwidge to Caccia, 18 June 1965, RG 1052/42, FO 371/183043, PRO. A similar picture of the development of contacts between London and Bonn emerges from correspondence in B31/298, PAAA Berlin.

56 Ponting, *Breach of Promise*, p. 16. Ponting argues that the make-up of the first Wilson Cabinet meant that 'in political terms Wilson and his supporters were outnumbered'.

57 Richard Crossman, *The Diaries of a Cabinet Minister. Volume 1: Minister of Housing 1964–66* (1976), entries for 20 November 1964 and 18 April 1965, p. 68 and p. 203. Wilson himself stated that 'a modern head of government must be the managing director … he must be completely *au fait* with … the work of all main departments'. See Wilson, *The Labour Government*, p. 45.

58 Telegram number 1016, Roberts to Foreign Office, 19 October 1964, RG 1051/51, FO 371/177928, PRO.

59 Palliser went on to indicate that Wilson shared the view of other colleagues that Erhard was 'a rather weak Chancellor' and that he saw Kiesinger as 'a pretty second-rate man'. As for Brandt, whilst Wilson got on well with the German Chancellor, 'they were not particularly close'. Interview material.

60 Foreign Ministry brief for the visit to London by the Federal Chancellor, 'Aufzeichnung über Premierminister Wilson-zur Person und zum Werdegang', 25 April 1966, B31/299, PAAA Berlin.

61 German Ambassador to the Foreign Ministry, 'Das Deutschlandbild der Briten', 22 March 1965, B31/285, PAAA Berlin. The Ambassador's impressions bear a striking resemblance to the description of the German character discussed on 24 March 1990 at Chequers at a meeting between Margaret Thatcher and a small group of historians – part of the German character was seen as being 'angst, aggressiveness, bullying, egotism, inferiority complex, sentimentality'. See Ash, 'The Chequers Affair', p. 65.

62 Richard Crossman, *The Diaries of a Cabinet Minister. Volume 3: Secretary of State for Social Services 1968–70* (1977), entry for 31 October 1968, p. 246.

63 'Aufzeichnung über Premierminister Wilson-zur Person und zum Werdegang', 25 April 1966, B31/299, PAAA Berlin.

64 'Herr Blankenhorn as London Envoy', *The Times*, 19 February 1965, p. 10.

65 'Europe, Power for Change', *The Guardian*, 4 March 1965, p. 10.

66 Gallup, *Gallup International: Volume 1*, p. 673.

67 Gallup, *Gallup International: Volume 2*, p. 957.

68 German Embassy to Bonn, 'Das Deutschlandbild der Briten', 22 March 1965, B31/285, PAAA Berlin.

69 Memorandum by Stewart, 'Policy Towards Germany', 5 August 1965, C(65) 119, CAB 129/122 (Pt. 2), PRO.

70 Gallup, *Gallup International: Volume 1*, p. 779.

71 *Hansard*, House of Lords, Fifth Volume of 1966–67 (21 November 1966), col. 775. Similarly, Viscount Montgomery asserted that 'the real danger in Europe is Germany'. See *ibid.*, col. 774.

72 *Ibid.*, col. 788.

73 Telegram number 2391, Germany Embassy, London to Bonn, 7 December 1966, B31/306, PAAA Berlin.

74 For one example of fears about the revival of extreme German nationalism expressed in popular culture, see John le Carré, *A Small Town in Germany* (1968).

75 Report of the Long Term Study Group, 'Regional Study on Europe', 23 October 1964, DO (O) (S), CAB 148/10, PRO.
76 Cabinet memorandum, 'Policy Towards Germany', August 1965, C (65) 119, CAB 129/122 (Pt 2), PRO.
77 'Europe, Power for Change', *The Guardian*, 4 March 1965, p. 10.
78 'Germany: Annual Review for 1965', 1 January 1965, RG 1011/1, FO 371/189155, PRO.
79 Wilson, *The Labour Government*, p. 117.
80 Organisation for Economic Co-operation and Development (OECD) figures published in *Europe: The Case for Going In* (1971), p. 12.
81 Commonwealth Trade, Commonwealth Secretariat, August 1970, in *Europe: The Case for Going In*, p. 44.
82 Tomlinson, *Economic Policy*, p. 49.
83 *Ibid.*, pp. 14–15. See also Wilson, *The Labour Government*, p. 5.
84 Wilson, *The Labour Government*, p. 6.
85 Prime Minister's visit to Germany, 6–9 March 1965, RG 1052/22, PREM 13/329, PRO.
86 Aufzeichnung des Staatssekretärs Carstens, 26 November 1964, *AAPD* (1964), II, p. 1407.
87 Record of a conversation between the Prime Minister and the Federal German Chancellor, 30 January 1965, RG 1051/15, FO 371/183042, PRO.
88 Memo from Sir Burke Trend, 2 March 1965, PREM 13/342, PRO.
89 Record of the meeting between the Prime Minister and the Federal Chancellor, 8 March 1965, PREM 13/342, PRO.
90 See in particular Jones, 'A Decision Delayed', pp. 569–595.
91 Denis Healey, 'British Defence Policy: A Lecture Given at the Royal United Services Institute (RUSI) on 22 October 1969', *Royal United Services Journal*, 656 (December 1969), p. 16.
92 Quoted in Jefferys, *The Labour Party*, p. 64.
93 Crossman, *Diaries: Volume 1*, entry for 15 June 1966, p. 540. Denis Healey also refers to it being true that 'Harold Wilson had illusions of grandeur about our post-imperial role in Asia and Africa; they endured even after his Cabinet had swung against it'. See Denis Healey, *The Time of My Life* (1990), p. 300. Oliver Wright, Wilson's Private Secretary from 1964 to 1966, suggests that 'Wilson was very much in favour of Britain's world role. He only relinquished it when he had to and then with regret'. Interview material.
94 Note from J. A. Thomson, Cabinet Office Planning Staff, to Sir Burke Trend, 'Foreign Affairs in the Next Two Years', 3 February 1969, PREM 13/2636, PRO. Sir Oliver Wright suggested a similar order of priorities during interview.
95 Cabinet memorandum, 'Policy Towards Germany', August 1965, C (65) 119, CAB 129/122 (Pt 2), PRO.

Chapter 2

Nuclear sharing in NATO: hardware or software?

The question of nuclear sharing within NATO was one of the more seemingly intractable problems confronting Harold Wilson and the in-coming Labour government. The solution that commanded the field in October 1964, having been advanced some four years earlier by the United States as a counter to the increasing number of Soviet medium-range ballistic missiles (MRBMs) capable of striking at NATO bases, and as tangible evidence of its commitment to the defence of Western Europe, was for a NATO multilateral force, the so-called MLF. The MLF concept envisaged a surface fleet of ships armed with Polaris nuclear missiles that would be jointly owned, controlled and financed by the subscribers.[1]

From the outset, however, the MLF proposal provoked different reactions, and not all of them favourable. By 1964, opinion within the American administration had polarised between those, principally in the State Department, who were enthusiastic MLF advocates, and others who were more dubious about the concept.[2] Significantly, however, a majority in Congress opposed the MLF. The position of the President was equivocal to say the least but, as George Ball, the Under-Secretary of State, later suggested, 'President Johnson became increasingly cool towards the idea'.[3] The German government was seemingly committed to the MLF, not because it offered the prospect of ownership of nuclear weapons (although whether such ownership was an aim that enjoyed meaningful support within German political and military circles was, and remains, open to question) but because it would strengthen the security guarantee of the United States. Nevertheless, the governing CDU was split on the proposal, with 'Gaullist' elements such as Franz Josef Strauss, the former Defence Secretary, opposing the force on military grounds and favouring 'a reorientation of German policy away from its Atlantic and American affiliations towards a Franco-German partnership'.[4] In Britain, the

Labour Party was known to have somewhat different ideas about defence policy than its Conservative counterpart and had already expressed opposition to the MLF concept. However, there was a cross-party consensus against the United States' proposal. As observed in an election survey, 'the Labour Party's view is that the MLF has little to commend it militarily and that it is politically undesirable in that it admits Germany to the nuclear circle'. However, in a comparison of the approach that both parties might adopt when in office, the report suggested that 'the Conservative Party [was] prepared to talk about the MLF, but might not be prepared to join it, while a Labour Government would not be prepared to join the force but might be prepared to talk about it'.[5]

In the event, under pressure from Washington to give Britain's formal response to the MLF proposal, the new government offered an alternative plan – for an ANF.[6] It is essentially on this aspect of British foreign policy, and the controversy that surrounded it, that this chapter focuses. The MLF/ANF debate must be considered against a background where Britain was concerned to settle the nuclear sharing problem within NATO, but in a way that would: meet the legitimate claims of its non-nuclear members for more involvement in Alliance nuclear strategy; avoid commitment to a surface fleet; prevent direct German control of nuclear weapons; and maintain progress towards an agreement with the Soviet Union on the non-dissemination of nuclear weapons. It will be argued here that Wilson and his ministers achieved these objectives by effectively blocking plans for the MLF and supporting alternative proposals – for the formation of NATO's NPG, the so-called 'software option', designed to ensure more effective consultation between the United States and its allies on nuclear policy.[7] Britain's handling of the nuclear sharing problem demonstrated sensitivity to Germany's concerns and a determination to maintain good relations with Bonn.

Britain, Germany and the MLF

There is a consensus that the impetus to create the MLF gathered momentum during 1963 and that a major contributory factor was the agreement reached at Nassau in December 1962 under which the United States would make available its Polaris missiles for Britain's planned submarine fleet.[8] The detail of the Nassau agreement has been well documented elsewhere and need not detain us here, but some comment is worth making. Nassau was seen by the Americans as a means of accommodating both Britain's wish to maintain an independent nuclear deterrent and a multilateral solution to NATO's nuclear sharing problem favoured by them, through integrating the

Polaris missiles offered to Britain into an Alliance nuclear force. In incorporating both concepts in the final communiqué at Nassau, however, the principals effectively allowed for different interpretations; in Britain's case, this encouraged expectations of a multinational structure for any future NATO nuclear force. As Alastair Buchan cogently argues, Britain's view about Nassau and the commitment of existing national forces 'was strengthened by the fact that an offer of American Polaris missiles was immediately made to President de Gaulle'.[9] Britain's interpretation of the Nassau agreement was seemingly further confirmed by the inclusion of the 'national interest' clause, under which forces assigned to a NATO nuclear MLF could be withdrawn for independent use when 'Her Majesty's Government [might] decide that supreme national interests [were] at stake'.[10] How could a MLF function effectively if one of the participants could withdraw its contingent at any time of its choosing? Whilst it can be argued that the ambiguity of Nassau was the justification for British governments, Conservative as well as Labour, to sponsor multinational concepts for an Alliance nuclear force, which effectively ensured that the MLF would never see the light of day, this point of view overlooks a more fundamental reason for Britain's attachment to the ownership of nuclear weapons. In an uncertain world, where a nuclear capability would enable Britain to have influence beyond what its economic and political standing would otherwise convey, the surrender of such a capability to a multilateral force made little sense. As Peter Riddell pointed out recently, 'uncertainty about American intentions was one of the main reasons why successive Prime Ministers, from Attlee, through Churchill and Macmillan to Wilson were so determined to retain a British nuclear deterrent'.[11]

Two developments in the wake of Nassau added greater urgency to the American drive to create the MLF. Firstly, on 14 January 1963, President Charles de Gaulle rejected both the offer of Polaris missiles made as a result of the Nassau agreement and vetoed Britain's first application to join the EEC. In this way, de Gaulle: made clear that France would not rely solely upon American nuclear weapons for the defence of NATO territory in Western Europe; suggested that by developing its own deterrent capability France could achieve the status of an independent nuclear power; and opened up the possibility that, by excluding a Britain seen as an American surrogate from membership of the EEC, Europe could develop its own security system, with France as its leading power.[12] However, it was perhaps a further development, following shortly after de Gaulle's announcement, that finally tipped the balance in persuading the Americans to push so hard for the MLF as the solution to NATO's nuclear sharing problem. The Franco-German Élysée Treaty due to be signed on

22 January 1963 raised fears in Washington of co-operation between the two countries in the nuclear field. The MLF, hardly an American priority before Nassau, now became the preferred solution to the political problems of the Alliance.[13] In other words, as Andrew Pierre argues, 'the MLF was promoted as a way to funnel the Federal Republic's supposed nuclear appetites, and to court her away from France by forging new German–American links'.[14]

The official records in Britain and Germany reveal differences over the MLF, within government and between political parties, to an extent no less than existed in America. In Britain, the concept of a MLF was not viewed with any enthusiasm by the Conservative government, or within the defence fraternity. As Earl Mountbatten, Britain's Chief of the Defence Staff (CDS), told General Sir Michael West, chairman of the British Defence Staff in Washington, 'this is, I fear, a subject on which opinion is very much divided ... by a great deal of ill-conceived and unsubstantiated "sludge" ... neither the Minister, the Chiefs of Staff, nor I see a practical military need or justification for any kind of MLF at all'.[15] Behind Mountbatten's caustic comments were more fundamental concerns. Whilst acknowledging that the political aim of the MLF was to provide a means by which the influence of the non-nuclear powers, notably Germany, could be brought to bear more effectively on the nuclear decisions of the Alliance as a whole, Mountbatten observed that this could be achieved only through changes in the existing political control arrangements and not solely by creating a military force of 'mixed-manned' weapons. He went on to add that the critical issue was the veto, and that he had every reason to believe that the Americans had no intention of sharing this with anyone else, no matter what they might have said to the Germans and others.

As to the Germans, the CDS could not see any attraction in the MLF to compensate them for the very considerable financial and outlay on crews which they would be required to make, unless it was the possibility that some sort of majority voting system would give them more influence over the ultimate decision on the use of the Polaris missiles. Mountbatten argued that the only way for members of the MLF to have the same kind of influence on the nuclear decision that Britain had as a manufacturer of warheads would be if the MLF governing body could act independently and not be subject to any overriding veto. This, however, would be pregnant with danger. In many ways, Mountbatten's letter served as an accurate pointer to the approach that Britain would come to adopt towards the MLF. Britain favoured a multinational approach to nuclear sharing which would enable it to retain its deterrent, albeit one that would be available to NATO under existing arrangements; Britain would resist contributing to any MLF that might be set up; and British policy must ensure that Germany had no direct control over nuclear weapons.

As to political differences in Britain, Pierre suggests that, during 1963, as American State Department officials brought pressure on the British to join the MLF, and contrary to the negative opinion of the Ministry of Defence (MOD) as to the military utility of the surface fleet, the Foreign Office formed the view that if the MLF were to be formed, Britain could not afford to remain outside and that to do so could impair relations with the United States. Furthermore, such a development would increase Britain's isolation in Europe, especially after de Gaulle's veto.[16] Nevertheless, as subsequent developments showed, ministers came to see that the way to derail the MLF and prevent the prospect of an American–German force would be to propose the creation of a jointly owned, managed and controlled force of nuclear weapons, but one based on existing land-based weapons systems, involving aircraft and missiles. As far as the Chiefs of Staff were concerned, such a force would be militarily practicable, less costly than nuclear armed surface ships and would meet the basic political requirement to give non-nuclear members of NATO fuller participation in the nuclear defence of the Alliance. In a meeting in Washington in April 1964, R. A. Butler, the Conservative Foreign Secretary, made it clear to Dean Rusk, his American counterpart, that the timing of the general election (planned for October 1964) made it impossible for the British to take a position on the MLF and that, whilst work could continue in the working group sitting in Paris, consideration should be given in parallel to the new British proposals.[17]

It is possible to conclude from these exchanges that, by early 1964, any differences between ministers and officials about Britain's attitude to the MLF had largely been reconciled. Certainly the timing of the general election was a convenient pretext for Britain to drag its heels over the MLF and to complicate the situation with its alternative proposals. Nevertheless, the fact that Britain offered an alternative to the MLF, albeit one that might perpetuate multinational divisions (in relation to the potential withdrawal of national forces), was evidence of the recognition in London that the non-nuclear members of NATO were justified in wanting a more influential role in the development of the Alliance's strategic policy, and that this required a British response. As Leader of the Opposition, Wilson was on record in March 1964 as being against 'the Polaris MLF'.[18] In his memoirs, Wilson claimed that the American proposal for the MLF had divided the previous Conservative government, in contrast to the united opposition presented by the Labour Party.[19] There is no doubt that Wilson and many of his colleagues did oppose the MLF but no more or less than members of the Conservative government, and in this regard it is significant that the counterproposals to the MLF presented by the first Wilson administration were founded on similar principles as, and marked lines of continuity from, those set out by Butler in April 1964 during his meeting in Washington.[20] Certainly convergence between the parties on defence policy had become evident to at least one respected British newspaper by the time of the general election. In an editorial article published just days before polling was due to start, *The Times* commented that the Conservative government had placed Britain's nuclear bombers at the disposal of NATO and had undertaken to do the same with the Polaris system when it came into service. The article went on to observe that, if elected, the Labour Party would follow substantially the same line and, as to the renegotiation of Nassau to which the Party was committed, this would 'probably mean no more than the commitment of the submarines to an allied force as an alternative to the multilateral force'.[21]

As a non-nuclear power, Germany regarded the MLF in a fundamentally different light from Britain. This was hardly surprising. Germany stood in the front line of NATO defences in Europe. Despite its growing economic and military strength, it was completely dependent upon the NATO Alliance, and principally the United States, for conventional and nuclear support to deter Warsaw Pact forces from launching an attack across its borders. Any proposal that seemingly tied the United States more tightly into defence arrangements in Europe would work to its advantage. But were there grounds for Germany to doubt America's commitment to Europe? In this context Buchan points to three factors that seemingly cast doubts over American intentions. The development by the United States of the new NATO strategy of 'flexible response', a subject we will deal with more fully in Chapter 5, and the delay it allowed before the use of nuclear weapons, seemed incompatible with German security requirements. Moreover, talk of a cut-back of American troops in Europe heightened concerns in Bonn that the Americans would withdraw completely at some stage in the future. Finally, the prospect of an arms control agreement in the context of bilateral Soviet–American discussions on Berlin raised fears in Bonn that arrangements might be agreed that ran counter to German interests.[22] Here, then, were sound reasons why the MLF was an attractive proposition for Germany: not only would it help strengthen the bond between Washington and Bonn, but it would also put Germany in a better light as a committed member of the Alliance. As Wilhelm Grewe, Chancellor Konrad Adenauer's Ambassador in Washington, observed, 'we did not feel we could afford to reject an American offer of nuclear sharing'.[23]

The MLF debate has given rise to the suggestion that there were other motives behind German support for the American proposals.

Was there a hidden agenda designed to lead to a national nuclear force? Was it this that provoked so much opposition in Britain, and not just in the Labour Party, to any prospect of a German 'finger on the nuclear trigger'? In a very balanced article, Pertti Ahonen explores the German nuclear question in some depth, discusses the arguments advanced by the two schools of thought on the subject and highlights the part played in the development of Alliance strategy by Strauss, which has been cited as evidence that 'the German Government consistently strove for an independent nuclear capability from the mid-1950s to the late 1960s and that the task of containing Germany dominated much of Western diplomacy during these years'.[24] Whilst it is beyond the scope of this book to add to this debate in any detail, there is no doubt that public statements by Strauss were a cause for some concern in Washington. Although Jane Stromseth asserts that 'Strauss' interest in greater nuclear control-sharing was expressed with clarity and urgency' and that he advocated 'general NATO control over all tactical nuclear weapons in Europe', her reference to a speech to the NATO Council in which Strauss warned that 'if NATO did not establish an MRBM force ... the British and French could easily find followers' might be viewed as evidence of Strauss' real intentions.[25]

Whilst there was some support within Germany for an independent national nuclear force, particularly given the position of Britain and of France in the wake of Nassau, there was never any serious likelihood that the possession of nuclear weapons would become official German policy.[26] In this context, German policy makers were well aware that the depth of concern within the Alliance, in the Soviet Union and throughout Eastern Europe, fostered by the experiences of two World Wars, demanded that strict controls be maintained over the rearmament of the Bundeswehr and that such controls would preclude the possession of nuclear weapons. Moreover, the German government would have known that the Soviet Union could well regard any suggestion of the possession of nuclear weapons by the Bundeswehr as a *casus belli*, a possibility that was totally incompatible with Germany's basic security aims. For these overriding reasons, it can be asserted, as Catherine Kelleher suggests, that 'for Bonn ... nuclear decision-making necessarily involved broader considerations than those of direct national possession or even strategic military preferences'.[27] Such references that were made by German politicians and officials to the possibility that, at some future stage, Germany might wish to possess or control nuclear weapons, and Bonn's lingering attachment to the MLF or some derivative thereof, as the nuclear sharing question ran its course, should be seen as little more than bargaining counters aimed at increasing Germany's influence in Washington, at securing greater involvement in NATO's nuclear strategy and at gaining leverage towards reaching an accommodation with the Soviet Union that might lead to reunification.

Britain, Germany and the ANF

The election of a Labour government under Wilson in October 1964 introduced a new and complicating dimension to the nuclear sharing debate. What nuclear sharing policy would the new government pursue? What was meant by Wilson's commitment to renegotiate the Nassau agreement? What were the implications for relations between London and Bonn? The answers to the first two of these three questions were set out in Labour's election manifesto, which, as well as confirming policy towards Nassau, asserted that the Party opposed 'the current proposal for a new mixed-manned nuclear surface fleet (MLF)' and that it would 'put forward constructive proposals for integrating all NATO's nuclear weapons under effective political control so that all partners in the Alliance [had] a proper share in their deployment and control'.[28] In expressing open opposition to the MLF, the Labour Party had put 'clear blue water' between it and a government that had no desire for a multilateral surface fleet but, for political and electoral reasons, was not prepared to say so. Nevertheless, a careful reading of the Labour manifesto leaves no doubt that, although there was criticism of the Conservative government's pretence of possession of an independent British deterrent and a promise to place emphasis on strengthening Britain's conventional forces, there was no explicit commitment to relinquish Britain's nuclear capability.[29]

What Labour's manifesto commitments would actually mean in practice became clearer after a flurry of diplomatic activity in the weeks following Labour's election victory. The question of Britain's retention of the Polaris fleet, and in effect whether Britain would retain a nuclear force, was settled within days of the election during an informal meeting between Wilson, Patrick Gordon Walker and Denis Healey (his Foreign and Defence Secretaries). As Wilson himself noted, 'we decided to go ahead with four of the projected five submarines, and to ensure their deployment as a fully committed part of the NATO defence forces'.[30] At meetings of ministers and officials held at Chequers over a weekend in late November 1964, called by Wilson to review defence commitments in the light of Britain's declining economic strength and to formulate policy on nuclear sharing, opinion was divided over whether Britain's first priority should be to maintain overseas commitments at the expense of the level of forces stationed in Europe. It was argued that any reduction of Britain's European commitments would send the wrong signals to the United States, lessen Britain's political influence in Europe and, in the

present circumstances (referring presumably to French disenchant-
ment with NATO and Germany's growing economic and military
strength), lead to a predominating German influence on European
defence. Such a situation would not serve Britain's best interests.[31]
The conclusion was drawn that if Britain were to maintain its three
major defence roles – nuclear deterrence, a contribution to NATO
and fulfilling 'overseas' commitments – a substantial reduction would
have to be effected in the scale on which they were maintained.

The implication of this assessment was that the defence budget at
its current level could not accommodate additional commitments and
that, as a consequence, any contribution to NATO nuclear sharing
arrangements would have to be found from within existing resources.
In other words, not only did the MLF make little military or political
sense, as Mountbatten had already argued, but also it would incur
costs that could be found only at the expense of other defence commitments.[32] By the time of a third meeting at Chequers, at which the
outlines of an ANF were considered, there was general agreement that
Britain should 'try to prevent the establishment of a mixed-manned
surface fleet [but] if it became clear that this aim was impossible ...
insist that the United States would undertake to maintain a veto on
the use of the fleet ... [and] resist pressure for any United Kingdom
contribution to the fleet'.[33]

In a briefing to the meeting, Gordon Walker outlined the results
of discussions he had held prior to Chequers with his counterparts
in Washington and Bonn. During his visit to Washington, he had
spoken in general terms, without commitment, about the form that
the ANF might take. Reactions had been more favourable than might
have been expected, given that the Foreign Secretary had made clear
Britain's opposition to a mixed-manned element in a NATO nuclear
force, whereas the commitment to the mixed-manned surface fleet
in both Washington and Bonn seemed as strong as ever, and in both
capitals there now appeared more flexibility as regards timing.[34]
Nevertheless, Gordon Walker assured the Americans that Britain
recognised the time had come for a decision and indicated that 'by
the time of anticipated Wilson visit to US, HMG [Her Majesty's
government] would be prepared for more definitive discussion'.[35] To
his colleagues at Chequers, Gordon Walker suggested that Britain's
policy towards nuclear sharing should be based on three long-term
objectives: to prevent a Franco-German nuclear alliance which would
result in the establishment of a European nuclear force; to prevent
a special alliance between the United States and Germany; and to
leave a place for France to join whatever arrangements might be
agreed. In short, Britain's alternative to the MLF must be sufficiently
attractive to Washington, Paris and Bonn but above all it must check

Germany's nuclear aspirations. Britain's proposals for nuclear sharing would therefore have to be presented in as positive a form as possible and on the basis that they were intended 'to strengthen NATO, to move towards a reduction in East West tension and to contribute to the non-dissemination of nuclear weapons'.[36]

In Bonn, Gerhard Schröder, the German Foreign Secretary, told Gordon Walker that Germany's attitude towards the MLF project had been set out by former Chancellor Adenauer and remained unchanged. Germany wanted to be part of an interdependent Alliance, with all types of weapon, conventional and nuclear, fully integrated, and regarded that objective as more important than having any special role or 'going it alone'. The MLF was militarily sound and offered an effective counter to Soviet MRBMs; in its integrated form it would tie in Alliance forces in the event that, at some future stage, force reductions in Germany might become a consideration. Such problems would become easier to settle when the MLF was in being, although, as Schröder emphasised, Germany wished to see Alliance forces retained at their present levels.[37] In response, Gordon Walker stressed that the new British government needed time to develop its ideas about an alternative to the MLF and to discuss these ideas with its Allies; there was no intention to drag things out or to present a *fait accompli*. The entire concept had to be discussed between the 'big three', meaning Britain, the United States and Germany. In very reassuring terms, the British Foreign Secretary confirmed that his government understood Bonn's motives for supporting the MLF, and agreed that Germany should have the same status as other members and be fully integrated in nuclear sharing arrangements. Care should also be taken that France could join as an equal partner at the appropriate time. However, Gordon Walker told his German counterpart that Britain had little taste for the surface fleet concept, and believed that the control arrangements would not give Germany equal status whilst requiring personnel resources that Britain could not provide.[38]

These were not the only points on which the two men had different opinions. Britain could not support a German–American-constituted MLF and would not favour, for the reasons already outlined, incorporating a surface fleet element within any new British proposals. Against this, whereas Britain envisaged including an agreement on non-proliferation and non-acquisition of nuclear weapons within its proposals, Schröder saw such an agreement as being linked with the German problem and a European security system, which meant that it could not be realised until Germany's nuclear defence had been guaranteed. Despite Gordon Walker's conciliatory message, it would have been clear to the German government from this conversation that, given Britain's overt opposition to the mixed-manned surface fleet and to any nuclear sharing arrangement that involved just America and Germany, Britain had taken a position that would make it very difficult, if not impossible, for the MLF as originally conceived to continue as the answer to NATO's nuclear sharing problem.[39] Nevertheless, the British government's thinking on the MLF, although in line with what the Labour Party had suggested whilst in opposition, was clearly not as bad as the Germans might have feared, and did not provoke any particular anti-British sentiments. According to Britain's Ambassador in Germany, Sir Frank Roberts, 'Erhard and Schröder had been particularly impressed by the warmth and sincerity of [Gordon Walker's] approach, by [his] clear desire to strengthen the Atlantic Alliance and to find a solution providing equal status for Germany'.[40]

Britain's proposed alternative to the MLF was finalised at Chequers. It envisaged a force comprising: a British contribution of V-bombers, except for those aircraft which were needed for existing commitments, and Polaris submarines; an American contribution of an equal number of Polaris submarines and possibly some Minuteman missiles based in the United States; some kind of mixed-manned and jointly owned element in which the non-nuclear powers could take part; and any force which France might decide to subscribe. There would be a possibility that some weapons systems, specifically aircraft and missiles, provided from national sources could constitute the mixed-manned element; and it was proposed the whole force would be under the command of a dedicated commander other than the Supreme Allied Commander Europe (SACEUR), and be responsible to a single authority on which all countries taking part would be represented. The authority would consist of the permanent representatives to NATO of the countries concerned and would provide the commander with political guidance, approve targeting and operational plans for the use of all weapons allocated to the force, take the decision to release nuclear weapons and develop doctrine on the role of strategic and tactical weapons. On the crucial question of how the force would be fired, the proposal was that although the United States, Britain and France, if it took part, would have a veto over the use of all elements in the force and over any changes which might at any time be proposed in the control system, the same would apply to any other participating country.[41] This proposal was clearly aimed to appeal to the Germans, who, as Schröder had already assured Gordon Walker, were still committed to a hardware solution as the best means of sharing in the Alliance's nuclear decision making.

Bearing in mind that the Chequers meeting was held just weeks after Labour's victory at the polls, the speed with which the new government was able to develop, refine and secure interdepartmental agreement to its ANF proposals was surprising to say the least. However, Wilson and his ministers were hardly starting with a blank sheet of paper, in that they were able to pick up from the point at which the previous administration had left matters in discussions with the Americans earlier in the year.[42] As Pierre correctly points out, in contributing V-bombers and Polaris submarines and avoiding the expense of new weapons, the proposals were 'extraordinarily similar to the [proposals] of the previous Government in that both were based upon the use of existing weapon systems'.[43] In other respects, however, they were somewhat different. Whilst in opposition, Labour had consistently criticised the Nassau agreement and what it saw as the 'sham' of Britain's nuclear independence. By offering to commit Britain's nuclear forces, and specifically Polaris submarines, to the Alliance for as long as NATO continued to exist, Wilson had seemingly fulfilled his pledge to renegotiate the Nassau agreement.[44] As he was later to observe, 'these vessels would be irrevocably committed to NATO as long as NATO lasted as an effective organisation. Only in the event of a break-up of NATO would they revert to British control.'[45]

Wilson's claim that the ANF proposals fulfilled Labour's commitment to renegotiate Nassau has widely been seen as a ploy that would satisfy election promises but would not actually change the *modus operandi* for Britain's nuclear forces. In this sense, it was also a device to contain criticism from the left wing of the Labour Party, when, with an overall parliamentary majority of five seats, the government's political survival literally hung on a thread. There was also, as Gerald Hughes makes clear, '[a] strong anti-German faction in the Labour party'.[46] That Wilson's problems with these Labour factions were recognised in Bonn could be seen by the reaction of Schröder to comments made by the British Prime Minister in the House that associated the Nassau agreement with stimulating nuclear appetites in other members of the Alliance, including Germany (see Chapter 1).[47] As Schröder was to say subsequently to Roberts, whilst 'he recognised the internal political difficulties with which Wilson had to contend ... his remarks had cast a shadow over the visit recently made by Gordon Walker'.[48] Nevertheless, by opting to continue with the Polaris programme, albeit with the force committed to NATO, Britain would still retain a nuclear deterrent, contrary to the impression that had been created prior to the election, and, by so doing, would continue to enjoy the status and influence that this would convey. Moreover, the claim that by committing the force to NATO Britain would, in effect, be renouncing the independence of its deterrent was hardly credible, in that the force would return to British control should the Alliance founder. As Stromseth, among others, makes clear, 'this did not differ significantly from the Nassau agreement's provisions for the withdrawal of the British Polaris force from NATO in cases where supreme national interests were at stake'.[49]

In one other way the ANF proposals were fundamentally different from the multilateral surface fleet concept and from the alternative discussed earlier in 1964 with the Americans by the then Conservative government. Labour's manifesto commitments contained the pledge that, if elected, the Party would reverse Britain's isolationist nuclear policy that had incited the French and encouraged the Germans to attain nuclear status, and take an initiative in the field of disarmament. Labour proposed appointing a minister with special responsibility for disarmament, who would initiate action that would stop the spread of nuclear weapons.[50] It was in this context that it was decided at the Chequers meetings that, under the treaty constituting the ANF, the nuclear members would undertake not to disseminate nuclear weapons and the non-nuclear members would undertake not to acquire them or exercise control over them. Germany had already undertaken not to manufacture nuclear weapons.[51] Now the ANF would, in effect, lock Germany into a full non-proliferation commitment by also closing the door to national ownership and control of nuclear weapons.[52] As Burke Trend, the Cabinet Secretary, was to suggest to Wilson, 'these [ANF] proposals are valuable militarily (since they make more strategic sense than the MLF) and politically (since they offer some prospect of containing German nuclear aspirations)'.[53]

Wilson, accompanied by Gordon Walker, Healey and senior officials, arrived in Washington on 7 December 1964 for two days of meetings with their American counterparts. Both at the time and subsequently, these meetings were seen as crucial to an agreement on the policies that both governments would pursue in areas such as East–West relations, nuclear strategy and arms control. Within these broad subject areas, the question of the MLF and the counterproposal made by the new British government for an ANF figured prominently in the discussions. It is not the intention here to repeat the detail of the exchanges that took place in Washington, since there are many informative accounts already available, but it is relevant to focus on those aspects that relate specifically to the NATO nuclear sharing problem and Anglo-German relations.[54] From these accounts, both official and scholarly, there is little doubt that the Washington meetings marked a significant stage in the development of a bilateral understanding between Washington and London on nuclear sharing, and that they effectively sealed the fate of the MLF. The same can be said about its British counterpart, the ANF.

In a preliminary meeting held in private, Wilson accepted that the comments he had made in the House shortly before the Washington visit had caused problems (and had upset the Germans) but he assured President Lyndon Johnson that his remarks did not represent a rejection of the MLF.[55] Both agreed that it was necessary to have an arrangement that tied in the Germans without giving them control of nuclear weapons. In this sense, the two men shared common ground. Perhaps the most significant comment made by the President, however, was that the United States would not take any adamant position on the MLF and had no intention of forcing the matter during the meetings that were to follow.[56] This was the clearest indication yet that America was no longer committed to the MLF and was in no hurry to pursue a 'hardware solution' to the nuclear sharing problem. An astute politician like Wilson would have appreciated that in his attempt to derail the MLF (which, in effect, Britain's counterproposal for an ANF represented), he would be pushing against an open door. The hardening in the President's position can be attributed to the influence of his National Security Adviser, McGeorge Bundy, who, prior to the meetings with Wilson and his team, advised Johnson not to press for the MLF. Bundy asserted that it would be opposed by France and the Soviet Union and would be likely to split the Alliance. Domestically also, there were many political, military and other informed voices raised against the proposed force. Overall, the MLF or the ANF would make such heavy demands on presidential time that he would be diverted from more important government business, for very little return. As Bundy went on to suggest, 'there will be plenty of opportunities for debate, discussion and delay, and for gradual and ceremonial burial'.[57]

The official record of the Washington talks makes interesting reading. At first sight, the minutes would indicate that American ministers fought hard to convince their British counterparts of the merits of the mixed-manned surface fleet and the necessity of British involvement, and that the British side fought equally hard in support of the ANF and to argue why, if America decided to persist with a mixed-manned surface fleet element, even as part of the ANF, Britain would still not wish to provide personnel to support the fleet. Johnson's contribution to the detailed discussion on nuclear sharing appears to have been minimal but this was probably deliberate, bearing in mind Bundy's earlier briefing and the fact that the President, unlike Ball, did not have a close attachment to the MLF. Johnson was almost certainly watching the reaction of Wilson and his ministers to the American pressure and would have noted the determination with which the British party argued against the MLF. For MLF advocates within the State Department, British participation in the mixed-manned fleet was essential since, in their view, this was the obvious route to ensure harmony among the European allies and, more important, the easiest way that 'the British can be forced out of the independent

nuclear business for their own good'.[58] Once discussion focused on
the detail of the ANF proposals set out in a paper tabled by Healey,
both sides agreed that it was essential to curb the possible growth
of German nuclear appetites and to spread a responsible attitude
towards nuclear weapons. In fact, the only point of major difference
between the two sides concerned British participation in the surface
fleet, which the Americans still believed should be an element in the
force. One explanation for their persistence on this point was the
wish to mask a reluctance to match the British offer to contribute
Polaris submarines to the ANF, or to permit mixed-manning of its
Minuteman missile system, with the implication that NATO would
have become involved in the control of US strategic forces. As Robert
McNamara, the American Defence Secretary, put it:

> the context of the Nassau discussions had clearly implied a mixed-
> manned seaborne fleet. The US Government was prepared to
> consider ways of contributing nationally manned forces, but the
> terms of assignment now envisaged (which were quite different from
> those of Nassau) gave the proposition a rather different colouring.[59]

In concluding the British case for the ANF, Healey claimed that the
proposals contained a substantial offer to the Germans: they would
be getting equality with the British in respect of control arrangements for the force; they would have part ownership through their
participation in any mixed-manned element (not of course a surface
fleet); and they would have a share in the targeting and planning
arrangements. Whilst this was true in principle, given the reluctance
of Britain to support the surface fleet and of the United States to
mix-man its Minuteman force, the fact that assigned forces would
revert to national control should the Alliance founder, and that the
United States would have an overriding veto, equality for Germany
would rest essentially on participation in the targeting and planning
of the force. As Healey was to say subsequently, 'Their [the Germans']
experience with the MLF should have taught both the European and
American governments a lesson of seminal importance – that there
can be no hardware solution to the quintessentially political problem
of nuclear sharing'.[60]

By the end of the discussion, it was apparent that the Americans
had decided not to insist on a hardware solution. As Johnson was subsequently to tell Rusk and McNamara, 'the US is not seeking to force
its own views on any European nation, but wishes rather to find a
way of responding effectively to the largest possible consensus among
interested European allies'.[61] In this context, further progress would
depend upon Bonn's reaction to the new proposals, since it was primarily to satisfy the political and military requirements of Germany,

and to prevent a Bonn–Paris nuclear axis, that so much American effort had been invested in the MLF. The extent of the shift in the American commitment away from the MLF was revealed in the suggestion by Rusk that 'Britain should proceed to unfettered discussion with the Germans similar to those with the Americans'.[62] In other words, whilst the Americans were apparently ready to consider new proposals for nuclear sharing, albeit in parallel with what was already on the table, it would be up to the British to sell their ideas to the Germans. As an article in the *New York Times* suggested, 'the time [had] come for hard, honest, objective discussions of the facts, uncomplicated by old personal and subjective considerations'.[63]

Exchanges between the British and German governments on nuclear sharing began immediately after Wilson's visit to Washington. At one level, these exchanges created an impression of constructive co-operation between allies anxious to find a compromise between the MLF and ANF proposals, whereas in reality fundamental differences continued to exist. As Gordon Walker made clear to his German counterpart, 'we do not care for the surface fleet concept and do not wish to have anything to do with it ... the contribution of our Polaris submarines is worth far more than our participation in the MLF'.[64] On the German side, Karl Carstens, Federal State Secretary, observed that 'the British proposals [had] positive elements ... [but] other points appear less convincing: the V-bombers [were] already old ... the existence of veto rights for all participants would undermine the credibility of the force'.[65] Moreover, in its formal response to the British proposals, the German government expressed serious reservations about the non-proliferation and non-dissemination aspects of the ANF concept and asserted that progress in these areas could be made only in a world-wide context.[66] The situation was further complicated by the differences within the German government that the ANF proposals brought out into the open. As Gordon Walker was to tell his Cabinet colleagues on 11 December 1964:

> the German Government were themselves divided on the issues involved ... they were acutely aware that if the French Government ... sought them to choose between some new and closer form of Atlantic interdependence and an independent Franco-German nuclear force, they might be exposed to serious political embarrassment ... they might well prefer ... to evade this unpalatable choice; and in that event it might be possible to postpone a final decision on the form of an ANF until the late autumn of 1965.[67]

In fact, reports that the German government was in no hurry to press for a decision on the MLF began to filter back to London soon after Gordon Walker's statement to the Cabinet. In a telegram sent a few days later, Roberts reported the detail of a conversation in which Rainer Barzel, the CDU majority leader, had suggested 'that the whole NATO nuclear problem should be swept out of sight until after the German election'.[68] More significantly, a Foreign Office discussion document prepared for Wilson's visit to Bonn in March 1965 reported the outcome of talks between Chancellor Ludwig Erhard and President Charles de Gaulle three months earlier and suggested that 'General de Gaulle's publicly expressed opposition ... to the MLF [seemed] to have removed the urgency hitherto attributed by the Chancellor to achieving a nuclear force agreement' and that, in return for modest concessions from de Gaulle (on European political co-operation and French agreement to a new Western initiative on German reunification), the Chancellor made it clear that 'a German decision on the MLF/ANF proposals [would] not be reached until after the elections'.[69]

It is possible to conclude, therefore, that, faced with a lessening of the American commitment to the MLF, French opposition, differences within CDU governing circles, particularly the Gaullist elements led by Strauss, who was a strong advocate of a nuclear armed federal Europe, and the approach of Bundestag elections, the Germans had decided to reconsider their options.[70] In that context, the need to respond to the British ANF proposals, and the delay this would cause, represented little more than a breathing space in what had become for Bonn a serious dilemma. Nevertheless, dilemma or not, the German government could still use the British intervention to its advantage by maintaining an explicit commitment to a hardware solution, whilst knowing that its principal NATO allies, the United States and Britain, were equally committed to providing Germany with a greater say in the nuclear defence of the Alliance.[71] However, as Kelleher rightly asserts, 'some initiative clearly was required, for to do nothing was to run the risk of further discrimination or sacrifice of German interests'.[72]

It was against this background that Wilson and Erhard began to prepare for their meeting in March 1965 as a follow-up to the MLF discussions in Washington. Shortly before the meeting, the German Chancellor, on a distinctly downbeat note, told Roberts that he supposed the Prime Minister would want to discuss the ANF, although Erhard regarded the subject as distasteful, particularly as there could be no question of German decisions before the election. In an honest assessment of the effect of the British proposals on Washington, Erhard went on to add that he 'was inclined to argue that the Americans had lost interest'.[73] Moreover, as one German regional newspaper commented at the time, 'Bonn has realised that ... Wilson's ANF would not serve the interests of the Federal Republic or Europe'.[74] That the ANF had fatally crippled the MLF as the solution to the NATO nuclear sharing problem was a view that was held not only in Bonn. In a defence debate in the House of Commons, just days before Wilson's visit to Bonn, Peter Thorneycroft, a former Conservative Defence Secretary, in a response to Healey's claim that the government's proposals had saved the Western Alliance from what threatened to be a crisis over the MLF, asserted that 'the Atlantic Nuclear Force ... will never happen ... the only engagement which this nuclear force has ever been in was to sink the MLF'.[75]

Given the political constraints acting on Erhard, it was hardly surprising that his discussions with Wilson on the MLF/ANF proposals were relatively low key. The Chancellor admitted that the nuclear organisation of the Alliance was a difficult subject in Germany. It touched on German domestic politics and on relations with France and, in these circumstances, he could not announce a joint Anglo-German initiative or even suggest that he agreed with the British proposals. For his part, Wilson suggested that they could progress on the machinery in which the subject would be discussed and readily agreed that there was no rush to make progress. On the other hand, and no doubt mindful that failure to do anything might put new impetus behind the MLF project, a development that would be most unwelcome to Britain, Wilson voiced concern about the danger of losing momentum. The two men simply agreed that the whole subject should be remitted to the appropriate NATO MLF working group sitting in Paris.[76] If Wilson's talks with Johnson in Washington had put a nail in the coffin of the MLF, Erhard's agreement to relegate the matter to the level of a NATO 'talking shop', rather than to move positively towards some form of compromise on the ANF, fatally undermined the hardware solution. A similar conclusion was reached by Buchan, who predicted in 1964 that 'if the MLF treaty were not ... completed before [the Bundestag] elections [it] would either become delayed until 1966 or become a prey to the growing dispute between the right and the moderate centre in Germany, or both'.[77]

The software solution

From this point, a hardware solution as the answer to the NATO sharing problem began to die a slow death. There are a number of factors that support this argument, principally those set out in Bundy's note to Johnson written just before the Wilson visit to Washington of December 1964, although the key decision was that taken by the Americans to distance themselves from the MLF.[78] With the President insisting to Rusk and McNamara that 'no agreement [could] be made with the UK that [did] not take account of the legitimate interests of Germany' and that 'we [would] never support any proposal for a nuclear force which [was] in fact directed against France', and given the position that each of these countries had taken towards NATO nuclear sharing, there was never any likelihood that a consensus would emerge.[79]

In fact, Labour, when in opposition, had already predicated the solution to the NATO nuclear sharing problem. In an article setting out the basis of Labour's defence policy should it win the general election, Gordon Walker suggested that what the new government wanted was:

> to participate ... in the formulation of the ideas, policy and strategy that ... make up the doctrine upon which any particular decision of the [US] President must depend. We would want to share in the decisions about ... nuclear weapons ... a Labour Government would want France and Germany to play the same role as Britain in the Western Alliance.[80]

In effect, Gordon Walker's views marked an intent to work for a 'return to basics', to the commitments offered to the Alliance by the United States on different occasions: through the 'Athens guidelines' adopted in 1962, which provided for Allied consultation regarding nuclear use, time and circumstances permitting; and again at the Ottawa meeting of NATO ministers in 1963, which provided for the broader participation by officers of NATO countries in nuclear planning at Supreme Headquarters Allied Powers Europe (SHAPE), and in the co-ordination of operational targeting and planning at Strategic Air Command (SAC) headquarters.[81] Implicit in Gordon Walker's remarks was the assertion that the United States had not lived up to these commitments and had singularly failed to take the non-nuclear allies into its confidence. As Harlan Cleveland, the American Ambassador to NATO, subsequently argued, 'it is fair to say that we [the United States] not only failed to consult, we were not even very good about telling our allies about plans made on their behalf to protect their national existence'.[82]

It is in this context, therefore, that Britain's proposals for the ANF must be seen. Not only were they designed to stop the MLF, but it is the contention here that they were also intended to focus attention on the need for the United States to engage in more meaningful nuclear sharing with its NATO partners. In the words of one brief prepared for the Washington meeting, one of Britain's key objectives was to 'foster the strength and unity of the Alliance as a whole by taking account of the position of those non-nuclear members who want to exercise greater influence on nuclear planning, policy and strategy'.[83] Also significant in this context were the frequent references in government papers to the real intention behind the ANF proposals. For example, as a brief for multilateral discussions in NATO, prepared by the Overseas Policy and Defence (OPD) (Official) Committee, suggested, 'the principal objective of the ANF is to establish continuous close consultation within NATO on nuclear policy and planning'.[84] Similarly, Wilson's report to Cabinet following his talks in March 1965 with Erhard significantly referred to the hope he had expressed that 'the Federal Government would be equally disposed to sponsor an Anglo-German initiative on the organisation of the nuclear capability of the North Atlantic Treaty Organisation'.[85] It is possible to conclude, therefore, that the Wilson government's underlying objective was, and remained, to ensure that the software option of consultation became the answer to NATO's nuclear sharing problem.

The success of Labour's opposition to the MLF and its strategy for solving the NATO nuclear sharing problem can be judged by the emergence in May 1965 of a proposal by McNamara for a Select Committee of Defence Ministers. In essence, this Committee would examine the means of improving and extending Allied participation in planning for the use of nuclear forces, including strategic nuclear forces, and to make recommendations as to how the procedures agreed after the Ottawa meeting in 1963 could be improved.[86] As Pierre argues, 'the next proposal ... a special committee of defence ministers to provide for close consultations in nuclear strategic planning, was quite similar to what Labour defence spokesmen had been suggesting since their early opposition to the MLF'.[87] This is not to imply that it was solely the British government's opposition to a hardware solution that prompted McNamara's move. Account must also be taken of the growing support within the American government to reach an agreement with the Soviet Union on the NPT, which, by early 1965, had become a crucial factor in the implicit rejection by the United States of a hardware solution to nuclear sharing within NATO. Nevertheless, the need for a solution remained, not least to satisfy German political and military concerns, and the Select Committee with its sub-group, the NPG, both with German representation, ultimately fulfilled that need.

Not that persuading Bonn to accept a consultative role as a substitute for the influence on American nuclear decisions in Europe that the common ownership and management of a nuclear weapon system might convey was quickly achieved. Erhard was still under domestic pressure and faced an election in September 1965, even though, as the *Westfalen Zeitung* suggested some months earlier, 'Bonn would no longer press for a nuclear force ... instead the Federal Republic would ask for involvement in Alliance nuclear planning'.[88] At a meeting in Washington in December 1965, Erhard continued to press the case for a hardware solution and, although Johnson agreed to consider new proposals presented by the German Chancellor, it was evident that no new weapons system was contemplated.[89] Given that the German proposals were, as Kelleher puts it, 'merely a warmed-over version of the original project, buttressed by familiar arguments and designed to resolve few if any of the previous objections or outstanding dilemmas at home or abroad', the Washington meeting effectively left the NPG as the only conceivable answer to NATO's nuclear sharing problem.[90] The point was clearly not lost on Wilson, who, in reply to Johnson's report of the meeting with Erhard, expressed his 'pleasure at the establishment of the Nuclear Planning Group of the NATO Special Committee which would help Erhard present the German position on nuclear problems'.[91] Nor was it lost on the Germans. As an analysis of opinion among NATO partners prepared at the end of 1965 by the Federal Defence Ministry suggested, 'the widely accepted solution for the Federal Republic to have joint nuclear responsibility would be through participation in the McNamara committee'.[92]

There is little to suggest that the nuclear sharing problem within NATO adversely affected Anglo-German relations. In practice, the focus of action centred on Washington, although this tended to shift towards London, Bonn and, to a lesser extent, Paris as the search for a solution intensified immediately after the election of Wilson's government. Kelleher suggests that the main decision centres remained Bonn and Washington but, although there is a case to support the inclusion of London in this category, especially as the Americans saw the participation of the British in the MLF as a *sine qua non*, a factor that was well appreciated by the Germans, it is evident that any final word would rest with Washington.[93] The point that flows from this line of reasoning is that Britain's role was a subordinate one, in the sense that the only country able to satisfy German nuclear aspirations was the United States. It is also significant that when Germany produced its proposals for nuclear sharing, in December 1965, these were unveiled in Washington rather than in London. Thus, despite resolute opposition to the MLF, Britain was never regarded as the principal obstacle to German ambitions. Following on from this point, Wilson and his ministers were always careful, in sponsoring the ANF as a better option than the MLF, to emphasise their concern about German sensitivities and to argue that Britain's proposals were designed to give Germany equal status and a more meaningful role in NATO nuclear strategy. Even though Britain never intended the ANF to be implemented, in favouring a consultative solution to the nuclear sharing problem, British ministers, and principally Healey, worked hard in support of McNamara to convince the Germans of the advantages of this option. For example, as both men told Kai-Uwe von Hassel, Germany's Defence Secretary, at a private dinner held before the first meeting of the Special Committee:

there exists no rational plan for the use of nuclear weapons now in Europe ... there is no realistic plan for selective use, and contingencies short of general war have not been thought through. Nor are there effective procedures for consultation at political level. [The] Special Committee was designed precisely to solve this problem.[94]

The nuclear sharing debate in NATO was bedevilled by half-truths and the fact that the principals involved were working to hidden agendas. By 1965 it was evident that the possibility of concluding an agreement on non-proliferation of nuclear weapons with the Soviet Union figured prominently in America's calculations, and that this would rule out any hardware solution to nuclear sharing. On the other hand, Germany clung persistently to participation in some form of NATO nuclear force, not only for domestic political reasons but also because this would increase pressure for its greater role in nuclear planning and because of the opportunity this might convey to trade renunciation of nuclear weapons as a bargaining counter on reunification.[95]

Wilson's government had domestic reasons for opposing the MLF but its alternative of the ANF was designed to maintain its position and influence as a nuclear power, to ensure that there was no suggestion of German access to nuclear weapons and to focus attention on the need for greater consultation within NATO on nuclear strategy. The key issue in the hardware debate was always the question of control. In this regard, there was considerable force in the claims made in 1964 by British ministers, in their meeting in Washington, that the MLF would not give Germany any effective control over nuclear weapons, especially with the overriding American veto. As Stromseth asserts, 'the NPG fostered ... a greater German understanding of American strategic analysis ... it also finally gave the Federal Republic a role in alliance nuclear matters commensurate with her substantial contribution in conventional forces'.[96] The nuclear sharing debate was shrouded in complexities, but Britain was instrumental in achieving an effective solution to the problem and in so doing skilfully avoided undermining relations with Germany. In 1965, the critical year for nuclear sharing, Roberts was able to report that 'for Anglo German relations [this] was a good year'.[97]

Notes

1 J. W. Boulton, 'NATO and the MLF', *Journal of Contemporary History*, 7, 3–4 (July–October 1972), p. 276.
2 See for example memorandum from Bundy, Special Assistant for National Security Affairs, to President Johnson, 8 November 1964, *Foreign Relations of the United States* (Washington, DC) (hereinafter *FRUS*) (1964–68), XIII, pp. 104–106.

3 George W. Ball, *The Past Has Another Pattern: Memoirs* (1982), p. 274.
4 Alastair Buchan, 'The Multilateral Force: A Study in Alliance Politics', *International Affairs*, 40, 4 (October 1964), pp. 619–637.
5 'Paradox of Defence Policy', *The Times*, 13 April 1964, p. 13.
6 Andrew J. Pierre, *Nuclear Politics: The British Experience with an Independent Strategic Force 1939–1970* (1972), p. 276. The timetable for a decision on the MLF had previously been discussed by British and American ministers, who, taking account of the general election in October 1964, assumed that 'the Working Group in Paris will continue work on plans and language which could be converted into charter form for decision in November or December 1964'. See memorandum of conversation, 26 April 1964, *FRUS* (1964–68), XIII, p. 43, fn 3(2).
7 Healey, *Time of My Life*, p. 307.
8 See for example Helga Haftendorn, *NATO and the Nuclear Revolution: A Crisis of Credibility, 1966–1967* (Oxford, 1996), p. 118; Jane E. Stromseth, *The Origins of Flexible Response: NATO's Debate over Strategy in the 1960s* (1988), p. 77; and Pierre, *Nuclear Politics*, p. 244.
9 Buchan, 'Multilateral Force', p. 626.
10 Pierre, *Nuclear Politics*, Appendix B, 'The Nassau Agreement', p. 346.
11 Peter Riddell, 'Not Quite a Poodle, Not Quite a Bulldog', *The Times*, 4 February 2002, p. 12.
12 Frédéric Bozo, 'Détente Versus Alliance: France, the United States and the Politics of the Harmel Report (1964–1968)', *Contemporary European History*, 7, 3 (November 1998), p. 345. Similar arguments are advanced by Haftendorn, *NATO*, p. 119.
13 Stromseth, *Origins of Flexible Response*, p. 79.
14 Pierre, *Nuclear Politics*, p. 245.
15 CDS to Chairman, British Defence Staff, Washington, 'The Multilateral Force', 25 February 1964, L181/08(1), DEFE 25/31, PRO.
16 Pierre, *Nuclear Politics*, p. 247.
17 Memorandum of conversation, 26 April 1964, *FRUS* (1964–68), XIII, p. 43.
18 Letter from General Sir Michael West to CDS, 9 March 1964, L181/08(1), DEFE 25/31, PRO.
19 Wilson, *The Labour Government*, p. 41.
20 See Healey, *Time of My Life*, p. 245.
21 'Not a Bomb Apart', *The Times*, 7 October 1964, p. 13.
22 Buchan, 'Multilateral Force', p. 629.
23 Quoted in Stromseth, *Origins of Flexible Response*, p. 83. In similar vein, there is evidence to suggest that one important motive for Germany's support for the MLF was the fact that it represented an important American goal. This claim was based on interview responses in which 'all but a very few respondents cited American desires as the primary reason for initial and continuing German support of the MLF'. See Catherine McArdle Kelleher, *Germany and the Politics of Nuclear Weapons* (New York, 1975), p. 264.
24 Pertti Ahonen, 'Franz-Josef Strauss and the German Nuclear Question, 1956–1962', *Journal of Strategic Studies*, 18, 2 (June 1995), p. 27.
25 Stromseth, *Origins of Flexible Response*, p. 82. See also obituary, 'Rudolph Augstein', *The Times*, 8 November 2002, p. 45.
26 For an excellent account of how Konrad Adenauer, German Chancellor, led Germany into the nuclear age and, in so doing, avoided any 'serious miscalculations', see Hans-Peter Schwarz, 'Adenauer und die Kernwaffen', *Vierteljahrshefte für Zeitgeschichte*, 37 (1989), pp. 567–593.
27 Kelleher, *Germany and the Politics of Nuclear Weapons*, p. 5.
28 Craig, *British General Election Manifestos*, p. 60.

29 *Ibid.*, p. 59. One leading member of the Labour opposition had seemingly committed the Party to a change in policy when he said 'we do not ... believe that Britain herself should seek to make or possess nuclear weapons', although he then cast doubt on Labour's real intentions by adding 'we do not intend to throw away the nuclear weapons that we now possess'. See Gordon Walker, 'Labour Party's Defense and Foreign Policy', pp. 392–393.

30 Wilson, *The Labour Government*, p. 40.

31 Minutes of a meeting held at Chequers, Saturday 21 November 1964, Misc 17/1st Meeting, CAB 130/213, PRO. See also Saki Dockrill, 'Britain's Power and Influence: Dealing with Three Roles and the Wilson Government's Defence Debate at Chequers in November 1964', *Diplomacy and Statecraft*, 11, 1 (March 2000), pp. 211–240.

32 CDS to Chairman, British Defence Staff, Washington, 'The Multilateral Force', 25 February 1964, L181/08(1), DEFE 25/31, PRO.

33 Minutes of a meeting held at Chequers, Saturday 21 November 1964, Misc 17/3rd Meeting, CAB 130/213, PRO.

34 *Ibid.*

35 Department of State to Embassy in Germany, 29 October 1964, *FRUS* (1964–68), XIII, p. 94. Arrangements had been made for Wilson to meet with Johnson on 7/8 December 1964 in Washington.

36 Discussion on the ANF, 21 November 1964, Misc 17/3rd Meeting, CAB 130/213, PRO.

37 Gespräch – Schröder mit Gordon Walker, 15 November 1964, *AAPD* (1964), II, pp. 1304–1309.

38 *Ibid.*

39 In practice, however, there was little likelihood that the Americans would agree to a bilateral nuclear force with the Germans. Although during the course of 1964 the Germans pressed for progress to agree a draft MLF charter, this was primarily to have an agreement in place before the United Nations General Assembly could adopt a resolution on non-proliferation of nuclear weapons that might require a suspension of the MLF concept, and to have something accomplished before any high-level meeting occurred between representatives of the German and Soviet governments. Whilst Erhard was prepared to sign an MLF treaty, he suggested that, even on a bilateral basis, it would spur others to accession and that consideration should be given as to what arrangements could be made to avoid creating the impression that the MLF was being placed solely on an American–German basis. See Erhard to Johnson, 30 September 1964, *FRUS* (1964–68), XIII, p. 79. The American position was referred to in a memorandum, dated 8 November 1964, which stated that the Germans had given the impression that the Americans might go ahead with them on the MLF, although Washington's official position was one of supporting this force on a multilateral basis. See McGeorge Bundy to Johnson, 8 November 1964, *ibid.*, p. 104.

40 Roberts to Secretary of State, 18 November 1964, PREM 13/26, PRO.

41 The detail of the British ANF proposals can be found in the Ministry of Defence briefing note for Wilson's meeting with Johnson in December 1964. See PMV (W) (64) 1, Copy 28, 27 November 1964, CAB 133/266, PRO.

42 Memorandum of conversation, 26 April 1964, *FRUS* (1964–68), XIII, p. 43.

43 Pierre, *Nuclear Politics*, p. 278.

44 Paragraph 9 of the Nassau agreement allowed for British Polaris submarines included in a NATO nuclear MLF to be recalled by Her Majesty's government where supreme national interests were at stake. See Macmillan, *End of the Day*, Appendix 4, 'Nassau Communiqué', p. 555.

45 Wilson, *The Labour Government*, p. 44.
46 R. Gerald Hughes, '"We Are Not Seeking Strength for Its Own Sake": the British Labour Party, West Germany and the Cold War, 1951–64', *Cold War History*, 3, 1 (October 2002), p. 67.
47 *Hansard*, House of Commons, 702 (23 November 1964), col. 936.
48 Gespräch – Schröder mit Roberts, 4 December 1964, *AAPD* (1964), II, p. 1443.
49 Stromseth, *Origins of Flexible Response*, p. 163. Similar arguments are advanced by Pierre, *Nuclear Politics*, p. 279; Ponting, *Breach of Promise*, p. 92; and Dockrill, 'Britain's Power and Influence', p. 231.
50 Craig, *British General Election Manifestos*, pp. 57–58.
51 The commitment was entered into as part of the Paris accords of 1954, which provided for German entry to NATO and the WEU. See Ahonen, 'Franz-Josef Strauss', p. 43, fn. 32.
52 See brief by the Ministry of Defence for Washington talks in December 1964, PMV (W) (64), CAB 133/266, PRO.
53 Letter from Burke Trend to Wilson, 25 November 1954, PREM 13/26, PRO.
54 The official account of the Washington talks is contained in PMV (W) (64)1, CAB 133/266, PRO; and *FRUS* (1964–68), XIII, pp. 137–156. Secondary accounts of the Washington meetings can be found, for example, in: Kelleher, *Germany and the Politics of Nuclear Weapons*, pp. 253–254; Susanna Schrafstetter and Stephen Twigge, 'Trick or Truth? The British ANF Proposal, West Germany and US Nonproliferation Policy, 1964–68', *Diplomacy and Statecraft*, 11, 27 (July 2000), pp. 161–184; Saki Dockrill, 'Forging the Anglo-American Global Defence Partnership: Harold Wilson, Lyndon Johnson and the Washington Summit, December 1964', *Journal of Strategic Studies*, 23, 4 (December 2000), pp. 107–129; Haftendorn, *NATO*, pp. 137–138; and Wilson, *The Labour Government*, pp. 47–51.
55 *Hansard*, House of Commons, 702 (23 November 1964), col. 936. Wilson commented that 'the MLF concept was a divisive force in Europe'.
56 Memorandum for the record, 7 December 1964, *FRUS* (1964–68), XIII, p. 139.
57 Bundy to Johnson, 6 December 1964, *FRUS* (1964–68), XIII, p. 134–137.
58 Bundy to Johnson, 8 November 1964, *FRUS* (1964–68), XIII, p. 105.
59 PMV (W) (64), 4th Meeting, 7 December 1964, CAB 133/266, PRO.
60 Healey, *Time of My Life*, p. 305.
61 National Security Action Memorandum, 17 December 1964, *FRUS* (1964–68), XIII, p. 164.
62 PMV (W) (64), 4th Meeting, 7 December 1964, CAB 133/266, PRO.
63 'President Urges Full US Effort to Reunify NATO', *New York Times*, 21 December 1964, p. 1.
64 Gespräch – Schröder mit Gordon Walker, 11 December 1964, *AAPD* (1964), II, p. 1501.
65 Runderlaß des Staatssekretärs Carstens, 11 January 1965, *AAPD* (1965), I, p. 53.
66 Stellungnahme der Bundesregierung, 18 January 1965, *AAPD* (1965), I, p. 100.
67 Conclusions of Cabinet meeting, 11 December 1964, CC 14(64), CAB 128/39, PRO.
68 Telegram number 1285, Roberts to Foreign Office, 17 December 1964, PREM 13/219, PRO. The German elections were scheduled for September 1965.
69 Foreign Office assessment, 'German Foreign Policy', 24 February 1965, PMV (G) (65) 17, FO 371/182999, PRO.

70 On the point about French opposition, see Kelleher, *Germany and the Politics of Nuclear Weapons*, p. 259. As to Strauss, in an interview published in the *Suddeutsche Zeitung*, the former Defence Secretary said he regarded the original MLF project worthy of consideration but only if it was supported by as many members of the EEC as possible and if the United States declared itself willing to place the MLF under any future European government. He expressed reservations about the ANF proposals and believed they derived from Labour Party ideas on foreign policy that were not compatible with plans for bringing continental Europe together into a political union with an open door for Britain. See telegram number 1287, Roberts to Foreign Office, 17 December 1964, PREM 13/219, PRO.
71 Wilson had made this quite clear to Erhard during the latter's visit to London in January 1965 for Sir Winston Churchill's funeral, when he asserted that Britain 'recognised the need for the full participation of Germany in the nuclear defence of the Alliance'. See record of conversation, 30 January 1965, RG 1051/15, FO 371/183042, PRO.
72 Kelleher, *Germany and the Politics of Nuclear Weapons*, p. 269.
73 Telegram number 190, Roberts to Foreign Office, 24 February 1965, PREM 13/220, PRO. George McGhee, American Ambassador in Bonn, had already reported German despondency about the MLF/ANF situation. He referred to the 'widespread feeling ... in all circles – government, diplomatic and press – that the US has abandoned interest in the MLF – that it is dead'. See McGhee to State Department, 9 January 1965, *FRUS* (1964–68), XIII, p. 171.
74 'Keine Utopien', *Westfalen Zeitung*, 9 March 1965, p. 1.
75 *Hansard*, House of Commons, 707 (3 March 1965), col. 1364.
76 Record of talks between Erhard and Wilson, 2 April 1965, RG 1052/22, PREM 13/329, PRO.
77 Buchan, 'Multilateral Force', p. 631.
78 Bundy to Johnson, 6 December 1964, *FRUS* (1964–68), XIII, p. 134–137.
79 See Johnson to Rusk and McNamara, 17 December 1964, *FRUS* (1964–68), XIII, p. 166.
80 Gordon Walker, 'Labour Party's Defense and Foreign Policy', pp. 393–394.
81 See Stromseth, *Origins of Flexible Response*, p. 73.
82 Harlan Cleveland, *NATO: The Transatlantic Bargain* (New York, 1970), p. 47. Quoted in Stromseth, *Origins of Flexible Response*, p. 74. On America's reluctance to consult its allies, see also Healey, *Time of My Life*, p. 306.
83 Brief for Washington talks, 27 November 1964, PMV (W) (64)1, CAB 133/266, PRO.
84 Brief for multilateral discussions, 20 April 1965, OPD (O) (ANF)(65), CAB 148/48, PRO.
85 Conclusions of a Cabinet meeting, 11 March 1965, CC 15(65), CAB 128/39, PRO.
86 Department of State to NATO capitals, 2 June 1965, *FRUS* (1964–68), XIII, p. 213.
87 Pierre, *Nuclear Politics*, p. 283.
88 'Bundesregierung ändert Kurs', *Westfalen Zeitung*, 9 January 1965, p. 1.
89 Johnson to Wilson, 23 December 1965, *FRUS* (1964–68), XIII, pp. 295–296.
90 Kelleher, *Germany and the Politics of Nuclear Weapons*, p. 268.
91 Wilson to Johnson, 5 January 1966, *FRUS* (1964–68), XIII, p. 296, fn. 3.
92 Analysis of opinion, 30 December 1965, B136/6822, Band V, BA Koblenz. Wilson apparently reached a similar conclusion when he advised Cabinet that 'Even the Germans were beginning to realise that it was better for them

to have more consultation and less hardware'. See Barbara Castle, *The Castle Diaries 1964–70* (1984), diary entry for 7 December 1965, p. 75.

93 Kelleher, *Germany and the Politics of Nuclear Weapons*, p. 246.

94 American mission to NATO to State Department, 29 November 1965, *FRUS* (1964–68), XIII, pp. 280–281. See also Healey, *Time of My Life*, p. 307.

95 See Christoph Bluth, *Britain, Germany and Western Nuclear Strategy* (Oxford, 1998), p. 181; and Theo Sommer, 'Bonn Changes Course', *Foreign Affairs*, 45, 3 (April 1967), p. 486.

96 Stromseth, *Origins of Flexible Response*, p. 150.

97 'Germany: Annual Review for 1965', 1 January 1966, RG 1011/1, FO 371/189155, PRO.

Chapter 3

The offset agreements and their impact on Anglo-German relations

One issue perhaps more than any other seemingly had the potential to seriously undermine relations between Britain and Germany during the period between 1964 and 1970. This was the dispute over the sterling exchange costs of the BAOR. It became an issue to the extent that the cohesion of the Atlantic Alliance was threatened, that differences between leading members of Harold Wilson's government and within the Labour Party were exposed and, important from the perspective of a study of Anglo-German relations, that the evident wish of both the London and Bonn to improve their understanding could have been undermined.[1] As Michael Stewart, the Foreign Secretary, suggested to one German minister in 1965, 'the exchange agreement is currently the most pressing problem affecting Anglo-German relations'.[2]

For Britain, the foreign currency needed to support the BAOR added to the problems faced by the government as it sought to stabilise the economy, maintain the value of sterling and meet Britain's defence commitments world-wide. The frequent threats by Wilson and his ministers to withdraw troops unless their demands were met, legitimate though these tactics might have been, touched a raw nerve within a German government committed to ensuring its own national security. The linkage between security and economics drawn by British ministers in their dealings with Germany over the exchange costs of the BAOR was by no means new. Rather, it reflected continuity in an approach adopted by their Conservative predecessors, albeit one that displayed a similar incompatibility with the attempts to make Europe the focus of British foreign policy.[3]

Whilst the nature of the dispute over the exchange costs of the BAOR might be viewed as evidence of bad relations between London and Bonn, it will be argued here that, at its worst, the dispute should be seen as little more than an irritant, and one that was managed in such a way as to ensure that it did not impair the real interests of both governments.

The offset agreements

Agreements with Germany over the exchange costs of the BAOR stemmed from the commitment entered into by Britain under the Brussels Treaty of 1954 to maintain a military presence in Europe.[4] Not only was this commitment aimed at providing future guarantees covering Germany's sovereignty and rearmament, but the presence of British forces on the European mainland was designed to provide a forward defence against any Soviet incursion into Western Europe, to increase British influence in the area and to encourage developments in Germany compatible with British interests. On this last point, there can be little doubt that British policy makers continued to have reservations about a resurgent Germany, and regarded the presence of British troops as part of a NATO force on German soil as the best means of locking a democratic Germany into the Atlantic Alliance.[5] As the OPD observed in 1967, when discussing the possibility of substantial British and American troop withdrawals, 'this would leave Germany in a dominant position in Europe … [and] this would be gravely damaging to [Britain's] interests and those of the Western Alliance'.[6]

In numerical terms, the commitment under the Brussels Treaty inherited by the Labour government of 1964 was to maintain an army of 55,000 ground troops in Germany, a force that was roughly one-quarter the size of its American counterpart.[7] Consequently, both countries had an interest in securing as large a financial contribution as possible from Germany towards the exchange costs involved in supporting these troops, once their official status changed in 1955 from an occupation army, when all their costs were paid directly by the occupied country, to an Allied force committed to the defence of NATO territory. The means by which this was done became known from 1961 onwards as the series of offset agreements, under which Germany undertook to provide balance of payments relief by means other than direct budgetary contributions.[8] In Britain's case, such relief took the form of purchases by Germany of armaments, goods and services to an amount equivalent to the costs in deutschmarks incurred by the BAOR for payments to German civil employees, services by German agencies and the demand by British service personnel and their dependants for German currency. However, as Hubert Zimmermann suggests, for a country like Britain struggling against increasing pressure on sterling, due in part to its role within the international monetary system:

military expenditures abroad, of which troop stationing was a
major component, were a conspicuous negative factor in the British
... balance of payments ... [and] they were an easy and popular
target.[9]

Labour's response to the 1964 offset agreement

Despite Britain's need to reduce the demand for foreign exchange, the
omens for squeezing more money out of the Germans were not good.
In the first instance, no previous offset agreement had allowed for
a full reimbursement of exchange costs. Also, by the 1960s, because
of the chequered past of British armaments sales to Germany and
aggressive selling tactics by the Americans for their own armaments,
the prospects for increasing British sales were unpromising to say the
least.[10] As Chancellor Kurt Kiesinger was to confirm in 1967, 'there
was really very little of value to the FRG in the way of military equipment which the UK had or could readily produce'.[11] Moreover, unlike
armaments exports, the sale of British goods and services to German
companies and civil authorities was subject to the constraints of
market forces, which were largely immune from manipulation by politicians. Furthermore, as a Treasury brief prepared in 1962 had made
abundantly clear, 'anything in the nature of "occupation costs" or
"support costs" – i.e. a direct payment in aid of the United Kingdom
defence funds would be politically unacceptable to the Germans'.[12]
Finally, Britain was bound by treaty to maintain the size of the BAOR
at prescribed levels and, although there were let-out clauses to
cover national emergencies or extreme financial difficulties, any concessions made by the NATO Council would require the agreement
of other members, who would almost certainly resist substantial
withdrawals from strategically important territory and the prospect
of making good any shortfall in NATO front-line strength.[13] Perhaps
the most telling pointer for ministers in this regard would have been
the fact that threats of troop withdrawals made by previous British
governments had been unsuccessful in securing full compensation for
Britain's exchange costs. Nevertheless, in the sense that they introduced an element of uncertainty in the minds of German negotiators,
threats of troop withdrawals had been and remained a legitimate
tactic, especially if they were likely to provoke similar action by the
United States. Indeed, 'the threat' was potentially the strongest card
that Britain could play.

The agreement negotiated in July 1964 by the outgoing Conservative administration, and inherited by Labour, differed markedly
from the previous two-year deal, struck in 1962. Whilst the latter
allowed for exchange cost relief amounting to some £55 million a

year, the former gave no specific cash commitment other than an undertaking to offset the exchange costs of the BAOR as far as possible. As John Boyd-Carpenter, Conservative Chief Secretary to the Treasury, admitted to the Cabinet:

> The draft Agreement is not as good as it might be, but it is better than having no Agreement at all ... the Germans have now dropped their previous proposal ... whereby we would recognise that they were unlikely to be able to make purchases at a higher level than DM350 [i.e. £31] million a year.[14]

This was an opinion that was not shared by Wilson or his ministers. During heated exchanges in the House, Boyd-Carpenter, by then in Opposition, continued to argue the merits of what he had negotiated and claimed that 'the agreement left the possibility of obtaining full recompense from the Germans'. Wilson scathingly dismissed this as 'a situation very unsatisfactory to this country'.[15] In theory, Boyd-Carpenter's claim was correct, but he chose not to mention that even the 1962 agreement was based on an understanding that allowed for compensation of no more than around 70% of Britain's exchange costs. On this basis, and given the difficulties experienced by the British negotiators, it was wishful thinking to expect the German government to exceed even this level during the period of the 1964 agreement. As James Callaghan, Chancellor of the Exchequer, suggested to the Prime Minister:

> In the absence of a target the Germans have no inducement to make a really significant contribution. The result is that in all fields affected – arms purchases, civil procurement and development aid – the Germans naturally put their own interests first, while British interests, if they come into the reckoning at all, do so only as a secondary consideration.[16]

Labour's policy for defraying the exchange costs of the BAOR gradually took shape. Already in November 1964, in response to a question in the House by one prominent left-wing Labour MP, Denis Healey, the Defence Secretary, expressed the opinion that 'there is a general feeling on both sides of the House that our responsibilities in this respect [that is, to maintain the strength of the BAOR] would be easier to carry if the West German Government were more prepared to make a substantial contribution to the support costs'.[17] Healey's moderate tone not surprisingly failed to satisfy left-wing opinion. As Michael Foot, another Labour MP, made clear:

> many of us think that the commitment by a previous Government to keep a British Army of this size in Germany ... was one of the most irresponsible commitments ever made by a British Government

... [we] would give him very strong support if he took up with our allies the question of reducing this figure ... to one commensurate with the country's economic position.[18]

Wilson gave a clearer indication of government thinking when he told the House that, although the foreign exchange costs of maintaining troops in Germany would be about £85 million, 'we can see no firm prospect of receiving more from Germany, by way of offset payments, than perhaps £25 million to £30 million ... this is an impossible situation'.[19] Other evidence of a hardening of government attitudes could be seen by reports in *The Times* that consideration was being given to reducing the size of the BAOR.[20] Although these suggestions were denied, the reports provoked a hostile reaction in Germany, where the *FAZ* published a leading article in which it 'sharply attacked Mr Wilson for the arrogant impression he has created abroad and warning that ... the British Government is considering not fulfilling its obligations'.[21]

What these early exchanges showed was that ministers would take a firm line and use the possibility of troop withdrawals as the means to concentrate the minds of their German counterparts. In circumstances where the government believed it was faced with a substantial deficit on the balance of payments, and with more of the same likely in 1965, the need for greater relief from the offset burden had become pressing.[22] But there were other factors that influenced government policy. Ministers had openly criticised the arrangements negotiated by their Conservative predecessors and were consequently obliged to demonstrate that they could do better; moreover, pressure from the left wing of the Labour Party at a time when the government's survival was at stake could simply not be ignored. Despite the 'gloss' of positive action, however, the policy adopted by Wilson and his ministers to secure more by way of offset payments, with the withdrawal of the BAOR as a bargaining chip, was little different from the position taken by their Conservative predecessors and demonstrated that political differences between the parties, despite heated exchanges in the House, were more apparent than real.

With the threat of troop withdrawals as the central plank of government strategy, Wilson visited Bonn in March 1965 for talks with Chancellor Ludwig Erhard. Here was the opportunity to put the Germans on notice that the new government meant business over offset payments. As John Diamond, the Chief Secretary to the Treasury, reminded Wilson:

the deficit is running at least at a rate of £60 million per annum ... the situation is deteriorating ... and the Chief Secretary does not believe the present gap can be sufficiently bridged unless we reduce the strength of our forces ... or the Germans ... contribute more.

Callaghan agreed with this line and saw 'no alternative but to press the Germans hard'. He warned Wilson that if the BAOR was withdrawn there would be difficulties in the form of 'substantial rehousing costs in the UK with industrial, social and budgetary consequences', but suggested it might have to be done and that there would be 'no harm in putting the wind up the Chancellor [Erhard] in the meantime'.[23]

Callaghan's suggestion on how to deal with the Germans reflected the harder line of the Treasury and exposed differences within the Cabinet. Burke Trend, the Cabinet Secretary, reminded Wilson of the difficulties concerning a threat to reduce British forces in Germany and advised him that 'we must do so by agreement with our allies, not unilaterally'. Merely bringing home the troops from Germany might help the balance of payments but it could hinder the budget; 'only repatriation and disbandment [would] really do the trick' and, critically in the light of Britain's economic problems, '[Britain] may need to enlist German political support for [its] next battle with the IMF'. For all these reasons, argued Trend, 'we should not face the Germans with the stark choice of finding more money or of seeing our forces reduced'.[24] Healey wrote to Wilson in support of Trend, making it clear that he would not wish at this stage of the defence review to go as far as Callaghan in negotiations with the Germans, and pointing out in particular that 'any withdrawal would be bound to create a serious and costly problem of re-deployment ... unless it were part of a wider plan to reduce our total force levels'.[25] Healey almost certainly had in mind the undertakings that he and Wilson had given to the Americans in December 1964 not to make unilateral reductions but 'to create conditions [in Europe] in which our allies would agree to reductions in our contribution'.[26] These were powerful arguments to counter the hawkish stance of the Treasury and posed an enduring problem for Wilson and his ministers. They needed to persuade the Germans to pay more for the BAOR but any threat of its withdrawal had to be carefully used if it was to have credibility.

It is clear from the record of Wilson's talks in Bonn that the efforts both sides made to ensure that relations between Britain and Germany were stabilised were, in the language of the Foreign Office, 'successful to a high degree'.[27] Wilson went out of his way to empha-sise the allies' commitment to the maintenance of the status of Berlin and to a solution to the German question but, whilst he found the Germans sympathetic towards British complaints about the burden of exchange costs, he detected little sign that they were prepared to meet his demands. As Erhard reminded his British visitors:

> it was unfortunate that the United Kingdom Government should
> feel so disappointed ... it would be even more unfortunate if ... the

> United Kingdom might henceforward be less willing to contribute
> to the defence of Germany, since this would appear to be incompat-
> ible with the spirit in which the Federal Government had recently
> tried to help the United Kingdom during a period of very heavy
> pressure on sterling.[28]

Clearly mindful of the advice he had been given in London, Wilson
took care in countering Erhard's argument to stress that his ministers
might be forced by public opinion 'albeit against their will to raise
the whole issue of force levels [within NATO] and to reconsider the
size of the British forces in Germany'.[29] Whereas Wilson's suggestion
that the terms of the present offset agreement be renegotiated for
its second year was not agreed, since, as Erhard reasonably argued, a
single year might prove even more unsatisfactory than a normal two-
year agreement, uncertainty about Britain's intentions persuaded
Erhard to compromise. As Helga Haftendorn rightly suggests, 'the
offset agreements ... can only be explained by the major military
threat to the Federal Republic ... as well as its great dependence for
its security on the continuing deployment of sizeable allied forces'.[30]

Erhard was not inclined to gamble with Germany's security and
this suggests why he accepted that Diamond should return to Bonn
in the spring for talks with Dr Rolf Dahlgrün, the German Minister
of Finance, on the working of the current agreement, and to agree
improved arrangements for the period ending April 1967. In a post-
talk report, Ambassador Frank Roberts enthused about the 'undoubted
success of the Prime Minister ... in consolidating Anglo-German
relations ... and in engaging the Chancellor's goodwill and energies
personally in the problem of making the Offset Agreement work'.[31]
Diamond made it clear in the House that the aim of the government
was 'to negotiate new arrangements in place of the totally inadequate
document that [the Prime Minister] had inherited from his predecessor'.[32] In a message to President Lyndon Johnson, Wilson referred
to 'some very tough sessions on the offset agreement'. As a reminder
to the Americans of the financial burden of Britain's defence commitments, and as a measure of the seriousness with which London still
viewed the situation, he added that 'we left the Germans in no doubt
that if we did not get satisfaction on this point, we should be forced to
agonizing re-appraisals'.[33]

Despite Bonn's fairly uncompromising line before talks in June
1965, Diamond did secure what Wilson's government claimed were
favourable changes to the terms of the 1964 agreement.[34] Although
the protocol detailing the changes included specific cash targets,
which was an improvement on the 'best endeavours' undertaking
given to Boyd-Carpenter by the Germans, Edward Heath, the shadow
Chancellor, rightly argued that Diamond's calculations included an

element of double counting and, in terms of a special credit facility, allowed for income that did not represent 'a firm undertaking'.[35] In effect, although Wilson had fulfilled his commitment to renegotiate the agreement, he had been no more successful than his Conservative predecessors in obtaining a full offset of the exchange costs of the BAOR. The principal weakness with the protocol, as with the agreements, was that the outcome would still depend upon Bonn's ability to find scope for arms purchases that it was unable or not already committed to obtain from its principal supplier, the United States, and to encourage imports from Britain.

The omens in this regard were not promising. In November 1965, the situation took a turn for the worse when Germany announced proposed cuts in its defence expenditure.[36] Although Gerhard Schröder, the German Foreign Minister, confirmed that, despite its own budgetary problems, Germany still hoped to meet the targets in the latest offset agreement, Britain's confidence that this would prove to be the case began to wane.[37] In particular, the announced cuts in expenditure served to reinforce the opinion held in Britain and the United States that Germany was not bearing a fair share of the cost of defending Western Europe.[38] There were other reasons for Britain's concern. It was already clear that, in return for America's support for sterling, Britain had pledged to maintain defence commitments that were patently beyond its means.[39] Perhaps more telling, however, was the fact that, despite international backing for the support of sterling that the Americans had organised, the outlook for Britain's balance of payments began to cause further concern in London. This suggestion is consistent with claims by Alec Cairncross, head of the government's Economic Service, that 'there was a growing feeling that devaluation in the course of 1966 was inevitable', a development that Wilson and his closest advisers would regard as a disastrous symbol of the government's failure to exercise effective management of the economy.[40] If Britain was to maintain defence commitments and defend sterling, then savings in public expenditure had to be found, and that meant Germany bearing a higher share of the costs of maintaining the BAOR. Thus, by January 1966, Stewart warned his American counterpart at a meeting in Washington that, in relation to the 1965 protocol, 'it was not certain that [Germany's] undertaking would be fulfilled' and that 'the percentage was too low for the United Kingdom which needed 100 per cent'.[41]

The tripartite negotiations

Britain's more trenchant attitude towards offsetting payments by Germany received a sympathetic response at the Washington meeting.

Robert McNamara criticised Germany's military force structure and defence budget and 'noted many signs that the FRG was moving away from their offset agreement with [the United States] ... and urged that the British talk bilaterally with the FRG on this problem and indicated that the US would also do this'.[42] Healey agreed that political pressure should be applied to the Germans but made the telling point that although 'the FRG looked the best place for the British to make savings ... redeploying forces to the UK would involve a large budgetary increase to provide facilities for the forces' but added that 'if no foreign exchange savings could be made, the British would be forced to make cuts in their forces in Germany'. Healey also gave an indication of the direction that strategic thinking in Britain was taking when he said that 'to reduce the BAOR would make it appear that the UK was opting for outside Europe rather than into Europe'.[43] In these comments Healey laid bare the constraints acting on Britain as it approached negotiations with the Germans on the exchange costs of the BAOR. Large-scale redeployments would not be possible in the short term since facilities simply did not exist to accommodate troops and families in Britain; and if Europe was to be the focus of Britain's political strategy in future, then a major crisis between Britain and its European partners, that even threats of a withdrawal from Germany would create, had to be avoided. The real significance of the Washington meeting, however, was the foundation it created for co-ordinated action by Britain and the United States to force the Germans to make higher offset provisions.

Britain's formal position on the BAOR was set out in the defence white paper issued in February 1966. It stated that Britain should 'maintain ... forces in Germany at about their existing level until satisfactory arms control arrangements have been agreed in Europe provided ... that some means [was] found for meeting the foreign exchange costs of these forces'.[44] An OPD working party described the foreign exchange costs of the BAOR as 'a continuing irritant in Anglo-German relations since 1955'. It exposed differences in departmental thinking and proposed negotiating tactics for Wilson at a forthcoming meeting with Erhard. The Foreign Office warned that any unilateral breach of Britain's treaty obligations in terms of troop withdrawals would 'do harm to [its] wider interests out of all proportion to the benefit it might bring to [Britain's] balance of payments' and argued that 'if [Britain] could not withdraw [its] forces ... [it] should not therefore threaten to do so'. The Treasury, on the other hand, concluded that the threat to withdraw troops was more powerful than it had ever been and proposed action to prepare for rehousing the troops withdrawn if the negotiations with Erhard did not 'give hope of a successful negotiation'.[45] Whilst the working party's report stressed the need to work with the Germans for a less damaging solution, it acknowledged that the balance of payments difficulties required urgent action. Against this background, and in the light of constant threats by ministers, it is reasonable to conclude that the Treasury view held sway. Any change in tactics at that stage would have undermined Britain's negotiating position. The problem for ministers, however, was how to convince the Germans, and the Americans, that the threat of large-scale troop withdrawals was real, notwithstanding that, in reality, accommodation constraints meant that this was not a viable option.

In March 1966, in a personal letter to President Johnson, President Charles de Gaulle announced that France proposed to withdraw from the NATO military structure. De Gaulle's earlier announcements, as in November 1964, when he said that 'France would not stay in NATO after 1969', and in February 1966, when he confirmed that 'France would review its relations with the Atlantic Alliance', made such an outcome inevitable.[46] Whilst it therefore came as no particular surprise, its effect was considerable, in that it undermined one of the core principles of NATO: its unity. This outcome was a possibility that Johnson expressed to Wilson both in May 1966, when, in the context of a visit to London by Erhard, he commented that 'a growing sense of uncertainty and insecurity on their [the Germans'] part could lead to a fragmentation of European and Atlantic relations which would be tragic for all of us', and again in August, when he told Wilson that he had 'become increasingly concerned during the past few weeks about the dangers of an unravelling in NATO'.[47] If Wilson saw in Johnson's genuine concern about the future of the Atlantic Alliance an opening that he might be able to exploit during negotiations over offset payments, he would most certainly have appreciated that American support would not be forthcoming for any action by Britain that might further undermine NATO solidarity, such as the unilateral withdrawal of troops. Whilst Washington's influence in London was to prove crucial as the Americans became increasingly involved in the offset dispute, the relationship with Germany had become even more important in Britain's diplomatic calculations. Not only would German support be essential for any further international rescue operation for sterling but, as Trend later emphasised to Wilson, 'we cannot ignore the repercussions on our approach to the EEC'.[48]

In his meeting with Erhard in May 1966, Wilson pointed to the disparity in defence spending by the two countries and referred to the commitment on the BAOR made in the defence white paper.[49] In a preliminary meeting with Erhard, Callaghan noted that 'the net cost in foreign exchange of keeping our forces in Germany ... amounted to some £50 million' and proposed that 'the German Government should make a contribution of such an amount in 1966'. Wilson took up this point by insisting that '[Britain] would only maintain [its] troops if the £50 million was met'.[50] For his part, Erhard insisted that the additional money could not be paid if the stability of the German currency was to be maintained.[51] Whilst Erhard suggested that 'there was no problem outstanding on the foreign exchange cost of British forces under the existing agreement expiring in April 1967', the only point of agreement between the two sides was that a meeting should be held between Callaghan and Dahlgrün, to arrange for a bilateral commission 'to examine all the various methods by which the problem might be satisfactorily resolved' and to 'report to the two Governments by 15 September 1966'.[52]

Ministers maintained the pressure on their German counterparts in the following months, still on the basis that troop withdrawals would be made unless Germany agreed to the full offset of the BAOR exchange costs. In June 1966, at a meeting with Kai-Uwe von Hassel, his German counterpart, Healey said that 'a tension was being created ... from the continuing lack of an effective solution to the problem of foreign exchange costs', whilst Callaghan left Dahlgrün in no doubt that 'if, as it seemed likely, there was no prospect of obtaining the total offset the British government wished, he might have to recommend courses of action to his Cabinet colleagues that he would much regret'.[53] Despite Britain's firm stance, the Germans were apparently not convinced by Callaghan's threat. In a despatch from Bonn, Roberts reported that:

> Dahlgrün had noted the careful form of words used ... that any implication that there might be substantial troop withdrawals was a British bargaining counter, since the present NATO crisis and the difficulties of accommodating our troops elsewhere made this unlikely.[54]

It was at this point that Callaghan, frustrated by the lack of progress with Dahlgrün, advocated a much harder line. Sensing that the Germans were employing delaying tactics and were seeking 'to link British and American demands', and had 'taken a decision not to provide budgetary support for either', Callaghan suggested to Wilson that, as it was 'unlikely that the Germans [would] agree to make any payments unless they are convinced that we are in earnest about this [troop withdrawals]', he should be authorised at his next meeting with Dahlgrün to threaten that 'if the German Government [did] not produce a satisfactory answer [Britain would] begin to withdraw troops immediately thereafter'.[55] Given the innate caution of the Foreign Office about the damage this approach would cause to Anglo-German relations, Stewart reminded Callaghan that the level of

Britain's forces was emphatically not 'something that could be settled simply between [Britain] and the Germans' and emphasised that the withdrawal of some British forces should not be done or threatened 'except in accordance with established NATO and WEU procedures and after proper consultation with our allies, especially the United States'.[56] The logic of Stewart's advice found support within Wilson's inner circle of advisers (principally from Healey and George Brown, First Secretary of State at the Department of Economic Affairs), to the extent that Callaghan was instructed to modify his approach. If the Germans did not meet British demands in the year 1967–68, Britain would have to 'propose forthwith through the prescribed NATO and WEU procedures very substantial cuts in [its] forces in Germany'.[57] This represented a more sustainable British position, in that it linked troop withdrawals and treaty obligations but still put the Germans on notice that Britain expected full compensation for the exchange costs of the BAOR.

Nevertheless, the situation caused Roberts to report from Bonn that 'if we [were] not careful, quite unnecessary harm may be done to Anglo-German relations over a wider field'.[58] In a flurry of diplomatic activity, Britain instructed its ambassadors to inform the WEU and NATO of the progress in negotiations with Germany aimed at eliminating the foreign exchange burden of maintaining the BAOR, to outline the measures that would be taken to reduce that burden, and to seek views on these and further measures that might prove necessary.[59] Britain's more reasoned but seemingly no less determined approach caused the alarm bells to start ringing in Washington. Within days, Francis M. Bator, the President's Deputy Special Assistant for National Security Affairs, sought advice from the President on two points: what should be done to 'dissuade the British from rushing ahead with sharp cuts in their forces in Germany (men and stocks) in a way which would probably start an unravelling process in NATO and increase domestic pressure for us to follow suit'; and 'what should [be done] about [America's] own offset with the Germans?'[60] Johnson's view was that only Bator's suggestion of tripartite negotiations would contain the situation. By adopting a more calculated approach, Britain encouraged Washington's involvement in the dispute, increased the pressure on the Germans and improved the prospects of alleviating its foreign exchange burden. In a more subtle way also, a tripartite approach to the problem would avoid any direct confrontation between London and Bonn at a time when German influence could be helpful as Britain reconsidered its policy towards Europe.

The bilateral commission was making no progress and the Germans were unwilling to enter trilateral negotiations until after Erhard's planned visit to Washington in September 1966, but Wilson and his ministers needed quick answers if a decline in Britain's balance of payments position was to be halted. The fall of the Erhard government that October, and the time that would be needed for its replacement, the Grand Coalition, to agree a policy on offset, only served to aggravate the situation from the British viewpoint. In November 1966, Johnson endeavoured to head off any precipitate British action, and gain time for the Germans, by offering a sweetener of $35 million worth of new orders in Britain for military equipment. Inevitably, this money came at a price, in that Britain would have to remain in the trilateral talks, which had by this time got underway under the chairmanship of John McCloy, former American High Commissioner for Germany, make no change in troop and supply dispositions in Germany, and work with the United States on changes that resulted from the talks.[61] Whilst Wilson had little difficulty in selling this 'deal' in Cabinet, it brought a predictable response from government critics on Labour's left wing. As a reflection of traditional left-wing hostility towards Germany and its refusal to bear a fair share of European defence, Michael Foot told the Commons that 'many of us on this side of the House find the continued stalling of the German Government on this subject, and the utterly feeble response of the British Government to it, totally intolerable'.[62]

The British government was facing other criticisms, too. Roberts alerted ministers to articles appearing in the German press referring to 'the alleged excessive cost of British troops here'.[63] This comment reflected the long-held view within German political circles that the British were living beyond their means and expected the cost to fall on the German taxpayer.[64] Perhaps the one member of the triumvirate with the most domestic pressure to contain, however, was the American President. In an angry telephone conversation with Senator Russell Long in September 1966, Johnson complained bitterly about the non-binding resolution offered by Senator Mike Mansfield and twelve other Senators recommending cuts in the size of American forces in Europe. Some week's later, Mansfield elaborated on the thinking behind the resolution. He and his supporters believed that the United States was the only country meeting its commitments in Europe and that, in terms of the extra $35 million for equipment purchases in Britain, 'he did not think it was a good idea to subsidise the British'.[65] Mansfield was not alone in holding the view that tension in Europe had lessened to an extent that the presence of so many American troops was unnecessary. In a note for the OPD in October, Trend referred to a comprehensive NATO force level plan and the possibility of 'a more realistic NATO strategy – which would be reflected in a reduction of our forces'.[66] Trend saw in this strategy the possibility of a deal with the Soviet Union under which there would

be agreed mutual and balanced force reductions in Europe and with
it a solution to the offset dispute with the Germans. But as Johnson
was to tell Long just weeks later, whilst putting out feelers to the
Russians on troop reductions, Mansfield's resolution had persuaded
the Russians that the West might be obliged to make troop reductions without the need for any concessions by the Warsaw Pact. In
the light of these domestic pressures, the three allies approached the
trilateral talks urgently, needing a solution that would reconcile what
on the face of it were irreconcilable objectives.

The beginning of 1967 saw the British government disappointed
by the apparent hesitation of the new German government to make
progress in the tripartite talks. Kiesinger was to tell Roberts in
January that 'balancing the budget was the first task now before his
government ... he had not personally yet been able to give proper
thought to the offset problem'.[67] Even greater doubt was cast in
British minds about the willingness of the Germans to react to
Britain's demands when Callaghan reported comments made to him
by Klaus Schütz, State Secretary of the German Foreign Ministry,
during a visit to London, to the effect that:

> the German economic outlook was so gloomy that he must warn
> [Britain] not to assume that the Germans could live up to their past
> promises ... they would fulfil their current agreement but would
> find it difficult to do anything after it came to an end ... this meant
> that the agreement already reached for offset of Deutschmarks 350
> million in 1967/68 would no longer stand.

As George Thomson, Chancellor of the Duchy of Lancaster and
Britain's representative at the tripartite talks, made clear in replying
to Schütz's comments, 'he could not over-emphasise the gravity of the
situation for Anglo-German relations and NATO as a whole'.[68]

Implied by this comment was the intent to withdraw troops and,
despite German doubts about Britain's agenda in this regard, it was
still London's strongest bargaining chip. But it was a ploy that the
Cabinet believed had to be used with care when it agreed that 'it
would be important for us ... to work in close concert with the United
States ... our action must moreover have full regard to our strategic
views on defence needs in Europe and the importance of not expos-
ing our allies and ourselves to military danger'.[69] The threat of troop
withdrawals had now been given much greater potency, by the linkage between the British threat and political pressure in the American
Congress resulting from the Mansfield resolution. Recognition of this
linkage could be seen in the comments of George McGhee, American
Ambassador in Bonn, during a conversation with Willy Brandt, the
German Foreign Minister, when he stressed that 'the British are so

committed to a troop reduction in the event the offset is not continued ... which would play into the hands of Senator Mansfield and
others seeking a reduction of US forces'.[70]

From this point, the negotiations quickly reached their climax. By
February 1967, Roberts was able to report comments by a spokesman
that 'the Federal Government had always fulfilled their obligations
... the current agreement would also be fulfilled. For the future
the Federal Government was concerned to achieve a fair offset in
British interests.'[71] But not everything was plain sailing as the parties
manoeuvred for position. In March, Thomson noted that, as a counter
to further German stalling, McCloy had warned that, 'if there were
British withdrawals of more than one Brigade it was his judgement
that Congressional pressure for Unites States' withdrawals would
become irresistible'. Thomson had backed this up by suggesting to
the Germans that, if they failed to come up with a substantial offer
of military procurement, withdrawals would take place. He found it
difficult to see 'on what basis [he] could be authorised by the British
Government to carry on the talks'.[72] To reinforce Britain's position,
Wilson wrote to Kiesinger on 14 March emphasising that, without a
substantial offer, 'massive withdrawals of British forces' would follow.
By this stage, however, a more conciliatory tone tempered British
demands, in that Wilson also suggested that force withdrawals could
be kept to a minimum if Germany was able 'to bring its contribution
in terms of purchases for 1967/68 up to the equivalent of £45 million
and for satisfactory arrangements to be made to cover the rest of
the gap'.[73] The pressure on Germany was maintained on the following day by a press release in which the government announced that
'plans for the accommodation of servicemen if they are withdrawn
from Germany [were] well advanced'.[74]

The offset agreement between Britain and Germany that eventually emerged in May 1967 from the tripartite negotiations allowed
for military orders from Germany 'amounting to DM 200 million ...
accountable (civil) purchases amounting to DM 250 million ... and
additional purchases in the United Kingdom ... of up to DM 100 million'.[75] This was broadly in line with Wilson's suggestion to Kiesinger,
although, unlike previous agreements, covered only a twelve-month
period. The tripartite talks also resulted in an agreed approach to the
WEU and NATO on the transfer of one brigade and one helicopter
squadron from the BAOR back to Britain – with both units to remain
committed to NATO – and an increase in American military orders in
Britain to supplement the $35 million already announced.[76] In these
various ways the gap referred to by Wilson was mainly closed, which
enabled Thomson subsequently to claim in the House of Commons
that, as well as some withdrawals of troops, 'the net foreign exchange

of our forces in Germany will this year be less than it has been for many years'.[77] More fundamentally, however, the main conclusion that could be drawn from the tripartite exercise was that it effectively marked a turning point in the whole offset saga. In particular, the possibility of full offset, if it ever existed, had been ruled out by the agreement that force levels would be determined only by security considerations, and by the fact that American financial intervention to offset the costs of the BAOR would almost certainly not be forthcoming in future.

The offset agreements of 1968 and 1969

Essential to an understanding of why British ministers and officials approached the offset negotiations with their German counterparts in 1968 and 1969 in such a fundamentally different way, and in order to place the agreements that were reached in context, it is necessary first to highlight the implications of three other developments during 1967 that were to have a major influence on the course of British foreign policy. In the space of several months following the signing of the trilateral agreement, Britain applied for membership of the EEC, announced far-reaching proposals in a defence white paper on the deployment of British forces east of Suez, and devalued the pound. The implication of these developments for Anglo-German relations, and for future bilateral negotiations over the exchange costs of the BAOR, were spelled out by Roberts when he advised London that:

> German Ministers know that it is in the interests of both countries for agreement to be reached ... we have also to take into account the fact that Germany has now acquired a central role in our attempt to enter the European Communities and that the Germans now realise that we have decided to make our main defence effort in Europe and no longer East of Suez.[78]

The message coming from Bonn was clear: negotiations with the Germans on offset payments would have to be conducted more in a spirit of compromise rather than by adopting the 'pay us in full or we withdraw' approach that had been the basis of British tactics since Labour came to power in 1964. In effect, Britain's bluff had been called.

Initially, however, as London and Bonn manoeuvred for position in advance of the 1968 negotiations, there were signs that Britain might again resort to familiar tactics. At a meeting in December 1967, Healey told Schröder, who was then German Defence Minister, that 'offsetting the costs of the British military presence in Germany was an important item in the political balance sheet' and that 'given the effect of devaluation on the costs of our forces in Germany, he saw the two Governments running into a major crisis over offset.'[79] Healey apparently found the talk with his German counterpart somewhat depressing and in a written summary prepared after the meeting predicted that 'there was little or no hope of any real progress either on the offset position in 1968/69 so far as purchases of defence equipment was concerned or on the longer term question of collaboration'.[80] In making his comment about collaboration, Healey had in mind the decision by ministers to support a new approach to the offset question, which would require an agreement with the Germans based on long-term arrangements for 'collaborative military research, development and production' and which would 'be in accord [with Britain's] European policy'.[81] Healey could hardly have been surprised by Schröder's reaction at their talks, since it was well known that collaboration could work only in the long term, bearing in mind the time that it would take to identify and prove the feasibility of projects that would meet both partners' requirements. Nevertheless, such a policy had much to commend it, in that it offered the real prospect of solving the offset problem and of producing projects that would have a wider European appeal. This last point was particularly relevant to Britain's European aspirations and the decision to focus its defence priorities on Europe.

Official documents covering the period leading to the start of offset negotiations in February 1968 reveal the difficulty that ministers and their advisers encountered in agreeing the British position. Moreover, for the first time in the history of the offset agreements, officials appeared to be more open in their criticisms of what had been achieved in the past in terms of 'real' offset payments and of how this had been presented to Parliament. An immediate difficulty was agreeing the basis on which an interim agreement should be constructed, given the new policy of working towards a collaborative venture in the longer term. In a memorandum to Roy Jenkins, who had replaced Callaghan as Chancellor of the Exchequer, Brown, now Foreign Secretary, suggested that 'we should be content to tide ourselves over the next financial year by building on the continuing elements from the last agreement' and that 'we should be ready to consider financial measures such as borrowing in order to reduce the gap'.[82] Whilst expressing reluctance to increase Britain's indebtedness, Jenkins supported the idea of some form of borrowing. But, in a radical break with past practice, he also proposed that the opportunity should be taken to drop civil purchases from the agreement. Jenkins argued that these were 'no real benefit to our balance of payments' and that, as devaluation had changed the basis on which the civil element had been built, it would be inconsistent to count as offset payments exports to Germany which had supposedly been influenced by Bonn and 'to suggest that there was still significant room for such influence would cast doubt on our own belief that after devaluation our exports were now fully competitive'.[83]

Ministers recognised, however, that there would be other problems in explaining this new approach. In the first place, not only would the Germans need considerable persuasion to drop civil purchases from the overall package but, as Jenkins reminded Brown, 'we have accepted civil public purchases as satisfactory in the past and it will not be easy to justify discarding them if the effect is merely to leave an equivalent gap'. In expressing such concern, Jenkins clearly had in mind the somewhat misleading claims that Labour ministers had already made in Parliament to the effect that, because of their robust stance in negotiations with Bonn, Britain's exchange costs had virtually been covered and the civil element was an important ingredient in achieving this objective. As Jenkins now openly admitted, although his predecessor had been asked in the House what proportion of these purchases would have taken place without an agreement, and had presumably fended off the question, he suspected that 'we should be hard pressed to give a satisfactory reply'.[84] Hugh Morgan, head of the Western European Department at the Foreign Office, also took up Jenkins' implied criticism of past agreements. As he suggested, 'the choice between leaving a substantial gap ... or trying to conceal it behind "window dressing" e.g. the civil purchases, would be a political decision for Ministers'.[85]

It was against this background that Fred Mulley, Minister of State at the Foreign Office, prepared for the start of negotiations. His instructions were to secure an agreement that, if possible, would: include a public commitment by the Germans to a longer-term collaborative partnership; exclude civil purchases; and provide maximum offset cover by a combination of German defence purchases from Britain and a substantial loan at preferential rates. The loan was to be justified on the basis that it would add only to Britain's medium-term indebtedness, and had become a serious consideration only because of devaluation and recent defence decisions.[86] Mulley's brief was significant by its moderate tone, the absence of any threat of troop withdrawals and the implication that Britain would rely on Germany's goodwill in order to reach a mutually satisfactory solution; as such, it marked a substantial departure from Britain's previous negotiating position. The signals coming from Bonn were mixed. Whereas Roberts believed there was evidence to show that the Germans would approach the negotiations in a constructive mood, he was unenthusiastic about the prospects for dropping the civil purchases element, as 'the Germans [would] expect us to make a corresponding reduction in our total target instead of asking them to cover by means of a loan most of the gap'. In Roberts' opinion, German finance ministers would expect 'civil purchases to feature in the agreement'.[87]

Roberts' predictions proved correct. The Germans appeared to recognise that they were in the driving seat and, although the negotiations were conducted in a friendly atmosphere, few concessions were on offer. Rolf Lahr, State Secretary at the German Foreign Ministry, again questioned whether savings could be made to the foreign exchange costs of the BAOR but insisted that Germany's own budgetary difficulties would rule out a full offset. The target for defence sales suggested by Mulley was too high, civil purchases had to be included and, whilst the principle of a loan could be considered, its level would depend upon the make-up of the package. Germany welcomed the offer of defence collaboration but this was for the long term and no commitment to specific projects could be given. Mulley was clearly in some difficulty to counter the German arguments. He accepted that Bonn was under no international obligation to provide 100% offset, agreed that civil procurement should be considered if that was what the German side wished and somewhat tamely emphasised that Britain sought a 'friendly and practical solution'.[88]

Mulley was obliged to report back to London that the package on offer was virtually the same as the previous year's, albeit 'with the addition of a loan of £20 million to compensate [Britain] for the absence of most, if not all, of last year's United States contribution'.[89] Although on instruction he managed to negotiate an increase to the figure for defence purchases, the Germans insisted that even this had to be subject to greater accountability. In the House, the minister claimed that the outcome was comparable to that in the previous year's trilateral agreement and that, in total, 'some 90 per cent of [Britain's] estimated foreign exchange costs in 1968–69 [would] be covered'.[90] What his comments did not reveal, however, was that the Cabinet had already agreed that in Parliament ministers would 'avoid a commitment to obtain 100 per cent offset' and 'be particularly careful to avoid creating difficulties with our European allies'.[91]

The calm that had by now descended on the costs of the BAOR encouraged British officials to express further misgivings about previous offset agreements.[92] In September 1968, Morgan appeared ready to contemplate the unthinkable when he suggested that rather than make another attempt to secure a long-term agreement with the Germans, or to reach another one-year agreement, and on the assumption that there would be no less help from the Germans without an agreement than with one, Britain could 'take the plunge and say that [its] relationship with Europe, especially on defence matters, [was] now such that the time [had] come to forget about offset accounting'.[93]

Logical though this third option might have been, it was politically out of the question, given the government's rhetoric and its insistence on reducing the BAOR exchange costs. Nevertheless, in May 1969 Trend reminded the Prime Minister that, although the general shape of the next package (along familiar lines) was beginning to take shape, 'some of this [had] been doubtfully valid and [had] been included for presentational reasons, eg. many of the civil purchases would have taken place anyway'.[94] Mulley's subsequent announcement in the House about the 1969 agreement was a relatively low-key affair. The package contained the usual ingredients, with arms procurements, purchases by German public authorities and, as in 1968, a loan on favourable terms. The only change was that the period would extend over two years, partly in recognition that it was still not possible to announce the longer-term collaborative arrangements that Britain sought to establish. Brushing aside further Conservative probing about civil purchases, Mulley felt able to describe the agreement as 'an improvement in a number of respects over the last agreement' and to claim that, in the round, 'over 88 per cent of our estimated foreign exchange costs in 1969–71 [would] be covered'.[95] More important to the government, however, was the fact that the terms of the agreement and the way in which it had been negotiated would do nothing to disturb the harmony in relations between London and Bonn. Perhaps the final judgement on the government's efforts was sounded by John Mendelson, a Labour MP, when he observed that 'this Government [was] not succeeding any more than the Conservative Government did in making a good offset agreement'.[96]

The offset agreements reconsidered

The offset problem was one of the more complex issues affecting Anglo-German relations during the 1960s. Its enduring nature and the war of words it generated, primarily from Britain, might be seen as evidence of something rather more than a difference between friends and allies. Britain's approach was seemingly contradictory, in that it was based on the threat of troop withdrawals when the presence of those troops on German territory served Britain's wider interests and when it demonstrated a commitment to Europe as ministers contemplated a second application for membership of the EEC. A further contradiction was that the accommodation in Britain required to house troops and their families, if withdrawn from Germany in the numbers threatened, could not have been made available in the timescale needed or at a cost to make such an option viable. This was well appreciated by the Germans. As a report in the *Frankfurter Rundschau* made clear:

a reliable source announced that the cost of building new accommodation for troops and families from BAOR would be an
unacceptable burden. The government could either demob the
troops, which would be politically and strategically impossible, or
leave them in Germany.[97]

Despite these contradictions, there was a certain logic in British tactics. Nonetheless, to some extent, ministers had talked themselves into
a corner. On taking office they denounced the arrangements for offset
payments they inherited from their Conservative predecessors and,
under pressure from Labour's left wing, announced they would secure
better terms. The threat of troop withdrawals served two purposes: it
touched on the sensitivities of a German government dependent for its
security on the Atlantic Alliance; and it would placate left-wing critics
who were hostile to the costs involved in maintaining the BAOR at
the levels prescribed by international treaty. The Labour government
elected in 1964 faced mounting balance payments problems and, if
the value of sterling was to be maintained, as Wilson and his close
associates agreed was to be the case within days of taking office, then
negative factors, such as the demand for foreign currency generated
by the BAOR, had to be eliminated.[98] Thus, troop withdrawals from
Germany and economic policy became inextricably intertwined.

The real potency of the threat of troop withdrawals became
evident only after the United States was drawn into the tripartite
negotiations. Up until this time, it could be said that, as a tactic,
it had persuaded the Germans to set targets for offset payments,
as opposed to offering their best endeavours to help with Britain's
exchange costs, although it had done nothing to remove the anoma-
lies in offset accounting. It had not secured a commitment for
increased arms purchases, in a situation where the United States
remained the principal supplier to the Bundeswehr, and it had not
brought about the removal of the absurdity of including as off-
sets public sector purchases that would probably have been made
regardless of any agreement. Nevertheless, once President Johnson,
under pressure from Congress to make corresponding reductions in
American armed forces in Germany, became involved in the offset
dispute, Germany was forced to make concessions. In a situation
where the Germans were suggesting that their own budgetary difficulties might prevent them making further offset agreements, the
risk that a British withdrawal might provoke a chain reaction proved
too great for the Bonn government to contemplate. After the tripartite negotiations, troop withdrawals as an issue dropped largely out
of sight as Britain announced its decision to seek membership of the
EEC, committed itself to withdraw from east of Suez and was forced
to devalue the pound. Significant also in this regard was the decision

by Britain and Germany to seek longer-term solutions, based on defence collaboration, to the offset problem.

In his excellent account of the background to and detail of the offset negotiations, Zimmermann argues with some force that whilst 'British and American troops ... were a major factor in the political relations between these countries and the Federal Republic ... less well known is the fact that these troops also held great importance for the international monetary relations of the Western world'.[99] However, he goes on to suggest that, in Britain's case, the government's position 'deprived the United Kingdom of any chance to make positive use of the troops for political or economic benefit'.[100] This is to some extent a counterfactual argument, to which there is no satisfactory answer, and it is difficult to identify what other policies Britain might have pursued. For example, there is nothing to suggest that, by abandoning the offset principle, even were this politically possible, Britain would have achieved any greater financial support from Germany; and, in terms of Britain's aspirations of a place in Europe, Zimmermann's argument overlooks the fact that, despite the German goodwill which undoubtedly existed, the route to membership of the EEC was effectively blocked as long as de Gaulle remained President of France. Indeed, it can be argued that it was precisely the threat of troop withdrawals that forced the involvement of the United States and ultimately led to the search for other ways, including defence collaboration, to offset the exchange costs of the BAOR.

The effect of the offset problem on relations between London and Bonn was not as great as might be supposed. Certainly the constant threat of troop withdrawals, at least up until the conclusion in 1967 of the tripartite negotiations, was an irritant and one that was not conducive to a harmonious atmosphere. However, the Germans were well aware of the constraints that stood in the way of significant reductions in the strength of the BAOR and, in any event, understood the economic and political imperatives that motivated such threats. Even more telling, however, was the fact that, notwithstanding the polemics, and the claims about worsening relations, the Germans never failed to enter negotiations with Britain over the exchange costs of the BAOR, agreements were always reached, albeit the sums involved remained broadly constant, and by 1970 the size of the BAOR was back to where it had been in 1964. The strength and validity of these arguments can be seen in the following comment by Barbara Castle, Labour's Secretary of State for Employment, at the time:

> I wanted to know why we couldn't insist on having real offsets instead of bogus ones ... I was as good as told that we had no bargaining power ... Harold maintained that we had got better terms than the Tories had ... Jim [Callaghan] added wryly that he had

stuck his neck out on offset costs at Cabinet's request ... only to
find that it cost more to rehouse at home the one brigade we did
withdraw. The Germans could always call our bluff again.[101]

By 1970 in his annual report, Sir Roger Jackling, British Ambassador
in Bonn, in relation to Anglo-German collaboration in the defence
field, commented on the multi-role combat aircraft and on the 'good
state of Anglo-German relations generally'.[102] The irritant of the
offset problem had clearly been removed.

Notes

1 The most comprehensive treatment of the offset problem is to be found in
works by German historians. See for example Hubert Zimmermann, *Money
and Security: Troops, Monetary Policy, and West Germany's Relations with the United
States and Britain, 1950–1971* (Cambridge, 2002); and Haftendorn, *NATO*,
Chapter 4. British historians by comparison have not shown the same degree
of interest, but see Young, 'West Germany', pp. 181–189.
2 Besprechungen – Bundesminister Scheel, London, 2 June 1965, *AAPD* (1965),
II, p. 939.
3 See for example Zimmermann, *Money and Security*, p. 79.
4 The British pledge took the form of an official declaration that became part
of the WEU Treaty of 1954. Under Article IV of Protocol II to the Revised
Brussels Treaty of 1954, Britain undertook to 'maintain the effective strength
of the United Kingdom forces which are now assigned to the Supreme Allied
Commander, Europe, that is to say four divisions and the Second Tactical Air
Force ... and not to withdraw these forces against the wishes of the majority of the High Contracting Parties'. Quoted in Working Party Report, 11
March 1966, OPD (O) (GC) (66)2, CAB 148/74, PRO.
5 See Trachtenberg, *Constructed Peace*, p. 220.
6 Minutes of OPD meeting, 7 March 1967, OPD (67) 10, CAB 148/30, PRO.
7 American troop strength reached 280,000 in 1962 but had fallen to 210,000
by 1968. Actual BAOR strength in 1964 was 51,000. Figures quoted in
Zimmermann, *Money and Security*, p. 248.
8 Between 1955 and 1960, Germany made a partial budgetary contribution
towards the exchange costs of the BAOR on a declining scale, with a conse-
quent progressive increase in the charge falling upon Britain's budget and
balance of payments. Treasury brief, 31 January 1968, RG 10/32 Pt D, FCO
33/179, PRO.
9 Zimmermann, *Money and Security*, p. 5.
10 For the background to British arms sales to Germany, see *ibid.*, pp. 57–68.
11 Telegram from Rostow to President Johnson, 6 March 1967, *FRUS* (1964–
68), XIII, p. 539.
12 Brief for Macmillan's talks with Adenauer, 9 January 1962, T 236/6753,
PRO.
13 The Germans calculated that the burden of filling gaps left by departing
elements of the BAOR would fall to the Bundeswehr; and it was unlikely
that they were capable of mounting an effective defence. See Harald
Rosenbach, 'Die Schattenseiten der "Stillen Allianz": Der deutsch-britische
Devisenausgleich 1958–1967', *Vierteljahrschrift für Sozial und Wirtschaftsgeschichte*,
85 (1998), p. 217.

14 Memorandum by Boyd-Carpenter, 22 July 1964, CP (64) 155, CAB 129/118, PRO. The figure of DM350 million was considerably less than the provision by the Germans under the 1962 agreement 'of DM600 million a year for a minimum period of two years' – see conclusions of a Cabinet meeting, 3 May 1962, CC 21(62), CAB 128/36, PRO.

15 *Hansard*, House of Commons, 706 (16 February 1965), cols 1008–1009.

16 Letter from Callaghan to Wilson, 11 December 1964, PREM 13/342, PRO.

17 *Hansard*, House of Commons, 703 (30 November 1964), col. 29. Healey was responding to a question by Emmanuel Shinwell, MP.

18 *Hansard*, House of Commons, 703 (30 November 1964), col. 30.

19 *Hansard*, House of Commons, 704 (16 December 1964), cols 420–421. In fact, Michael Foot's question was but one instance of a constant stream of critical questions posed by left-wing Labour members in the House. See for example *Hansard*, House of Commons, 787 (23 July 1969), cols 1732–1733.

20 'Denial of Proposals to Reduce Strength of BAOR', *The Times*, 30 November 1964, p. 10.

21 'Denial of BAOR Cut Doubted', *The Times*, 1 December 1964, p. 8.

22 See Wilson, *The Labour Government*, p. 5. In a leading article one newspaper described Germany as 'the wealthiest country in Europe with the largest gold and exchange reserves' and Britain as having 'the largest short-term debt'. The article went on to suggest that if Britain made little progress in bilateral negotiations, other measures, including troop withdrawals, should be kept in mind. 'Support Costs: A Last Effort', *The Times*, 10 March 1965, p. 10.

23 Letters from Diamond and Callaghan to Wilson, 25 February 1965, PREM 13/342, PRO.

24 Trend to Wilson, 2 March 1965, OPD (65) 47, PREM 13/342, PRO.

25 Healey to Wilson 'Bonn Discussions – March 1965', 2 March 1965, PREM 13/342, PRO.

26 Record of talks in Washington, second meeting, 7 December 1964, PMV (W) (64), CAB 133/266, PRO.

27 Record of discussions, Prime Minister's visit to Germany, 6–9 March 1965, PREM 13/329, PRO.

28 Record of meeting in Bonn, Monday 8 March 1964, PREM 13/342, PRO. On German support for sterling, Saki Dockrill confirms that, in November 1964, 'the United States, the [German] Bundesbank and other European central banks intervened to avert a sterling crisis with an aid package of $3,000 million'. See Saki Dockkrill, *Britain's Retreat from East of Suez: The Choice Between Europe and the World* (Basingstoke, 2002), p. 56.

29 *Ibid.*

30 Haftendorn, *NATO*, pp. 241–242.

31 Report on the Bonn talks, RG 1052/22, 2 April 1965, PREM 13/329, PRO.

32 *Hansard*, House of Commons, 710 (12 April 1965), col. 965.

33 Message from Wilson, 11 March 1965, *FRUS* (1964–1968), XIII, pp. 190–191.

34 Diamond to the Prime Minister, 'Anglo-German Offset Agreement', 29 June 1965, PREM 13/934, PRO. The main changes were: an extension of one year to March 1967 with a relatively firm commitment of *c.* £54 million; promise of a cheque for £42 million as a payment on account, bringing the second year's payments up to £50 million; finance for 'additional' British exports of £23 million from the frozen arms account in London, plus an additional sum from German bankers; and an agreed statement that performance under the current agreement 'would not fall short of expectations'.

35 *Hansard*, House of Commons, 715 (1 July 1965), cols 831 and 836.

36 Roberts to Foreign Office, 11 November 1965, PREM 13/934, PRO.

37 Gespräch – Schröder mit Stewart, 19 November 1965, *AAPD* (1965), III, p. 1772.
38 In evidence before the Federal Defence Committee, the German Defence Minister quoted from British sources to demonstrate that the United States spent 8.5% of GDP on defence, Britain spent 6.9%, whilst Germany spent 4.5%. See Rosenbach, 'Die Schattenseiten', p. 223.
39 Ponting, *Breach of Promise*, pp. 80–83.
40 Cairncross, *Managing the British Economy*, p. 142.
41 Record of a meeting between Stewart, Healey, Rusk and McNamara, 27 January 1966, PREM 13/934, PRO. In similar vein, at a meeting with McNamara on the same day, Healey emphasised that 'unless help with our foreign exchange problem was forthcoming British defence costs in Germany would have to be cut'. *Ibid*.
42 Memorandum of conversation, 27 January 1966, *FRUS* (1964–68), XIII, p. 304.
43 *Ibid*., p. 305.
44 *Statement on Defence Estimates*, 1966, Cmnd 2901, p. 6.
45 Working Party on Foreign Exchange Costs of BAOR, OPD (O) (GC) (66) 2 (Final), 11 May 1966, CAB 148/74, PRO.
46 See Embassy in France to Department of State, 30 November 1964, *FRUS* (1964–68), XIII, p. 125; and Haftendorn, *NATO*, p. 224.
47 Johnson to Wilson, 21 May 1966 and 26 August 1966, *FRUS* (1964–68), XIII, p. 457.
48 Trend to Wilson, 27 January 1967, PREM 13/1525, PRO.
49 Record of meeting, 24 May 1966, PREM 13/934, PRO. Wilson pointed to the disparity in expenditure on defence, 6.9% of gross national produce by Britain against Germany's 4.7%, and claimed that Germany had cut defence expenditure in 1965 whilst Britain's was still rising.
50 *Ibid*.
51 Deutsch–Britische Regierungsbesprechung, 24 May 1966, *AAPD* (1966), I, p. 696.
52 Record of meeting, 24 May 1966, PREM 13/934, PRO.
53 Record of meeting between Healey and von Hassel, 6 June 1966, and notes of a meeting, 30 June 1966, PREM 13/934, PRO. See also Blankenhorn an das Auswärtige Amt, 1 July 1966, *AAPD* (1966), II, pp. 909–910.
54 Bonn to Foreign Office, 11 July 1966, PREM 13/934, PRO.
55 Callaghan to Wilson, 15 July 1966, PREM 13/934, PRO.
56 Stewart to Callaghan, 18 July 1966, PREM 13/934, PRO.
57 Proposed statement agreed for use by the Chancellor in the discussions with Dahlgrün, 21 July 1966, PREM 13/934, PRO.
58 Bonn to Foreign Office, 5 August 1966, PREM 13/934, PRO.
59 Foreign Office to UK delegation to NATO, 18 August 1966, PREM 13/934, PRO. The proposed measures included: a reduction in the personal foreign exchange expenditure of British forces and British-based civilians; and a major change in the logistic support for British forces. The Ambassadors were also told that 'the outcome of the Mixed Commission is likely to show that ... we shall need to withdraw some troops as well ... we shall welcome the views of our Allies on ... achieving ... a saving of some £10 million this way.' See telegram number 1341, 12 August 1966, PREM 13/934, PRO.
60 Briefing memorandum, 23 August 1966, *FRUS* (1964–68), XIII, p. 453.
61 Johnson to Wilson, 15 November 1966, *FRUS* (1964–68), XIII, p. 492.
62 *Hansard*, House of Commons, 738 (12 December 1966), col. 46.
63 Roberts to Foreign Office, 5 August 1966, PREM 13/934, PRO.

64 See Frank Roberts, *Dealing with Dictators: The Destruction and Revival of Europe 1930–70* (1991), p. 256.
65 Memorandum of conversation, December 1966, *FRUS* (1964–68), XIII, p. 509.
66 Note for the OPD Committee, 18 October 1966, OPD (66) 102, PREM 13/936, PRO.
67 Roberts to Foreign Office, 17 January 1967, PREM 13/1525, PRO.
68 Foreign Office to Bonn, 24 January 1967, PREM 13/1525, PRO.
69 Conclusions of a Cabinet meeting held on 26 January 1967, CC 3(67), CAB 128/42 (Pt 1), PRO.
70 Embassy in Germany to Department of State, 27 January 1967, *FRUS* (1964–68), XV, p. 484.
71 Roberts to Foreign Office, 22 February 1967, PREM 13/1525, PRO.
72 Report by Thomson on tripartite talks, 9 March 1967, PREM 13/1526, PRO.
73 Message from Wilson to Kiesinger, 14 March 1967, PREM 13/1526, PRO.
74 Government press release, 15 March 1967, PREM 13/1526, PRO.
75 Telegram number 636, Washington to the Foreign Office, 21 April 1967, PREM 13/1526, PRO.
76 Details of the agreements affecting the exchange costs of British and American forces stationed in Germany and troop redeployments from the BAOR are shown in Aufzeichnung des Ministerialdirigenten Thieme, 28 April 1967, *AAPD* (1967), *II*, p. 685.
77 *Hansard*, House of Commons, 746 (2 May 1967), col. 332.
78 Roberts to Foreign Office, 31 January 1968, RG 10/32 (D), FCO 33/179, PRO.
79 Note of a meeting between Healey and Schröder, 13 December 1967, PREM 13/2661, PRO.
80 Letter MO 12/5 from Euwen Broadbent (Healey's Private Secretary) to D. J. D. Maitland (British Embassy, Bonn),13 December 1967, PREM 13/2661, PRO.
81 Burke Trend to the Prime Minister, 27 July 1967, PREM 13/1526, PRO. This refers to a report by officials prepared for the OPD Committee. The decision by ministers to approve this new approach as the 'means of meeting the foreign exchange costs of our forces in Europe' was relayed by the Foreign Office to Bonn in telegram number 2087, 1 August 1967, PREM 13/1526, PRO.
82 Foreign Secretary to Chancellor of the Exchequer, 25 January 1968, PREM 13/2661, PRO.
83 Chancellor to Foreign Secretary, 30 January 1968, PREM 13/2661, PRO.
84 Chancellor to Foreign Secretary, 5 February 1968, RG 10/32 (D), FCO 33/179, PRO.
85 Morgan to Lord Hood, 31 January 1968, FCO 33/179, PRO.
86 See telegram number 472, Foreign Office to Roberts, 2 February 1968, FCO 33/179, PRO.
87 Roberts to Foreign Office, 6 February 1968, RG 10/32 (D), FCO 33/179, PRO.
88 Anglo-German offset negotiations – record of meeting, 8 February 1968, RG 10/32 (D), FCO 33/179, PRO.
89 Memorandum by Minister of State for Foreign Affairs, 18 March 1968, RG 10/32 (F), FCO 33/181, PRO.
90 *Hansard*, House of Commons, 762 (1 April 1968), col. 33.
91 Conclusions of a Cabinet meeting, 15 January 1968, CC (68) 7, CAB 128/43 (Pt 1), PRO.
92 This calm was disturbed on the night of 20 November 1968 by an incident involving Wilson and Herbert Blankenhorn, the German Ambassador in

London. Faced with further pressure on sterling caused in part by the strength of the Deutschmark, Wilson saw the answer to the problem resting in a German revaluation. After consultation with Jenkins, Wilson summoned Blankenhorn to Downing Street late at night to give vent to his feelings and demand that Bonn be advised accordingly. Different versions of what followed exist but one version, following a deliberate leak by officials in Bonn, had Wilson threatening to withdraw troops from Germany. This was subsequently denied by Wilson in the House. Wilson's version was supported by Jenkins – see Roy Jenkins, *A Life at the Centre* (1991), p. 265 – and by Blankenhorn – see Blankenhorn an Brandt, 20 November 1968, *AAPD* (1968), II, p. 1498–1500. At an informal meeting with Blankenhorn a few days later, Wilson sought to calm matters by suggesting that it was high time that London and Bonn resumed co-operation on more important matters. See Aufzeichnung des Bundeskanzlers Kiesinger, 2 December 1968, *AAPD* (1968), II, p. 1547.

93 Morgan to Taylor (Bonn), 24 September 1968, RG 10/32 (H), FCO 33/183, PRO.
94 Briefing note for the Prime Minister by Sir Burke Trend, 14 May 1969, PREM 13/3220, PRO.
95 *Hansard*, House of Commons, 787 (23 July 1969), col. 1728.
96 *Ibid.*, col. 1732.
97 'Britische Truppen am Rhein Billiger als zu Hause', 23 July 1965, *Frankfurter Rundschau*, see B136/3144, BA Koblenz.
98 See Wilson, *The Labour Government*, pp. 5–7.
99 Zimmermann, *Money and Security*, p. 2.
100 *Ibid.*, p. 341.
101 Castle, *The Castle Diaries*, diary entry for 15 May 1969, p. 652.
102 Report by Sir Frank Roberts, 'Germany: Annual Review', 1 January 1970, WRG 1/1, FCO 33/1010, PRO.

Chapter 4

Britain, Germany and the Harmel report

The Harmel exercise undertaken in 1967 by the members of NATO can be considered as fundamental to the continued existence of the Atlantic Alliance. Not only had the Alliance been shaken by President Charles de Gaulle's announcement in March 1966 of his intent to withdraw France from the military organisation of NATO, but in January 1964, as Germany's Defence Minister suggested when outlining the German government's position on the problems of *détente* and security, 'an uneasiness similar to that of 15 years ago can now be observed among the public ... they are questioning the value of further defense efforts, now that the door seems to be open for a policy of détente over years to come'.[1] By 1966, therefore, in circumstances where the French considered that the structure of NATO no longer met their needs and where there was a distinct possibility that France would withdraw completely from the Alliance in 1969, when its mandate was due for review, where the prospect of *détente* with the Soviet Union seemed better than before and where there was considerable doubt among Alliance members that the United States would use its strategic nuclear forces to defend Europe, the need for NATO to identify a *raison d'être* that would meet these and other challenges that might arise in the future had become pressing.[2] As Helga Haftendorn succinctly comments, 'the problem which had developed for NATO was how to harmonize in the future an active *détente* policy with the Alliance's principal task: guaranteeing the security of its members through credible military deterrence'.[3]

It was against this background that the Harmel exercise was born. Haftendorn's work provides an excellent exposition of the way the exercise was conducted and the negotiations that led to the publication in December 1967 of the Harmel report by the North Atlantic Council.[4] The aim here, however, is not to repeat the full detail of Haftendorn's account, although there will clearly be a need to draw from it and other interpretative material, but rather to put the Harmel exercise into the context of the state of the Alliance in the mid-1960s and to discuss the implication of this and other factors for Anglo-German relations. Given other and more pressing problems that demanded the attention of British policy makers in 1967 – not the least being the reassessment of Britain's defence priorities, the decision to apply for membership of the European Communities and the unrelenting pressure on the pound – it is hardly surprising that, initially at least and in the terms suggested, a reappraisal of the role of NATO, including an assessment of its future tasks, was hardly the stuff to set pulses racing in London. Nevertheless, as President Lyndon Johnson made clear to Harold Wilson in the wake of de Gaulle's decision to leave NATO's military organisation, 'now that France is no longer taking part in this joint effort there is a grave danger that Germany will over time feel that they have been cast adrift ... we cannot risk the danger of a rudderless Germany in the heart of Europe'.[5] Such concerns about Germany were by no means confined to the American President. In the higher reaches of British society similar doubts existed. During a defence debate in November 1966 in the House of Lords, the Earl of Arran asserted that '[he] still regard[ed], as [he had] always regarded, Germany, and not Russia, as our potential enemy'.[6] Although this somewhat extremist opinion was strongly countered by government spokespersons, it was consistent with the view that the unity of NATO not only was of supreme importance to the security of Western Europe but was also the best means of keeping a resurgent Germany anchored firmly to the West. For these reasons, Britain could not afford for Harmel to go wrong, which was why British influence on key aspects of the exercise was so marked. Moreover, the experience of joint Anglo-German responsibility for one main part of the Harmel report, albeit at official level, and the good level of understanding that developed between the officials involved as the work progressed, would clearly do no harm to relations between London and Bonn at a time when Europe had become the focus of British foreign policy and for which a good understanding with Germany was seen as a key factor. Nevertheless, it is necessary to put the importance of Harmel into proper perspective. In practice, although important, it was only one part of a web of problems which NATO had to face in the 1960s: problems to do with nuclear sharing, with troop deployments in Europe, particularly those involving the United States and Britain, and with achieving agreement on a new strategic concept of flexible response. Whilst Harmel should be seen more as a significant landmark in the evolution of NATO into a more confident and resilient partnership of member states, it will be argued here that, insofar as it helped to breathe new life into the Atlantic Alliance at a moment of crisis, and in so doing served interests that were of fundamental importance to both London and Bonn, it was also a positive development in Anglo-German relations at the time.

Background to the Harmel study

There were several factors that together motivated the NATO Council at its meeting in December 1966 to agree 'to undertake a broad analysis of international developments' and 'to determine the influence of such developments on the Alliance and to identify the tasks which lie before it, in order to strengthen the Alliance as a factor for a durable peace'.[7] As we have already made clear, one important consideration was the announcement by de Gaulle in March 1966 that France intended to withdraw from the military structure of NATO. This announcement, in which he claimed that 'the changes which have taken place or in process of occurring since 1949 in Europe, Asia, and elsewhere ... no longer justify insofar as that concerns [France] the arrangements of a military nature',[8] heightened uncertainty about whether the French would remain in NATO when the North Atlantic Treaty came up for renewal in 1969 and created considerable misgivings among members of the Alliance. However, the French announcement by itself was not necessarily a reason for the Alliance to undertake such a root-and-branch reassessment of its future tasks as the Harmel exercise was designed to be. As Haftendorn puts it:

> there is much to suggest that this crisis had already passed its peak in December 1966 when the NATO ministers commissioned the report.... [Members] had found ways and means of managing NATO's expulsion from France. The removal of the seat of NATO from Paris to Brussels and of its headquarters (SHAPE) ... had presented few political problems and had been concluded ... as scheduled.[9]

Rather, Haftendorn suggests that Harmel was undertaken to resolve NATO's conflict of priorities between security and *détente*, and in support points to the belief held by some NATO members that the Soviet threat had subsided and the concern of others that co-operation with Eastern European states and the Soviet Union might undermine the principal purpose of the Alliance.[10] This line of reasoning is supported by a number of tactical considerations, including the pertinent fact that 'for reasons of domestic politics the Belgian government [and it was the Belgian Foreign Minister who subsequently proposed the study], which had just agreed to the transfer of NATO's seat to Brussels, wanted to show itself especially committed to *détente* policy'.[11]

Frédéric Bozo, on the other hand, cogently argues that 'France's increasingly disruptive NATO policy was perhaps the most direct and immediate origin of the Harmel exercise, if only because de Gaulle's actions had, by then, become the most evident symptom and the most effective catalyst of the overall crisis in the Alliance'.[12] Whilst Bozo accepts that factors such as the emerging *détente* in Europe and public opinion within NATO countries, which was then increasingly seen by decision makers and politicians with a growing awareness, or fear, of an eroding support for the Alliance, he goes on to assert that it was de Gaulle's grand vision of East–West relations, his concept of '*détente, entente* and co-operation', which was perceived as a way to overcome the logic of opposing blocs in the West and in the East, and his challenge to the American-dominated Atlantic status quo, that constituted a major threat to NATO's integrated structure and to its nuclear underpinning. As Bozo puts it, 'the Gaullist challenge, as many then started to realise, was no longer just a military and a strategic one but was increasingly a political one: what was at stake was no longer solely the workings of NATO, but its very legitimacy'.[13] According to Bozo, the American diplomatic reaction to issues raised by the Gaullist challenge, the diminishing perceptions of Soviet threat (which meant an equally diminishing military role for NATO) and whether NATO could be kept cohesive in an era of relaxed East–West relations involved the United States seeking answers to what was 'an essentially political problem: that of NATO's functions in a new international setting'.[14] Indeed, by the spring of 1966, Johnson was being advised that 'emphasizing, clarifying, and implementing NATO's political function [were] central to its cohesion during the present strains'.[15]

Whilst it is not necessary here to argue in any depth the relative merits of the arguments presented above, both Haftendorn's and Bozo's accounts make similar points about the Harmel exercise, and agree that, by 1966, there was widespread recognition that NATO had reached a cross-roads in its development. The perception that the threat from the East had diminished clearly merited a response by the West if public opinion was to remain supportive of an organisation that had its origins in the onset of the Cold War. As NATO ministers were to acknowledge, 'the Allies had already been able to initiate a policy of détente towards the countries of the East ... made possible by the general evolution of relations between East and West in Europe, and also by the balance of forces resulting from the continued cohesion of the Alliance and its readiness for defence'.[16] However, unco-ordinated attempts by NATO members to improve bilateral understandings with the Soviet Union and Eastern European states might also undermine Alliance cohesion. On this point, it is significant that, during 1966, Germany launched its Peace Note initiative, and Britain submitted to NATO a proposal for a Declaration on Europe.[17] Furthermore, given the signs of greater flexibility coming from Bonn, there was a need to build a consensus on the German question. Thus, it was timely for NATO to take stock and reach agreement on how it would manage in future a strategy of *détente* that took these factors into account. The disruptive nature of French tactics added to the urgency of this requirement.

Bozo's account draws extensively from French and American official documents. He suggests that Harmel's significance 'can best be understood through the prism of Franco-US relations in the context of the 1966 crisis'.[18] It is true, as Bozo argues, that officials in the US State Department believed that 'de Gaulle's challenge to NATO … [was] based on the presumption that he, acting alone, [could] do more to promote European *détente* than can NATO' and that, as a consequence, 'NATO … must demonstrate its capability to serve as a serious forum for the consideration of new problems which still beset our common relations with the Communist world'.[19] On the other hand, his account readily acknowledges that Belgium's proposal for a redefinition of NATO's tasks, tabled by Pierre Harmel, the Belgian Foreign Minister, in December 1966 at the NATO Council meeting, was motivated by two concerns: 'to reassert the long-term necessity of the Alliance after the turmoil of 1966, and to make NATO's transfer to Belgium acceptable to domestic public opinion'.[20] Haftendorn's account is more broadly based, although if there is any bias in presentation and argumentation it can probably be attributed to the influence on her thinking of access to 'recently declassified documents from German and American sources' and the assistance she received from 'a number of German and American colleagues'.[21]

The US State Department's 'Scope' paper drafted for the NATO Council meeting held in December 1966 explicitly and implicitly captures the arguments made by both historians. Perhaps the key point in the debate, however, was that made in the context of East–West relations, to the effect that 'thoughtful examination within NATO … of bilateral activities and future possibilities revealed a considerable variety of views'.[22] This observation supports the assertion advanced here, that it was a combination of factors that together motivated the proposal made by Harmel, but that individual Alliance members approached the exercise from different standpoints. One overriding objective of all members, although not necessarily of France, was to maintain the cohesion of NATO in what was perceived to be an era of *détente*. This was certainly the case with Britain and Germany.

British and German attitudes towards the Harmel exercise

Britain's attitude towards Harmel can best be considered through the prism of its policies towards Europe. By November 1966, when

Wilson made his historic statement in the House in which he announced the plan to hold discussions with each of the heads of government of the Six, with the clear intention and determination to gain membership of the EEC, Britain was on course to move towards an economic and political union with its European allies. From this moment on, Britain's role in the world as a major European power, resting upon the twin pillars of membership of the European Communities and of NATO, became the focus of British foreign policy. The Long Term Study Group in its Regional Study on Europe had already advised the government that Europe was vital to Britain's defence and economic interests.[23] Wilson's action over an approach to the EEC demonstrates that this and similar advice had been well taken, and supports the assertion that the cardinal importance of Harmel to the British government was essentially the opportunity it provided to show that, by working for the future of NATO, Britain was underlining its commitment to Europe. As John Adam Watson, an Assistant Under-Secretary at the Foreign Office and Britain's nominated rapporteur for the Harmel exercise, confirmed: 'the British attitude [towards Harmel] was largely governed by the wish to keep Britain at the centre of the European stage.... Ministers were generally pleased that Britain was involved in the exercise as a way of showing the British commitment to Europe.'[24]

There were other factors that had a bearing on Britain's attitude towards the Harmel exercise. For example, Watson confirms that although Harmel was seen as 'an opportunity to breathe new life into the Alliance ... public opinion was an important factor'.[25] There is little to suggest that public opinion in Britain at the time was stridently critical about NATO or perceived it to be a failure as an instrument of *détente*. The Campaign for Nuclear Disarmament (CND), which favoured unilateral rather than multilateral disarmament and was opposed to NATO, had by the time of the election of Wilson's government in 1964 already lost much of the support it had harnessed in the early 1960s and, as Paul Byrne suggests, 'the young people who had been its most active supporters turned their attention elsewhere – to the student movement and the Vietnam war in particular'.[26] Whilst ministers may have believed that a majority of the public at home supported its policies on nuclear deterrence, the same was not necessarily true of public opinion towards NATO elsewhere in Europe. In this context, Sir Bernard Burrows, Britain's permanent representative to NATO, told his ambassadorial colleagues that 'the Alliance could not endure beyond 1969 unless it were capable of conveying its political objectives to a broader public'.[27] More pointedly, at a meeting in the wake of Harmel at which he briefed Her Majesty's representatives in Eastern Europe on the future role of NATO,

Michael Stewart, the Foreign Secretary, admitted that 'there was a distinct feeling among many people in the West, particularly among the young, that NATO should be more concerned with a policy of *détente*; they needed to be convinced that the alliance's defensive role was not an anachronism'.[28]

Within British government circles there was also the realisation that the image of Britain as a staunch ally within the framework of the Alliance was being tarnished by its dispute with Germany over the BAOR, particularly its threats to withdraw troops (see Chapter 3). The inconsistency between Britain's approach to Europe and its actions within NATO was brought home to ministers by Lord Harlech, Conservative defence spokesman in the House of Lords, who suggested in November 1966 that it was 'surely inevitable that the six members of the European Economic Community will entertain serious doubts about our change of heart in favour of Europe when they see Britain behaving badly about the defence of Western Europe'.[29] David Vital made a similar point when he asserted at the time that 'in the case of Britain it [is] principally her insistence on making the presence of the bulk of her troops conditional on the financial assistance of her allies in maintaining them that [has] aroused doubts about her commitment to NATO'.[30] In such circumstances, therefore, support for Harmel was an opportunity for Britain to demonstrate a clear wish to maintain the cohesion of the Alliance and to avoid becoming involved in a further dispute to the detriment of NATO. As Watson put it: 'Ministers were relatively indifferent about the outcome of the Harmel study ... [they] wanted it to concentrate on the future of NATO ... [and] welcomed the chance it provided for Britain to co-operate with Germany over an important part of the exercise'.[31]

The Germans were also initially sceptical about the Harmel exercise. For one thing, the Grand Coalition between the CDU under Kurt Georg Kiesinger and the Sozialdemokratische Partei Deutschlands (Social Democratic Party of Germany; SPD) under Willy Brandt had only recently assumed office and, at the time of Harmel's approach to the NATO Council, was still in the process of agreeing its foreign policy priorities. Also, it seems clear that 'there was a prevailing scepticism whether a theoretical study could really strengthen the Alliance'.[32] On the other hand, Bonn would do nothing that would undermine the cohesion of NATO or impair its relations with the United States. As Watson made clear: 'For the Germans NATO was absolutely vital since it was the guarantee of their security ... without NATO they were naked. It was important to the Germans that NATO was strengthened and this was the role that Harmel was designed to fulfil.'[33]

Despite its initial uncertainties, therefore, Bonn gave unconditional
support to Harmel's proposal for a new NATO study when it was made
to the North Atlantic Council. A successful outcome to the exercise
would not only help ensure that NATO's mandate would be renewed
in 1969, which was a matter of critical concern to the Germans, but
under Bonn's influence meaningful Harmel recommendations would
provide an agreed basis for NATO's involvement in *détente* and, more
importantly, ensure that the Alliance would pursue co-ordinated policies that might overcome the division of Germany. Even under Allied
prompting, like the suggestions made by Wilson during his first visit
to Germany, in March 1965, Bonn had been slow to move away from a
policy that envisaged German reunification as a precursor to *détente*.[34]
However, with the advent of the Grand Coalition, and the insistence
of the SPD partner that the government work more meaningfully
towards eliminating political tensions and containing the arms race,
'the Federal Republic had joined in the Western *détente* dialogue and
put itself in a position to influence this dialogue in its interests'.[35]
As Theo Sommer, the respected German left-liberal commentator,
was to point out at the time, when discussing the new government's
approach to East–West relations:

> the Grand Coalition has left the trenches of the cold war. It has
> scrapped the old concept that reunification must precede *détente*, as
> well as the philosophy that any step toward relaxation of tension in
> Europe must be linked with a step toward German unity.[36]

Thus, the combination of a more broadly based and politically
stronger German government and the opportunities offered by the
review of NATO's future tasks makes it possible to argue that, for
Germany, the Harmel exercise was potentially of supreme importance
and would prove to be a constructive factor in the development of its
Ostpolitik. As Brandt was to comment in October 1967, as German
Foreign Minister, in an obvious reference to Harmel, 'we strive for a
period of *détente* in order to establish a firm basis for the security of
Europe; we seek to solve the German question too.'[37]

Bonn's attitude towards the Harmel exercise was governed by one
further important consideration. In January 1963, Konrad Adenauer
had signed the Élysée Treaty between Paris and Bonn and, in
Germany's eyes, this was viewed as 'a fundamental prerequisite for
European integration and for Bonn's continued aim of establishing
a Political Union'.[38] Although Bonn's relations with Paris during the
years of Ludwig Erhard's government had been marked by growing
irritation and recrimination, due principally to the 'Atlanticist' lean-
ings of leading members of the German administration, the Grand
Coalition quickly announced its intent to mend fences with the

French. In the words of Kiesinger, when he addressed the Bundestag shortly after his appointment as Chancellor, 'the decisive role in the future of Europe depends upon the development of the German–French relationship'.[39] Thus, whatever course Harmel was likely to take, notwithstanding French opposition, it was important to Bonn that France was associated with the outcome, as long as this did not provoke a dispute with the Americans and that nothing was done to disturb the Franco-German axis. A. J. Nicholls noted that:

> The close Franco-German relationship in Europe became a con-
> sistent feature of West German foreign policy to put alongside
> its commitment to the American security system of NATO. Even
> though the two policies were not always easy bedfellows, they
> formed the basis of Bonn's western policy, her *Westpolitik*.[40]

The Harmel study

Harmel's proposal to the NATO Council represented a line of continuity in moves aimed at redefining the Alliance's purpose. The start of this movement can be traced back to 1956 and to the *Report of the Committee of Three on Non-Military Cooperation in NATO*, more usually known as the 'Three Wise Men's Report'.[41] Like Harmel, the 1956 study aimed at redefining the objectives and needs of the Alliance, and to make recommendations which would strengthen NATO's internal solidarity, cohesion and unity. In many ways, however, the study was ahead of its time. In being tasked to consider co-operation between Alliance members in the political, economic, cultural and information fields, the study group was in effect being invited to recommend an outcome that would inevitably amount to a supranational charter. Although the report that emerged from the study argued that the 'deterrent role of NATO ... [could] be discharged only if the political and economic relations between its members [were] cooperative and close',[42] its detailed recommendations for the mid-1950s were too radical, and it was hardly surprising that, visionary though it might have been, the report was quietly shelved.

Nevertheless, the prediction by the Three Wise Men that unless the Atlantic community could develop greater unity, the framework of co-operation in NATO, which was so vital to its advancement, would be endangered proved to be an accurate assessment of the situation that confronted the Alliance when a stock-taking study of the Harmel type was proposed. Even before Harmel was mooted, there was a general feeling that the Alliance would benefit and gain strength from a fresh look at its aims and objectives. In 1964, for example, the Canadian government had proposed the appointment of a special committee to study the goals and tasks of the Alliance.[43] There can be little doubt, nevertheless, that President Johnson's address to the National Conference of Editorial Writers in October 1966 was central in prompting fresh debate. Johnson had stressed that the United States and its European allies must move ahead on three fronts: 'first, to modernise NATO ... second, to further the integration of the Western Community [and] third, to quicken progress in East–West relations'.[44] This constituted a firm response to the challenge to NATO and America's role in Europe posed by de Gaulle. Thus, it would have come as no surprise to NATO members when Harmel, building on the Canadian initiative, having taken soundings from the Johnson administration and reacting to Belgian public opinion, proposed a study of the future tasks which faced the Alliance, and of its procedures for fulfilling them, in order to strengthen the Alliance as a factor for a durable peace.[45] In agreeing that the Organisation would have an active role in promoting *détente*, NATO members (apart from France) expected that this would fashion a coherent role for the Alliance in the field of East–West relations that, in turn, might ultimately lead to ending the divisions in Europe and, at some future stage, to that affecting Germany. As officials in the German Foreign Ministry suggested to their Foreign Minister, Brandt, the objective must be 'so to change the position in central Europe that it will be possible to surmount the Iron Curtain and solve the German question'.[46]

Despite NATO ministerial endorsement of Harmel's proposal, doubts remained about its real purpose and, in particular, whether the review would lead to anything substantive. Regarding the purpose, there is little doubt that:

> [besides his] concern for the continued existence of the Alliance, which had been seriously shaken by de Gaulle's actions, Harmel's motivation no doubt stemmed from Belgian politics. He was intent on convincing the critics of Belgium's commitment to NATO ... that this engagement in the Alliance was in no way in contradiction to the government's desire for a relaxation of tensions in East–West relations.[47]

The assertion that Harmel's proposal was strongly influenced by the need to appease public opinion within Belgium is given credibility by the reaction of British officials. Following the NATO Council meeting of 11 January 1967, staff of the British delegation advised the Foreign Office that 'it is rather depressing to find the Belgians, having launched the initiative, are now calling upon others to give it substance by producing ideas'.[48] A few days later, in a memorandum to Lord Hood, a Deputy Under-Secretary of State at the Foreign Office, John Barnes, the head of the Western Organisations and Coordination Department, reiterated the point made by the delegation to NATO and added that 'they [the Belgians] seem to see it partly as a public relations exercise to improve NATO's image, and partly as a means of bringing M. Spaak back into the NATO act'.[49] Despite these reservations on the part of officials, the brief for the Prime Minister's visit to Belgium later in the month carried the additional and more positive pointer that 'there is a genuine Belgium wish to breathe new life into the Alliance, both in its internal organisation and in its part in East–West relations, and in particular to help it to surmount the dangerous date of 1969, when members first have the right to give notice of withdrawal'.[50]

The importance of public opinion, however, was a vital consideration, and not just in Belgium, especially if NATO solidarity was to be reinforced in the way that most of its members intended. It remained a compelling spur for NATO and one to which those members engaged in the study constantly referred. For example, Harlan Cleveland, America's permanent representative to NATO, most tellingly drew the connection between Harmel and NATO's image. In December 1966, in a telegram to the State Department, in the aftermath of the North Atlantic Council meeting, he suggested that the study 'can become a serious effort by governments ... to reformulate our collective aims in a way that fits the increasing fluid international situation, and is more likely to appeal to the generation that does not remember why we got into the Atlantic Alliance to begin with'.[51]

Whilst the hopes for Harmel which were expressed by Cleveland were widely shared throughout the Alliance, doubts about the value of the exercise, such as those voiced by British officials, continued to persist, and not just in London. Even as late as May 1967, some five months into the Harmel study, Hans Ruete, the Director of Political Division II in the German Foreign Ministry, still believed that it was impossible to tell whether 'Harmel would remain an exercise that NATO governments would take forward only with half seriousness and a clear regard to public opinion, or if it would become a searching examination of the Alliance'.[52] In fact, an answer to this question only gradually emerged. The problem initially, following the NATO ministerial decision of December 1966, was the failure to reach an accord between the fifteen member states on how the Harmel exercise should be conducted and, in particular, what subjects should be studied. Solving this problem proved to be a time-consuming task and was not finally settled until the following April, when the real work got underway. A positive start was made at the North Atlantic Council meeting of 15 February 1967, when it was agreed that the Council would direct the exercise and be responsible for it. An open-ended Special Group of representatives would be designated by governments under the chairmanship of the Secretary-General. The Special Group was to have a two-phase remit: to study the development of political events as it affected the purposes of the Alliance; and then to recommend the future tasks of the Alliance. It would be able to establish such special procedures, sub-groups and rapporteurs as it deemed necessary to complete the two-phase approach.[53] Although the Special Group met for the first time on 6 March, London's frustration with the slow rate of progress can be judged by the tone of a telegram from the Foreign Office to the British delegation to NATO, with comments on the outcome of the meeting, which welcomed 'the signs that at least some members of the Special Group are anxious to come to grips with questions of substance rather than dwell on broad analyses' but found it 'disappointing that so much attention is still being paid to procedural questions'.[54] Nevertheless, there was one predominant reason behind the Council's agreement that the procedure adopted should be flexible. As Belgian representatives made clear to Eugene Rostow, the American Under-Secretary of State, in recommending that the work on substantive issues should be delayed to a later and second stage, 'they [wished] to avoid frightening off any hesitant government ... [and] they [were] also anxious to give the French as small a target as possible until the exercise [was] well under way'.[55]

Furthermore, agreement was not easily reached on the question of sub-groups and rapporteurs. After a meeting on 13 March 1967, Burrows reported to Barnes that 'there was a good deal more uncertainty about the machinery for conducting these studies ... the Germans had reservations to the idea of setting up special sub-Groups' and that the German representative was 'doubtful about the idea of national rapporteurs'.[56] In part, this German caution can be attributed to the concern in Bonn not to fall out of step with Paris – France had by now withdrawn from NATO's military organisation and the French had severe reservations about sub-groups and most other things to do with Harmel – and to the fact that the Grand Coalition still needed time in which to formulate and agree its approach to Harmel, particularly on the subject of the German problem.[57] Even when these difficulties had been overcome, and agreement was reached within the Special Group on the subjects to be studied, the suggestion by Germany that it should provide the rapporteur to deal with the German problem did not attract universal support. It is clear, however, that the Germans offered this proposal in order to make their allies more familiar with their thinking about the German question and a European peace settlement and considered that, for this reason, 'it would be advantageous if the position of rapporteur on this question ... was allocated to them'.[58] To the embarrassment of the British representative, however, the Norwegian and Danish representatives made it clear that Britain should lead on this subject and, specifically, the 'Norwegian made it pretty clear that he would have great difficulty in accepting a list [of rapporteurs] on any other basis'.[59] As Haftendorn pointedly confirms, 'the reason for the objections to naming a German rapporteur on East–West relations was that Bonn's position on the German question was not shared by all members'.[60]

The compromise that was reached allowed for Britain and Germany to take joint responsibility for 'sub-group 1', under which Britain would deal with East–West relations in the light of an analysis of the foreign policy of the Soviet Union, whilst Germany would deal with European security, the German problem and the nature of a European settlement. Other sub-groups were also appointed: number 2 to deal with intra-Alliance relations, with Paul-Henri Spaak, Belgian Minister of State, as rapporteur; number 3 to cover general defence policy, with Foy Kohler, American Deputy Under-Secretary of State, as rapporteur; and number 4 to report on relations with other countries, with Constantijn Patijn, Professor in International Relations at the University of Utrecht in the Netherlands, as rapporteur. With this agreement, the Special Group cleared the way for the Harmel exercise to begin in earnest, which by this time had become somewhat pressing, given the deadlines set by the Council, although the methodology adopted up to then accorded with the staged approach originally envisaged by the United States and Belgium. Whilst Watson was able to report satisfactory progress after the preliminary meetings of the four sub-groups and 'that we have also established a useful working arrangement with the Germans', there was considerable significance in his other comment, to the effect that 'most delegations seem to agree with British ministers that the crux of the problem is the role of the Alliance in the context of the East–West *détente*'.[61] This assessment in particular underscores why NATO members were anxious to have the work on this part of the study under British leadership, so as to moderate the influence of German thinking on how NATO policy towards the Soviet Union and Eastern Europe should develop.[62] It was also a clear indication that the work of this sub-group would be crucial to a successful outcome of the exercise as a whole.

The period up until the ministerial meeting in December 1967 and the completion of the Harmel exercise was marked by a growing consensus among NATO members on the need to demonstrate a unity of purpose and a commitment to managing *détente* in Europe. In a brief for the NATO ministerial meeting held on 13–14 June, officials at the Foreign Office confirmed that 'the final report of the Special Group should be ready for our next meeting in December' and went on to suggest that 'our objective must be to make our alliance as forward-looking as possible, so that we may be seen to be doing everything we reasonably can both to ensure our own security and increase political cohesion among ourselves'. Nevertheless, the word-ing of the brief was forthright in suggesting that 'we do not want just a public relations exercise ... but a real attempt to reinvigorate the cooperative activities of the allies'.[63] Officials also began to focus on the public relations aspects of Harmel and in particular on the need for the Alliance to make a much greater impact on public opinion in NATO countries. Cleveland confirmed that this opinion was shared by other members when, in the aftermath of a Special Group meet-ing in November, he reported that 'it has become clear that concern about educating member country public, particularly youth, is very widely shared among Allied governments'.[64]

In British political circles, opinion varied as to how a stronger NATO identity was to be created. In suggesting specific themes for the rapporteurs to develop, Barnes at the Foreign Office was overtly anxious to force the pace on recommendations – for example, the foundation of NATO scholarships and even the foundation of an Atlantic university – that could result from the Harmel exercise.[65] In his response, however, on which Barnes made the hand-written comment 'cold douche', Burrows agreed with the 'point about the need for some publicity pegs, in order to ensure that the exercise makes its full impact on public opinion', but caustically dismissed Barnes' proposals as 'gadgets' and asserted that 'it would be better to concentrate on the definition of policies of the Alliance for the 1970s and to show that NATO is now essential for the *détente*, just as it has been and still is for defence'.[66] It was apparent that Barnes' ideas were essentially a throwback to the Three Wise Men's report, and that to have brought them into the equation at that stage could well have diverted attention from the real issues confronting NATO, and invited the criticism of 'window dressing'. In any event, that Burrows' views had more in common with the feeling among other NATO members and the realities of the Harmel exercise can be seen by the inclusion in the final communiqué of the Council meeting that approved the Harmel report of the unequivocal statement that 'the ultimate political purpose of the Alliance [was] to achieve a just and lasting peaceful order in Europe accompanied by appropriate security guarantees'.[67] This was in essence the ultimate appeal to public opinion, just as it answered the concerns expressed by Fred Mulley, Minister of State at the Foreign Office, to Harmel in October 1967 when they agreed it was important to work for a positive result. As Mulley so rightly put it, 'the Fourteen could not accept the scandal of failure to define the objectives of the Alliance after a year's work'.[68]

Official documents suggest that what might have been seen by some NATO members at the outset as merely a public relations exer-cise developed a momentum of its own as work within the sub-groups got underway. Reporting on the NATO ministerial meeting in June 1967, Watson advised Lord Hood that 'the Belgians and Dutch, and the Scandinavians and Americans said that the possibilities of the exercise had opened up since it started' and that 'a constructive group is beginning to emerge'.[69] In the Foreign Office brief for that meeting, officials commented to the effect that 'all our representatives on the Special Group are well aware of the importance of making sure that the final report points the way clearly towards constructive political action in the future'.[70] More tellingly, in November in a telegram to the State Department, Cleveland noted that 'the broad consensus on key issues which began to take form in subgroup sessions has begun to be converted into Alliance doctrine' and that 'the exercise has evidently been a soul searching exercise for at least half the Allies'.[71]

There were, on the other hand, quite different reactions to the Harmel exercise. At ministerial level, the French in particular were openly hostile; at sub-group level, however, French officials seemed more co-operative, albeit to ensure that the outcome resulted in policies their ministers could accept.[72] As Watson was to observe, 'the French difficulty is a real one: but the French do not want a stronger and healthier NATO: so that it will be virtually impossible to please them.'[73] But in the Harmel context it is difficult to escape the conclusion that French tactics were a ploy to neutralise the outcome of the exercise. On the assumption that Paris had no intention of making a complete break with its allies, and recognising the inevitability of the consensus that developed between the other members and that further concessions to its viewpoint were unlikely, the fact of French endorsement of the Harmel findings at the December 1967 meeting of NATO ministers becomes more understandable.[74] The Harmel report, in the form of a summary based on the sub-groups' findings, which was the compromise arrangement that was devised to satisfy the French, was subsequently published as an annex to the final communiqué of that ministerial meeting, which, given French ambivalence and the concessions that were required from all members, must in itself be regarded as an achievement by, and an endorsement of, the Alliance.[75] Whereas the 1956 Three Wise Men's report was, as we have already seen, widely regarded as a step too far at the time, Harmel, with its popular appeal, its demonstration of Alliance unity and, more fundamentally, its emphasis that 'Military security and a policy of *détente* are not contradictory but complementary', offered a blueprint for the future – an assertion that is supported by NATO's declaration in the 1970s of a twin-track strategy, based on a determination to deter aggression but with a will to negotiate, with its distinct Harmellian overtones.[76]

Harmel reassessed

Opinions vary as to the success of the Harmel exercise. For example, in September 1967, when outlining his thoughts on how the final Harmel report should be drafted, Dean Rusk, the American Secretary of State, emphasised that 'we continue to attach major importance to … [avoiding] negotiated language representing lowest common denominator of fifteen national positions'.[77] In December, following the NATO Council meeting and the discussion on the report itself, Rusk was more upbeat in his observation, saying that 'the value of the Harmel exercise goes beyond the report itself … the analytical process … has had great utility in clarifying Alliance thinking; in bringing the members closer together on some fundamental propositions, and in laying out [an] agreed framework for future political consultations'.[78] In an even more positive assessment, Bozo suggests that 'the development of East–West relations in the wake of the Harmel report demonstrated its validity not only in the context of the 1960s, but for the remaining two decades of the Cold War'.[79] On the other hand, however, *The Times* was more critical and in one article asserted that 'in spite of some fine phrases, the report provided little in the way of concrete measures to keep the alliance true to its declared aim. The main reason for this is that to get French approval it had to be watered down a great deal.'[80] Whilst it was true that the method of presentation of the Harmel report adopted by the NATO Council reflected concessions to the French, French endorsement of Harmel effectively conceded that the Alliance had a political role in promoting *détente* in Europe.

In that context, therefore, the outcome of the Harmel exercise can be viewed as positive. However, whereas the NATO Council final communiqué on Harmel asserted that 'the Atlantic Alliance has been a co-operative grouping of states' and that 'Their cohesion and solidarity provide an element of stability within the Atlantic area', in practice the relations between its members were much more complicated than this claim suggests.[81] This was particularly true in the case of Anglo-German relations. Moreover, as the experience of the Harmel negotiations showed, it would be a mistake to attempt any assessment of these relations in isolation and without taking account of the wider interests of both countries. At the level of the subgroup, there is ample evidence to show a high degree of co-operation between the British and German representatives, primarily because both sides believed Harmel to be important, although not necessarily for the same reasons. As Watson confirms, 'relations with my German counterparts were good … I was told to get on with the Germans'.[82] In London, ministers saw Harmel as the means of 'showing public opinion ... that the alliance [was] not an old-style cold-war crusade against a Communist attack which may never come, but [was] up-to-date and constructive in terms of *détente* as well as water-tight in terms of defence and deterrence'.[83] But whereas British negotiators were briefed to work towards a positive outcome, this would not be at the expense of a damaging split with the French. In this sense, London and Bonn shared similar objectives, but for different reasons. Early on during the Harmel exercise, Burrows and Lord Hood recognised that 'the UK would not wish to provoke an Anglo-French dispute ... because of our application to join the EEC'.[84] Britain's approach to Europe clearly coloured British thinking about Harmel, just as it did about most other bilateral dealings with the Germans at the time, and influenced the approach to it of ministers and officials. It was almost certainly the same factor that the French took into account when finally accepting the Harmel report. Having effectively vetoed the second British application to join the EEC in November 1967, why provoke yet another dispute by frustrating the completion of Harmel? As Rusk suggested, 'France undoubtedly went along in part because of solidarity among key members of Fourteen, but [the] existence of [the] UK/EEC problem may also have played [an] important role, [the] French not wanting to add [a] new NATO dispute to [a] UK/Common Market dispute'.[85]

In Bonn, Harmel was seen as an opportunity, within a clearly defined political role for NATO, to add greater credibility to its *détente* initiative and to ensure that the German problem would be considered an essential part of any European settlement.[86] Over time, Harmel would become the *leitmotif* of German foreign policy in relation to the East. As Timothy Garton Ash succinctly puts it, 'West German policymakers never tired of citing Nato's Harmel report as the bible of East–West relations. Here they said was a common definition of common goals to be realised through common instruments.'[87] Nevertheless, just as Britain was anxious to avoid a damaging split with France, so too would the Germans not allow Harmel to damage their relations with the French.[88] This line of reasoning is also supported by Watson's assessment of comments made by Brandt: 'they [the Germans] want the protection that the Alliance affords them; and to ensure that the East/West *détente* keeps their problems in the centre of the discussion. This is really why they are at the same time so anxious to keep in with the French.'[89] Thus, a significant and consistent feature of diplomatic exchanges throughout the Harmel exercise was the determination of the Germans not to create any impediment in their relationship with the French. For Germany, therefore, Harmel was an exercise in balancing relations. As Sommer noted when discussing German foreign policy, 'the new government [the Grand Alliance] refuses to be talked into making a choice between Paris and Washington ... it does not consider Franco-German friendship a bar to continued close relations with America'.[90]

Thus, the French connection was a crucial factor in determining the attitude of both London and Bonn towards Harmel and in that sense to one another. Beyond this, the Harmel exercise was completed after the resolution of the offset negotiations of 1966/67, and at a time when Britain and Germany had begun to search for a solution to the exchange costs problem, which would remove a source of irritation in their relations, and might be seen in its outcome as further evidence of the wish of both governments to maintain the basically sound relationship they had established from October 1964 following the British general election. Frank Roberts, the Ambassador in Bonn, in his annual assessment of Anglo-German relations at the end of 1967, felt the need to warn London about:

> a growing feeling [in Germany], especially in business and financial circles influenced by their contacts in the United Kingdom, that our economic ills are deep-seated, our social attitudes too complacent and the measures hitherto taken inadequate to put our house in order. This more pessimistic assessment of the 'English sickness' is the greatest single danger to Anglo-German relations and could affect German zeal in supporting our 'post veto' European policies.

Nevertheless, Roberts still felt able to refer overall to 'the satisfactory picture of Anglo-German relations'.[91] Despite the slight shadow cast by Roberts' remarks, it is still necessary not to overlook the fact that both governments regularly stressed the importance they attached to a good bilateral relationship and had put in place practical measures to ensure that this was the case. Thus, Harmel should be considered both as a key landmark in the development of NATO and as a positive factor in Anglo-German relations during the 1960s. It was one further element, admittedly small, in Britain's turn towards Europe and the policy of friendship with Germany.

The NATO Council could fairly claim in its announcement about Harmel that 'The exercise has shown that the Alliance is a dynamic and vigorous organisation which is constantly adapting itself to changing conditions'.[92] It had successfully faced the challenged posed by France and, in so doing, effectively ensured its longer-term viability. By its policy of linking security and *détente* it broadened its public appeal, emphasised NATO's political role and, in so doing, brought added coherence to its dealings with the Soviet Union and its Eastern European satellites. One of the by-products of the Harmel exercise was that it promoted a better understanding between London and Bonn about an eventual settlement in Europe, although this must be

seen in a context where France still figured prominently in Germany's
calculations. Harmel occurred at a time when Britain and Germany
were already working to foster their relationship and, in that it provided an opportunity for both governments to co-operate during an
important phase of Alliance diplomacy, it should be considered as a
relevant factor in their relationship at the time.

Notes

1 Kai-Uwe von Hassel, 'Détente Through Firmness', *Foreign Affairs*, 42, 2
   (January 1964), p. 184.
2 The term *détente* is used in its broad sense as meaning the reduction in tension between the West, that is the United States and its Western European
   allies, and the East, meaning the Soviet Union and members of the Warsaw
   Pact.
3 Haftendorn, *NATO*, p. 321.
4 *Ibid.*, pp. 320–385. The Harmel report itself comprised four 'full reports by
   the rapporteurs on the future tasks of the Alliance': Report of Sub-group
   I, East–West Relations; Report of Sub-group II, Les Relations Interalliees;
   Report of Sub-group III, General Defence Policy; Report of Sub-group IV,
   Relations with Other Countries (the full text of the four reports is presented
   in the language in which they were drafted). It is available at the NATO on-
   line library, www.nato.int/archives/harmel/harmel.htm (last accessed May
   2007). The Final Communiqué of the North Atlantic Council, Brussels, 13–
   14 December 1967, at which the Harmel report was approved is reproduced
   as Appendix 1, taken from the NATO on-line library, www.nato.int/docu/
   comm/49-95/c671213b.htm (last accessed May 2007).
5 Telegram from President Johnson to Prime Minister Wilson, 21 May 1966,
   FRUS (1964–68), XIII, p. 396. In his reply on 26 May, Wilson 'expressed his
   agreement with the need to maintain the closest unity of action with the
   West Germans in the difficult period ahead'. *Ibid.*, p. 398, fn. 6.
6 *Hansard*, House of Lords, Fifth Volume of Session 1966–67 (30 November
   1966), col. 775. In the same debate, Viscount Montgomery of Alamein
   expressed similar sentiments. *Ibid.*, col. 774. It is, however, important to put
   these comments in the context of recent election in Germany, in which the
   right-wing Nationalist Party had made unexpected gains. There is also evidence that among the British public there was a degree of concern about
   German nationalism. In a public opinion poll published in December 1967,
   for example, 31% of those asked thought that there was some chance that
   Nazism or something like it would again become powerful in Germany. See
   Gallup, *Gallup International: Volume 2*, p. 957.
7 Final Communiqué, North Atlantic Council, Paris, 15–16 December 1966.
   Available at the NATO on-line library, www.nato.int/docu/comm/49-95/
   c661215a.htm (last accessed May 2007). As to the timetable for the completion of the Harmel exercise, the report by the rapporteurs confirms that at
   the December 1966 ministerial meeting it was agreed that a preliminary
   report would be examined at the spring 1967 ministerial meeting (to be held
   in June) and the Ministerial Council at its meeting in December 1967 would
   draw the appropriate conclusions that emerged from the enquiry.
8 Letter from President de Gaulle to President Johnson, 7 March 1966, *FRUS*
   (1964–68), XIII, p 325.

9 Haftendorn, *NATO*, p. 401. Haftendorn's reasoning is consistent with comments made in a State Department paper prepared for the December NATO ministerial meeting that 'despite these uncertainties [i.e. the atmosphere of transition and ferment in Western Europe] the Alliance in 1966 has met de Gaulle's challenge'. See Scope paper, 7 December 1966, *FRUS* (1964–68), XIII, p. 504.
10 See Scope paper, p. 505.
11 Haftendorn, *NATO*, p. 398.
12 Bozo, 'Détente Versus Alliance', p. 344.
13 *Ibid.*, p. 346.
14 *Ibid.*, p. 347.
15 Memorandum by Acheson Group, 3 June 1966, *FRUS* (1964–68), XIII, p. 407.
16 NATO Archives, The Harmel Report, 13–14 December 1957, Report of Sub-group I: East–West Relations. Available at www.nato.int/archives/harmel/harmel01.htm (last accessed May 2007).
17 On the German Peace Note, see Chapter 7, note 36; on the British Declaration on Europe, see Chapter 7, note 48, and Appendix 2.
18 Bozo, 'Détente Versus Alliance', p. 343.
19 Department of State to Embassy in Germany, 2 February 1966, *FRUS* (1964–68), XIII, p. 399.
20 Bozo, 'Détente Versus Alliance', p. 349.
21 Haftendorn, *NATO*, p. vi.
22 Scope paper, p. 505.
23 Report of the Long Term Study Group, 23 October 1964, CAB 148/10, PRO.
24 Interview material.
25 *Ibid.*
26 Paul Byrne, 'Pressure Groups and Popular Campaigns', in Paul Johnson (ed.), *20th Century Britain: Economic, Social and Cultural Change* (1996), p. 454.
27 Haftendorn, *NATO*, p. 329.
28 Record of meeting, 10 May 1968, *Documents on British Policy Overseas, Series III. Volume I: Britain and the Soviet Union, 1968–1972* (1997) (hereinafter *DBPO III I*), p. 44.
29 *Hansard*, The House of Lords, Fifth Volume of Session 1966–67 (30 November 1966), col. 729.
30 David Vital, *The Making of British Foreign Policy* (1968), p. 34.
31 Interview material.
32 Haftendorn, *NATO*, p. 323. Haftendorn elaborates this point by arguing that Bonn's scepticism arose from the view that 'not all the allies wanted closer political consultation within NATO and would therefore be unlikely to support proposals to that effect'. *Ibid.*, p. 327.
33 Interview material.
34 During his visit, Wilson suggested to Erhard that 'when one talked about German reunification one could only see this taking place as a result of more relaxed feeling between East and West'. See record of the talks between Wilson and Erhard, RG 1052/22, 2 April 1965, PREM 13/329, PRO.
35 Helga Haftendorn, *Security and Détente: Conflicting Priorities in German Foreign Policy* (New York, 1985), p. 121.
36 Theo Sommer, 'Bonn Changes Course', *Foreign Affairs*, 45, 3 (April 1967), pp. 477–91.
37 Willy Brandt, 'Détente Over the Long Haul', *Survival*, 9, 10 (October 1967), p. 311.
38 Haftendorn, *NATO*, p. 323.

39 Address by Chancellor Kiesinger to the German Bundestag, 13 December 1966. Gisela Oberländer (ed.), *Dokumente zur Deutschlandpolitik, Volume 1, 1 December 1966 to 31 December 1967* (Frankfurt am Main, 1984), p. 59.
40 Nicholls, *The Bonn Republic*, p. 168.
41 *Report of the Committee of Three on Non-Military Cooperation in NATO*, 13 December 1956, NATO on-line library, www.nato.int/archives/committee_of_three/ CT.pdf (last accessed May 2007). The members of the Committee of Three were the Foreign Ministers Dr Gaetano Martino (Italy), Mr Halvard Lange (Norway) and Mr Lester Pearson (Canada).
42 *Report of the Committee of Three on Non-Military Cooperation in NATO*, paragraph 9.
43 Haftendorn, *NATO*, p. 376, fn. 7. This initiative reflected the underlying belief of the Canadian government that the improvement in East–West relations justified a review of NATO's organisation. See also memorandum of conversation, 18 March 1964, *FRUS* (1964–68), XIII, p. 27.
44 Editorial note, 7 October 1966, *FRUS* (1964–68), XIII, p. 482. See also Frank Costagliola, 'Lyndon B Johnson, Germany, and "the End of the Cold War"', in Warren I. Cohen and Nancy Bernkopf Tucker (eds), *Lyndon Johnson Confronts the World: American Foreign Policy 1963–1968* (Cambridge, 1994), p. 175.
45 See Appendix 1, paragraph 1.
46 Aufzeichnung des Ministerialdirigenten Ulrich Sahm, 17 February 1967, *AAPD* (1967), I, p. 302.
47 Haftendorn, *NATO*, p. 321.
48 Letter from G. E. Millard to E. J. W. Barnes, 11 January 1967, WN 29/1/1, FCO 41/210, PRO.
49 Memorandum from Barnes to Lord Hood, 17 January 1967, FCO 41/210, PRO. Paul Henri Spaak had been NATO's Secretary General from 1957 to 1961.
50 Brief for Prime Minister's visit to Brussels, 27 January 1967, FCO 41/210, PRO.
51 Cleveland to Department of State, 17 December 1966, *FRUS* (1964–68), XIII, p. 525.
52 Aufzeichnung des Ministerialdirektors Ruete, 26 May 1967, *AAPD* (1967), II, p. 786.
53 Telegram Number 53, British delegation to NATO to Foreign Office, 15 February 1967, WN 29/1/1, FCO 41/210, PRO.
54 Telegram Number 470, Foreign Office to British delegation to NATO, 10 March 1967, FCO 41/210, PRO.
55 Circular telegram from the Department of State to the posts in the NATO capitals, 11 February 1967, *FRUS* (1964–68), XIII, p. 533.
56 Letter from Sir Bernard Burrows to Barnes, 13 March 1967, WN 29/1/1, FCO 41/210, PRO.
57 The attitude of France was an enduring problem throughout the Harmel exercise. However, whilst Germany regarded Harmel as being very important, Brandt made clear that every effort should be made to avoid 'a confrontation with the French Government'. See Gespräch Brandt mit Brosio, 9 October 1967, *AAPD* (1967), II, pp. 1347–1349.
58 Aufzeichnung-Ruete, 26 May 1967, *AAPD* (1967), II, p. 786.
59 Burrows to D. M. Day, Private Secretary to Foreign Secretary, WN 29/1/1, FCO 41/210, PRO.
60 Haftendorn, *NATO*, p. 331.
61 Internal memorandum from Watson to Mr Thomson, Lord Hood and Mr Barnes, 21 April 1967, WN 29/1/1, FCO 41/211, PRO.
62 As proof of British influence, Watson confirmed that the work of sub-group 1 – 'The chapter on East–West relations, the Détente, and a European

settlement' – and 'that on Practical Steps and Procedures' – were 'joint efforts', although 'these chapters contain[ed] rather more of our ideas than German ones'. Letter to Burrows, 4 September 1967, WN 29/1/1, FCO 41/212, PRO.

63 Brief number 2 for the NATO ministerial meeting, 13–14 June 1967, WN 29/1/1, FCO 41/212, PRO.

64 Cleveland to Department of State, 23 November 1967, *FRUS* (1964–68), XIII, p. 642.

65 Barnes to Burrows, 6 July 1967, WN 29/1/1, FCO 41/212, PRO.

66 Burrows to Barnes, 12 July 1967, WN 29/1/1, FCO 41/212, PRO.

67 See Appendix 1, paragraph 9.

68 Telegram Number 348, British delegation to NATO to Foreign Office, 27 October 1967, WN 29/1/1, FCO 41/213, PRO.

69 Watson to Lord Hood, 13 June 1967, WN 29/1/1, FCO 41/212, PRO.

70 Brief number 2 for NATO ministerial meeting, 13–14 June 1967, WN 29/1/1, FCO 41/212, PRO.

71 Cleveland to State Department, 23 November 1967, *FRUS* (1964–68), XIII, p. 641.

72 Watson to Lord Hood, 21 September 1967. Watson advised Hood that 'The French were cooperative over sub-Group 1.... The French representative told me [Watson] privately that the important thing for his government was to avoid hard commitments ... or anything which implied a commitment to remain in the Alliance after 1969'.

73 Watson to Lord Hood, 31 July 1967, WN 29/1/1, FCO 41/212, PRO.

74 Ruete an Bonn, 15 December 1967, *AAPD* (1967), III, pp. 1668–1669. This gives a German Foreign Ministry perspective on French tactics during the Harmel exercise.

75 See covering comments to the Harmel report: 'Full Reports by the Rapporteurs on the Future Tasks of the Alliance', at the NATO on-line library, www.nato.int/archives/harmel/harmel.htm (last accessed May 2007).

76 *Ibid.*, paragraph 5.

77 Rusk to State Department, 6 September 1967, *FRUS* (1964–68), XIII, p. 609.

78 Rusk to Department of State, 14 December 1967, *FRUS* (1964–68), XIII, p. 652.

79 Bozo, 'Détente Versus Alliance', p. 360.

80 'NATO Policy on Europe', *The Times*, 15 December 1967, p. 4.

81 See Appendix 1, paragraph 6.

82 Interview material.

83 'France and the Atlantic Alliance', 20 November 1967, OPD(67) 87, CAB 148/34, PRO.

84 Account of a meeting between Burrows and Lord Hood, R. E. Parsons (Foreign Office) to G. E. Millard (British Delegation to NATO), 27 September 1967, WN 29/1/1, FCO 41/212, PRO.

85 Rusk to Department of State, 14 December 1967, *FRUS* (1964–68), XIII, p. 651.

86 See Appendix 1, paragraph 8.

87 Ash, *In Europe's Name*, p. 41.

88 Gespräch – Brandt mit Brosio, 9 October 1967, *AAPD* (1967), II, pp. 1347–1349.

89 Watson to Lord Hood, 14 November 1967, WN 29/1/1, FCO 41/214, PRO.

90 Sommer, 'Bonn Changes Course', p. 482.

91 Report by Sir Frank Roberts, 'Germany: Annual Review for 1967', 3 January 1968, RG 1/1, FCO 33/91, PRO.

92 See Appendix 1, paragraph 3.

Chapter 5

NATO nuclear strategy and the adoption of 'flexible response'

By 1964, the debate within NATO over nuclear strategy, of which nuclear sharing (Chapter 2) was but one element, was in full swing. At issue was the question of deterrence and how, should it break down, the Alliance would respond to any Soviet incursion into Western Europe. In this context, it is worth recalling the basic mission of the Alliance as set out in the Three Wise Men's 1956 NATO report: 'the foundation of NATO ... is [and remains] the political obligation that its members have taken for collective defence: to consider that an attack on one is an attack on all which will be met by the collective action of all'.[1] However, as the report went on to make clear, 'the ways and means by which the obligation is to be discharged may alter as political or strategic conditions alter, as the threat to peace changes its character or direction'.[2] By the early 1960s, with differences surfacing between the United States and its European allies on the balance that should be set between nuclear and conventional forces, and with the suspicion, if not the recognition, among European members of the Alliance that, in the light of the threat to the North American continent posed by Soviet strategic nuclear weapons, the United States would not risk the use of its strike forces in the defence of Europe, the dilemma facing NATO members was how to ensure that the basic mission of the Alliance would be met. In other words, how could the threat to initiate the use of nuclear weapons to deter a Soviet attack in Western Europe remain credible, in circumstances where both political and strategic conditions had clearly changed?

It was essentially to address this dilemma that, in the early 1960s, the American government presented its proposals for a move away from existing NATO strategy.[3] In the event of Soviet aggression, NATO's response in future would incorporate greater flexibility, in which conventional defences would be strengthened so that commanders would have a wider range of options, with the use of strategic nuclear weapons as a last resort. By this time, there was almost universal agreement within NATO that the Soviet Union would be most unlikely to launch a pre-emptive nuclear strike against the United States, because of the risk that this would entail for the Soviet homeland, and that a more likely scenario would see any conflict develop after an incursion into German border territory by the Soviets using their stronger conventional forces. The problem facing the Alliance, however, as Jane Stromseth suggests, was how 'to design a unified military strategy that satisfies the often diverging interests of a disparate set of allies'.[4] Against this background, this chapter will discuss the factors that eventually led to the formal adoption by NATO in 1967 of a revised nuclear strategy, that of flexible response, and how this and subsequent developments, primarily that relating to guidance on the use of tactical nuclear weapons as part of the concept of flexible response, affected Anglo-German relations. It will be shown that, in the main, there was a large measure of agreement between London and Bonn about nuclear strategy. Although this was conducive to a better understanding between the two governments, which had in any event developed by 1964 and was being fostered thereafter, agreement on nuclear strategy reflected more a convergence of interests than a deliberate attempt by either side to act in unison for political gain.

Early developments in NATO's nuclear strategy

During the 1950s and 1960s, NATO strategy passed through several formative stages. The basis for its development can be seen in the strategic guidance agreed in December 1952 under the document codename Military Committee (MC) 14/1.[5] The strategy represented a compromise between American beliefs that any Soviet attack should be met in kind and European views that any conventional attack should be matched by simultaneous use of American strategic nuclear forces. Nevertheless, Britain in particular was unhappy with the force goals of additional ground forces that were required of the European members of NATO under MC 14/1, and proposed that greater reliance should be placed on nuclear weapons so as to produce personnel economies. As a consequence of British pressure, and comparable thinking by the newly elected administration of Dwight D. Eisenhower in the United States, NATO moved towards a strategy based upon massive nuclear retaliation. Document MC 48, which was agreed in December 1954 by the North Atlantic Council, 'was built on the assumption that there was one, and only one, way in which the Soviets could be prevented from overrunning Europe in the event of war, and that was through the very rapid and massive use of nuclear weapons, both tactically and strategically'.[6]

Within the American administration, President Eisenhower was the staunchest advocate of MC 48, and throughout his presidency he continued to believe that 'strategic nuclear weapons were the dominant instrument of warfare, and that primary reliance should be placed on America's ability to fight a general nuclear war'.[7] Eisenhower's philosophy even embraced the concept of nuclear sharing since, as Marc Trachtenberg demonstrates, the 'MC 48 strategy implied that the European armies needed to be equipped with nuclear weapons'.[8] Although this is not the place to elaborate on these aspects of Eisenhower's conceptual thinking, it is safe to assume that, by the 1960s, if not before, any implicit proposals for providing Germany with control of nuclear weapons would have faced insurmountable opposition from the American Congress, and from the principal European members of NATO, led by Britain. MC 48, the strategy of massive retaliation, met the wish of the Europeans to emphasise the use of nuclear weapons for the defence of NATO territory but, as Beatrice Heuser suggests, the all-or-nothing nature of the concept was viewed in many quarters as both 'flawed and dangerous'.[9] As a consequence, acceptance that conventional forces, which were in any event needed under MC 48, might still contain local conflicts in Europe led NATO to modify its strategy to incorporate a more inclusive role for its non-nuclear elements. MC 14/2, approved by the North Atlantic Council in May 1957, introduced greater symmetry into NATO strategy and, with its move away from massive retaliation, represented a 'halfway house between MC 48 and the flexible response strategies of the 1960s and beyond'.[10]

The accession of John F. Kennedy to the White House at the beginning of 1961, on a ticket that included a commitment to the reform of American defence strategy, held out the promise of a change in Alliance nuclear strategy, in line with the position previously adopted by critics of massive retaliation. As Heuser argues, 'Kennedy and his advisers ... wanted to reduce reliance on nuclear weapons as much as possible, and to regain a monopoly, or at least a veto, on all nuclear use within the Alliance'.[11] This assertion explains why the Americans were so anxious to see Britain, and if possible the French, become part of the proposed MLF, and it clearly ruled out any suggestion of German control over nuclear weapons. The thrust of strategic thinking within the new administration soon became clear. Following a reappraisal of military strategy, Kennedy announced three basic objectives for American defence policy: 'strengthening the nuclear deterrent; creating more flexible non-nuclear options; and enhancing central control over nuclear weapons'.[12] As for NATO, Kennedy quickly appointed Dean Acheson, a former Secretary of State, to conduct a review of the political, military and economic problems of the Alliance in what must be seen as an attempt to influence NATO strategy in line with the new thinking in Washington. Acheson's report, which was submitted to the President in March 1961, contained a number of salient points, which, according to the Chiefs of Staff in Britain, if adopted would materially affect the then current NATO strategy. These were that:

> the nuclear threshold should be raised and conventional forces strengthened so that NATO would be able to hold off for some two or three weeks with conventional forces alone any Soviet aggression ... persistence in the aggression beyond these limits would mean nuclear war ... the first priority would be the rapid build-up of conventional forces to meet present commitments, including modernisation and improved mobility ... use of nuclear weapons under American control in Europe would be authorised if the shield [i.e. conventional] forces were subjected to nuclear attack or to a conventional attack beyond their capacity to contain.[13]

The message coming from Washington was clear: 'nuclear weapons should serve only to deter the enemy ... the defence of Western Europe should be effected with conventional forces only, if this were at all possible'.[14]

The next hurdle for the Kennedy administration to negotiate was that of convincing its sceptical European partners of the need for NATO to adapt to this new thinking (i.e. that Soviet conventional aggression would not automatically trigger a nuclear response). In this context, in May 1962 Robert McNamara, the American Secretary of Defense, set out the new strategic concept formulated by Washington to a NATO Council meeting at Athens.[15] Whilst he stressed that the United States would still respond with nuclear weapons to a nuclear attack, or to a massive Soviet conventional attack which could not be countered with conventional weapons, McNamara made clear to his audience that, owing to its non-nuclear deficiencies, the Alliance would have to accept the responsibility and the consequences of initiating the use of nuclear weapons. Given the capability that NATO possessed in both strategic and tactical nuclear weapons, McNamara asserted that the nuclear superiority enjoyed by the West was such that an all-out Soviet attack was most unlikely. Nevertheless, and recent events in Berlin were cited as an example, nuclear threats by the West would lack credibility to deter lesser actions by the Soviets.[16] As a consequence, the Defense Secretary was in no doubt that 'for the kinds of conflicts ... most likely to arise in the NATO area, non-nuclear capabilities appear to be clearly the sort the Alliance would wish to use from the outset'.[17]

In the following month, McNamara repeated what the United States expected from its NATO partners in a speech at a more public forum, at Ann Arbor. He argued that, given the current balance of nuclear power, which America confidently expected to maintain in the years ahead, a surprise nuclear attack was simply not a rational option for any enemy. Nor would there be any logic in an enemy resorting to the use of nuclear weapons as an escalation of a limited engagement in Europe or elsewhere. This was the case for deterrence in its purist form. However, these arguments did not necessarily mean that nuclear war could not take place. There was always the possibility of a miscalculation or a mistake by an aggressor that could lead to an act that was difficult to explain on a rational basis; and NATO strategy had to be framed with these contingencies in mind. That this possibility was of real concern at the time can be seen in such Cold War popular culture as the 1965 James Harris film *The Bedford Incident*, in which unauthorised action by the commander of an American destroyer provokes nuclear retaliation by a Soviet submarine. The remedy was to ensure that, for the conflicts most likely to arise in the NATO area, the response must not be limited to nuclear weapons alone. Consequently, the United States demanded that its NATO allies 'undertake to strengthen further their non-nuclear forces, and to improve the quality and staying power of these forces'; in this way, the Alliance '[could] be assured that no deficiency [existed] in the NATO defence of this vital region, and that no aggression, small or large, [could] succeed'.[18]

The outcome of McNamara's diplomacy was the adoption by the NATO Council of guidelines for the use of nuclear weapons, in line with the new American strategic thinking.[19] The guidelines set out the circumstances under which NATO would use nuclear weapons and the extent of consultation that might be possible before their release was authorised. As Christoph Bluth makes clear, however, 'the guidelines were very general and did not discuss particular contingencies, nor did they deal with specific weapons systems or targeting policy'.[20] In this context, it is relevant to note that, at Athens, McNamara had suggested that, whilst battlefield nuclear weapons were an essential part of the NATO armoury, if only for the purposes of demonstrating a will to employ such weapons, their use would probably lead to general war. Underpinning the new strategy was the concept of forward defence by NATO conventional forces capable of holding any Soviet non-nuclear attack less than all-out. Only in circumstances where a break-through occurred by the massive application of Soviet power would Alliance nuclear action follow. The guidelines were widely seen as the best compromise that could be obtained within an Alliance whose members had different views of the nature of the Soviet threat. As one analyst suggests:

> the Nuclear Guidelines represented a compromise ... between the views of the US which wanted to induce its European allies to make

substantial changes in NATO's strategic concept, and the desires of the Europeans who were greatly disturbed about this and wanted assurances that the USA would use nuclear weapons in their defence in virtually any military conflict.[21]

Britain, Germany and NATO nuclear strategy before 1964

To be sure, the reactions in Britain and in Germany to McNamara's proposals were motivated by different concerns. Unlike Germany, Britain was a nuclear power with an 'independent' deterrent and enjoyed a status that could be derived only from this fact. In any accommodation with the Soviet Union relating to nuclear weapons, for example an agreement on a non-proliferation treaty, Britain would be a key player. Leading political figures in Britain had consistently held the view that possession of nuclear weapons offered increased international influence. In this context, and some two years after a similar assertion by the former Prime Minister, Clement Attlee, George Brown, the then shadow Defence Secretary, told the House: 'if we still have visions of retaining influence in the world ... and if we see ourselves influencing the circumstances in which the deterrent might be used, I do not see how we can do without it'.[22] Nevertheless, influence was not the only factor that persuaded Britain towards the possession of nuclear weapons. The Suez debacle in 1956 probably contributed as much as anything else to focusing attention on Britain's defence weakness and dependence on the United States, although, as Andrew Pierre rightly points out, 'the deterrent strategy enunciated in the 1957 Defence White Paper was in its broad fundamentals virtually the same as that proposed by the Chiefs of Staff in 1952 ... and written into every defence statement since 1954'.[23] Moreover, possession of nuclear weapons would also, it was supposed, mean that Washington would have to take on board British views.[24] However, although Britain's membership of the nuclear club was designed in the hope that it would bestow a degree of freedom of action from the United States, and would provide added security in the event that the nuclear guarantees provided by its more powerful ally were called into question, Britain's security ultimately rested on the military effectiveness of NATO and the commitments offered to it by the United States. In the words of the 1966 defence white paper, 'the security of these islands still depends primarily on preventing war in Europe. For this reason, we regard the continuation of the North Atlantic alliance as vital to our survival.'[25]

For Germany there was no question of nuclear status. As Pertti Ahonen makes clear, 'Bonn's potential in the nuclear field was particularly restricted because in 1954 the country had voluntarily pledged to refrain from producing nuclear weapons on its territory'.[26] Moreover, one important and largely continuous aspect of American, and indeed British, policy since the 1950s was to ensure that Germany never possessed nor gained independent control over nuclear weapons. As we have already argued (Chapter 2), there is little to suggest that German policy makers ever regarded nuclear status as a realistic objective, but there is evidence that for Franz Josef Strauss, German Defence Minister at the time of McNamara's proposals for a more flexible approach to NATO strategy, Germany's renunciation of an independent nuclear status depended upon 'NATO continuing to be in a position to carry out its protective function'.[27] Nevertheless, if Germany was not to enjoy the status that nuclear weapons would bring, the Federal Republic was still important in terms of overall NATO strategy. After all, it was essentially on German territory that NATO and the Warsaw Pact forces faced one another and if there was a Soviet incursion, planned or otherwise, then it was likely to be the Federal Republic that would be the first to face invasion. Like Britain, Germany was dependent upon the nuclear guarantee provided by the United States; but, unlike Britain with its sea barrier to hinder a conventional attack, the Federal Republic, with its exposed geographical position, was acutely sensitive to any change of Alliance strategy that might endanger its territory. Any use of so-called 'battlefield' nuclear weapons, an element of flexible response, was also likely to devastate West Germany. Effective deterrence was therefore crucial as far as the Federal Republic was concerned.

Against this background, it is unremarkable that reactions in London and Bonn to McNamara's proposals were somewhat less than enthusiastic. However, NATO nuclear strategy had aroused mixed feelings in both countries even before the Athens meeting, although this was hardly surprising given the fundamental change to perceptions of warfare that the nuclear age had brought about. In Britain, as Sir Michael Quinlan, a former Permanent Under-Secretary at the Ministry of Defence, was to suggest to an audience of senior military officers and officials:

> we need to perceive the basic truth underlying the *Copernican* insight in this field ... that truth is that the advent of nuclear weapons has done something quite fundamental ... to the entire nature of war ... the result is that some of the old categories of military appraisal ... have simply ceased to apply.[28]

Britain's concept of increased reliance on the deterrent power of nuclear weapons to prevent major aggression, announced in the 1957 defence white paper, whilst generally supported within the country, was not without its critics.[29] Writing in the *New Statesman*, Patrick

Blackett, a former scientific adviser to the government, criticised what he described as an incoherent and unintelligible defence policy and argued that the policy of greater emphasis on nuclear weapons would 'disrupt NATO planning for adequate land strength ... force NATO to rely increasingly on tactical nuclear weapons ... [and] mean the destruction of Great Britain'. The solution advanced by Blackett was that, in an era of nuclear parity, the European members of NATO could survive, not by jointly owned nuclear forces or with individual nuclear forces, but only by accepting that an American safety-catch on all its nuclear weapons was much more stable. However, for this stability to be ensured, 'it [was] essential for Britain to renounce her own nuclear forces otherwise their spread to other countries [would] never be checked'.[30] Given the political and strategic importance that the British government attached to the creation and continuation of an independent nuclear deterrent, there was no prospect that arguments such as those advanced by Blackett would motivate a change in defence policy. In the light of subsequent developments, Blackett's arguments clearly had some validity but whether other countries, for example France, would have been persuaded to follow a similar course after a British unilateral declaration to relinquish its nuclear weapons must be open to considerable doubt. Whatever the case, and this is a debate that is beyond the scope of this book, the stance articulated in the 1957 defence white paper, and in particular the commitment to place a stronger emphasis on nuclear deterrence and to end conscription, marked a radical shift in policy and brought another dimension to moves within NATO to introduce more flexibility into nuclear strategy.

America's pressure for a revised NATO strategy, based on Acheson's report and McNamara's proposals, caused considerable misgivings in London.[31] In the case of Acheson, the Chiefs of Staff questioned the rationale of a proposal for stronger conventional forces to hold off any Soviet aggression for two or three weeks. Not only was there little or no reasoning to justify the proposal, but also it was difficult to envisage either side accepting defeat after such a conventional battle without first resorting to nuclear weapons. Moreover, the larger the conventional battle, the less there was that could be gained from the discriminate tactical use of nuclear weapons. NATO members were being asked to provide additional personnel and financial resources. The Chiefs concluded that, from a military viewpoint, they were 'unable to accept that the strategic concept ... would lead to an improvement in the security of NATO'.[32]

The main stumbling block, however, was the emphasis on increased conventional forces, which clearly conflicted with the accent on nuclear deterrence made as a result of the 1957 defence white paper and which, in the opinion of the Chiefs of Staff, would mean that 'the costs for the United Kingdom could not be faced without a complete reappraisal of our defence policy'.[33] Moreover, in his speech at Ann Arbor, and obviously with Britain in mind, McNamara argued that 'limited nuclear capabilities, operating independently, [were] dangerous, expensive, prone to obsolescence, and lacking in credibility as a deterrent'.[34] Whilst Britain was unable to increase defence spending on additional conventional forces, and was not prepared to relinquish its nuclear deterrent, there was no fundamental objection to greater flexibility in NATO nuclear strategy. However, in their consideration of the Mottershead report, produced early in 1961 by a working party under Frank Mottershead, a senior official, set up by the British government to study the problem of institutions and strategic theory as an alternative to the MLF, the Chiefs of Staff noted that, for effective deterrence in Europe, NATO forces must be 'deployed, organised, equipped and controlled in such a way that the Soviets could never be certain that they would by aggression unleash a major war'. Moreover, as long as this manifest capability was maintained, hostilities were unlikely to break out except 'by accident or by miscalculation of NATO's determination'.[35] The core of Mottershead's concept rested on deterrence, and within that to attempt to exclude the possibility of an accident or miscalculation leading to all-out war by using tactical nuclear weapons discriminately to impose a pause. Nevertheless, the Chiefs concluded that, whilst the concept did offer a good prospect of allowing an intermediate stage between conventional resistance and full military use of nuclear weapons, 'it did not alter the need for NATO force requirements to be determined primarily by the shield-deterrent role', nor did it change the fact that 'the scale of aggression that the forces could hold for the period of the pause required by the concept would be limited'.[36] Thus, whilst Britain was prepared to support McNamara's concept of a more flexible nuclear strategy, the British reaction to America's proposals demonstrated an underlying concern that too great an emphasis on conventional forces would undermine the credibility of deterrence.

In Germany, the arguments within NATO for stronger conventional forces were an echo of similar assertions made previously by Konrad Adenauer's administration. Only when the risks of emphasising conventional defence, at a time when both the United States and Britain were looking to nuclear strategy as a means of reducing reliance on personnel, became apparent during the 1950s did Germany adopt a policy of nuclear deterrence. By deciding in 1958 to equip the Bundeswehr with tactical nuclear weapons, albeit with the warheads under American control, and to reduce its conventional capability, Germany hoped to 'strengthen the American security guarantee, enhance the Federal Republic's status as a reliable ally, improve German military effectiveness within NATO and ensure that German forces would not be in an inferior position relative to the forces of other European allies'.[37] Thus, McNamara's proposals for more flexibility in NATO's nuclear strategy, involving greater emphasis on conventional capabilities, caught Germany in the midst of a force adjustment. However, this was not the only reason for German unease. In a context where foreign policy differences surfaced between America and Germany, principally over Kennedy's apparent willingness to reach agreements with the Soviet Union over Berlin and arms control, McNamara's proposals added to the doubts that were beginning to form in Bonn about the reliability of Washington's security guarantees.

McNamara's flexible response proposals were strongly opposed by Strauss, the German Defence Minister. In many ways Strauss was a formidable personality and a man who was no stranger to NATO strategy. As Hans-Peter Schwarz argues:

> it was obvious that between the years 1956–1962 the Federal Defence Secretary played a decisive role ... of all the members of Adenauer's Cabinet he had the best overview of the relationship between the peaceful and military uses of atomic energy within the Alliance ... and didn't hesitate to identify himself with the objective of involving the Federal Republic by one means or another with the international development of atomic weapons.[38]

Like his British counterparts, Strauss understood that a nuclear exchange in Europe would be disastrous for all concerned, that the principal aim of defence policy should be to prevent war and that the only way to achieve this objective was through nuclear deterrence. In Strauss's opinion nuclear weapons had changed 'from the absolute weapon of waging war to the absolute weapon against war'.[39] As a mark of Strauss's intense interest in nuclear weapon deployments, it is significant that he became one of the chief advocates of a NATO nuclear force and was instrumental in influencing the American-inspired proposals for the MLF.[40] Despite Strauss's advocacy of deterrence as the foundation of NATO strategy, 'he recognised the need for graduated deterrence and a balance of conventional and nuclear capabilities. But he rejected the idea of an extended conventional defence on German territory.'[41] In this context, Strauss poured cold water on the concept of a pause during which negotiations resulting in a withdrawal of Soviet forces could take place. As Strauss himself put it: 'Does anyone believe that if a dividing line between atomic and conventional weapons is allowed, the democracies will then say "if you don't go back ... then tomorrow at six o'clock, total

atomic war begins with which we will drive you back"....'[42] Strauss's
colourful period as Defence Minister ended in December 1962 as
a consequence of the so-called *Der Spiegel* affair but, although this
brought to an end the more open disagreements with proposals
for a revised NATO strategy, Germany's unease with the thrust of
American nuclear policy remained unchanged.[43]

By 1963, there are grounds for saying that there was little difference between the respective British and German positions on NATO
nuclear strategy, with *The Times* claiming that 'British and German
strategic thinking was now proceeding ... on the same lines'.[44] In
particular, both governments believed that deterrence must remain
central to NATO strategy, were unconvinced about the strong
emphasis on conventional forces inherent in McNamara's proposals,
notwithstanding recognition that such forces should be capable of
dealing with relatively minor Soviet incursions into NATO territory,
and retained considerable doubts about the concept of a pause to
allow negotiations leading to a return to the status quo should such
an incursion take place.

Britain, Germany and NATO nuclear strategy after 1964

The election of Wilson's government brought little change in official
attitudes in Britain towards NATO nuclear strategy. In opposition,
Labour's criticisms about defence spending, particularly on conventional forces in an era of nuclear deterrence, were remarkably
in tune with the commitments expressed in the 1957 white paper.
Three years later, the government's decision in 1960 to cancel the
Blue Streak missile system caused the Labour Party to split over
opposition to Britain's independent nuclear deterrent and support for
unilateral disarmament and withdrawal from NATO. By the time of
the 1964 general election, the Labour Party was committed to the renegotiation of the Nassau agreement, opposed the MLF but favoured
strengthening Britain's conventional forces (see Chapter 2).[45] Like
other commitments in Labour's election manifesto, the one about
conventional forces was somewhat ambiguous, especially so since,
from the outset, the new government was forced to reduce defence
expenditure.[46] It is worth recalling also that the Party brought with
it a left wing that contained anti-German elements, although, as we
have noted (Chapter 1), once elected Wilson and his ministers made
the improvement of Anglo-German relations one of their priorities.

Nevertheless, the key questions once Labour took office were:
would the new government give up Britain's nuclear weapons, as its
criticisms of the 'independent deterrent' implied and, if so, how would
this affect Britain's approach to NATO's nuclear strategy? Writing

in *Foreign Affairs*, Patrick Gordon Walker, Labour's shadow Foreign Secretary, seemingly provided answers to both questions. He claimed that whilst Labour accepted the need for a Western deterrent, the Party:

> [did] not believe that Britain herself should seek to make or possess nuclear weapons ... [and did] not accept that [Britain] must continue to buy an American weapon as a sort of status symbol [and that] an essential feature of [the Party's] defence policy would be ... to improve [Britain's] conventional forces.[47]

Intended or otherwise, Gordon Walker seemed to be saying that a Labour government would adopt two essential elements of McNamara's proposals for NATO nuclear strategy: firstly, by removing Britain's independent deterrent it would acquiesce to American control of all NATO nuclear weapons; and secondly, by improving Britain's conventional forces, it would *a fortiori* accept a range of options to respond to any Soviet incursion into NATO territory rather than assume an early use of nuclear weapons. However, the real architect of Labour's defence policies was Denis Healey, who, as a former army officer and a man who had taken a deep interest in nuclear strategy during the opposition years, had developed a reputation as a heavyweight in this field within defence and academic circles. It is also relevant that Healey, who was immediately appointed Defence Secretary following the 1964 election, remained in his appointment throughout the time of the first two Wilson administrations, bringing a degree of continuity and expertise to the defence portfolio rarely seen in British politics at the time. As Healey himself put it, 'Since the early fifties, I had been working with men on both sides of the Atlantic, many with unique military experience, trying to understand the unprecedented problems created for strategy and diplomacy by nuclear weapons.'[48]

Within days of the election victory, Wilson, in conjunction with Gordon Walker and Healey, reached the decision that Britain should continue with an order for four of the five Polaris submarines on the basis that 'in the light of the information [then] available ... it was clear that production of the submarines was well past the point of no return: there could be no question of cancelling them, except at inordinate cost'.[49] At a Chequers meeting in November 1964 called, *inter alia*, to discuss Britain's defence problems and to prepare ministers for the December meetings with Johnson and his advisers in Washington, proposals for the ANF were formulated, which included the assignment to NATO, without recall, of Britain's nuclear forces (see Chapter 2). In Wilson's eyes this effectively disposed of Labour's commitment to renegotiate the Nassau agreement and of the party

political controversy about 'the pretence that Britain had an "independent" nuclear weapon'.[50] With the key policy decisions taken about
Britain's deterrent, the detail of nuclear strategy could be left to
Healey and his advisers, although within the tight constraints of
Britain's precarious financial situation. As Pierre rightly argues,
'the dominating question of defence policy during Labour's years in
power was how the nation's military capabilities could be brought into
balance with its economic resources and foreign policy objectives'.[51]
Healey summed up the problem and his solution to it as follows:

> my problem as Secretary of State ... was to plan an orderly reduc-
> tion of the defence expenditure programmed, and to insist that
> the political Departments made the reductions in our defence
> commitments.... In 1964 ... our forces were already considerably
> overstretched by their existing commitments. If [we were] to bring
> our commitments effectively into line with a diminished capabil-
> ity [we] would have to ensure that our commitments were reduced
> proportionately more than our armed forces.[52]

In the early 1960s, Healey by his own admission wanted to encourage 'a shift in the strategy of NATO ... away from deterrence by the
nuclear tripwire, towards defence by conventional forces adequate
in strength to resist anything but an all-out attack by the Warsaw
powers'.[53] At first sight, this might seem to support McNamara's
concept of flexible response set out in the proposals he presented to
the Athens meeting in 1962, but Healey never completely endorsed
the conventional aspects of flexible response. Instead, whilst he saw
the need for sufficient conventional strength to deal with the possibility of small-scale local operations or frontier incidents, he had no
doubt that:

> NATO could not forgo reliance on nuclear escalation in case of
> large-scale attack without an increase in European military budgets
> which [was] beyond the realm of practical possibility ... it [was] far
> from clear that NATO would be acting wisely in seeking to achieve
> security ... through the building of a Maginot Line of conventional
> forces.[54]

Moreover, he was somewhat critical of McNamara's proposals in that,
although he saw their purpose as being to dissuade the European
allies from over-reliance on nuclear weapons, he suspected that his
American counterpart really intended 'to dispense with the need for
using nuclear weapons in Europe altogether, if the enemy did not
use them'.[55] As Healey also argued, 'a large scale conventional war of
movement would involve destruction for the people living in the area
of the battlefield no more tolerable in prospect than that imposed by a

strategic nuclear exchange'.[56] Healey understood the concerns in this regard of countries on the front line, particularly Germany, and saw his task, as NATO members struggled to secure a compromise agreement on nuclear strategy, as acting 'as a bridge between McNamara ... and the Germans who really wanted to go back to the strategy of massive nuclear retaliation, triggered by a tripwire on their Eastern frontier'.[57] By 1966, in a summary of Britain's position, Healey's officials were advising ministers that:

> the United Kingdom believes that a new ... concept is needed which places emphasis on deterrence rather than on actually fighting a war in Europe ... we believe that NATO requires a range of capabilities, extending from non-nuclear forces which by their deployment are bound to become engaged as soon as aggression takes place, through tactical nuclear weapons ready for use if conventional forces do not suffice, to the ultimate sanction of strategic nuclear forces ... NATO's limited resources would be better devoted to such measures as improving mobility and reinforcement capability, so that a limited attack[could be] identified and held long enough for a decision to be taken on the use of nuclear weapons.[58]

In Germany, the appointment of Kai-Uwe von Hassel as Defence Minister in place of Strauss and of Ludwig Erhard as the successor to Adenauer as Chancellor brought a shift in emphasis towards a more Atlanticist outlook in German foreign policy. As Heuser puts it, 'von Hassel, like Foreign Minister Schröder ... Erhard and indeed the Socialist (SDP) opposition party, were far keener on co-operation with the Americans than with de Gaulle'.[59] Nevertheless, basic differences with the Americans over the concept of flexible response as the answer to NATO's nuclear strategy remained. Writing in *Foreign Affairs*, von Hassel provided a clearer insight into the position of the German government with regard to the problems of *détente* and security. The Defence Minister restated the essential principles of German foreign policy: that the NATO Alliance would remain the basis of all their efforts to maintain freedom and territorial integrity; that a close friendship with France would still be necessary for the political integration of Europe; and that the division of Germany, as a principal cause of tension between East and West, must be ended. As to Germany's security, von Hassel emphasised that the aim of any type of defence policy must be to maintain deterrence from any kind of military aggression, and that this required determination to meet such aggression with appropriate means and with a degree of flexibility that would prevent an enemy from calculating NATO's reaction in advance. Whilst this appeared to endorse McNamara's concept of flexible response, von Hassel qualified his comments with the rider that 'NATO had to be capable of employing nuclear weapons ...

[whilst this] did not mean to say that employment of nuclear weapons should be the rule ... any evident lack of resolution ... might prove disastrous and signify complete failure of the deterrent'.[60]

Von Hassel elaborated some months later on Germany's attitude towards nuclear strategy. In expressing concern about the risks in setting the nuclear threshold too high, he argued that an extended conventional conflict could create the conditions whereby an aggressor might make acquisitions that would improve a bargaining position at the expense of the West. The solution here was to utilise atomic demolition munitions (ADMs) or even battlefield nuclear weapons at an early stage of any attack.[61] What these glimpses of German thinking demonstrate is an attempt to come to terms with the dynamics of NATO nuclear strategy, albeit from a position of dependence upon an ally determined to ensure greater flexibility in the options open to the Alliance.

The further evolution of NATO nuclear strategy – MC 14/3

The catalyst for movement within NATO to resolve differences over nuclear strategy came with the withdrawal in 1966 of France from NATO's military organisation. Without going over in any detail ground already well covered about the reasons for the French action, it is only necessary to say here that it was based on the rejection of American leadership of the Alliance and, in an era where conditions of military stability prevailed and the threats of direct aggression seemed remote, a fundamentally different view of East–West relations in Europe.[62] French military specialists argued that the strategy of nuclear deterrence had been undermined by a lack of credibility and that for this reason France refused to accept the principle of flexible response. What needed to be done was 'to keep the enemy's mind in a state of uncertainty ... [and in order] to enable several methods of deterrence to be used simultaneously, there [had to] be several centres of decision'.[63] With France's withdrawal from the NATO military command structure, the way was clear for the Alliance to reach a common position on nuclear strategy. However, as Britain's defence white paper for 1967 put it:

> none of the NATO governments is willing to pay for the forces which SACEUR would need to carry out his mission as hitherto defined ... NATO defence ministers finally agreed to instruct their advisers to revise NATO strategy in the light of the forces which governments would undertake to make available.[64]

The comment in that white paper to the effect that strategy must be designed to fit the forces that would be made available was a continuous strand in Britain's attitude towards NATO policy. As Healey was also to tell the House, 'NATO would be compelled to resort to nuclear weapons within days of an attack ... [and] within days of starting to use nuclear weapons, organised warfare would become impossible'.[65] Healey, and it was the Defence Secretary who was orchestrating Britain's approach to NATO strategy, 'never believed that the Soviet Union was bent on military conquest of Western Europe', although he did not dismiss the possibility of border incursions and for this reason 'NATO did need conventional weapons at least large enough to control such incidents'.[66] In an elaboration of Britain's position, Healey was to tell a German audience that:

> while there are still deficiencies in some of NATO's forces ... NATO could not forego reliance on nuclear escalation in case of large-scale attack ... for countries like Germany which are in the front line, deterrence is the only acceptable strategy ... to reject an all-conventional strategy for the defence of Western Europe is not however to deny that conventional forces at roughly the present level have a vital role to play in NATO's strategy of deterrence by the threat of escalation.[67]

It would only be on this basis that Britain would justify support for NATO's shift to a policy of flexible response.

A similar consistency ran through German reactions towards the concept of flexible response. Whilst the German government was prepared to strengthen its conventional forces, this would only be on the basis that nuclear weapons remained an essential component of deterrence. There could be no question of extended conflict on German soil and the possibility of conceding territory to an aggressor was politically unacceptable. As Wilhelm Grewe, the German permanent representative to NATO, was to put it, 'it would be impossible for any German Defence Minister to agree to mention the possibility of loss of territory ... it would cause grave embarrassment'.[68] Moreover, the Germans held deep-seated reservations about the use of tactical nuclear weapons. In a report on the discussions at a NATO ministerial meeting held in 1967, Hans Ruete, Director of Political Division II in the German Foreign Ministry, referred to German military studies which had demonstrated that:

> tactical nuclear weapons would have adverse psychological effects upon friendly forces as well as on the civilian population; the first use of nuclear weapons by NATO could provoke the Warsaw Pact to respond with a world-wide offensive; and, the time needed for release authorisation was too great.

Similar problems had also been identified with the use of ADMs, 'a subject that was extremely sensitive in German internal politics and had to be handled carefully especially in dealings with the Press'.[69] Of particular concern was the question of consultation with a host nation before authorisation of the use of nuclear weapons. As Ruete was to put it, 'the influence of the host nation on the decision to release nuclear weapons is an important question for Germany'.[70] As well as clarification of the conditions under which tactical nuclear weapons were to be used, this was a matter that had to be settled before Germany would give agreement to the revised nuclear concept of flexible response.

NATO defence ministers eventually adopted the strategy of flexible response in December 1967, after long, protracted and detailed discussions by ministers and officials within bilateral and multilateral meetings. Officially labelled 'MC 14/3', the achievement was seen by American Secretary of State Dean Rusk as 'a set of institutionalised arrangements enabling [members] realistically to tie together nuclear and conventional strategy, force planning and available resources'.[71] The essential ingredients of the concept were described as a manifest determination to defend against all forms and levels of aggression by means of a flexible response. In the event that deterrence failed, three types of response would be open to NATO: direct defence, which would seek to defeat aggression at the level at which the enemy chose to fight; deliberate escalation, which would seek to defeat aggression by raising the scope and intensity of combat, to the point where the aggression was contained, but without resort to nuclear weapons; and a general nuclear response, that is, massive nuclear attacks not only to contain the conventional attack but also to strike at the enemy's nuclear weapons. In a subsequent assessment of the strategy, Healey said that 'he did not agree with every single item in MC 14/3 but he did regard it as a very great step forward and he hoped that all could approve it in a spirit of compromise'.[72] The extent of that compromise can be seen in a summary of the results of the ministerial defence and nuclear meetings of NATO held on 1 January 1968. Sir Bernard Burrows, Britain's permanent representative to NATO, reported that:

> the Germans have several difficulties with the new strategy of flexible response which seems to involve possible loss of territory in the early stages and makes them doubt the reality of the American nuclear guarantee ... in the UK view ... the possibilities of conventional defence are limited and excessive dependence on these could reduce the efficacy of deterrence by threat of escalation.[73]

In a compromise, each side has to make concessions in order to achieve progress and that proved to be the case in the sometimes tortuous negotiations leading to the agreement on flexible response. The

American objective was to place greater emphasis on conventional weapons to deal with any major Soviet aggression in Europe, so as to avoid the use of nuclear weapons, although, over time, McNamara came to recognise that the European allies would refuse to make the improvements in their conventional forces on which his vision of flexible response depended. Germany remained opposed to the weakening of deterrence that too great an emphasis on conventional defence might create and to the possibility of conceding territory through an extended conventional conflict. For these reasons, the Germans firmly believed in forward defence and, where appropriate, in the early use of strategic nuclear weapons. The British also believed that deterrence was fundamental to NATO's nuclear strategy, but remained convinced that a conventional conflict was in any event unlikely. Britain was not prepared, nor financially able, to provide extra conventional resources for NATO, particularly so at a time when it was pressing the Germans to contribute more towards the exchange costs of the BAOR. Overall, agreement on flexible response was a compromise between the initial American objective of establishing conventional forces at a level capable of responding to a major Warsaw Pact attack without resort to nuclear weapons, and the European preference to maintain NATO's conventional capability at its prevailing level and for the potential rapid employment of nuclear weapons.[74]

NATO strategy and tactical nuclear weapons

Despite the agreement on a revised nuclear strategy, areas of uncertainty remained. For example, as Healey made clear, 'Flexible Response had obvious weaknesses ... European Defence Ministers ... discovered that nuclear warfare was not as simple as they imagined ... they never got beyond listing a series of options in very general terms, with no attempt to define which might be appropriate in what circumstances'.[75] One key weakness in this regard was political guidance on the use of tactical nuclear weapons. In establishing the McNamara Special Committee and its offshoots (see Chapter 2), NATO had the ideal forum in the NPG for resolving issues relating to the use of battlefield nuclear weapons, including areas of particular concern to the European allies, not least Germany, such as the deployment of ADMs and host nation consultation. The formation of the NPG marked the culmination of the nuclear sharing debate within NATO, and served the specific purpose of providing European members of NATO, and Germany in particular, with a more direct role in the formulation of Alliance nuclear policy. As well as providing an essential bridge in resolving differences between strategic thought in America and Europe, the NPG ultimately became an important medium to facilitate the growing convergence of British and German interests.

Both Britain and Germany had already conducted studies on the use of tactical nuclear weapons and were therefore tasked by the NATO defence ministers with drawing together all the work that had been done in this area, to form political guidelines as part of the overall concept of flexible response. This was a development that was viewed with some satisfaction in both countries, since, 'for the first time, two European allies, including non-nuclear Germany, were given responsibility for preparing a policy study on the use of nuclear weapons'.[76] As far as British officials were concerned, 'it [is] a useful innovation which will tie the Germans even more closely into the work of the NPG and will ensure that they do not feel their views are being ignored'.[77] Work on the draft guidelines proceeded quickly and, in May 1969, following discussions within the NPG, the British delegation to NATO was able to report that 'we are within measurable distance of reaching an agreement on Guidance ... we should pursue this aim rigorously'.[78]

As evidence of the good relationship between the British and German officials involved, Burrows sent a follow-up despatch in which he reported the remarks of the German permanent representative:

> the draft before you is the first example of the results of joint work between two NPG members. You may therefore be interested to know ... this progress worked ... extremely well. From the relatively short time needed ... it follows that the British and the German delegations were very much in accord from the outset.[79]

This accord, inspired by Healey and his German counterpart, Gerhard Schröder, led to agreement within the NPG in November 1969: firstly, on *Provisional Political Guidelines for the Tactical Use of Nuclear Weapons*; and secondly, as an extension of the Athens guidelines, on improved consultative procedures to address host nation concerns about the release of nuclear weapons. The guidelines did not resolve the question of the timing of the use of nuclear weapons, nor did they settle the complex issue of follow-on measures.[80] Instead, as the Anglo-German report that led to the *Guidelines* emphasised, 'the use of nuclear weapons that would be needed [in the event of Soviet aggression] ... to restore NATO's deterrent would depend upon what had been the aim of Soviet aggression and the Soviet's appreciation of NATO's likely response'.[81] As to consultation, it was agreed that 'special weight ... would be given to those countries most directly involved, including the country from or on whose territory nuclear weapons would be fired, the country providing the delivery vehicle and the country providing the nuclear warhead'.[82] In both

Britain and Germany there was satisfaction about the outcome of the work within NATO on defining how and in what circumstances tactical nuclear weapons might be used. As a report in *The Times* on the 1970 defence estimates put it:

> Political guidelines for the initial tactical use of nuclear weapons ... have been agreed and procedures for consultation ... have been refined. Both these achievements are the result of thorough and detailed work by NATO as a whole; but in framing the guidelines the United Kingdom and Germany played the leading part. We believe that NATO strategy ... offers the best available security for the Alliance.[83]

As for the Germans, in a report on the political situation in Britain during 1969, the German Embassy in London observed:

> Healey and his German counterpart had achieved close co-operation. Both sides see in NATO the only instrument for European defence, in which the British are doing more than we are [i.e. Germany] for a closer partnership of the Europeans within the Alliance in order to offset the effects if the Americans chose to withdraw their forces from Europe.[84]

There can be little doubt that the NPG was an effective forum for direct European participation in decision making on nuclear strategy, and the work largely conducted by Britain and Germany on tactical nuclear weapons bears out this assertion. In a review of the NPG since the 1960s, one informed observer asserts that it 'has been a notably successful mechanism – in a real sense a useful confidence trick'.[85] It is also true that the NPG provided an ideal opportunity for British and German co-operation, particularly at the time when Europe had assumed a greater importance in Britain's defence priorities.

NATO nuclear strategy and Anglo-German relations

A constant theme running through the accounts of NATO's efforts to agree an acceptable nuclear strategy in the wake of McNamara's proposals for a more flexible response to conflict in Europe is how British and German interests had converged. Such convergence of interests, particularly evident in their agreement about the primacy of deterrence and resistance to a strategy that envisaged a greater role for conventional forces, was already underway prior to the 1964 British general election and became more evident thereafter, once NATO initiated the detailed work that resulted in the strategy document MC 14/3 and the guidelines for the use of tactical nuclear weapons.

To be sure, one of the prime reasons for Britain's attitude towards NATO during the time of the Labour governments was the perceived importance of Europe to Britain's economic, political and strategic interests. As financial necessity motivated the withdrawal from commitments in the Middle East and Asia, and as Britain adjusted its role in the world, so Europe assumed a higher priority. Healey told a press group when introducing the 1969 defence white paper that 'the defence decisions of the previous three years set the seal on the transformation of Britain from a world power to a European power'.[86] Whilst we have argued elsewhere that throughout the Labour years Britain's policy towards Europe was based on a close relationship with Germany, there is little evidence to suggest that it was this factor alone that motivated British and German attitudes and mutual understanding in formulating nuclear strategy. Clearly, the reorientation of British defence policies, and the British decision in 1967 to apply for membership of the EEC, which required that Britain demonstrate a greater commitment towards Europe than it had in the past, were factors in a greater European gloss to Britain's defence initiatives, but it is relevant to ask whether this would have been any different had Britain not made its turn towards Europe. In strategic terms, Britain did not agree with all the facets of McNamara's concept of flexible response; it did not accept that nuclear decision making should rest exclusively with Washington; financial strictures meant that it was in any event poorly placed to strengthen its conventional forces in the way that had been suggested; and, finally, it was already a European power in the sense that its security depended upon the effective functioning of the NATO Alliance. Nevertheless, by its wholehearted endeavour towards achieving agreement on a revised NATO nuclear strategy, and by the commitment of ministers such as Healey along with his permanent officials, Britain demonstrated that it was a truly European power in military, political and strategic terms. However, Britain's approach was motivated as much by its own interests as it was by an attempt to gain support for its membership of the EEC. Although Britain and Germany approached nuclear strategy from different perspectives, 'the political and economic pressures which shaped British defence policy came to coincide with German perceptions of the requirements for the adequate deterrence of the Soviet threat'.[87] The outcome facilitated the understanding between London and Bonn and was a positive factor in Anglo-German relations.

The success of NATO in implementing the strategy of flexible response, especially at a time of crisis following the French withdrawal from the Alliance's military organisation, can be seen as one of its most noteworthy achievements. Flexible response was a compromise but it was instrumental in bridging the gap in strategic thinking between America and its European allies. In an appropriate commentary on British foreign policy, Joseph Frankel suggests that:

> the politics of interdependence is most conveniently conducted within the framework of international institutions. This is easy to grasp and to formulate in theory but it is extremely difficult to shape in practice. The only organization that gave little rise to difficulties was NATO, as its pattern is so similar to traditional alliances. Here Britain was both a moving spirit and one of the most faithful adherents.[88]

Britain was a key player in achieving the consensus on flexible response. The agreement on NATO nuclear strategy breathed new life into the Alliance and marked an important stage in the development of Anglo-German understanding.

Notes

1 See Part III, paragraph 5 of the *Report of the Committee of Three on Non-Military Cooperation in NATO*, 13 December 1956, NATO on-line library, www.nato.int/archives/committee_of_three/CT.pdf (last accessed May 2007). See also Chapter 4 (p. 108).
2 *Ibid.*, paragraph 6.
3 For detailed coverage of NATO strategy, see for example: Beatrice Heuser, *NATO, France and the FRG: Nuclear Strategies and Forces for Europe, 1949–2000* (1997); Stromseth, *Origins of Flexible Response*; and Trachtenberg, *Constructed Peace*.
4 Stromseth, *Origins of Flexible Response*, p. 5.
5 See Heuser, *NATO*, pp. 31–33.
6 Trachtenberg, *Constructed Peace*, p. 158.
7 *Ibid.*, p. 185.
8 *Ibid.*, p. 175.
9 Heuser, *NATO*, p. 35.
10 Trachtenberg, *Constructed Peace*, p. 188.
11 Heuser, *NATO*, p. 43.
12 Stromseth, *Origins of Flexible Response*, p. 30.
13 'Mr Acheson's Concept of Conventional Operations', 27 April 1961, COS (61) 138, DEFE 5/113, PRO.
14 Heuser, *NATO*, p. 45.
15 See address by Secretary of Defense McNamara at the ministerial meeting of the North Atlantic Council, Athens, 5 May 1962, *FRUS* (1961–63), VIII, pp. 275–281.
16 For discussion of nuclear weapons and the 1961 Berlin crisis, see Lawrence Freedman, *The Evolution of Nuclear Strategy* (Basingstoke, 2003), p. 282.
17 See address by Secretary of Defense McNamara at the ministerial meeting of the North Atlantic Council, Athens, 5 May 1962, *FRUS* (1961–1963), VIII, p. 280.
18 Robert McNamara, 'The Western Debate: The American Conclusions', *Survival*, 4, 5 (September–October 1962), p. 196. (McNamara's speech at Ann Arbor on 16 June 1962.)

19 The guidelines are set out in Bluth, *Britain, Germany*, p. 108. It should be noted, however, that the guidelines did not constitute a formal change to NATO's strategic concept detailed in MC 14/2. See Heuser, *NATO*, p. 47.

20 Bluth, *Britain, Germany*, p. 109.

21 Haftendorn, *NATO*, p. 33.

22 *Hansard*, House of Commons, 564 (13 February 1957), col. 1293. See *Hansard*, House of Commons, 537 (2 March 1955), col. 2175, for Attlee's comments.

23 Pierre, *Nuclear Politics*, p. 95.

24 Heuser, *NATO*, p. 91.

25 *Statement on the Defence Estimates 1966*, Cmnd 2901, p. 5.

26 Ahonen, 'Franz-Josef Strauss', p. 29.

27 See memo of a conversation between Rusk, Schröder, and Strauss, 22 November 1961, Secretary of State files 1961–62, National Security Archive, Washington. Quoted in Ahonen, 'Franz-Josef Strauss', p. 29.

28 Michael Quinlan, 'NATO Nuclear Philosophy', talk at Royal College of Defence Studies, 26 October 1982. Emphasis added.

29 Public opinion was consistently in favour of Britain possessing nuclear weapons. For example, in a poll conducted in December 1957, 52% of those asked believed that Britain should concentrate on building up strength in atomic weapons whilst 8% favoured a build-up of conventional weapons. In October 1961, of those asked whether Britain should give up its H-bombs even if other countries did not, only 21% agreed whilst 61% disagreed. See Gallup, *Gallup International: Volume 1*, p. 435 and p. 604.

30 P. M. S. Blackett, 'Thoughts on British Defence Policy', *New Statesman*, 5 December 1959, p. 790.

31 See 'Mr Acheson's Concept of Conventional Operations', 27 April 1961, COS (61) 138, DEFE 5/113, PRO.

32 *Ibid.*

33 *Ibid.*

34 McNamara, 'Western Debate', p. 195.

35 'NATO Strategy and Nuclear Weapons – Military Implications of the Mottershead Report', 3 May 1961, COS (61) 146, DEFE 5/113, PRO. On the Mottershead report, see also Heuser, *NATO*, pp. 48–51.

36 'Military Implications of the Mottershead Report', 3 May 1961, COS (61) 146, DEFE 5/113, PRO.

37 Stromseth, *Origins of Flexible Response*, p. 123.

38 Schwarz, 'Adenauer und die Kernwaffen', p. 568.

39 Strauss's speech in the Bundestag, 10 May 1957, quoted in Ahonen, 'Franz-Josef Strauss', p. 28.

40 Although not strictly relevant to the discussion about the background to flexible response, it should not be forgotten that Strauss contemplated other policy options for Germany besides the acquisition of nuclear weapons for the Bundeswehr. They were: a NATO nuclear force free from an US veto; and the European option that led to the FIG (France, Italy and Germany) agreement for joint nuclear weapons production. See Heuser, *NATO*, pp. 148–151.

41 Stromseth, *Origins of Flexible Response*, p. 130.

42 Kelleher, *Germany*, p. 160.

43 The so-called *Der Spiegel* affair occurred in October 1962 when Strauss ordered the arrest of the editor (Rudolf Augstein) and some of his staff on the charge that an article referring to NATO plans and the use of nuclear weapons exposed state secrets and threatened German security. See 'Rudolf Augstein: Obituary', *The Times*, 8 November 2002, p. 45; and Bluth, *Britain, Germany*, p. 118 fn. 31.

44 Interview with British Defence Secretary, Peter Thorneycroft, *The Times*, 10 September 1963.
45 Craig, *British General Election Manifestos*, pp. 43–60.
46 See Healey, 'British Defence Policy', pp. 15–22.
47 Gordon Walker, 'Labor Party's Defense and Foreign Policy', pp. 392–395.
48 Healey, *Time of My Life*, p. 252.
49 Wilson, *The Labour Government*, p. 40. Wilson's explanation has been disputed. According to one account, 'Internal Whitehall estimates put the total cost of cancellation at about £40 million out of a projected total cost of over £300 million. Early cancellation would thus have produced substantial savings. Costs were not, therefore, the reason.' See Ponting, *Breach of Promise*, p. 88.
50 Wilson, *The Labour Government*, p. 40.
51 Pierre, *Nuclear Politics*, p. 275.
52 Healey, 'British Defence Policy', p. 15. The success of Healey's commitment might be judged by comment made in 1969 by one of his Cabinet colleagues to the effect that 'we've managed to lop our commitments without cutting the defence budget or defence status nearly enough'. See Crossman, *Diaries: Volume 3*, diary entry for 3 March 1969, p. 393.
53 Healey, *Time of My Life*, p. 245.
54 Denis Healey, 'NATO, Britain and Soviet Military Policy', *Orbis*, 13, 1 (spring 1969), p. 51.
55 Healey, *Time of My Life*, p. 310
56 Healey, 'NATO', p. 51.
57 Healey, *Time of My Life*, p. 310.
58 'Tripartite Talks – NATO Strategy', paper by R. J. Andrew, Head of Defence Secretariat 12, 25 October 1966, DS12/206/9, DEFE 24/32, PRO.
59 Heuser, *NATO*, p. 131.
60 Von Hassel, 'Détente Through Firmness', p. 190.
61 Kai-Uwe von Hassel, 'Organizing Western Defense: The Search for Consensus', *Foreign Affairs*, 43, 2 (January 1965), pp. 210–211.
62 Detailed accounts of French attitudes towards NATO nuclear strategy can be found, for example, in Stromseth, *Origins of Flexible Response*, pp. 96–120; and Heuser, *NATO*, pp. 93–123.
63 André Beaufre, 'The Sharing of Nuclear Responsibilities: A Problem in Need of Solution', *International Affairs*, 41, 3 (July 1965), p. 416. At the time of writing this article General Beaufre was Director of the Institut Français d'Études Stratégie.
64 *Statement on the Defence Estimates 1967*, Cmnd 3203, p. 3.
65 *Hansard*, House of Commons, 742 (27 February 1967), cols 111–112.
66 Healey, *Time of My Life*, p. 309.
67 Denis Healey, 'On European Defence', *Survival*, 11, 4 (April 1969), pp. 110–115. (Healey's address to the 6th International Wehrkunde meeting on 1 February 1969.)
68 Telegram number 465, British delegation NATO to Foreign Office, 4 December 1967, WN 30/3/3 (Pt F), FCO 41/229, PRO.
69 Aufzeichnung des Ministerialdirektors Ruete, 25 September 1967, *AAPD* (1967), II, p. 1302.
70 *Ibid.*, p.1300.
71 Telegram Rusk to State Department, 14 December 1967, *FRUS* (1964–68), XIII, p. 651.
72 Telegram number 62, Sir Bernard Burrows to Foreign Office, 15 December 1967, WN 30/3/3 (Pt F), FCO 41/229, PRO.

73 Memo by Sir Bernard Burrows, 1 January 1968, WN 30/3/3 (Pt F), FCO 41/229, PRO.
74 Stromseth, *Origins of Flexible Response*, p. 176.
75 Healey, *Time of My Life*, p. 311.
76 Haftendorn, *NATO*, p. 172.
77 Letter to Lord Hood, 16 October 1968, WDN 24/1/1, FCO 41/428, PRO.
78 Telegram number 283, British delegation NATO to Foreign and Commonwealth Office, 14 May 1969, WDN 24/7, FCO 41/433, PRO.
79 Telegram number 141519Z, UK NATO to FCO, 14 May 1969, WDN 24/7, FCO 41/433, PRO.
80 Further consideration of these points by the NPG delayed the agreement on the final version of the provisional guidance.
81 Anglo-German paper on tentative political guidelines, March 1969, WDN 24/7, FCO 41/433, PRO.
82 Stromseth, *Origins of Flexible Response*, p. 185.
83 'Britain's Strength Highest in Western Europe', *The Times*, 20 February 1970, p. 4.
84 Politischen Jahresbericht 1969, German Embassy to Foreign Office in Bonn, 2 February 1970, B 31/ Band 369, PAAA Berlin. The reference to Britain's efforts to inspire greater co-operation among European members of the Alliance almost certainly derives from efforts to set up the Eurogroup of NATO members. See Healey, *Time of My Life*, p. 316.
85 Michael Quinlan, 'NATO Nuclear Philosophy'. The NPG still meets when necessary at ambassador level and twice a year at the level of ministers of defence.
86 Quoted in Pierre, *Nuclear Politics*, p. 299.
87 Bluth, *Britain, Germany*, p. 140.
88 Joseph Frankel, 'The Intellectual Framework of British Foreign Policy', in Karl Kaiser and Roger Morgan (eds), *Britain and West Germany: Changing Societies and the Future of Foreign Policy* (1971), p. 101.

Chapter 6

Britain, Germany and
the Non-Proliferation Treaty

Throughout the period from 1964 to 1970, an international agreement on measures that would prevent the proliferation of nuclear weapons, not least into the hands of Germany, was a prime foreign policy objective of the Labour governments. In this context, it is significant that the day before Harold Wilson entered Downing Street as the newly elected Prime Minister, the Chinese had detonated their first nuclear weapon, a development that would be bound to cause regional anxieties, and might provoke nuclear proliferation, and not just in Asia.[1] Initially, the Labour government pursued its non-proliferation policies through two channels: firstly, through the device of the ANF, an initiative that we have discussed in Chapter 2; and secondly, through the appointment of a Minister of Disarmament with the task of 'helping forward the United Nations disarmament programme'.[2] However, as we will emphasise here, the ANF non-proliferation initiative was little more than window dressing. The main focus of Britain's non-proliferation policy was, from the start, to support the United States in the construction of a treaty that would have universal application.

The road towards an international agreement on an NPT proved a difficult one to travel. The main obstacles seemed to have been overcome in July 1968, when, after prolonged negotiation, the treaty was opened for signature in Washington, London and Moscow; but the prime objective of securing the signature of Germany to the treaty was finally achieved only in November 1969, after the election of Willy Brandt as German Chancellor and 'after Bonn had obtained further clarification on its rights and obligations'.[3] The saga of the NPT involved a *mélange* of complex and interlocking problems: for example, the question of nuclear sharing within NATO and how the interests of the non-nuclear powers, and not just those in NATO, would be guaranteed by the nuclear powers; the question of nuclear safeguards, with its overtones of commercial espionage, and how the inspection regimes operated by the International Atomic Energy Agency (IAEA) could be made compatible with procedures employed by the European Atomic Energy Community (EURATOM); and how Britain could protect its interests, but in such a way that would support its efforts to demonstrate a commitment to Europe. Whilst the NPT was essentially a treaty designed by the United States and the Soviet Union, it will be argued here that Britain's effort to ensure that agreement was reached between the principals was strongly influenced by its position as a potential member of the European Communities. Central to this strategy was a good relationship with Germany.

The Labour Party and nuclear weapons

The Labour Party and the issues surrounding nuclear disarmament were no strangers. There are many accounts of how, before October 1964, the Labour Party was badly divided over Britain's nuclear strategy and nuclear disarmament.[4] Whilst it is beyond the scope of this chapter to dwell at any length upon these divisions and disputes, a brief flavour of the nature of the debates that took place within the Labour movement during the years before 1964 is relevant to an understanding of how Wilson's government approached the question of proliferation of nuclear weapons. Within the Party, Denis Healey was a key figure during the 1950s and early 1960s in influencing thinking about defence and the moral, political and military implications of nuclear weapons.[5] From his detailed account of his involvement in the internal debates within the Labour Party, it is apparent that Healey was primarily interested in nuclear strategy but, although he was concerned about the spread of nuclear weapons, he was never a supporter of unilateral nuclear disarmament. He was associated with the movement that led to the formation of CND, and with scientists such as Patrick Blackett, who had been an appointee to the Advisory Committee on Atomic Energy, formed in 1945 by Clement Attlee's government, and who was known for his expertise on nuclear weapon development.[6] Blackett had become one of a group that included Healey, formed to prompt Western governments to act on what was perceived to be the danger of the imminent prospect of nuclear stalemate. In a forthright article published in 1959 in the *New Statesman*, Blackett advocated that Britain renounce its own nuclear forces and argued, in the context of the 1957 defence white paper, that the effect of current British defence policy would be to encourage the spread of nuclear weapons (see Chapter 5).[7]

Although CND established itself as a powerful force within the Labour Party, its support came mainly from the trades union movement and left-wing MPs and its influence can easily be exaggerated.[8] In his memoirs, Healey was scathingly critical of CND and blamed it for many of the divisions within the Party during the late 1950s and 1960s over nuclear weapons and about NATO membership, and for 'the Punch and Judy show between Multilateralism and Unilateralism into which the argument ... degenerated'.[9] The decision in 1960 of the Labour Party conference to ignore the advice of the leadership and reject any defence policy based on the threat of the use of strategic nuclear weapons was symptomatic of the struggle between the unilateralists and multilateralists. It must also be seen in the context of the contest for control of the Labour movement. Significant in this respect was the role of Wilson, who tried to span the gap between the two factions in a bid to unite the Party within the context of the leadership contest arising from the sudden death of Hugh Gaitskell. In fact Wilson was unsuccessful in his manoeuvrings to establish a unifying policy on nuclear weapons and in any event there was never any suggestion that he was serious about unilateralism, an assertion that would certainly be borne out by subsequent events.[10]

The Labour Party therefore approached the 1964 election with a defence policy that represented a compromise after the defeat suffered by the leadership at the 1960 Party conference. The policy agreed at the 1961 conference reversed the unilateralist stance of the previous year but called for an end to the attempt by Britain 'to remain an independent nuclear power since this neither strengthened the alliance nor was it a sensible use of resources'.[11] By the time of the election, Labour was still split between the unilateralists and multilaterists, although Wilson, by now Party leader, had papered over the cracks within the movement by a commitment to renegotiate the Nassau agreement in order to prevent the waste of 'the country's resources on endless duplication of strategic nuclear weapons'.[12] We have already discussed in Chapter 2 the controversy over the real objective behind Labour's election pledge to renegotiate Nassau, but it is worth emphasising that sensitivity about nuclear weapons continued to run deep within the Party. Whilst the leadership was able to use the ANF as the pretext under which Britain maintained a nuclear deterrent, albeit one that was no longer supposed to be independent, the Party was united on the question of control of nuclear weapons and, in particular, on the need to secure a treaty on non-proliferation. In this context, senior Labour personalities across the political spectrum had consistently warned of the dangers of nuclear proliferation. In 1958, for example, Richard Crossman had questioned 'how can we possibly prevent the Germans, the French and every other nation in the alliance saying "what the British demand for themselves, we demand for ourselves"',[13] whilst in 1961 Healey suggested that 'if the possession of atomic weapons spreads inside the Western Alliance, it is certain to spread outside it ... action to stop the spread of nuclear weapons is not only vital, but extremely urgent'.[14] Labour's election manifesto was therefore specific on the point: Britain's possession of nuclear weapons carried with it the grave dangers of encouraging proliferation to countries not possessing them, including Germany, and a Wilson government would consequently 'do everything possible to halt this dangerous trend'.[15]

Britain, Germany and nuclear non-proliferation

Once in office, the immediate appointment of Lord Chalfont, a minister dedicated to handling the disarmament portfolio, was evidence of the Labour government's wish to demonstrate its credibility as an administration committed to halting the spread of nuclear weapons. However, as one Cabinet member later commented, Chalfont's appointment 'always seemed a dangerous gimmick and it backfired. Chalfont was never politically at home in a Labour Government and once out of office he came out of his true colours as a Conservative.'[16] This criticism of Chalfont's appointment on the grounds of gimmickry had some force, in that the new minister's responsibilities had already been covered within the portfolio allocated to the Minister of State under the previous Conservative administration. Nevertheless, in his memoirs Wilson justified the appointment on the grounds that 'the minister should be under the general control of the Foreign Secretary – but with strong and expert connections with the Defence Department ... [and] Alun Gwynne Jones [defence correspondent of *The Times*] raised to the Lords as Lord Chalfont ... brought his considerable expertise and ability to the task'.[17] Leaving aside Chalfont's suitability for the appointment, Wilson needed to hold the Labour Party together at a time when he was under electoral pressure with a small parliamentary majority and in circumstances where he had given specific pledges about Britain's deterrent and nuclear proliferation. A ministerial appointment dedicated to the latter aspect of foreign policy was a strong signal that the Prime Minister was determined to honour the Party's election pledges.

The government's proposals for an ANF as its preferred alternative to the MLF was the way the government chose to honour its election pledge on the other aspect of foreign policy, namely Britain's deterrent. We have already argued in Chapter 2 that the ANF proposals were designed to block the MLF. Whilst there were political advantages in including non-proliferation provisions in the ANF proposals, ministers must have appreciated that they would do little to prevent the spread of nuclear weapons. It is true that the

ANF, if implemented in full, would have provided another obstacle to Germany in any serious search for a hardware solution to the NATO nuclear sharing problem, but it is difficult to see how, in any event, Germany would have gained access to nuclear weapons, even without the ANF. The Soviet Union was even more stridently opposed to any suggestion of Germany gaining control of nuclear weapons than Britain, France and the United States. As Andrei Gromyko, Soviet Foreign Minister, made clear in response to an assurance by Patrick Gordon Walker, Britain's Foreign Secretary, that the ANF proposals would maintain the existing safeguards on the use of nuclear weapons, 'the plans for a NATO nuclear force [were] very dangerous.... The Soviet Government could not agree to or tolerate any form of German access to nuclear weapons.'[18]

Nevertheless, Susanna Schrafstetter and Stephen Twigge argue that, despite the interpretation in standard accounts:

> the British ANF proposal was not solely a cynical manoeuvre to block the MLF but represented a serious diplomatic initiative by the new Labour government which, if successful, would have achieved a number of pressing policy objectives ... [including] a non-proliferation treaty (NPT) to fix West Germany's status as a non-nuclear power.[19]

To be sure, the ANF proposals did contain provisions for an agreement for the non-proliferation of nuclear weapons by the nuclear powers and for the non-acquisition of such weapons by the non-nuclear powers but, although these were the fundamental requirements of a non-proliferation regime, they would apply only to those NATO members prepared to join the ANF and were not intended to embrace the comprehensive safeguards of a full NPT.[20] It is hardly surprising that official documents make no specific mention of any hidden agenda behind Britain's policy objectives in advancing the ANF proposals. In fact, the impression can be formed from the way that officials approached the task of formulating the detail that the ANF concept was meant to be taken seriously, and clearly this was the objective if the proposals were to form the credible centrepiece of Wilson's discussions with President Lyndon Johnson in December 1964. Indeed, as Saki Dockrill argues, 'Militarily, the ANF was more credible than the MLF, and the Chiefs of Staff, who were opposed to the latter, accepted the ANF project in principle.'[21]

In terms of non-proliferation, the ANF could never be the complete alternative to an international agreement, and in that sense it is hard to accept the claim advanced by Schrafstetter and Twigge that 'in curtailing West German nuclear ambitions, the proposal addressed Soviet concerns on the control of nuclear forces within NATO and advanced the prospects for a global nonproliferation treaty based on the ANF framework'.[22] Whilst the ANF was designed to block the MLF, Russian spokespersons repeatedly made clear that the Soviet Union would oppose any suggestion of German access to nuclear weapons, and that would include Germany's participation in a NATO MLF. As an article in *The Times* put it:

> Nothing apparently will convince them [the Soviets] they are wrong – at least as regards the Multilateral Force, and Atlantic Force proposed by the British. Very possibly therefore they hope to sign a non-proliferation agreement that will effectively rule out any such scheme.[23]

Whatever the Russian motives were for this stance, the fact remained that any nuclear force would prevent progress towards a global NPT, which was a foreign policy objective of both superpowers, as well as of Britain. Thus, the purpose of the ANF as a vehicle for a global NPT must be questionable to say the least, particularly so when, within months of producing its alternative to the MLF, Britain announced proposals for a full treaty and its intention to table a draft NPT at a meeting of the Eighteen Nation Disarmament Conference (ENDC) in Geneva.[24] Why complicate the NATO force negotiations if the intention was to press forward with disarmament proposals that would render the ANF provisions unnecessary in this regard? The answer to this question may well rest in the comment made by Burke Trend, the Cabinet Secretary, to Wilson at the end of November 1964, just two days before the Chequers meeting held to discuss the ANF proposals. As Trend put it, 'in the context of the proposal for the Atlantic Nuclear Force … if we try … to obtain too many concessions … we may only arouse suspicions about our motives for proposing it'.[25]

Whilst Germany supported the principle of the non-proliferation of nuclear weapons, its approach to disarmament was coloured by a deep suspicion of the Soviet Union. Moreover, the attitude of the German government in 1964 remained one of determination to link progress on an easing of tension in Europe, of which controlled disarmament would be but one feature, with progress to end the division of Germany. In an article in *Foreign Affairs*, Kai-Uwe von Hassel, the German Defence Minister, summarised German thinking as follows:

> All efforts to improve the political structure of the world and to strengthen security in Europe must proceed from the recognition of the fact that the division of Germany is one of the most serious causes of tension and insecurity. If a détente in the relations between East and West is to be more than a mere pause in the cold war, that particular cause of tension must be removed.[26]

At the same time, however, Germany's association with the MLF project had been held by the Soviet Union to be evidence of its nuclear aspirations. We have already discussed how the Germans regarded participation in a MLF as an opportunity for involvement in NATO nuclear decision making and as recognition of its growing status within the Alliance. The Soviet opposition to the MLF was regarded not only as an attempt to exercise a veto in NATO nuclear strategy but also as a direct threat to the aspirations of Germany. In this context, Bonn could point to its declaration of renunciation in 1954, under which Germany undertook not to produce nuclear weapons on its territory, and its submission to international controls, as evidence of a clear commitment to non-proliferation. Although the Germans claimed that they had no wish to possess nuclear weapons, this act of renunciation gained credibility only when, in 1967, the newly elected Chancellor, Kurt Georg Kiesinger, publicly pledged that his country sought 'neither national control nor national ownership of atomic weapons'.[27]

There were other factors that informed Germany's approach towards agreement on the non-proliferation of nuclear weapons. In the text of an interview, published in December 1964 in the *Suddeutsche Zeitung*, Franz Josef Strauss, Germany's former Defence Minister and still an influential voice within the governing CDU, set out his views on the MLF project. As Strauss put it, 'the Federal Republic wanted maximum security – no national nuclear capability – a German voice on nuclear questions … and above all a "European clause" so that the project would contribute to the unity of Continental Europe'. Strauss's views were coloured by the recent announcement of Britain's ANF proposals, the negative attitude of France to any form of MLF and to American leadership of NATO, and by what he described as the effect of socialist theory on British foreign policy, which rested upon 'the classic socialist view of disengagement of the power blocs as the key for ending the East/West conflict'. As Strauss saw it, the Labour Party's ideas on an approach to *détente* with Moscow, of which an East–West agreement on the prevention of a further spread of nuclear weapons was one element, were incompatible with 'plans for bringing Continental Europe together into a political union with an open door for Britain'.[28]

The Bonn government's position was set out in its official reaction to Britain's ANF proposals.[29] The problem of the non-proliferation of nuclear weapons had to be considered in a world-wide context, and therefore any declaration by the German government required under any ANF charter would be unlikely to improve the international situation. Moreover, it was for consideration that the Alliance could take advantage of the Soviet Union's obvious intention to place constraints

on the involvement of Germany in nuclear defence and use this to
forge a positive policy on the German question. Finally, bearing in
mind the declarations that were already in existence, it would be
necessary to ensure that the conditions were not created that would
prevent the possibility of a European nuclear force at some stage in
the future. Thus, given the importance attached to the European
option by Germany and Britain's growing interest in membership of
the European Communities, and the part that Bonn might play in
that endeavour, the actions of both countries during the negotiations
to agree an NPT would be certain to affect their relations.

Towards an NPT

It would be wrong to assume, however, that Britain's commitment
to non-proliferation developed in 1964 with the election of a Labour
government. Non-proliferation of nuclear weapons had been a factor
in international relations for some years before Wilson appointed
Lord Chalfont as the minister with responsibility for disarmament.
As J. P. G. Freeman puts it, 'as the Labour Party took office, the issues
before the ENDC were no different in kind or in particular after
October 1964 from what they had been before. There was no dramatic
change of route or destination because Labour had moved into the
driving seat.'[30] Whilst the appointment of Chalfont gave a new look
to the Labour ministerial team, marked a fresh determination in
Britain's efforts to halt the proliferation of nuclear weapons and was
consistent with the view within the Party that a Labour government
should be proactive in the field of disarmament, the fact remains that
before Labour took office, Britain and the United States were already
co-operating on the text of a draft NPT.[31] Even Wilson's eye-catching
proposal for a non-proliferation commitment as part of the ANF package was not as original as it may have seemed. In August 1964, for
example, officials in the American Arms Control and Disarmament
Agency (ACDA) were already speculating whether the United States
'should support and encourage appropriate efforts which may develop
among participants in the MLF to register a commitment on non-
acquisition in connection with adherence to the MLF'.[32] It was this
speculation about a non-acquisition clause that went to the heart of
the non-proliferation debate. As an ACDA non-dissemination paper
conceded, 'for more than a year, the United States has been trying
to persuade the USSR to accept a non-proliferation agreement. The
MLF has been cited by the Soviets as the only obstacle to reaching
such an agreement.'[33]

Nevertheless, these bilateral contacts underlined the fact that it
would be the United States and the Soviet Union that would be the

main players if any agreement covering global non-proliferation were to be reached. Moreover, if other countries were to be persuaded away from the acquisition of nuclear weapons, then it would clearly be necessary for the two superpowers to lessen tension by agreements covering the wider arms control field. However, both bilateral and ENDC negotiations involving the superpowers had become somewhat stuck over the principle of a NATO nuclear force, and particularly with the participation in it of Germany. The new urgency that entered into the equation during October 1964 was generated not by the appearance of a Labour government in London but by the first Chinese atomic test. As William Foster, Director of the ACDA, commented in an article published in July 1965 in *Foreign Affairs*, 'it is clear that the Chinese tests have had an unsettling effect throughout much of Asia and particularly in India'; he went on to say that whilst the Chinese might decide they had much to gain by accepting the concept of peaceful coexistence, and so might be brought into arms control and disarmament agreements, 'the alternative … [was] bleak indeed'.[34]

America's response to the Chinese nuclear test was to commission a presidential task force under Roswell Gilpatric, a former Deputy Secretary of Defense, with the remit to study means to prevent the spread of nuclear weapons.[35] In his report submitted two months later, Gilpatric recommended that the United States 'should intensify … efforts for a non-proliferation agreement and seek the early conclusion of the widest and most effective possible international treaty on non-dissemination and non-acquisition of nuclear weapons' and that the government 'should continue urgent exploration of possible alternatives to an MLF/ANF which would permanently inhibit Germany from acquiring nuclear weapons but would nevertheless assure that, in the absence of German reunification, West Germany would remain as a real ally on the Western side'.[36] Gilpatric went on to recommend that, in order to ensure peaceful atomic energy programmes did not contribute to the proliferation of nuclear weapons capabilities, the United States should insist on adequate safeguards for all peaceful programmes and that, to this end, efforts should be made to ensure the acceptability, one to the other, of EURATOM and IAEA safeguards.[37] The message from Gilpatric was clear. If the President wanted to reach an early agreement with the Soviet Union on an NPT, and according to Gilpatric this was very much in the interests of the United States, Germany would have to settle for something other than the MLF/ANF as a means of participation in nuclear decision making and could not expect progress on reunification as a precondition. The United States, and its Alliance partners, for their part, should be prepared to accept internationally recognised safeguard controls over their civilian nuclear facilities.

Whilst there was little in the Gilpatric report that might worry Britain, especially as any non-proliferation agreement, even on the terms suggested, would meet one of the key objectives of the Labour government and serve to confirm Britain's status not only as a nuclear power but also as an important player in negotiations that might lead to a treaty, for Bonn the outlook was somewhat bleak. Not only would Germany come under American and Soviet pressure to commit to proliferation restrictions, and be denied what it perceived as a stronger role in shaping Alliance nuclear policy, unlike Britain it would be permanently confined to the lesser status of a non-nuclear power. In the words of one historian, 'Bonn ... regarded the Non-Proliferation Treaty as a sword of Damocles that hung over NATO's non-nuclear members and that would deny them nuclear co-determination before it had even been established'.[38]

The initial actions of the British government in respect of nonproliferation seemed indicative of an intent to inject movement in the ENDC process, but to do so without any particular regard for the likely impact upon bilateral relations with Germany. In a meeting with his German opposite number, Gordon Walker advised Gerhard Schröder of the commitment of the new British government to conclude an agreement on the non-proliferation and non-acquisition of nuclear weapons.[39] Although Gordon Walker expressed understanding for Schröder's reaction, that any agreement on non-proliferation was bound up with the German problem and the European security system, and that Germany would not make any declaration in this regard until the MLF project had become a reality, other British reactions were less reassuring. In a proposed statement on the official German position on the non-dissemination of nuclear weapons, whilst expressing support for measures to prevent further dissemination of nuclear weapons into the national control of individual states, the Germans pointed out that their renunciation of the production of nuclear weapons, made in 1954, had not received a favourable response from the Soviet Union nor had it brought benefits in terms of a non-dissemination agreement and the MLF project, with accession to the former coming after completion of the latter. In an internal Foreign Office discussion paper, British officials referred to this linkage as misguided and concluded that 'the German statement repeats the familiar arguments against a non-dissemination agreement *now* and is a further indication that we must expect great difficulty with them if a non-dissemination or non-acquisition agreement becomes possible'.[40]

Moreover, German opinion was not reassured by an impression created by Healey, during a television interview, to the effect 'that the British were more interested in pushing non-dissemination ... than preserving the basic principles of the MLF'.[41] This impression was seemingly confirmed when Lord Chalfont bluntly told a senior German official in July 1965, in response to a question about the effect of a NPT on the MLF/ANF project, that 'he considered non-proliferation to be more urgent than a multilateral nuclear force'.[42] Nevertheless, Germany was too important to Britain for policies to be pursued that would diminish the understanding between the two governments. As Michael Stewart, the new Foreign Secretary, suggested to his Cabinet colleagues:

> the position of the German Government is crucial towards an East/ West détente ... there is a clear case ... for taking the Germans into our confidence on arms control and disarmament matters ... we need to dispel the long-standing fears that we are trying to make a settlement with the Russians at the expense of the German claim to national unity. We must try to persuade them that progress towards reunification can only be made in an atmosphere of East/ West détente, and that the right arms control measures can contribute towards the creation of such an atmosphere, even if they are not linked with provisions for immediate progress towards German reunification.[43]

Germany's apparent attachment to a hardware solution to NATO's nuclear sharing problem remained a complication during 1965 and 1966, as the Americans, with British support, struggled to find a formula on non-proliferation that would satisfy the Soviet Union but at the same time meet German concerns. In reality, the Washington summit between Johnson and Wilson in December 1964 marked the end of the MLF project but, until there was an acceptable alternative that would give the non-nuclear partners in the Alliance some say in nuclear decision making, both the United States and Britain had to pay lip service to support for a force based on either the MLF or the ANF, or a combination of the two. This dilemma came into sharp focus during 1965, when, following negotiations between the two nuclear powers, Britain announced its intention to present its draft version of an NPT to the ENDC.[44] In the normal course of events, this proposal would have been welcomed in Washington but, after examination of the British draft, the Americans expressed reservations and suggested that it would be premature to launch the document without further discussion by the North Atlantic Council. In particular, the Americans were concerned that by rejecting their proposed amendments, the British were ignoring the possibility of sharp disagreements within the Alliance. In circumstances where 'the UK draft treaty could not receive support from at least the United States and the Federal Republic of Germany ... even more unfortunate developments would be bound to occur'.[45]

This warning was sufficient to persuade the British side to confine discussion of the draft within the North Atlantic Council and not to table it immediately at the ENDC.[46] In the opinion of the Americans, the draft would complicate the evolution of the MLF/ANF under the so-called 'European clause' by requiring maintenance of the veto by one of the existing nuclear powers. What was clear, however, was that if the British wanted to progress with a draft NPT tabled to the ENDC at Geneva, this would have to be in conjunction with the American amendments.[47] As a report in *The Times* confirmed, 'it was no good putting forward British plans in international negotiations however sincerely they believed in them and however well they had prepared them if they could not rely on the support of the Western alliance'.[48] Moreover, the Germans were less than impressed with the British draft. In a discussion with Dean Rusk, the American Secretary of State, the German Ambassador in Washington, Heinrich Knappstein, expressed concern that, according to the *Washington Post*, reports from London indicated that 'the US may decide ... that a non-proliferation treaty [was] more vital than going ahead with the projected Atlantic nuclear fleet' and that 'the United States would support the English draft'. The Ambassador repeated Germany's objection to the concept of an NPT before its essential preconditions had been met and added that for the Germans 'the British draft non-proliferation proposals were not acceptable'.[49]

Why, then, did Britain pursue the question of a draft treaty in the face of American and German opposition, and at a time when, following Wilson's visit to Bonn in March 1965, efforts were being made by ministers to maintain the impetus behind improving relations with Germany? Britain's motives were almost certainly political. Although there was no doubting Labour's sincerity about the need to contain the proliferation of nuclear weapons and, in that context, its determination to breathe life into the Geneva negotiations, the government's approach was largely motivated by domestic considerations. The force of this argument rests on the fact that the Labour government was committed to a renegotiation of the Nassau agreement and to ending the myth of Britain's independent deterrent.[50] Thus, having taken the decision to retain Britain's deterrent and to cut only one of the five Polaris submarines, albeit on the basis of committing the Polaris fleet and most of the V-bomber force to NATO, and having agreed with Johnson in Washington to prevent the further proliferation of national nuclear capabilities and to open the way for future initiatives towards disarmament (commitments that were repeated in Parliament a few days after a briefing to the Cabinet), Wilson badly needed an arms control initiative to divert attention from his change of position on the deterrent and to satisfy his left-wing critics that he was serious about non-proliferation.[51] On the question of the deterrent, as Andrew Pierre rightly suggests:

> those who hold power, whether politicians in office or civil servants, also [view] the nuclear force as an important bargaining asset and instrument of diplomacy. This was particularly true ... as it became increasingly uncertain that the dispersion of nuclear capabilities could be arrested. The Wilson government was acutely aware of this: to cancel the Polaris submarine programme unilaterally, that is without a suitable quid pro quo, would not have improved Britain's bargaining power in the arena of international politics.[52]

As to the question of non-proliferation, and the attitude of Wilson's critics within the parliamentary Labour Party, an official in the British Embassy in Washington observed in March 1965 that:

> disarmament was not the live political issue in the US that it was in the UK. The government has now practically given up the idea of abandoning the UK nuclear deterrent and it had squeaked through the defence debate with a five-vote margin; as a result the government must be increasingly mindful of the Labour left wing. Something has to be said from time to time to keep the Labour left-wing in check.[53]

The main problem area dividing British and American viewpoints remained the incompatibility of the proposed NPT with NATO nuclear sharing arrangements based on some form of MLF. Whilst the Americans maintained in public that NATO nuclear sharing arrangements were not disseminatory, Britain was now convinced that the ANF should be officially dropped in favour of a NPT. British ministers had always argued that the ANF as such would not place nuclear weapons directly under the control of the Germans, and therefore was non-disseminatory, but the principal concern that had arisen during the NPT negotiations with America was that 'the UK was not prepared to subscribe to a treaty which might have allowed a future European entity to inherit an MLF and apply majority decision-making'.[54] The difficulty for both governments was that, whilst remaining publicly committed to a MLF in order to appease German sensitivities, if somewhat half-heartedly, any public shift of policy to abandon this form of nuclear sharing would not only add to the crisis within NATO, perpetrated by the French, but would also hand the Soviet Union an opportunity to exploit Allied differences. As Foster put it to Chalfont, 'non-proliferation continued to have top priority ... but we also continued to support our basic commitment on MLF/ANF. Until after the German election, at least, any discussion in this field [would be] very difficult for the present German government.'[55] The American draft NPT that was presented to the ENDC in August 1965 was designed to satisfy the various points raised by Alliance members, particularly those argued with such force by the British, and was accepted as the basis for further consideration, although some areas of difficulty were identified. Firstly, non-nuclear powers asked that any treaty should embrace a commitment by the nuclear powers to take positive nuclear disarmament measures; and secondly, the Soviet Union asserted that, notwithstanding the text of the treaty that would prohibit the transfer of nuclear weapons to any non-nuclear state, NATO nuclear sharing arrangements, including the NPG, would amount to nuclear weapons proliferation.

By the end of 1965, the Soviet Union had formulated its own version of a draft treaty. During a flurry of bilateral meetings between ministers and officials of the United States and Soviet Union, it was evident that, although both countries were anxious to conclude an agreement on non-proliferation, the Soviets still regarded as unacceptable any suggestion of nuclear sharing that, either directly or indirectly, 'would bring nuclear weapons within the reach of West Germany'.[56] The position taken up by the Soviets caused considerable consternation in Washington, particularly as it implied that all NATO nuclear sharing arrangements would be prohibited, including those that provided for the transfer of weapons delivery systems (principally from the United States), as well as the planning committee. In part this was a reflection both of a lack of clarity about the Soviets' real intentions and of the uncertainty in Soviet minds about American plans for nuclear sharing with its NATO partners. McGeorge Bundy, National Security Adviser, told the President that the situation presented an opportunity for a breakthrough. He seized upon the point about Soviet uncertainty and commented:

> it is clear that the Germans no longer really expect that we will support an MLF, and I believe that if you and Erhard could reach a firm agreement in December, that no new weapon systems is necessary, the way might be open toward a non-proliferation treaty and toward a new collective arrangement for command control and consultation in NATO.[57]

Although Johnson did not follow the course of action recommended by Bundy, the official record of Chancellor Ludwig's Erhard's meeting with the American President leaves little doubt that any lingering attachment that the Germans might have had to a MLF, or in other words a new weapons system, received no encouragement.[58]

In many ways, 1966 proved to be a defining period for the NPT negotiations. During that year, new governments were elected in Britain and Germany. In Britain, Wilson received a new mandate with an overall majority of ninety-seven seats, and thus became less restricted by the internal party constraints under which he had operated during the first eighteen months of government. Later in the year, the Erhard government was removed from power and was replaced by the Grand Coalition headed by Kurt Kiesinger, the CDU Chancellor, with the SPD leader, Willy Brandt, as his deputy and Foreign Minister. Within NATO, the Alliance was shaken by, but quickly surmounted, the challenge of the French withdrawal from the military organisation; France would not, in any event, be bound by any non-proliferation agreement. The year also brought the formal abandonment by NATO of the so-called hardware nuclear sharing option and the institutionalisation of the NPG, to provide Alliance members, but particularly Germany, with a say in nuclear decision making.

The advent of the new German government brought fresh thinking about East–West relations, a new confidence about the role of Germany in the world and, most importantly, a willingness to make concessions in order to foster *détente* with the Soviet Union. In the context of non-proliferation, Kiesinger emphasised in his first major policy statement that 'the German Government advocates a consistent and effective peace policy, apt to remove political tension and to check the arms race. We shall co-operate in any proposal for arms control, for a reduction of armaments and disarmament.'[59] Whilst Britain remained committed to securing an early agreement on an NPT, one event in 1966 above all others brought a new dimension to British calculations and strongly influenced the way ministers and officials conducted negotiations to protect British interests: Wilson's decision to determine whether the conditions were right for Britain to reapply for membership of the EEC, and subsequently to pursue membership, became inextricably linked with the conclusion of an agreement on the non-proliferation of nuclear weapons.

Finding the right language

In a series of bilateral meetings during 1966, and in the early months of 1967, the United States and the Soviet Union edged closer to agreement on non-proliferation. The most important areas where difficulty was being experienced in the negotiations were on the proposed Article 1, dealing with the controls that would prevent proliferation, and on the proposed Article 3, covering international safeguards to prevent the diversion of nuclear energy from peaceful uses to nuclear weapons. Agreement on Article 1 in particular was delayed by the problem of finding the right language that would satisfy two demands: on the one hand, the American position, to leave NATO with options for nuclear sharing and to enable the succession of any federal European state to the nuclear status of one of its former components; and, on the other hand, the Soviets' insistence that not only was any hardware solution to NATO nuclear sharing unacceptable, particularly as it applied to Germany, but also that they would not openly endorse a federal Europe either with or without nuclear weapons.

By May 1966, the Americans were expressing frustration with the Soviet approach, although, as Foster confirmed to Rusk, 'in private conversations ... Soviet and Bloc representatives have now shown awareness of the need to accommodate any non-proliferation treaty to the reality of continued consultations and ... to the reality of present nuclear arrangements in NATO'. Nevertheless, there was no way of knowing whether the Soviets were seeking serious nego-tiations. As Foster suggested, 'as a result of increased tensions over Vietnam, this may not be the case'.[60] In Britain, there was a degree of sympathy for the Soviet position on hardware and on the European option, but Britain, aware of its status as a nuclear power and key Alliance partner, and mindful of its growing interest in membership of the European Communities, adopted a policy of exerting influence over its more powerful ally by quiet diplomacy. A note handed to State Department officials by Sir Patrick Dean, British Ambassador in Washington, confirmed that Britain had always considered that 'a non-proliferation treaty should exclude the possibility of nuclear dissemination to associations of States ... the only such option strictly compatible with non-proliferation would be a fully federated European State, which would acquire by succession the nuclear status of either France of the United Kingdom or both'.[61] The way ahead suggested by the British was a fresh attempt at consultations within NATO before an approach to the German government.

Probing by the Americans revealed little in the way of change in the German attitude. In a meeting in Bonn in July 1966, Foster dis-covered splits in the ruling CDU faction on the hardware solution to the problem of nuclear sharing in NATO and disagreements between the main political parties. A report for the State Department on the meeting suggested that 'Chancellor Erhard [had] little independent conviction on the issue' whilst Schröder and von Hassel 'held firm in asserting that the Germans still seek a hardware solution'.[62] As to the other political parties, the SPD had rejected the MLF concept whilst the Freie Demokratische Partei (Free Democratic Party; FDP) had never given it support. By September, and prior to a meeting between Johnson and Erhard, the Americans prepared to compromise with the Soviet Union over the wording of an NPT. Not only was the administra-tion concerned about the danger of further nuclear proliferation but 'as an NPT became increasingly important as a way of mitigating the Vietnam war's negative repercussions and of getting the Soviets to exercise a moderating effect on North Vietnam, many members of the administration were increasingly willing to accept these strains [i.e. within NATO]'.[63] In a memorandum to the President, Foster asserted that it would be possible to negotiate an agreement with the Soviet Union which would not interfere with the NPG type of consultative arrangement, and which would not need changes to existing bilateral NATO nuclear arrangements. This would require, however, that the United States formally to announce that it would not transfer ownership of nuclear warheads to Germany or to any association of states. Foster recommended that Johnson should tell Erhard about the latest American thinking, prior to his visit to Washington later in the month, so that, once an understanding was reached with the Germans, 'the United States would be ready to undertake serious negotiations with the Soviet Union'.[64]

In fact, serious negotiations between the principals got under way just days before Johnson's meeting with Erhard in Washington. At a meeting between Rusk and Gromyko and their officials, it became apparent that it had become largely a question of finding 'the right language to express [their] agreement without involving extraneous matters'.[65] However, Gromyko did confirm that the question of consultation within the NPG (involving the Germans) in connection with an NPT was no longer an issue and indicated that existing arrangements were also unlikely to cause difficulty. His major concern remained nuclear weapons in the national hands of non-nuclear states, either directly or because of their participation in an alliance, and if an answer could be found to this problem then there could be real progress. It is evident from the tough stance that Johnson took during his meeting with the German Chancellor that the decision to compromise with the Soviet Union had effectively already been taken, and that all the subterfuge over a hardware solution to NATO nuclear sharing was at an end. After further bilateral contacts, agreement was quickly reached between the United States and the Soviet Union that a treaty would include an Article 1 that would not disturb existing NATO nuclear arrangements and would not bar succession by a federated European state to the nuclear status of one of its former components.[66]

The discussion between the superpowers up to the point that agreement on an NPT became possible had centred on the controversial Article 1 and, in particular, what would constitute proliferation. Once this hurdle had been cleared, attention focused on the wording of Article 3 and the subsidiary question of international safeguards. Reporting on his discussions with the Soviet representatives, Foster indicated that there appeared to be a good opportunity to take a positive step towards preventing the clandestine diversion of peaceful nuclear programmes to military purposes, but only if the members of EURATOM were willing to accept the application of IAEA safeguards, perhaps after a transitional period. As with Article 1, the wording of the proposed safeguards article would be crucial. The Soviet position was that a binding safeguards article would be acceptable if: it specified IAEA safeguards and did not call for inspections of nuclear weapons parties; and inspection of Germany was not entrusted to a group of NATO allies (in other words, under EURATOM auspices). If Eastern European states were to be inspected by the IAEA, there had to be equality of treatment for NATO allies, and especially Germany, with their subjection to the same international inspection regime. Given what was perceived as the rigidity of the Soviet position, Foster suggested that, as the United States attached major importance to inclusion of a meaningful safeguards article, America's allies should be told that, upon the entry into force of the treaty, 'EURATOM and IAEA would exchange technical information on their respective safeguards procedures with a view to facilitating the application of IAEA safeguards in the EURATOM countries'.[67] This would be an unwelcome development for members of the European Communities and, potentially so, for applicant members like Britain.

At the beginning of 1967, during a meeting with Burke Trend and Sir Solly Zuckerman, Chief Scientific Adviser, held to discuss tactics before Zuckerman's planned visit to Germany, Wilson directed that British policy towards the NPT should be to support 'the proposed control provisions [i.e. the American proposal for mandatory international safeguards in Article 3 of the Treaty] ... but that we should lie low and leave the running to be made by the United States'.[68] Not only did this recognise that Britain's role would be confined to that of influencing the superpowers as far as this was possible but also, given the growing importance of Europe in Britain's political calculations and the need for German support if Britain's application to the EEC was to succeed, Wilson's directive was based on the knowledge that Germany in particular would have serious concerns about the proposed provisions of Article 3, in terms of mandatory international safeguards and their impact upon EURATOM. Therefore, great care would have to be taken if Britain was to retain German goodwill in support of an approach to Europe and if, at the same time, Germany was to be persuaded towards the key British objective of securing an NPT, and one with verifiable safeguards.[69] As the Foreign Office had already realised:

> several EURATOM countries, notably Germany and Italy, as well as the EURATOM Commission, [had] expressed the view that acceptance of this article would mean a serious blow to EURATOM. They [believed] that the replacement of EURATOM safeguards by the

IAEA system would mean that their civil nuclear facilities would be exposed to the risk of commercial espionage from inspectors who were nationals of the nuclear states.[70]

Nevertheless, in a note to the Prime Minister's office with advice on what Britain might do to secure an NPT, and at the same time to demonstrate concern as a European power that the interests of EURATOM should be safeguarded, the Foreign Office emphasised that 'the last thing we wish to do is to destroy EURATOM ... which ... we shall wish to join' and claimed that 'there is no reason why the creation of a worldwide IAEA should permanently disrupt EURATOM ... it is already becoming clear that an agreement between the two organisations will be necessary'.[71] This last point was taken up during an exchange of views between Zuckerman and Dr Swidbert Schnippenkötter, the German government's representative for disarmament and arms control on the ENDC, when the latter argued that 'on the political level the EURATOM problem was not insoluble ... the technical problem was to reconcile EURATOM and IAEA safeguards system ... to involve the least amount of control and minimum amount of intrusion'. He went on to stress that 'reconciliation and cooperation between IAEA and EURATOM was necessary anyway, quite apart from the non-proliferation treaty'.[72]

In response to the argument raised by the Germans that an important political question was the degree of discrimination between nuclear and non-nuclear states, and the suggestion that the Western nuclear states which would sign the treaty should be prepared immediately to submit to the same degree of safeguards in their civil programmes as they were asking the non-nuclear states to accept, Zuckerman was able to confirm that Britain had already publicly announced a willingness to go along with a world-wide international system, provided that Britain was not the only nuclear state expected to do so. But, more pointedly for Britain's European aspirations, he emphasised that 'the impetus towards the Common Market was gaining force. The longer we delayed the more the Americans would gain in the technological field. We had a lot to contribute to EURATOM.'[73]

The clear impressions the British took from these exchanges were that the Germans were slowly shifting ground, having recognised that safeguards would have to be organised on an international basis and that, as an issue, they had become a political rather than a technical problem. In this context, it was also clear to the British that, in attempting to obtain the best possible bargain, the Germans would, as Michael Palliser, his Private Secretary, told Wilson, 'probably sign the Treaty' and that Britain had a clear interest in being seen to be 'as helpful to them ... as we can'.[74] By spring 1967, under German pressure and with British coaxing, the Americans agreed to offer the application of IAEA safeguards to their civilian nuclear activities. As American Vice President Hubert Humphrey told George Brown, by now British Foreign Secretary, 'on the question of reconciling IAEA safeguards with the EURATOM system, the US government were prepared to consider various ways of making the Treaty acceptable to both the European countries and the Russians'.[75] Later in the year, when advising Palliser on progress in the NPT negotiations, as well as stressing the policy objective of maintaining a balance between Britain's position as a European power, in particular the present position as an applicant for membership of the European Communities, and Britain's strong desire to see the successful completion of an NPT, Derek Day, Brown's Assistant Private Secretary, felt able to report that 'we have been reasonably successful in persuading the Europeans that we are aware of their anxieties. The Germans for example have twice congratulated us on the way in which we were showing ourselves to be good Europeans over this.'[76] Wilson's directive that Britain should adopt a low profile and act as a potential EEC member appeared to be paying dividends.[77]

Nevertheless, difficulties still remained to be settled before the path to an agreed NPT could be successfully negotiated. Even after tortuous exchanges between Washington and Moscow, as well as between the United States and its European partners, and the agreement reached on the contentious issue of international safeguards, Bonn continued to express reservations about other aspects of the proposed NPT. The breakthrough with the safeguards Article came in September 1967, when Adrian Fisher, acting Director of the ACDA, advised Rusk that 'the Soviets [had] proposed a compromise Article III dealing with safeguards' and that they were 'prepared to permit arrangements under which IAEA could make use of the Euratom system in performing the task of verification under such an Article'.[78] It was essentially a question of agreeing language that did not explicitly recognise EURATOM.[79] Not only did this make the connection between IAEA and EURATOM that had been suggested by Zuckerman and Schnippenkötter during their talks in Bonn in March 1967, but as part of this compromise the Soviets also announced their readiness to concede a period during which agreements with the IAEA could be negotiated.[80] In a briefing given to the OPD, Fred Mulley, Minister of State at the Foreign Office, described Britain's role in the negotiations leading to the ENDC agreement and said that the proposed treaty:

> embodied a number of revised provisions on which we had taken the initiative. Owing to our wish not to prejudice our position *vis a vis* the members of the European Atomic Energy Community ... we had not publicised the role we had played, but in fact we had done much to bridge opposing views.[81]

By this statement, Mulley attributed success to the policy of caution adopted during the NPT negotiations, and made clear yet again the considerable importance attached by Britain to extending its influence among the member states of the EEC. In this context, good relations with Germany remained central to British calculations since, as Wilson had told Chancellor Kiesinger referring to his tour of European capitals in early 1967, 'the outcome of our talks [on EEC entry] would depend to a great extent on the exercise of German influence in Paris'.[82]

Finalising the NPT

Finalising the NPT with the Germans, particularly with Kiesinger, was not proving easy, especially as the exchanges between respective ministers revealed differences between the German Chancellor and his Foreign Minister. During a visit to London in April 1967, Brandt set out German concerns about aspects of the NPT in relation to safeguards, interpretations relating to existing arrangements within NATO about nuclear sharing, and in particular the existence of the NPG, and the need to ensure that the treaty would not rule out the creation of a European state which would acquire nuclear status by succession from its former nuclear constituents. Brown was supportive on most of the issues raised by Brandt, although he had to make it clear that, although Britain was certain the treaty would not bar the creation of a European state, it would rule out the creation of a nuclear association of national states. Whilst Britain would not countenance any suggestion of Germany acquiring nuclear weapons through some form of association, and this was clearly understood by Brandt, it was evident that, at the end of their exchanges, both ministers were 'happy to note the extent to which they found their views in harmony'.[83] A less harmonious exchange took place in February 1969, after Britain had already signed and ratified the NPT, notwithstanding the invasion of Czechoslovakia. During talks in Bonn, Kiesinger suggested to Wilson that, despite assurances from the Soviet government, there was still the danger that the Soviets might claim 'to retain the right of intervention under the "enemy states" articles in the United Nations Charter'. He declined to accept Wilson's argument that this was irrelevant to the question of the NPT, 'since the essential security assurance for the Federal Government ... was provided by NATO and the US commitment to NATO'.[84]

Disagreements in the German camp became even more evident during a meeting between Wilson and Brandt later in the day, when the German Foreign Minister confirmed that, although Kiesinger wanted to sign the treaty, he was under pressure not to do so by Strauss and his supporters. Brandt emphasised that 'he did not attach much importance to the "enemy states" argument and expressed full agreement with Wilson's assertion that the real key to German security ... was in NATO'.[85] That there were political differences between Kiesinger and Brandt are also revealed by the tone and nature of a 'note for the record' that Kiesinger felt it necessary to write in December 1968, in which he set out clear guidelines for Brandt on the future conduct of German foreign policy and the co-operation he expected from his Foreign Minister.[86] This was symptomatic of what *The Guardian* had referred to as 'an immoderate public debate [within Germany ... and] the battle within the grand coalition ... [which would] provide the coalition with its sternest test yet of its durability'.[87] Germany finally signed the NPT in November 1969, immediately after Brandt became Chancellor in a new SDP/ FDP coalition government, and almost simultaneously with new initiatives by Bonn towards Eastern Europe.[88] In conjunction with Bonn's signature, Britain issued what *The Times* described as:

> an assurance to Germany that the so-called 'enemy states' clauses of the United Nation's charter [did] not give Russia any unilateral right to use force against Germany ... and that Germany as a full and equal partner in the North Atlantic Treaty would be defended by her NATO allies ... in case of an attack on her.[89]

Anglo-German relations and the NPT

It is not the place here to analyse the impact of the NPT in the fields of arms control and disarmament. Whilst the treaty was largely a reaction by the superpowers to the Chinese nuclear test in 1964, and to the proliferation of nuclear weapons that this might provoke, the fact that a treaty emerged at all might be viewed as a triumph after such long and tortuous negotiations – particularly as it established a link, albeit tenuous, between non-proliferation and disarmament. Both Britain and Germany gained from the treaty. By skilful and patient diplomacy, Britain influenced the negotiations in a way that enabled it both to demonstrate a commitment to Europe and to foster relations with Germany. For Bonn, the treaty maintained the discrimination between the nuclear 'haves' and 'have nots' and, in that sense, perpetuated Germany's status as a second-class power. By 1969, however, with an SPD Chancellor in Bonn anxious to take the first steps towards a new and more active *Ostpolitik*, signature of the NPT was tangible evidence of Germany's clear commitment to *détente* in Europe, and began a series of events that changed the whole nature of East–West relations.

It would be hard to show beyond doubt that the successful outcome of the NPT negotiations resulted in better relations between London and Bonn. Nevertheless, the approach adopted by both governments, and particularly by Britain, was symptomatic of the efforts being made by them both, against a backdrop of the political and economic integration of Europe, to heal the divisions of the past. As Willy Brandt so succinctly put it, when addressing a British audience in 1967, 'I must say that in the relations between Germany and Great Britain, the community of important interests is so great that by comparison individual, passing differences play a subordinate part'.[90]

Notes

1 See the account in Wilson, *The Labour Government*, p. 2.
2 *Ibid.*, p. 11.
3 Haftendorn, *Security and Detente*, p. 192.
4 See for example Healey, *Time of My Life*, pp. 234–248; J. P. G. Freeman, *Britain's Nuclear Arms Control Policy in the Context of Anglo-American Relations, 1957–68* (1986), Chapters 2 and 3; and Pierre, *Nuclear Politics*, Chapter 8.
5 Healey, *Time of My Life*, p. 234.
6 See Freeman, *Britain's Nuclear Arms Control Policy*, p. 29; Pierre, *Nuclear Politics*, p. 72; and Healey, *Time of My Life*, p. 237. Blackett became an adviser at the Ministry of Technology during the time of first Wilson government.
7 Blackett, 'Thoughts on British Defence Policy'.
8 See Freeman, *Britain's Nuclear Arms Control Policy*, Chapter 3.
9 Healey, *Time of My Life*, p. 242.
10 See Pierre, *Nuclear Politics*, p. 205; and Frank Parkin, *Middle Class Radicalism: The Social Base of the British Campaign for Nuclear Disarmament* (Manchester, 1968), p. 136.
11 *Report of the Sixtieth Annual Conference of the Labour Party* (1961), p. 8, quoted in Pierre, *Nuclear Politics*, p. 207.
12 Craig, *British General Election Manifestos*, p. 59.
13 *Hansard*, House of Commons, 583 (27 February 1958), col. 634.
14 *Hansard*, House of Commons, 635 (27 February 1961), col. 1220.
15 Craig, *British General Election Manifestos*, p. 59.
16 Castle, *Diaries*, diary entry for 21 October 1966, p. 177, fn. 1.
17 Wilson, *The Labour Government*, p. 11.
18 Record of conversation between Patrick Gordon Walker and Andrei Gromyko, 9 December 1964, PREM 13/104, PRO.
19 Schrafstetter and Twigge, 'Trick or Truth?', p. 162.
20 Details of the non-proliferation aspects of the ANF are contained in Misc 17/3rd and 4th Meetings, 22 November 1964, CAB 130/213, PRO.
21 Dockrill, 'Britain's Power and Influence', p. 232. In making this assertion, Dockrill draws from Cabinet minutes, 26 November 1964, CC (64) 11th Meeting, CAB 128/39 Pt 1, PRO.
22 Schrafstetter and Twigge, 'Trick or Truth?', p. 163.
23 'Russian Reasons', *The Times*, 19 July 1965, p. 11.
24 'NATO Support for Britain', *The Times*, 26 July 1965. According to the article, 'there was a general feeling of sympathy among NATO members for Britain's draft treaty ... [Lord Chalfont] will also outline the proposals at the ... conference which resumes in Geneva'.

25 'Possible Reductions in British Defence Expenditure', Trend to Wilson, 19 November 1964, Misc 16, CAB 130/213, PRO.
26 Von Hassel, 'Détente Through Firmness', p. 184.
27 Kurt Kiesinger, 'German Foreign Policy', *Survival*, 9, 2 (February 1967), p. 47.
28 Text of an interview with Strauss on 16 December 1964, published in the *Suddeutsche Zeitung*. Quoted in Bonn telegram 1287, Sir Frank Roberts to Foreign Office, 17 December 1964, PREM 13/219, PRO.
29 Stellungnahme der Bundesregierung, 18 January 1965, *AAPD* (1965), I, pp. 100–101.
30 Freeman, *Britain's Nuclear Arms Control Policy*, p. 197.
31 Memorandum from the Acting Deputy Under-Secretary of State for Political Affairs to Secretary of State, 25 August 1964, *FRUS* (1964–68), XI, p. 115.
32 Draft position paper, 14 August 1964, *FRUS* (1964–68), XI, p. 99.
33 *Ibid.*, p. 103.
34 William C. Foster, 'New Directions in Arms Control and Disarmament', *Foreign Affairs*, 43, 4 (July 1965), pp. 587–601.
35 National Security memorandum, 25 November 1964, *FRUS* (1964–68), XI, p. 126.
36 Report by the Committee on Nuclear Proliferation, 21 January 1965, *FRUS* (1964–68), XI, pp. 173–182.
37 *Ibid.*, p.181.
38 Haftendorn, *NATO*, p. 115.
39 Gespräch – Schröder mit Gordon Walker, 15 November 1964, *AAPD* (1964), II, p. 1307.
40 'Non-Dissemination of Nuclear Weapons', statement made by the German delegation to NATO Political Committee, 28 January 1965, IAD 1052/27, FO 371/181386, PRO.
41 Telegram from George McGhee to State Department, 9 January 1965, *FRUS* (1964–68), XIII, p. 171. According to McGhee, Schröder cited Healey's BBC interview of 20 December 1964 as evidence of Britain's position. Sir Frank Roberts, British Ambassador in Bonn, who advised the Foreign Office that 'the view still prevalent in political and press circles is that the United States has lost interest and that both ANF and MLF are virtually dead', shared McGhee's opinions. See Roberts' memo, 12 January 1965, PREM 13/329, PRO.
42 'Oberst Hopf … an das Auswärtige Amt', 21 July 1965, *AAPD* (1965), II, p. 1233.
43 Memorandum by the Secretary of State for Foreign Affairs, 'Policy Towards Germany', 5 August 1965, C(65) 119, CAB 129/122 (Pt 2), PRO.
44 Memorandum of conversation, 22 March 1965, *FRUS* (1964–68), XI, p. 195.
45 Telegram from Dean Rusk to Michael Stewart, 22 July 1965, *FRUS* (1964–68), XI, p. 230.
46 Message from Stewart to Rusk, 23 July 1965, *FRUS* (1964–68), XI, p. 232, fn. 3.
47 See memorandum of conversation, Lord Chalfont and William Foster, 1 August 1965, *FRUS* (1964–68), XI, pp. 233–235; and editorial note, *FRUS* (1964–68), XI, pp. 235–237. These documents confirm the 'arrangement' agreed by Chalfont and Foster, which the former asked 'to be kept in the closest confidence', to table the British draft together with American and Canadian amendments. The editorial note confirms that 'the text of a draft non-proliferation treaty [was] negotiated by the American, British, Canadian and Italian representatives of [ENDC] … [and that] the United States would sponsor this text and table it at the [ENDC] meeting on 17 August'.

48 Report on a House of Lords debate, *The Times*, 29 July 1965, p. 5.
49 Botschafter Knappstein an das Auswärtige Amt, 9 July 1965, *AAPD* (1965), II, pp. 1155–1159.
50 Craig, *British General Election Manifestos*, p. 59.
51 For details of Wilson's report on his Washington visit, see conclusions of a Cabinet meeting, 11 December 1964, CC 14(64), CAB 128/39, PRO.
52 Pierre, *Nuclear Politics*, p. 303.
53 Quoted in Freeman, *Britain's Nuclear Arms Control Policy*, p. 210. Chalfont made the point about the linkage between statements in Parliament and action on non-proliferation in conversation with Foster on 1 August 1965. In this conversation, Chalfont admitted that the British government may have read too much into Foster's article in *Foreign Affairs* (see note 34) and, as a consequence, 'have promised too much too soon in the House of Commons and with the press'. See *FRUS* (1964–68), XI, p. 234. Chalfont's reference to commitments made in the House of Commons were almost certainly based on Wilson's comments, following his meeting with President Johnson in December 1964, to the effect that the British had agreed 'to cooperate in finding the arrangements which best meet the legitimate interests of all members of the Alliance while maintaining existing safeguards on the use of nuclear weapons and preventing their further proliferation'. See *Hansard*, House of Commons, 704 (16 December 1964), col. 433.
54 Freeman, *Britain's Nuclear Arms Control Policy*, p. 220.
55 Memorandum of conversation, 1 August 1965, *FRUS* (1964–68), XI, p. 234.
56 Memorandum from Acting Director ACDA, Jacob Beam, to Rusk, 4 November 1965, *FRUS* (1964–68), XI, p. 263.
57 Memorandum from Bundy to Johnson, 25 November 1965, *FRUS* (1964–68), XI, p. 264.
58 See memorandum of conversation, 20 December 1965, *FRUS* (1964–68), XI, p. 289.
59 Kiesinger, 'German Foreign Policy', p. 47.
60 Memorandum from Foster to Rusk, 25 May 1966, *FRUS* (1964–68), XI, p. 324.
61 Aide-mémoire from the British Embassy to Department of State, 1 June 1966, *FRUS* (1964–68), XI, p. 326.
62 Telegram from the Embassy in Germany to Department of State, 2 July 1966, *FRUS* (1964–68), XIII, p. 428.
63 Haftendorn, *NATO*, p. 150.
64 Memorandum from Foster to Johnson, 15 September 1966, *FRUS* (1964–68), XI, p. 362.
65 Memorandum of conversation, 24 September 1966, *FRUS* (1964–68), XI, p. 382.
66 Memorandum from John McNaughton, Assistant Secretary of Defense, to McNamara, 15 October 1966, *FRUS* (1964–68), XI, p. 395. Gromyko also made it clear that any text which met three basic conditions would be acceptable: no transfer of warheads to non-nuclear states; no transfer of nuclear warheads to alliances made up of nuclear and non-nuclear states; and no transfer of warheads to alliances of non-nuclear states. See *FRUS* (1964–68), XI, p. 397.
67 Memorandum from Foster to Rusk, 11 January 1967, *FRUS* (1964–68), XI, p. 420.
68 Note for the record, meeting held by the Prime Minister with Sir Burke Trend and Sir Solly Zuckerman on 1 March 1967, PREM 13/1888, PRO.

69 Wilson also directed Zuckerman to make the point to the Germans that
    Britain would help to transform EURATOM and that this was 'a powerful
    argument in favour of German support for British entry'. *Ibid.*
70 Safeguards in a Non-Proliferation Treaty, PREM 13/1888, PRO.
71 *Ibid.*
72 Record of a meeting between Zuckerman and Schnippenkötter, 3 March
    1967, PREM 13/1888, PRO.
73 Record of a meeting between Zuckerman and Dr Stoltenberg, 4 March 1967,
    PREM 13/1888, PRO.
74 Note from Palliser to Wilson, 14 March 1967, PREM 13/1888, PRO.
75 Record of a conversation between the Foreign Secretary and the Vice President
    of the United States, PREM 13/1888, PRO. During a visit by Willy Brandt to
    London on 13 April 1967, Brown confirmed that 'the United Kingdom was
    seriously considering the possibility of offering, with the Americans, to accept
    safeguards on our civil military activities', PREM 13/1888, PRO. Both offers
    were announced at the North Atlantic Council meeting on 20 April 1967
    – see telegram number 148, British delegation to Foreign Office, 20 April
    1967, PREM 13/1888, PRO.
76 Day to Palliser, 2 October 1967, PREM 13/2441, PRO.
77 See Note for the record, meeting held by the Prime Minister with Sir Burke
    Trend and Sir Solly Zuckerman on 1 March 1967, PREM 13/1888, PRO.
78 Memorandum from Fisher to Rusk, 5 September 1967, *FRUS* (1964–68), XI,
    p. 508.
79 Day to Palliser, 4 December 1967, PREM 13/2441, PRO.
80 On 18 January 1968 the United States and the Soviet Union presented to
    the ENDC identical draft treaties, which included an international safeguard
    clause. Limited space prevents the inclusion here of the details of the Treaty
    on the Non-Proliferation of Nuclear Weapons but the full text can be found
    in Freeman, *Britain's Nuclear Arms Control Policy*, pp. 260–265.
81 Minutes of OPD Committee meeting, 30 January 1968, OPD (68) 2nd Mtg,
    CAB 148/35, PRO.
82 Wilson, *The Labour Government*, p. 367.
83 Record of a meeting between the Foreign Secretary and the Federal German
    Foreign Minister, 13 April 1967, PREM 13/1888, PRO.
84 Record of meeting between the Prime Minister and Federal German Chan-
    cellor, 13 February 1969, PREM 13/3002, PRO. Notwithstanding Wilson's
    assurances 'the three Western [nuclear] powers issued a statement [in
    September 1968] asserting that Articles 53 and 107 of the UN Charter, the
    enemy states clauses, gave no state the right to intervene unilaterally in the
    Federal Republic of Germany'. See Haftendorn, *NATO*, p. 153.
85 Record of conversation between the Prime Minister and German Foreign
    Minister, 12 February 1969, PREM 13/3002, PRO. The ACDA had already
    reported differences between Kiesinger and Brandt in May 1967. See tele-
    gram number 1530, British Embassy Washington to Foreign Office, 8 May
    1967, PREM 13/1888, PRO.
86 Aufzeichnung des Bundeskanzlers Kiesinger, 2 December 1968, *AAPD* (1968),
    II, pp. 1546–1548.
87 'Bonn Sets Out Its Demands Over Nuclear Treaty', *The Guardian*, 21 February
    1967, p. 7.
88 Botschafter Allardt an das Auswärtige Amt, 28 November 1969, *AAPD*
    (1969), II, pp. 1353–1355. At the signing ceremony the German Ambassador
    deposited a statement on behalf of Germany which included the following
    interpretations: signature of the NPT did not imply recognition of the East

Germany; security guarantees under United Nations Resolution 255 would apply without restriction to West Germany; the NPT would not hamper the unification of European states; parties to the NPT would commence without delay negotiations on disarmament, especially with regard to nuclear weapons; and safeguards agreements with the IAEA could be concluded individually and together with other states. See 'Signature and Ratification of Non-Proliferation Treaty', 8 January 1970, DS 5/5, FCO 66/188, PRO.

89 'Germany Renounces Use of Nuclear Weapons', *The Times*, 29 November 1969, p. 1.

90 Address by Willy Brandt, Foreign Affairs Club, London, 12 April 1967, B31/307, PAAA, Berlin.

Chapter 7

Détente, Ostpolitik and Anglo-German relations

A review of international relations in the 1950s and 1960s would show that Germany's policies towards Eastern Europe varied according to both the prevailing state of East–West relations and the make-up of the government in Bonn. For some, the policies pursued by Germany should be considered in the context of 'the phrase *Politik der kleinen Schritte* i.e. being content with small steps in the right direction ... the signposts were there for all to see: sovereignty ... unification ... and European integration'.[1] In practice, however, things were never as simple as this progression implies. Whereas the first step was safely negotiated with the integration of Germany into the Atlantic Alliance, by 1964, with the advent of a Labour government in Britain, there were sharp disagreements between the political parties in Germany, and between it and its principal allies, on the means whereby the second objective, that of unification, might be attained.

For Britain, the way ahead was clear. A settlement in Europe and agreement on a solution to the German problem could come only after an improved *détente* with the Soviet Union and a relaxation of tension in East–West relations. *Ostpolitik*, the policy that was designed by Germany to take the strain out of its relations with its eastern neighbours, and to lead to unification, is normally associated with Willy Brandt but, as one prominent German politician asserted, '*Ostpolitik* ... [was] not the result of a radical break with the past but rather the logical outcome of an evolution that started in the mid-sixties'.[2] During the period 1964–70, *Ostpolitik* passed through three discernible phases: the first, up to 1966, that of adapting to the failure of past policies to achieve unification; the second, from 1966 to 1969, with the arrival of the Grand Coalition, and Brandt as Foreign Minister; and the third, after October 1969, when Brandt was elected Chancellor. Britain could support *Ostpolitik* as long as it had no adverse effect upon the West's interests, particularly those relating to the status of Berlin.

It could also pay lip service to the ultimate objective of *Ostpolitik*, that of reunification, although, as a Conservative Foreign Secretary had suggested, 'we have a treaty commitment to German reunification but little national interest in expediting it'.[3] Within these limitations, Britain could be an advocate for *Ostpolitik* not only because of the prospect of improved East–West relations but also because Britain would need Germany's support for any attempt to join the EEC. As the discussion in this chapter suggests, *Ostpolitik* increasingly became a factor in consolidating a good understanding between Britain and Germany.

Ostpolitik in context

The development of *Ostpolitik* can best be considered in the context of the relationships that existed during the mid-1960s between Germany and its major partners in the Western Alliance, in other words with Britain, France and the United States, and, more crucially, with the Soviet Union. There were sound reasons why Britain was an important ally for Germany. Britain was a nuclear power with substantial military assets stationed on German soil and formed an important part of the protective shield on which German security depended. Britain also acted as a strategic link between Europe and the United States, and could serve to influence American policy in ways that might work to Germany's advantage. Of potential although uncertain value were Britain's contacts with the Soviet Union. These could conceivably prove helpful to German attempts to achieve a settlement in Europe and facilitate an agreement leading to reunification.[4] In an assessment of the prospects for East–West relations made in February 1969, for example, one OPD memorandum noted that whilst Britain acting alone might not achieve much *vis-à-vis* the Soviet Union, 'as an influential member of the [NATO] Alliance, and in due course, of a united Western Europe, we have a very considerable part to play'.[5]

France, on the other hand, was an important partner for quite different reasons. The links that developed between the two countries following the signing of the Franco-German Élysée Treaty in 1963 seemed to guarantee that the days of enmity between them were finally over and, as events subsequently proved, provided the *leitmotif* by which Paris and Bonn were able to assert their leadership of the EEC.[6] Nevertheless, President Charles de Gaulle's disruptive tactics within NATO and his concept of *détente*, based on a Europe from the Atlantic to the Urals in which neither the security blocs nor American predominance in NATO would play any part, and which presumed that he, acting alone, could do more to promote *détente* than NATO, threatened to seriously inhibit relations between Bonn and Washington and, for this reason, proved unwelcome to the Germans.[7]

In the words of Adam Watson, Britain's nominated rapporteur for the Harmel exercise (see Chapter 4): 'for obvious reasons the Germans would not quarrel with France although they had no enthusiasm for de Gaulle's vision of a Franco-Soviet accord'.[8]

By the early 1960s, persuaded by the dangers of confrontation that had arisen over access rights to West Berlin and during the Cuban missile crisis, the United States and the Soviet Union moved to place their relationship on a more conciliatory basis. For both countries, the avoidance of a nuclear confrontation was of supreme importance. The United States was the ultimate guarantor of Germany's security through its status as a superpower, its nuclear and conventional commitment to its defence and that of West Berlin, and a deterrent to any potential Soviet aggression in Western Europe. However, as Sir Frank Roberts, the British Ambassador in Bonn, made clear:

> as soon as United States policy started to veer ... in the direction of a relaxation of tension with the Soviet Union ... [the Germans] regarded the shift ... with considerable uneasiness and convinced themselves without difficulty that it must either imply acceptance of the *status quo* in Europe, and therefore in Germany, or that it must lead to unilateral concessions from the Western side, which would inevitably be at the expense of the Federal Republic.[9]

In this context, it was the Soviet Union that held the key to any potential *détente*, defined by the British Foreign Office as the 'search for secure and peaceful East–West relations leading in time to a European security settlement'.[10] However, as one senior British official made clear, 'we must bear in mind that ... the Soviet objective all the time is to hamper the future development of unity in Western Europe, to divide NATO and get the Americans out of Europe'.[11] Moscow's purpose was to ensure that the countries of Eastern Europe remained oriented economically as well as politically towards the Soviet Union and, significantly for *Ostpolitik*, that Germany remained divided. As Michael Stewart, the Foreign Secretary, suggested in May 1969, in a detailed assessment of the longer-term prospects for East–West relations:

> Deep-rooted Soviet fear and distrust of Germany will continue to play a central part in Soviet policy ... the Soviet Union uses 'German Revanchism' as a convenient stick to beat the West ... deep-rooted and persistent fears ... could make the Soviet leaders as suspicious of good relations between the two Germanys as they are now determined to prevent reunification.[12]

Ostpolitik 1964–66

It was against this backdrop that, in March 1965, Prime Minister Harold Wilson visited Germany for talks with Chancellor Ludwig

Erhard. As suggested in Chapter 2, some of the discomfort felt in Bonn about the attitude of Britain's new government towards NATO nuclear sharing, and principally concerning Wilson's comments about German access to nuclear weapons, had been dispelled by the time of the visit, although uncertainty still existed about the broad thrust of future British foreign policy. In terms of Anglo-German relations, press reports in Germany suggested that a crucial test for the ruling CDU of British intentions would be 'whether the new Cabinet maintain[ed] the previous line on West Berlin and the German question'.[13] The reasons for this conditional attitude were not difficult to identify. In 1961, for example, a Labour Party conference had passed a resolution which proposed an agreement on access to West Berlin which would include recognition of the existing 'eastern frontiers of Germany ... [and] a measure of *de facto* recognition of the regime in East Germany'.[14] Moreover, some two years later, after becoming leader of the Labour Party, Wilson expressed similar sentiments.[15] Coming on top of Harold Macmillan's apparent willingness in the late 1950s to contemplate recognition of East Germany and trade away Western rights in Berlin, the sensitivity of the Germans over British intentions at the time of Wilson's visit becomes more understandable.[16] Nevertheless, as the Germans would themselves come to appreciate, 'Wilson was a pragmatist ... he had adapted to the realities of foreign and defence politics ... for example, his earlier inclination to recognise East Germany had been replaced by an official non-recognition policy'.[17]

By early 1965, there were indications that, under the pressure of a growing *rapprochement* between the superpowers, and with an awareness that the country was no nearer its goal of reunification, the German government was prepared to consider alternative policies towards Eastern Europe. In a stocktaking message to the Foreign Secretary of July 1965, Roberts provided confirmation of German unease. Firstly, he reported that there was an 'uncomfortable feeling in certain circles, mainly on the Right, that the Americans [were] not prepared to disturb their relations with the Soviet Union for the sake of German reunification'. Secondly, he suggested that the Germans were 'all too well aware that the prospect of reunification [was] getting daily more remote [and] that the DDR's claim to be a separate state [was] becoming more valid'.[18] Up to this point, Germany's *Ostpolitik* had been based on two principal features: firstly, the Hallstein doctrine, under which Bonn sought to isolate East Germany, by the decree that diplomatic recognition of it by a third country would be considered an unfriendly act; and secondly, *Alleinvertretungsrecht*, which asserted that only West Germany was entitled to represent the whole German people.

In a press release in February 1965, the German government announced that 'in the interests of reunification ... it [was] endeavouring to reach a settlement with [its] neighbours in the East and that this policy which was initiated with the establishment of trade missions [would] be energetically pursued'.[19] Further evidence of a greater flexibility in Germany's approach towards its *Ostpolitik* could be seen in an article in *Foreign Affairs* in which Gerhard Schröder, the Foreign Minister, contemplated the establishment of diplomatic relations with all or some East European countries. However, no doubt mindful of the reaction of right-wing elements in the CDU and the mood in the country at the time, he insisted that 'no German Government could abandon the policy of reunification ... territorial questions [could] only be settled in a peace treaty for the whole of Germany ... [and that] our right to be the sole representative of Germany in international affairs [could be] neither impaired nor even endangered'.[20]

During Wilson's visit to Bonn, the seeds were sown for a British approach towards *Ostpolitik* that might encourage Germany to adapt more readily to the realities of East–West relations, without undermining efforts to improve the understanding between the two governments. Wilson's brief for the talks with Erhard outlined the main aims of the visit and suggested tactics. In terms of East–West relations, Wilson was advised that he should:

> convince the Germans that [Britain was] not contemplating disengagement or the surrender of positions of strength ... [and] persuade them towards accepting more readily the proposition that only measures leading towards an East–West *détente* could create an atmosphere in which progress towards reunification would be a practical proposition.[21]

As a preliminary to the meetings with Erhard, Wilson paid a symbolic visit to Berlin, during which he set out to dispel any doubts about his government's policy towards West Berlin and the recognition of East Germany. In a speech to a German audience, Wilson 'gave a categoric assurance that there was no question of any reduction in the British commitment to Berlin and expressed determination to follow a policy aimed at German reunification on the basis of free elections'.[22] During the talks in Bonn, Wilson welcomed the possibility of a fresh diplomatic initiative in Eastern Europe that the German government was contemplating, and suggested that this would mean a change of emphasis away from the Hallstein doctrine, since German reunification could take place only as a result of a more relaxed feeling between East and West. There were, however, limits to what the British could and would do to find a solution to the German problem.

Whilst the German Chancellor emphasised that the more independent the 'Soviet Zone' (i.e. East Germany) became of West Germany
the less hope there would be of eventual reunification, Wilson firmly
told his German counterpart that:

> although he understood that the Federal Republic regarded trade
> with the Soviet Zone as a special form of inter-German trade ...
> if the British Government placed difficulties in the way of British
> exporters doing trade they would come under heavy pressure from
> public opinion and from industrialists who claimed that they were
> losing orders to the Federal Republic.[23]

Nevertheless, Wilson had set the seal on British policy and in the process had, as Roberts reported, 'transformed German attitudes towards
the British Labour Government'.[24] Britain would uphold Western
rights in Berlin, move in step with Bonn on the German problem,
and withhold recognition of East Germany, but on the basis that the
West German government faced up to the realities of the situation
in Eastern Europe and accepted that *détente* had to be a precondition
for reunification. This was the approach that Britain would maintain
throughout the period of the Labour governments of 1964–70 and
must be considered as a positive factor in relations between the two
governments. As Stewart was to make clear to his Cabinet colleagues:

> we need good relations with Bonn. If we are to have these we must
> ... continue to support the German claim to peaceful reunification;
> maintain strong forces in Germany; defend the Allied position in
> Berlin; and refuse to recognise East Germany in any way.[25]

Sensing a certain frustration within Germany over *Ostpolitik*, and
the lack of progress to achieve reunification, Roberts composed two
despatches to the Foreign Office in which he analysed the situation
in some detail and outlined the direction that British foreign policy
might take in response.[26] To some extent, Roberts' initiative was
reminiscent of his analysis of Anglo-Soviet relations submitted to the
Foreign Office in 1946 whilst acting Ambassador in Moscow, in what
became known as the 'Other Long Telegram', after the despatch com-
piled by George Kennan, Roberts' American counterpart in Moscow.[27]
Roberts was clearly acting within his remit as an Ambassador by
reporting unusual circumstances, although, insofar as it was an
attempt to influence policy towards Germany, it was significant that
the remedies he recommended were general rather than specific and,
apart from suggesting an initiative to create a wider European unity,
were consistent with existing British policy.[28] The nub of Roberts' case
was that although the Germans had achieved security and prosperity,
unification was as far away as ever, and de Gaulle had dashed their

hopes of becoming part of a larger European unity. In this situation, the Germans were increasingly inclined to blame the Allies for this impasse and were looking for new directions their policy might take. Moreover, the frustration that had built up had stimulated national-ist tendencies, as evidenced by the rise in support for a newly formed nationalist party, the Nationaldemokratische Partei Deutschlands (National Party, NPD), and although there seemed little likelihood of a revival of German nationalism the situation might, over time, require remedial action by Britain and America.[29]

As far as Roberts was concerned, it was of very great long-term importance that the multilateral and bilateral links that tied Germany to the West be reinforced. He believed it was necessary to implement a scheme that would encompass: strengthening NATO and eliminating differences between Germany and its partners; find-ing a solution to the problem of German participation in the control and use of nuclear weapons; and making a further attempt both to resolve the problem of Britain's relationship with Europe and to focus German attention on the advantages of an organisation based on a wider membership than the Six. He believed that:

> a comprehensive approach on these lines would have a positive appeal to many Germans and would do much more than counter General de Gaulle. It would restore balance between Europe and the Atlantic, it would help the Germans find their bearings and widen their political horizons and, above all, it would enable the United Kingdom to play its proper role in the Western Community of nations as the nodal point between America, Europe and the Commonwealth.

In his view, given America's involvement in South East Asia and the attitude of de Gaulle, 'no other western nation besides the United Kingdom [was] in a position to put forward a scheme of comparable scope'.[30]

Roberts' proposals received a decidedly cool reaction from Foreign Office officials, however. John Barnes, head of the Western Organisa-tions and Coordination Department, saw dangers in centring German attention on European and NATO problems, since this might enhance Bonn's position in NATO at Britain's expense. In essence, he believed that British policy for strengthening Germany in the West 'must be combined with a policy of strengthening Germany's interest and activ-ity in the East'.[31] Bernard Ledwidge, head of the Western Department at the Foreign Office, characterised Roberts' remedies as being on familiar lines, but firmly opposed any suggestion of a wider European unity rather than the bridge-building proposals on which officials were working, especially as the Germans might see this as a ruse to divert their attention from reunification. Like Barnes, Ledwidge saw advantage in terms East–West *détente* in encouraging the Germans to persevere with new attempts to expand relations with countries in Eastern Europe, 'provided they did not conduct ... a blatant exercise in driving wedges between the Soviet Union and Eastern Europe'.[32] These comments revealed the basis of British policy. Britain would encourage the Germans towards initiatives that would improve *détente*, but reunification, if it was to happen at all, would be for the long term.

By 1966, there was a growing consensus between the political parties in Germany, and understanding by the public, that a different form of *Ostpolitik* would have to be considered if progress was ever to be made towards reunification. As *The Economist* perceptively observed:

> the Germans have begun to realise that the Adenauer version of the doctrine of 'negotiation from strength' is sterile. For one thing, western strength cements the east European countries to Russia in a joint refusal to negotiate about what really matters – east Germany ... so a *détente*, far from seeming a barrier to reunification, has gradually begun to look to Germans as the only available hope of achieving it.[33]

An indication of these developments can be gleaned from an article by Schröder in *Foreign Affairs* of October 1965, in which he also referred to the need to take advantage of a more receptive attitude in Eastern Europe to contacts with West Germany, although he warned that fear and mistrust of German intentions still had to be overcome. Nevertheless, although the article repeated familiar tenets of German foreign policy, such as not jeopardising long-term objectives, in other words reunification, for the sake of some short-lived progress towards a *rapprochement* with Eastern Europe, Schröder's idea was that, through confidence-building measures, it would be possible to 'establish relations between East and West based on mutual trust ... to remove, first of all, the minor sources of tension, but subsequently the major ones as well'.[34] As well as espousing this gradualist approach, he gave a fairly clear indication that the Hallstein doctrine need not be a bar to progress along these lines. Roberts felt that there were risks that Germany's sense of frustration about reunification could add to its vulnerability to pressure from France and Moscow to accept solutions that would not be in the West's interests. For this reason, as Roberts suggested to the Foreign Secretary, 'Germany was Britain's most important European ally ... it [would be] important to remain very close to the Germans ... to ensure that [their] Eastern policies continue to be patient, restrained and reasonably co-operative'.[35]

In March 1966, against a background in which Bonn's allies were urging a more flexible approach in its *Ostpolitik*, with the belief within German political circles that the time was right for new thinking about the German problem, and the suggestion from contacts with the Soviets that they might be more receptive to a diplomatic initiative designed to improve East–West relations, Germany decided to launch its so-called Peace Note.[36] In essence, the German initiative must be seen primarily as a public relations exercise, designed to counter criticism at home and to convince its allies that it was serious about *détente* and willing to distance itself from entrenched positions in order to move the process forward. The Note itself, as Schröder admitted to Stewart, 'contain[ed] little new but it gather[ed] together into a single text and in a positive form a number of useful reaffirmations of German policy'.[37] It stressed Bonn's commitment to peace and countered Moscow's claims, which found echo among East European states, that it was aggressive and revanchist, and it proposed arms control measures that might lead to a solution to outstanding questions in Europe, including the German problem.

An interesting feature of the Peace Note was that it managed to be both reassuring and controversial at the same time. It opened with the striking statement to the effect that the German people wanted to live in peace and freedom, that their greatest task was to overcome the division under which they had suffered for many years and to complete this mission by peaceful means. In language that the Germans thought might reassure Poland and Czechoslovakia, it asserted that Germany continued to exist in the borders of 1937, as other borders had not been recognised by a freely elected all-German government, and that the Munich accords of 1938 had been negated by Hitler's actions and had no further territorial relevance. Significantly, the Note made no mention of East Germany or the Hallstein doctrine, and it pointedly excluded East Germany from the arms control measures proposed.[38] In other words, 'the German government also believed it had to uphold its basic positions on the German question. This was registered with particular clarity in the fact that the DDR was not among the recipients of the Note.'[39]

There were mixed reactions from the British government. Although Helga Haftendorn, for example, who has written in detail on the circumstances surrounding the Note and the reaction to it, is technically correct in suggesting that 'in official statements and in their responses the Federal Republic's allies, with the exception of France, welcomed the German initiative', the reality in the case of Britain was somewhat different.[40] The official position was to welcome the Note, but behind the scenes British officials had considerable misgivings. For example, Sir Geoffrey Chilton, Ambassador in Warsaw, suggested that 'the tenor and phraseology of Section 2 of the Note [including relations with Poland] will cause a storm of anger in Poland ... it could hardly be more tactless for a peace initiative'.[41] Whilst Stewart, in instructing Roberts on how to react to the German proposals, admitted to being in a quandary, since the draft version of the Peace Note he was sent was 'a bit clumsy and, particularly in its references to Poland and the Soviet Union, likely to be counterproductive', he also doubted 'whether the text as a whole [would] prove to be very effective propaganda either in the West or in the East'.[42]

Nevertheless, despite these reservations, Britain could hardly complain about an initiative that provided tangible evidence of Bonn's commitment to do what Britain and other NATO countries had been urging it to do: namely, to adopt a more flexible approach in its *Ostpolitik* and to work towards a lowering of tension in East–West relations.[43] In this context, even if there were questions about ends and means, there can be little doubt that Stewart was sincere when he told Herbert Blankenhorn, the German Ambassador, on 25 March 1966 that 'Her Majesty's Government welcomed their initiative and would say so in public'.[44] Notwithstanding British doubts, which were kept strictly private, and adverse reaction among Eastern European states, the effect of Bonn's proposals was to encourage the Soviet Union to express interest in Germany's offer to exchange 'renunciation of force' declarations, and in that sense it imparted an impetus to *Ostpolitik*. By tactful diplomacy, Wilson's government remained in step with its German counterpart and, in so doing, earned its thanks and drew a positive reaction from the German press.[45] This was critically important at a time when Britain was reconsidering its role in Europe, and when the support of a friendly Germany was considered an essential precondition to a successful outcome of an application for membership of the European Communities.

In March 1966, as Bonn was finalising its Peace Note, Britain was drawn towards launching a *détente* initiative of its own. During a conversation with Howard Smith, head of the Foreign Office Northern Department, Zdenek Trhlik, the Czechoslovak Ambassador in London, suggested that the British and the Czech governments might issue a joint statement, in the form of a set of principles, which aimed at lowering the tension that the Ambassador believed had developed in Europe. In support of this claim, Trhlik cited NATO nuclear sharing plans and persistent statements from Germany about reunification. Given that there had been no previous indication of Czech thinking along these lines, British officials gave the proposal a cautious reception. If the Czechs were willing to enter into fairly free political talks, there might be advantage in discussing such matters. However, as Smith made clear to the Ambassador, Britain would have nothing to do with statements that implied either criticism of Germany or recognition of East Germany: '[Britain] knew perfectly well that ... Germany was doing nothing and intended doing nothing to aggravate international tension and that the ... Germans were quite certainly not going to threaten the use of force'.[46] Nevertheless, despite the reservations of his officials, the Foreign Secretary was not prepared to dismiss the Czech proposal out of hand. Although he was not sure about the real motives behind the proposal, Stewart insisted that 'it was an initiative he did not wish to discourage'.[47]

By May 1966, concerned to avoid any possibility that a statement of principles could be exploited for propaganda purposes against the Alliance, and particularly against Germany, British officials had converted the Czechoslovak proposals into a 'Declaration on Europe', which, after agreement on the text had been reached within NATO, would be a document that members of the Warsaw Pact and European countries belonging to neither bloc might support.[48] In practice, however, it would be the reaction of the United States and Germany that would ultimately determine whether the document would receive NATO backing. In this context, the Americans expressed concern that, by concentrating solely on Europe, the text could facilitate efforts by the Soviet Union to exclude the United States from a role in the settlement of European problems and, instead of Britain trying to agree a text with Communist states, it would be 'a better course for NATO countries to issue a declaration ... which would respond to some of the more constructive passages in recent Warsaw Pact statements ... dealing with general principles of co-existence and closer contacts'.[49] As for the Germans, whilst Hans Ruete, Director of Political Division II in the German Foreign Office, was concerned that the phraseology and ideas echoed too much concepts which the Communists had made their own, and that this might cause misunderstandings in the West, the official reaction was that the Germans were 'well disposed towards [the] initiative, [recognised] its possibilities and [were] grateful for being consulted in advance'.[50] Central to German thinking was the consideration that, whilst it was questionable as to how the Declaration could improve matters, Germany would not wish to be seen as an obstacle to reducing tension and would support the initiative, in the spirit of its recently published Peace Note.[51] It was also no coincidence that, as Schröder told George Brown, now Foreign Secretary, 'the Federal Republic was contemplating establishing diplomatic relations with Rumania ... and placed great store on British support'.[52]

Nevertheless, Britain remained determined to proceed with the Declaration and to complete consultations in NATO on that basis. Although the Americans continued to express misgivings, by the end of 1966 agreement had been reached in NATO that Britain should proceed on a unilateral basis and circulate a draft copy of the Declaration to the Czechs and a number of other Eastern European states. By this stage also, it had become clear that the British government had set considerable store on the possibilities that this initiative might open up in terms of improving East–West relations. As Brown told the House of Commons:

> There is a change of political climate in Europe, and we by reacting constructively to this new situation are helping the process forward … we are doing this on our own initiative for a declaration on a code of conduct to which all nations of East and West will be able to subscribe.[53]

In the event, the response from the Czechoslovak and Polish governments was disappointing, so that, by the middle of 1967, it had become clear that the initiative would not make progress.[54] A further obstacle was that, within NATO, the pendulum had swung in the direction of a collective approach towards East–West relations on the basis of the Harmel exercise. By November 1967, in an about-turn on policy, a government spokesman told the House of Commons that:

> real progress in improving relations with the countries of Eastern Europe can best be made in close consultation and cooperation with our allies … a successful outcome of what is called the Harmel review will enable us the better to serve the second and perhaps more important purpose – the political purpose – of the alliance.[55]

There are several points to make about the Declaration on Europe. It is somewhat surprising that, as an exercise in Cold War diplomacy, it has attracted little or no attention from historians. Even if a verdict on the conduct of British policy in this regard is a negative one, the Declaration was an important strand in the efforts that were being made during the 1960s that, it was hoped, would ultimately result in a settlement in Europe. It is not entirely clear why Britain decided to act upon the Czech suggestion, since, as the OPD appreciated at the time, 'a statement which was to command the agreement of both eastern and western European countries could not contain radically new or dramatic ideas'.[56] Moreover, as Stewart made clear to Sir Evelyn Shuckburgh, Britain's permanent representative to NATO, 'we must bear in mind the possible connection of this initiative with the long term Communist aim of easing the Americans out of Europe'.[57] Whilst official documents do not provide explicit reasons, they do suggest motives for Britain's actions. For example, in expressing disagreement with the reservations regarding the Declaration of the British Ambassador in Prague, Smith argued that 'this overlooks the fact that we wish to have a European policy'.[58] In similar vein, when asked for a reaction to the draft Declaration, Trhlik suggested that the Czech government 'were left with the impression that it was designed to secure certain exclusively British purposes such as entry into Europe'.[59] Although this suggestion was subsequently denied, it is certainly possible that a Declaration launched at a time when Britain was turning more towards Europe might be expected to help underline Britain's European credentials, and would help fill the policy void identified by Smith. Britain's commitment to Europe was a point emphasised by Wilson's Private Secretary when he reminded the Prime Minister that 'all our tactics so far [towards an application for membership of the EEC] have been calculated so as to make it difficult for France on the one hand to argue that Britain is not really European'.[60] What the whole exercise did demonstrate was Britain's concern to be regarded as a serious player in the movement towards establishing *détente* in Europe and, as with contacts with Bonn on the Peace Note, to ensure that good relations were maintained with Germany as Europe moved higher in its priorities.

Ostpolitik and the Grand Coalition

By the autumn of 1966, it was evident that Schröder's attempt to improve Bonn's relations with Eastern European states had made little progress in the face of the Soviet Union's insistence on recognition of East Germany and acceptance of existing borders, or in other words maintenance of the status quo, as prior conditions. In this situation, it would take a form of *Ostpolitik* that took account of the realities as they were to instil a greater dynamic into a European *détente*. The conditions for this dynamic were seemingly created at the end of November 1966, when the CDU/SPD Grand Coalition under Chancellor Kurt Georg Kiesinger replaced the Erhard government. With Brandt, the SPD leader, installed as Vice Chancellor and Foreign Minister – a man with a record of a more flexible attitude towards East Germany during his days as Mayor of Berlin, and now able to exert influence on Germany's policies towards the East as the price for SPD support for the new administration – the scene was set for a different approach to relations with the other part of Germany and Eastern Europe.[61] As Stewart's brief for Brandt's visit to Britain in October 1966 put it, 'there are signs of the possibility of movement in East–West relations which we think should be vigorously exploited ... we have been encouraged by ... signs of evolution in German thinking on the question of reunification and dealings with East Germany'.[62]

In December 1966, in his first major policy statement, Kiesinger outlined the new shape of German foreign policy. Its basis was a consistent and effective peace policy, designed to remove political tension and to check the arms race. He repeated the offer to the Soviet Union to exchange declarations renouncing the use of force, made in Schröder's Peace Note, and proposed to include in the offer the problem of the division of Germany. Kiesinger stated that Germany wanted reconciliation with Poland, but made clear that only an all-German government could determine territorial boundaries; and, whilst he stressed that the Munich agreement was no longer valid, he underlined the fact that a solution had to be found to the problem of the expellees and refugees from the former Sudetenland. As to East Germany, Kiesinger still argued that his government was the only one entitled to speak for all Germans, although he emphasised that Bonn wished to 'ease the situation, not harden it ... to bridge the gulfs not deepen them'.[63] In April 1967, in a reaction to Kiesinger's policy statement, Theo Sommer claimed to detect a new sense of vigour and purpose about the Grand Coalition. He referred to several sweeping changes relating to the new government's *Ostpolitik*: the quiet dismantling of the Hallstein doctrine and its replacement by the 'birthmark theory', under which it would be possible to have ties with countries that had never had any choice about links with East Germany; and the scrapping of the old concept that reunification had to precede *détente*. As Sommer put it, 'there [were] ... more and more German politicians who would be prepared to accept the statement that the goal of German policy must be reunification – or else the creation of conditions that make reunification superfluous or at least its absence tolerable'.[64]

In an article written over a year after Kiesinger's policy statement, Brandt set out his vision of Germany's *Ostpolitik*. Many of the commitments referred to by the Chancellor were repeated, but in one important respect there was a difference of emphasis. According to Brandt, Europe was moving towards a peaceful transformation of historic dimensions and, as he saw it, there was a specific inter-relationship between the German problem and European development generally. Rather than reunification being a possibility that could be negotiated in the short term, Brandt speculated that 'overcoming the division of Germany [would] be a long process whose duration no one [could] predict'.[65] This difference was symptomatic of the problems inherent in a coalition within which one of the partners, the SPD, held an underlying philosophy which required that Germany's policy towards the East should go much further than the CDU would be prepared to countenance. Evidence as to what might be described as friction between the partners over *Ostpolitik* can be seen in the action taken by Kiesinger in December 1968, to hold private talks with Brandt on the conduct of German foreign policy. The Chancellor insisted that, in future, 'dealings with the Soviet Union required the closest co-ordination between the two men'.[66] The documents are not more forthcoming on the nature of the problem, but at its nub was almost certainly an aspect of *Ostpolitik*. To be sure, the fact that the Chancellor felt the need to speak in this way to his Foreign Minister, and to record such a sensitive conversation, was unusual to say the least, and indicated his annoyance at activity of which he was obviously unaware. As A. J. Nicholls suggests, 'once Brandt became foreign minister … there were numerous contacts with the Soviet bloc at all levels … this aroused suspicions in the Federal Chancellery and Brandt became more and more irritated by the restrictions put upon his freedom of action within the coalition'.[67]

Perhaps the overriding feature of the statements by Kiesinger and Brandt, and of the conclusions drawn by Sommer, was the resolve by the Grand Coalition to make *Ostpolitik* an instrument of change in East–West relations. In essence, this is substantially the same point as that made by Haftendorn, who argues that 'the government announced a more independent … German *détente* policy … this became possible once Bonn had eliminated the conflict of aims between alliance policy and policy on Germany and had turned the Federal Republic onto the *détente* course of the allies'.[68] Another feature of the new approach was the acceptance that the effect of *Ostpolitik* hitherto had been to isolate East Germany and of the need to convince the Soviet Union that the objective of *Ostpolitik* was not to destabilise relations between members of the Warsaw Pact. As Brandt claimed, 'it is not our goal nor even a peripheral intention of our new Eastern policy to isolate the GDR, nor do we intend to create or exploit differences between the Soviet Union and her allies'.[69]

During 1967, and in the course of exchanges on a 'renunciation of force' agreement, it became clear that the price expected by the Soviet Union had broadened from a bilateral understanding to one that included a resolution of major differences between Germany and Eastern European states. In short, Bonn would be expected: to recognise East Germany; to recognise the demarcation line between the two parts of Germany and the Oder–Neisse line as national borders; and to renounce any ambition to obtain nuclear weapons.[70] In sum, this was clearly a price that Germany could not afford to pay. Nevertheless, *Ostpolitik* did yield gains, in that diplomatic relations with Rumania and Yugoslavia were restored, attempts were made to normalise relations with Czechoslovakia and hopes existed that an understanding with Poland on borders might be reached. The complexity of the issues involved, however, given the intermingling of renunciation of force agreements with other *Ostpolitik* factors such as recognition of East Germany and territorial borders, and with the tensions between the partners in the Grand Coalition, necessarily placed limits on the progress that might realistically have been expected. Moreover, in August 1968, and confronted by the realisation that *Ostpolitik* had to some extent undermined its grip on Eastern Europe, the Soviet Union, aided and abetted by armed forces from other Warsaw Pact countries, intervened to quell liberalisation tendencies in Czechoslovakia. Whilst the Czechoslovak crisis brought the *détente* process to a halt, this was always likely to be temporary, since there still remained common interests between East and West, transcending ideological differences, in maintaining an understanding on vital questions, not the least those affecting developments in Europe. As to Germany, as a British assessment put it, 'the Czech crisis and its aftermath [would be] unlikely to put a stop to their *Ostpolitik* but ... there is a growing feeling ... that the Federal Republic must at least come to *de facto* terms with East Germany ... reunification will become an even more distant objective'.[71]

In Britain, the advent of a Grand Coalition committed to improving relations with the Soviet Union and with Eastern European states was widely welcomed. In this context, for example, *The Times*, in commenting on Kiesinger's policy statement of December 1966, suggested that any effort to place greater emphasis on *détente* would depend upon Germany's willingness to abandon old thoughts on Eastern Europe and nuclear sharing, but concluded that 'if movement in Bonn [was] slow it [was] at least in the right direction'.[72] Politically, however, there were other considerations for the British government. Almost coincidental with the agreement by the CDU and SPD to form their Grand Coalition, Wilson announced Britain's intention to enter the EEC, should the outcome of a fact-finding mission that he would undertake to each of the member countries prove positive.[73] Given that ministers believed that support from Germany was essential for the success of Britain's EEC application, it was inevitable that, from a British viewpoint, there would be a direct link between its EEC diplomacy and support for *Ostpolitik*. This linkage, together with the uncertainty created by a growing assertiveness in German foreign policy, and the direction that a more flexible form of *Ostpolitik* might take, formed lines of continuity in British foreign policy throughout the remaining years of the second Labour government, and beyond.

At a crucial meeting of the Cabinet in April 1967, following Wilson's visits to EEC member countries, ministers were told that 'the prospect of access to a larger market ... could reasonably be expected to have a dynamic economic effect and make it much easier to carry out ... the social and industrial changes which were essential to ... [Britain's] economic strength in future'. In his concluding comments, Wilson stressed that, politically, there was a grave danger that failure to join the Community might leave Britain 'confronted with a situation in which a resurgent Germany might dominate Western Europe'.[74] These statements encapsulated British concerns. Not only was membership of the EEC important for the future well-being of the country but it would also serve to ensure that no one else, and especially Germany, would become the leading power within the Community, with all that implied. As Burke Trend, the Cabinet Secretary, suggested to the Prime Minister, 'we have a somewhat similar concern [to France] about the danger of German predominance on the Continent, whether militarily or economically'.[75]

In his annual review of Germany for 1967, Roberts drew a connection between Britain's EEC application and *Ostpolitik*. In the context of Britain's application, Roberts was able to highlight the increasing European line in British foreign policy, of which one important part was 'strong British support in Warsaw Pact capitals for Bonn's new Eastern policy', and he commented that this was one reason why there was 'no discordant note in Anglo-German relations'.[76] Earlier in the year also, in an address to the Königswinter Conference, Brandt outlined several related factors that were significant for Anglo-German relations.[77] In drawing attention to Britain's potential membership of the EEC, Brandt pledged Germany's readiness to support its entry and then, in moving on to discuss East–West relations, stressed that 'the Federal Republic [was] resolved to pursue honestly and consistently its policy of safeguarding peace and *détente* ... [and] that it [was] necessary for [the] allies to ... give their political and moral support'. To make the point clear, Brandt added that he knew Germany could 'count on Great Britain'.[78] That there was a clear connection between Britain's turn towards Europe and *Ostpolitik*, and that this was a fact that was also well appreciated by the Germans, was underlined by the points made by the Chancellor's staff, in an internal brief on Anglo-German relations prepared for his visit to Britain in October 1967. Not only were relations assessed as being good, but also the connection was made that 'as the British had great hopes of German help in the EEC question, in return therefore, they were more than ever prepared to support German objectives with *Ostpolitik*'.[79]

A major feature of Kiesinger's foreign policy statement of December 1966 was the emphasis he placed on restoring relations with France, after the differences that had emerged during the Erhard years.[80] Despite these differences, the Franco-German alliance remained the cornerstone of Bonn's *Westpolitik*, being fundamental to the economic and political integration of Europe. In terms of *Ostpolitik*, however, there were other reasons for a closer relationship with France. One of these, Roberts asserted, 'was the belief of the Grand Coalition ... that the French [could] help Bonn in Moscow and other Eastern capitals'.[81]

Roberts qualified this assessment. France could choose to add recognition of the DDR to recognition of the Oder–Neisse line and this could do great harm. In this situation, it would be difficult to avoid the conclusion, implied in Roberts' report, that advocacy based on strong British support in Warsaw Pact capitals for Bonn's new Eastern policy combined with American security guarantees to Germany would carry more weight in Moscow.[82] This is not the place to argue the relative merits of British and French influence in Moscow, and the truth may be that neither was predominant on the question of *Ostpolitik*, but during this period Britain, more than France, through its closer relationship with the United States, was well positioned to act as an interlocutor between the two superpowers. To be sure, Britain did seek to represent Germany's interests in Moscow but there is little to suggest that this had any marked effect on the Soviet Union's reaction to German overtures.[83] However, and this was the crucial point in the debate about influence, whilst Britain strongly favoured both an easing of tension in Europe and *détente* with the Soviet Union, this was not to say that ministers would be content to see the Germans, or anyone else for that matter, set the agenda for East–West relations as they affected Europe. In February 1969 in particular, Trend and his planning staff identified the growing importance of Germany in the international scene and argued that 'it [was] very much in [Britain's] interests to see that German policies on [the German question] did not get out of hand'.[84]

Brandt's *Ostpolitik*

The outcome of the German elections of September 1969 can be seen as a significant development for two principal reasons: firstly, the formation of the SPD and FDP coalition brought to an end the role of the CDU and their Christlich Soziale Union (Christian Socialist Union; CSU) partners as a government alliance of some twenty years' standing; and secondly, and more crucially, the appointment of Brandt as Chancellor provided a turning point in Germany's *Ostpolitik*. In one sense, timing was on Brandt's side, since he was able to build on the dialogue with the Soviet Union that had already resumed in July 1969 on a renunciation of force agreement, and could probe an apparent willingness of the Soviet Union to work for a genuine *détente* in East–West relations. In a meeting in November 1969 with the new German Chancellor, Stewart suggested that there were several reasons for the Soviet Union's newfound flexibility. Whilst he believed that the West could be on the threshold of better relations with the Soviet Union, he assessed that the real Soviet objectives for a more active dialogue were 'to bury the memory of the invasion of Prague, to enhance the

position of the DDR, and to divide Europe and the USA'.[85] In further
exchanges between the two men on a Soviet proposal for a European
security conference, Brandt confirmed that Germany would partici-
pate only if the United States was not excluded and, as evidence of
his new brand of *Ostpolitik*, asserted that West Germany would be prepared to accept the participation of East Germany, since 'it would be
unrealistic to hold a conference of this sort without the DDR'. Whilst
this would not be with a view to changing Bonn's fundamental standpoint on recognition of the other part of Germany, Brandt agreed with
Stewart that, on this whole question, 'it was imperative to proceed
slowly and carefully'.[86] From a British viewpoint, Stewart's caution
reflected Britain's concern to keep in step with the Germans as their
Ostpolitik unfolded and to make sure that it went in a direction that
was conducive to Western interests. As Sir Roger Jackling, the British
Ambassador in Bonn, suggested at the time, 'HMG [should] continue
to offer firm support for *Ostpolitik* because it appear[ed] to coincide
with [Britain's] aim of reducing tensions in Europe and because we
need close bilateral relations with the Federal Republic'.[87]

The thrust of Brandt's remarks to Stewart reflected what he had
said in October 1969, as part of his first official statement as Federal
Chancellor. In this statement, Brandt admitted that the relationship
between the two parts of Germany had to be improved, since not only
was this in the interests of the German people but it also would have
significance for Europe and for East–West relations. As to the sensitive issue of recognition of East Germany, however, Brandt emphasised
that this would not be possible, and justified this on the basis that
'while two states might exist in Germany, they were not foreign territory for one another; their relationship could only be of a special
kind'.[88] In practice, Brandt's *Ostpolitik* was intended to normalise
Germany's relations with the Soviet Union and its Eastern European
allies and in that way to heal the divisions that had been created in
1945 by the defeat of Germany. Unlike Schröder's form of *Ostpolitik*,
Brandt's strategy was to launch a 'dialogue simultaneously with the
Soviet Union, with Eastern Europe, and with East Germany ... [and
not] to drive wedges among the members of the Warsaw Pact'.[89]

There was immediate evidence of Brandt's determination to press
ahead with his progressive style of *Ostpolitik*. Germany signed the NPT
and opened negotiations with the Soviet Union on a renunciation of
force agreement. As part of a comprehensive package of measures,
Germany also offered talks with Poland on a renunciation of force
agreement and agreed to a meeting of the heads of government
of the two German states. The nature and pace of this diplomatic
activity, and ultimately its prospect of success, relied heavily upon
the unqualified support of its Alliance partners. Whilst Bonn would

still be dependent upon the United States to guarantee its security, British support would also be important. As Jackling commented:

> there can be little doubt that the present Chancellor attaches par-
> ticular importance to the support of Great Britain ... the fact that
> we are prepared to encourage his efforts to improve relations with
> their Eastern neighbours is of help to the Bonn Government in set-
> ting aside the French claim to act as the Federal Republic's sole
> mentor in such matters.[90]

To some extent, Brandt's diplomacy took Britain by surprise. Above all, with its *Ostpolitik*, the new German government launched an initiative that created great uncertainty, not the least in the minds of its allies, about how and when it would end. Whilst the official position was to welcome without reservation the fact that Germany had seized the nettle of normalisation of its relations with the Soviet Union and Eastern European states, behind the scenes the British government was concerned about the knock-on effect that *Ostpolitik* might have for its official position on the legitimacy of East Germany and, in particular, for the maintenance of Allied rights in Berlin.[91] In terms of reunification also, Britain could express overt support, safe in the knowledge that it was likely to become an issue only in the longer term. Nevertheless, from a British viewpoint, *Ostpolitik* can be seen to have held particular attractions. There was certainly no indication that ministers shared the viewpoint of their American counterparts that 'the SPD, for all the undoubted reasonableness of Herr Brandt and Helmut Schmidt, [was] still suspicious of the West and of rearmament and [hankered] for reconciliation with East Germany' or, like the French, '[resented] the possibility that Bonn would succeed in the field of East–West relations that they [had] hitherto liked to consider their preserve'.[92] British ministers recog-nised the need for Germany to take full account of Allied rights, and to that end ensured that their officials involved in the Bonn Study Group, the three-power group charged with proposing safeguards for Allied rights regarding Germany as a whole, and Berlin in particular, represented this concern.[93] Moreover, there was an acknowledgement in British political circles that as long as there was proper and timely consultation by the Germans, the Allies had the means and were better placed to look after their own interests. Thus, as Britain scaled down its world role, a supportive stance for *Ostpolitik* opened up the possibility of an even closer relationship with Germany, which by 1970 had become a major force within Europe, and which could work to Britain's advantage as it pursued its objective of membership of the European Communities. As the Conservative Foreign Secretary, Sir Alec Douglas Home, put it in February 1971: 'quite apart from

... the merits of Herr Brandt's Ostpolitik, we need to maintain the best possible relations with the Federal Government in the interests of our negotiations with the EEC'.[94]

British policy reconsidered

A major objective of British foreign policy during the Wilson years was to have a close relationship with Germany. As Stewart told his Cabinet colleagues in August 1965, 'if we can secure German cooperation our prospects of shaping Western Europe's economic and political future to the designs which suit us best will be greatly improved'.[95] Within this framework, Britain's reaction to Germany's *Ostpolitik*, in its three distinct phases, was informed by two principal considerations: firstly, to have influence on Germany's initiatives, initially to encourage Germany to adapt more reasonably to the realities of a divided Europe, and later to avoid concessions that went beyond what Brandt claimed was 'gambled away long ago', and always on the basis that Western interests in Europe, and particularly in Berlin, were not compromised;[96] and secondly, as an act of self-interest, to secure Germany's support for Britain's turn towards Europe and, more specifically, its entry into the EEC. At the same time, Germany needed the backing of its allies, and saw in Britain an understanding partner that would support the aims and objectives of its *Ostpolitik*. The success of British strategy can be judged by an assessment of Anglo-German relations made in March 1970 by Brandt's officials in preparation for his visit to London. They pointed out that 'Germany's *Ostpolitik* had the approval and support of the British Government ... in political and military terms Germany was a very important European ally of Great Britain ... Germany's approval and help were necessary for Britain's entry into the European Communities'.[97] As to Britain's policy objective, despite occasional differences of emphasis, a close relationship with Germany existed throughout the period 1964–70, and there can be little doubt that Britain's support for *Ostpolitik* was another contributory factor.

Notes

1 Kettenacker, *Germany since 1945*, p. 53.
2 Helmut Schmidt, 'Germany in the Era of Negotiations', *Foreign Affairs*, 49, 1 (October 1970), p. 45.
3 Sir Alec Douglas Home to Prime Minister, 2 February 1971, WRG 3/513/713, FCO 33/1416, PRO.
4 See record of discussion, Wilson and Brandt, 14 April 1967, PREM 13/2667, PRO.
5 'The Longer Term Prospects for East–West Relations After the Czechoslovak Crisis', 18 February 1969, OPD (69) 8, CAB 148/91, PRO. In an earlier

assessment, the Foreign and Commonwealth Office commented that German reunification could only be the outcome of a long period of *détente*. See 'The Longer Term Prospects for East–West Relations After the Czechoslovak Crisis', 20 January 1969, OPD (69) 1, CAB 148/91, PRO. See also note 3.

6 Nicholls, *The Bonn Republic*, p. 168.

7 For a more detailed account of de Gaulle's *détente* theories, see Bozo, 'Détente Versus Alliance', pp. 343–360.

8 Interview material.

9 Sir Frank Roberts to Michael Stewart, 'The Federal Republic of Germany's Position Within the Western Alliance', 5 July 1965, RG 1022/18, FO 371/183006, PRO.

10 'The Longer Term Prospects for East–West Relations', 15 May 1969, *DBPO III I*, p. 151.

11 Sir Thomas Brimelow to Sir Duncan Wilson, 14 July 1969, *DBPO III I*, p. 177.

12 'The Longer Term Prospects for East–West Relations', 15 May 1969, *DBPO III I* p. 147.

13 Telegram number 1013, Roberts to Foreign Office, 17 October 1964, RG 1051/51, FO 371/177928, PRO.

14 F. W. S. Craig (ed.), *Conservative and Labour Party Conference Decisions 1945–1981* (Chichester, 1982), p. 236.

15 See Larres, *Uneasy Allies*, p. 87.

16 For a detailed account of Macmillan's attitude towards Germany and Berlin see Lee, 'Pragmatism Versus Principle?', pp. 113–130.

17 Aufzeichnung über Premierminister Wilson, 25 April 1966, B31/299, PAAA Berlin.

18 Roberts to Stewart, 'The Federal Republic of Germany's Position Within the Western Alliance', 5 July 1965, RG 1022/18, FO 371/183006, PRO.

19 Press release, 2 February 1965, RG 1022/4, FO 371/183006, PRO.

20 Gerhard Schröder, 'Germany Looks at Eastern Europe', *Foreign Affairs*, 44, 1 (October 1965), pp. 15–25. See Haftendorn, *Security and Detente*, p. 165, for comment about CDU opposition to Schröder's plans to follow a course 'receptive to and supportive of the Western policy of *détente*'.

21 Steering brief for Prime Minister's visit to Germany, 26 February 1965, PREM 13/329, PRO.

22 Record of discussions, 2 April 1965, RG 1052/22, PREM 13/329, PRO.

23 *Ibid*.

24 *Ibid*.

25 Memorandum by the Foreign Secretary, 'Policy Towards Germany', 5 August 1965, C(65) 119, CAB 129/122 (Pt 2), PRO.

26 Roberts, 'The Federal Republic of Germany's Position Within the Western Alliance', 5 July 1965, RG 1022/18, FO 371/183006, PRO. See also Roberts, 'German Foreign Policy in the Light of Recent Developments', 11 November 1965, RG 1022/29, FO 371/183006, PRO.

27 See Sean Greenwood, 'Frank Roberts and the "Other" Long Telegram: The View from the British Embassy in Moscow, March 1946', *Journal of Contemporary History*, 25 (1990), pp. 103–122.

28 See Roberts to Stewart, 'The Federal Republic of Germany's Position Within the Western Alliance', 5 July 1965, RG 1022/18, FO 371/183006, PRO.

29 *Ibid*. Roberts referred to mounting worries about de Gaulle's policies and intentions. He asserted that these policies were totally divergent from German policies and seriously inhibited relations between Germany and the United States as Germany's effective protecting power.

30 *Ibid.* See also Roberts, 'German Foreign Policy in the Light of Recent Developments', 11 November 1965, RG 1022/29, FO 371/183006, PRO.
31 E. J. W. Barnes to Lord Hood, 19 July 1965, RG 1022/18, FO 371/183006, PRO.
32 W. B. L. Ledwidge to Lord Hood, 15 July 1965, RG 1022/18, FO 371/183006, PRO.
33 'Fingers Over the Wall', *The Economist*, 6 August 1966, p. 521.
34 Schröder, 'Germany in Era of Negotiations', p. 20.
35 Roberts to Stewart, 11 November 1965, RG 1022/29, FO 371/183006, PRO.
36 A draft of the full German text of the Peace Note is included in 'Note der Bundesregierung (Entwurf)', 7 March 1966, *AAPD* (1966), I, pp. 262–270. See also telegram number 349, Roberts to Foreign Office, 18 March 1966, RG 1022/4, FO 371/189172, PRO.
37 Brief for Stewart's meeting with Herbert Blankenhorn, German Ambassador in London, 23 March 1966, RG 1022/7, FO 371/189172, PRO.
38 Note der Bundesregierung (Entwurf), 7 March 1966, *AAPD* (1966), I, pp. 262–270.
39 Haftendorn, *Security and Detente*, p. 167.
40 *Ibid.*, p. 170. Haftendorn's book was written in 1985, before the release of official British documents that cast a rather different light on the reaction in London to the Peace Note.
41 Telegram number 153, Sir G. Chilton to Foreign Office, 22 March 1966, RG 1022/7, FO 371/189172, PRO.
42 Stewart to Roberts, 18 March 1966, RG 1022/5, FO 371/189172, PRO.
43 The brief (dated 23 March 1966) for Stewart's meeting with Herbert Blankenhorn, the German Ambassador, emphasised that 'the note ... shows welcome evidence of a more positive German attitude towards East–West relations which we want to encourage', RG 1022/8, FO 371/189172, PRO.
44 Stewart to missions, 29 March 1966, RG 1022/11, FO 371/189172, PRO.
45 Telegram number 71, Roberts to Foreign Office, 30 March 1966, RG 1022/12, FO 371/189172, PRO. This report stated that 'The German press in general have tended to greet the German Peace Note enthusiastically and somewhat uncritically ... *Mittag* claims that for the first time in many months the Federal Government is acting rather than reacting in foreign policy matters ... the approval voiced in ... London was widely respected and welcomed.'
46 Letter from Howard Smith to Denis Greenhill, Deputy Under-Secretary of State at the Foreign Office, 8 March 1966, N1075/1, FO 371/188497, PRO. The letter lists the set of six principles proposed by the Czechs. There had also been inconclusive discussions within the United States administration some months earlier, about issuing a 'Statement of Agreed Principles' on Europe as an alternative to a German initiative on reunification. See letter from Barber to Spiers, 16 December 1965, *FRUS* (1964–68), XV, pp. 344–345.
47 Letter from Stewart to Sir Cecil Parrott, Ambassador in Prague, 17 March 1966, N 1075/2, FO 371/188497, PRO.
48 The text of the British–Czechoslovak Declaration on Europe, FO 371/188501, PRO, is given in full in Appendix 2. See also Britische Entwurf zu einer 'Code of Behaviour' für die Europäische Politik (Declaration on Europe), Bonn, 25 October 1966, B31/299, PAAA Berlin.
49 Telegram number 2118, Washington to Foreign Office, 20 July 1966, N 1075/50, FO 371/188499, PRO.
50 Telegram number 1041, Bonn to Foreign Office, 16 July 1966, N 1075/46, FO 371/188499, PRO.
51 Gespräch zwischen Schröder und Brown, 4 November 1966, *AAPD* (1966),

II, p. 1469, fn. 35. See also Besuch von Aussenminister George Brown, 3/4 November 1966, B31/299, PAAA Berlin.

52 Gespräch zwischen Schröder und Brown, 4 November 1966, *AAPD* (1966), II, p. 1469.

53 *Hansard*, House of Commons, 737 (6 December 1966), col. 1172.

54 Brief for the visit of George Thomson, Foreign Office Minister of State, to Poland, 17–21 July 1967, N 2/1 (Pt B), FCO 28/2, PRO. 'The main gist of the Czech comment was that our draft was not sufficiently political … their suggested insertions were merely aimed to imply acceptance of the status quo in central Europe, including to some extent the position of East Germany.' In a meeting with Thomson, Jozef Winiewicz, the Polish Foreign Minister, said that 'he doubted whether the time was ripe … the Poles were working on the terms of a draft Treaty on European Security.' *Ibid.*

55 Statement by Fred Mulley, Minister of State, Foreign Office, *Hansard*, House of Commons, 753 (2 November 1967), col. 465.

56 Minutes of an OPD meeting, 5 July 1966, OPD (66) 31st Mtg, CAB 148/25, PRO.

57 Stewart to Sir Evelyn Shuckburgh, 12 May 1966, N1075/13, FO 371/188497, PRO.

58 Howard Smith's comments on letter from Sir Cecil Parrott to Michael Stewart, 2 April 1966, N 1075/10, FO 371/188497, PRO.

59 Telegram number 13, 11 January 1967, N 2/1 (Pt A), FCO 28/1, PRO.

60 Michael Palliser to the Prime Minister, 21 October 1967, PREM 13/1527, PRO.

61 See Roberts to Foreign Office, 'Germany: Annual Review for 1967', 3 January 1968, RG 1/1, FCO 33/91, PRO, in which the Ambassador makes the point that 'a more flexible eastern policy was the main foreign policy requirement of the SPD in entering the Big Coalition'.

62 Brief for Secretary of State, 21 October 1966, RG 1053/95, FO 371/189217, PRO.

63 Kiesinger, 'German Foreign Policy', p. 49. The full text of Kiesinger's major policy statement is give as Regierungserklärung des Bundeskanzlers Kiesinger, 13 December 1966, Oberländer, *Dokumente zur Deutschlandpolitik*. An extract was later published in *Survival* (Kiesinger, 'German Foreign Policy').

64 Sommer, 'Bonn Changes Course', p. 491.

65 Willy Brandt, 'German Policy Towards the East', *Foreign Affairs*, 46, 3 (April 1968), p. 481.

66 Aufzeichnung des Bundeskanzlers Kiesinger, 2 December 1968, *AAPD* (1968), II, p. 1546.

67 Nicholls, *The Bonn Republic*, p. 210.

68 Haftendorn, *Security and Detente*, p. 173.

69 Brandt, 'German Policy Towards the East', p. 480.

70 *Ibid.*, p. 483. In his article, Brandt sets out these conditions and provides an indication of how they were being, or might be, met.

71 'The Longer Term Prospects for East–West Relations After the Czech Crisis', 15 May 1969, *DBPO III I*, p. 146.

72 'Bonn Peeps over the Ramparts', *The Times*, 14 December 1966, p. 11.

73 Telegram number 230, Foreign Office to British delegation, Brussels, 9 November 1966, 1051/66, FO 1108/8, PRO.

74 Conclusions of a meeting of Cabinet, 20 April 1967, CC (67) 22, CAB 128/42 (Pt 2), PRO.

75 Burke Trend to Prime Minister, May 1966, C47A, CAB 165/151, PRO.

76 'Germany: Annual Review for 1967', 3 January 1968, RG1/1, FCO 33/91, PRO.

77 On the Königswinter Conferences, see Roberts, *Dealing with Dictators*, p. 239.
78 Address by Willy Brandt, 10 March 1967, RG 9/1, FCO 33/151, PRO.
79 Stand der deutsch–britischen Beziehungen, 11 October 1967, B136/3045, BA Koblenz.
80 See Sommer, 'Bonn Changes Course', p. 481.
81 'Germany: Annual Review for 1967', 3 January 1968, RG1/1, FCO 33/91, PRO.
82 *Ibid.* See also Chapter 8 (p. 212).
83 In February 1969, for example, Kiesinger thanked 'the British Government for the clear and firm support accorded to the Federal Government's eastern policy'. See meeting between Wilson and Kiesinger, 12 February 1969, PREM 13/2675, PRO.
84 Trend to Palliser, 7 February 1969, PREM 13/2636, PRO.
85 Gespräch – Brandt mit Stewart, 14 November 1969, *AAPD* (1969), II, p. 1286. Stewart placed less value on an alternative scenario in which the Soviets sought a relaxation of tension because of worries about controlling their satellites and dealing with the Chinese border dispute.
86 *Ibid.*, p. 1288.
87 Jackling to Foreign Office, 25 June 1970, *DBPO III I*, p. 243, fn. 1. Jackling had already provided an assessment of the new German foreign policy in which he asserted that 'close Anglo-German relations are most obviously important … in the context of the forthcoming negotiations for the enlargement of the EEC'. See 'New German Foreign Policy', 10 December 1969, WRG 3/548/7, FCO 33/588, PRO.
88 See Klaus von Beyme (ed.), *Die großen Regierungserklärungen der deutschen Bundeskanzler von Adenauer bis Schmidt* (München, 1979), p. 254.
89 Schmidt, 'Germany in the Era of Negotiations', p. 46. See also Roberts, *Dealing with Dictators*, p. 250.
90 Jackling to Stewart, 10 December 1969, WRG 3/548/7, FCO 33/588, PRO.
91 *Ibid.*
92 *Ibid.* Jackling's assessment was evidently well in tune with mainstream Foreign Office thinking. In a brief on *Ostpolitik* prepared for ministers in February 1971, over half a year after the demise of the Wilson government, the Foreign Secretary stated that 'we had been less jealous than the French … and we have not shared all the American preoccupations about the potential side effects of *Ostpolitik*'. See Foreign Secretary to Prime Minister, 2 February 1971, WRG 3/513/713, FCO 33/1416, PRO.
93 On the work of the Bonn Study Group, see WRL 2/15, FCO 33/1150, PRO.
94 Foreign Secretary to Prime Minister, 2 February 1971, WRG 3/513/713, FCO 33/1416, PRO.
95 Memorandum by the Foreign Secretary, 5 August 1965, C (65) 119, CAB 129/122 (Pt 2), PRO.
96 Brandt's comments were made in the context of the Moscow Treaty. See special edition of the *Bulletin* of the Presse und Informationsamt der Bundesregierung, Number 109, 17 August 1970.
97 Gespräch über die Reise des Herrn Bundeskanzler nach London, undated, B31/370, PAAA Berlin.

Anglo-German relations and Britain's policy towards the European Economic Community

Looking back on the 1960s and the time of the Wilson governments there can be little surprise at the turn of events that brought about Britain's second application for membership of the EEC. Although President Charles de Gaulle's veto in 1963 stopped Britain's turn towards Europe dead in its tracks, the economic and geopolitical imperatives that had motivated Britain's first application did not simply disappear. Rather, by the time Labour took office in October 1964, neither the economic advantages that membership of a trading bloc the size of the EEC would convey nor the importance of a potential boost to Britain's status from being part of a European power bloc had diminished, and in the eyes of those members of Wilson's government supportive of Britain's membership of the Community another application remained attractive and, indeed, was perceived as necessary. To Labour's pro-EEC faction, therefore, the question was not one of whether the government elected in 1964 would seek membership of the EEC but when the decision to do so could be made. This viewpoint is not intended to dispute the claim made by John Young to the effect that 'when Harold Wilson became Labour premier in October 1964, another application to "enter Europe" seemed unlikely'.[1] Wilson and many in his party had opposed Britain's original application and, when the new government took office, there was little to suggest that much, if anything, had changed in this regard.

Wilson's attitude towards Europe was therefore pivotal and is the key to understanding the reaction of his governments to events. Some accounts of the period suggest that the Prime Minister was indifferent towards Europe and that it was only in 1966 that he came 'to see a new initiative as valuable and the European Community as less of a threat to national sovereignty than he feared'.[2] Whilst Wilson had become overtly pro-EEC by 1966, it will be argued here that, by a pragmatic, step-by-step reaction to events, very much in line with what was seen in the 1960s as 'the long-established tradition of the [British] ... approach to policy-making',[3] and in a demonstration of continuities across the period from the approach to Europe adopted by Harold Macmillan's government up to 1963, Wilson progressively developed an EEC strategy from the time he took office that resulted in a second British application in 1967 and which, once de Gaulle had resigned as President of France in 1969, had positioned Britain to move towards membership.[4] It will also be shown that the linchpin of Britain's strategy towards Europe was a close bilateral understanding with the government in Bonn.[5]

Britain and the EEC: 1964–66

Inevitably, the background to Wilson's attitude is far more complex than the opening comments to this chapter imply. It is typical of his approach to politics that uncertainty still exists as to his real attitude towards Europe, notwithstanding the claim by John Dickie that he 'had privately come to the conclusion before he won the 1964 election that Britain's future lay inevitably with the European Community'.[6] What is not in doubt, however, is that the Labour Party under Wilson's leadership fought and won the 1964 general election on a manifesto that promised closer links with Britain's European neighbours but with the caveat that a future Labour government would ensure that the Commonwealth would remain Britain's prime responsibility.[7] This was hardly the stuff of a wholehearted commitment to joining the Common Market; rather, it was symptomatic of a political party more intent on fostering Britain's traditional links. There were, however, good reasons for Wilson's initial caution about the EEC. Not only was his party split on the subject but, given the parliamentary difficulties he faced with such a small majority, and the distinct possibility that at some stage in the not too distant future he would need to renew his mandate, a new European initiative was not a viable option. But there are other grounds for questioning the extent of Wilson's supposed antipathy towards the EEC. Wilson has been widely credited for his astuteness as a politician.[8] In an assessment of him in April 1966 by the German Foreign Ministry, tribute was paid to his intelligence and exceptional tactical skill in surviving in office despite such a narrow parliamentary majority and to his masterful but cold-blooded pragmatism in dealing with increasing problems at home and abroad.[9] As a former economics don also, Wilson could hardly have failed to appreciate the growing importance of Europe to Britain's trading patterns and the implications of their focus on West European markets. In this context, Andrew Moravcsik argues with some force

that 'from 1955 through 1970 it remained undisputed inside and outside the government that commercial considerations were sufficient
to force a British bid for membership over the long term. There was
uncertainty only about timing.'[10] It is not the place here to debate the
primacy of political factors or the economic case as being the main
reason behind Britain's application to join the EEC, notwithstanding Young's cogent arguments supporting the former, although some
comment would be appropriate.[11] There is a strong argument for
the political but it would be wrong to dismiss the economic case too
lightly. Whilst the EEC was turning into a political force and Britain
clearly had aspirations to influence its future development, particularly as it realised it would have to scale down its world role, the same
could be said about the Community's economic standing, given the
trend towards regional economic co-operation and the growing interdependence across the world economy. Within the government at the
time, it was appreciated that membership of EFTA simply would not
serve British interests over the longer term and, therefore, assuming
the costs were acceptable, both the economic and political benefits of
entry into the EEC became increasingly attractive. It is also relevant
to note that there is a strong interconnection between economics
and politics, and in governmental decisions it is often difficult to dis-
entangle the two. Finally, by way of confirmation of Wilson's attitude
towards the EEC, the Labour minister Richard Crossman suggests
that, by 1969, the Prime Minister was '*still* fanatically convinced of
the need to go in ... he clearly thinks it's right to do everything possible to get us into Europe'.[12]

Despite the constraints under which Wilson was initially obliged
to act, there is evidence to suggest that, from the outset, he carefully prepared the way for an eventual British application to join the
EEC. In this context, he appointed politicians as Foreign Secretary
who were supportive, to varying degrees, of British membership of
the EEC and he did nothing to discourage probing by ministers and
officials about attitudes within the EEC towards British membership.[13] One of Wilson's close associates, for example, recorded that:

> Douglas Jay [President of the Board of Trade and a staunch anti-
> Marketeer] ... warned that we must watch the Party's drift into the
> Common Market. The pressures that way were unrelenting, not
> only on the part of officials but also of George Brown [Secretary of
> State for Economic Affairs] who, despite the PM's warnings about
> talking to the press, had given a long interview to the *Guardian*
> implying that revisions of policy were going on.[14]

Wilson may have indeed created an impression of indifference about
membership of the Common Market, but he used the period up

until the general election of March 1966 to ensure that nothing was done which would stand in the way of Britain's formal move towards Europe by way of a second application, when he judged that the time to make it was right.

From the outset, bilateral contacts with the German government provided a pointer to the main features of British policy towards EEC membership. These were to express a definite but cautious interest and to use the support of Germany to overcome French opposition. Already in November 1964, Patrick Gordon Walker, the Foreign Secretary, told Gerhard Schröder, his German counterpart, that 'Britain considered itself as a part of Europe and, whilst it would be impossible to start negotiations when the risk of another veto existed, Germany could play an important role in future developments'.[15] The 'European question', as the Foreign Office described it, was one of several key issues that were to be discussed in March 1965 during Wilson's first visit to Bonn. As Wilson's brief suggested, 'the aim in these talks will be to establish a good personal relationship between the Prime Minister and the Chancellor' and, specifically on the European question, 'to re-affirm our desire to have a voice when decisions about the political and economic future of Europe are being considered ... we should leave the Germans in no doubt that we think it ... unwise to discuss European co-operation without Britain'.[16]

Whilst there was every likelihood that the aim of establishing a rapport between the two leaders would be achieved, there was real concern in London that the EEC might develop in ways contrary to Britain's interests. In particular, the talks between Chancellor Ludwig Erhard and Wilson exposed differences between the two sides about political union within Europe. As Helga Haftendorn strongly emphasised, 'From the standpoint of the Federal Republic, the European Community has always been three things: Common Market and Economic Community; multilateral framework for eliminating the Franco-German security conflict; and pioneer for a political union of Western Europe'.[17] On this last point, although Wilson advocated measures that would solve the problems caused by the 'present division of Europe between the Six and Seven' (respectively the EEC and the EFTA), he could not agree to 'supranational solutions'. In contrast, Erhard argued that his theory of a strong, supranational Europe 'called for a united Europe extending far beyond the Six'.[18] Nevertheless, according to Frank Roberts, the Ambassador in Bonn, the visit 'achieved undoubted success in consolidating Anglo-German relations' and, significantly in the context of a British move towards Europe based on a London–Bonn axis, 'the reaffirmation in the communiqué and during the talks of the importance of strengthening the links between EFTA (the European Free Trade Area) and the

EEC should also provide a helpful point of reference in future to help us to secure German support for any proposals we may decide to put forward'.[19]

In March 1966, with Labour ahead in the opinion polls, Wilson sought a new mandate. In his personal account, he refers only to two issues of major government policy that featured in the election campaign, the second of which was the Common Market (the first concerned negotiations with Ian Smith, the leader of the breakaway government of Rhodesia). According to Wilson, having dismissed in fairly derogatory terms opposition claims that the government had received encouragement from the French government 'for an enlarged Community to include Britain', he went on to insist that 'we will negotiate our way into the Common Market, head held high, not crawl in. And we shall go in if the conditions are right.'[20] Labour's election manifesto, *Time for Decision*, was only slightly more forth-coming on the EEC than the 1964 version, since, notwithstanding what might be viewed as its encouraging noises about Europe, Wilson could still not afford to expose the divisions within the Party during a campaign that was designed to exploit the reassuring signals that were coming from the opinion polls.[21]

In the event, Wilson's tactics were successful, but Europe as an issue failed to capture the imagination of the public. In a Gallup opinion poll taken once the result of the election was known, Labour's Common Market policy received no mention in the main reasons for the Party's victory, whilst only 1% of those asked believed that the Conservatives' policy on the Common Market – to work for entry at the first favourable opportunity – contributed to their defeat. However, in a further poll on the issue of Europe and the Common Market, the Conservatives achieved a clear majority among those asked to choose between the parties. That public opinion had clearly shifted, and would remain in favour of the Common Market, can be seen by the reaction to a poll in March 1966, in which 59% of those asked indicated that they would be in favour of Britain joining the EEC, a figure that by August had increased to 71%.[22] Wilson's clear mandate from the 1966 election, even though the EEC as an issue was not in the forefront of the campaign, and the strength of public opinion are cogent reasons why, *a fortiori*, the Prime Minister was able to be more overt henceforth about a strategy that from the outset can be seen as having been designed to take Britain into Europe.[23]

There were many positive signals about British intentions towards the EEC during the remaining months of 1966, leading up to a special meeting of the Cabinet in October at Chequers (see below), and Wilson's statement in the House in November in which he announced 'a new high-level approach ... to see whether the conditions exist ...

for fruitful negotiations'.[24] As one of his close associates commented, 'it looks to me as though he is right in thinking that there are reasonable chances of a new approach to Europe. As he sees it, the difficulties of staying outside Europe and surviving as an independent power are very great compared with entering on the right conditions.'[25] The first indication of a more overt interest in Europe came with the announcement of Wilson's new Cabinet after the March 1966 election and the appointment of George Thomson, a known pro-European, as the Chancellor of the Duchy of Lancaster with specific responsibility for European affairs, in support of the Foreign Secretary, Michael Stewart. Wilson explained to Parliament that Thomson was 'to seize every opportunity … to probe in a very positive sense, the terms on which we would be able to enter the European Economic Community'.[26] The pairing of Stewart and Thomson to spearhead Britain's Europe initiative, and the appointment of First Secretary George Brown to chair a new committee charged with examining the economic and social implications of Britain joining the EEC, brought a positive response from Bonn.[27] As Roberts was to report, 'the [German] Minister of Economics … noted with great interest and pleasure the new responsibilities … the Federal Government had long wanted British membership and they were now more than ever convinced it was a vital necessity.'[28]

Following a worsening economic situation in the summer of 1966, and the implementation of a package of deflationary measures designed to shore up the value of sterling, a package that stopped short of the devaluation that some members of Wilson's government and their advisers believed to be inevitable, and the ministerial reshuffle that took Brown to the Foreign Office, the way was cleared for the action that Roberts had pressed upon London.[29] As Wilson summarised the situation, 'we seemed to be drawing nearer to the point where we would have to take a decision about Europe, and George Brown seemed to me the appropriate leader for the task that might lie ahead'.[30] Although Wilson hints at other reasons behind the appointment, Brown's pivotal role in British policy on Europe is confirmed by Michael Palliser, Wilson's Principal Private Secretary for Foreign Affairs from 1966, who indicated that the Prime Minister was convinced that Britain should be a member of the EEC, and one reason for appointing Brown was because he believed that he was pro-European, and this would be an advantage.[31]

It was against this background that Wilson called a meeting of ministers at Chequers to discuss the outcome of the work that had gone on in committee on the question of closer relations with Europe and to agree the next steps. Although ministers agreed to Wilson's suggestion that he and the Foreign Secretary should visit

the six EEC capitals in order to take soundings about Britain's position, they were not asked at that stage to decide on an application
for membership. On this crucial point, Wilson remained cautious
and committed to his step-by-step strategy; he was intent on keeping his Cabinet together, although it contained anti-Marketeers, and
careful to ensure that a commitment to enter Europe would gain the
support of a majority of the Labour Party. On 10 November, Wilson
made his historic statement in the House. He announced the plan to
hold discussions with each of the heads of government of the Six and
insisted that 'the Government [was] approaching the discussions ...
with the clear intention and determination to enter [the] EEC if ...
our essential British and Commonwealth interests [could] be safeguarded'. To dispel any further doubt, Wilson added the words 'we
mean business'.[32] This commitment brought an immediate response
from Bonn. Roberts reported that State Secretary Rolf Lahr 'received
the news with great pleasure ... his government had done a great
deal of preparatory work ... Her Majesty's Government could rely on
the steady support and understanding of the Federal Government'.[33]

Britain and the EEC: 1967–70

The visits by Wilson and Brown to EEC capitals occupied the first
three months of 1967. Although the focus here will be on the visits to
Paris and Bonn, it is clear that the one common factor that emerged
from all the visits was, as Clive Ponting points out, that 'de Gaulle did
not want enlargement and ... the other five would not take him on'.[34]
In Paris, de Gaulle told Wilson that the participation of Britain in
the Community would present great problems in view of its different
economic interests, monetary arrangements and contacts with the
outside world. If Britain could not enter the Community, de Gaulle
invited the British to consider two alternatives: either something
entirely new, involving the dismantling of the EEC and making a
new arrangement to include Britain; or an agreement for association
between Britain and the Community. In offering these alternatives,
de Gaulle would have known that the former would not be acceptable
to other members of the EEC, even if Britain was favourably disposed,
and that with the latter, as Wilson said at the time, 'any form of
limited economic association could [not] generate the political unity
which lay at the heart of the decision he [Wilson] was seeking'.[35]

Given this background, there are grounds for questioning why
Wilson apparently found his talks with de Gaulle not wholly discouraging and why, as Crossman puts it, 'George and Harold both thought
that they had begun the major job of charming the General'.[36] In
emphasising time and time again that the whole character of the

Community would be changed by Britain's entry, de Gaulle clearly announced his opposition to a second application. However, for Wilson to back off before his other visits, or for him to have made public the doubts that he must have felt, would have placed Labour at an electoral disadvantage against a pro-Europe Conservative opposition, and ignored the grain of public opinion in favour of EEC membership. It would also have left Britain outside an increasingly influential and powerful political and economic bloc. Even more important was the fact that, without a leading role shaping the future of Europe, Britain ran the risk of isolation, forced to relinquish its commitments east of Suez and of diminished importance as an ally of the United States. The logical counter was to strengthen Britain's involvement in Europe through EEC membership, notwithstanding de Gaulle's opposition. As one prominent regional German newspaper suggested, 'London no longer has the alternative of a closer relationship with the USA ... Great Britain is turning inwards to Europe'.[37] Typical also of the advice that the Prime Minister had been getting from officials was that from Palliser, who, some months after the Paris visit, put it to Wilson that 'there are very strong reasons, in terms of major British interests, why we should keep up the maximum pressure consistent with avoiding the direct "non" and thereby begin the process ... of translating Western Europe into a force for world rather than simply continental influence'.[38]

From a British viewpoint, the visit to Germany was the most important of those to the other 'Five' that Wilson and Brown would make. Put simply, the British team had high hopes of a positive reaction from their German counterparts and a specific commitment of help. Wilson himself made clear the importance of Bonn to British strategy at the opening of his talks when he 'stressed that the outcome [of Britain's bid for entry] ... would depend to a great extent on the exercise of German influence in Paris'.[39] But to what extent could London count on Bonn to exercise its influence and what weight would this have with de Gaulle? Wilson's assumption that the Germans would help almost certainly stems from the cumulative effect of comments in favour of British membership of the EEC frequently made by German ministers and officials since October 1964, and the fact that a Britain fully committed to Europe would provide for Bonn a useful counterweight to French domination within the Community.[40] As to the likely effect of German influence, whilst Burke Trend, the Cabinet Secretary, advised the Prime Minister that the French held the key to Britain's entry to the EEC, he also argued that 'they are not likely to turn it in the direction we desire, except under very strong pressure and we must rely heavily upon pressures from the Five as well as our own to that end'.[41] The implication here was that, as the strongest economy within the EEC, and with a growing military capability, Germany could provide the lead that the remaining four members of the Five would almost certainly follow in bringing pressure to bear upon the French President.[42] However, as Willy Brandt was later to comment, 'Wilson came away [from Paris] under the misapprehension that a strong word from Germany was all that was needed to bring the General to his senses'.[43]

Nevertheless, there were mixed signals coming out of Bonn before the visit. On the one hand, Wilson faced the uncertainty of having to deal with a new German Chancellor, in the form of Kurt Georg Kiesinger. The latter, in a declaration made on 13 December 1966, confirmed not only that the EEC should be open to those European states prepared to accept its conditions of membership, but also that Germany would welcome the participation of Britain and other countries of EFTA in the Communities. He went on to confirm that Germany wanted to develop and strengthen its relationship with Britain. Despite these reassuring words, Kiesinger also stressed the importance of the understanding between Germany and France and how this was crucial for the future of Europe.[44] Despite these mixed signals, and on a positive note, Roberts reported that Lahr had said that Germany would be able to help. In Lahr's view, if Britain could quickly reach an understanding with the Five about the sort of terms that would be acceptable to them, it would be impossible for the French to frustrate the collective will. Although Roberts had no doubts about the sincerity of Lahr's belief and judged him to be 'the shrewdest and toughest judge of French intentions and tactics in the Community that the Germans can put in the field', he suggested that there were commercial interests that motivated German offers of help. The Germans would certainly see a strong advantage to them 'in our accession before the agricultural finance arrangements [were] finalised [i.e. in 1969], just as they have the strongest material reasons for not wanting the gulf between the EEC and EFTA to grow wider'. Roberts referred back to a conversation in which Lahr told the Chancellor of the Duchy of Lancaster that, 'in the event of her accession the United Kingdom would be bearing, together with Federal Germany, the heaviest financial burden. This made the prospect of our joining particularly attractive to the Germans.'[45] Just as Wilson's advisers were suggesting that membership of the EEC had become a major British interest, so senior German officials saw British membership as being very much in the interests of Germany.

Wilson's visit to Bonn occurred a few weeks after the new German Chancellor had travelled to Paris for talks with de Gaulle. According to Kiesinger, these talks had been designed to revive Franco-German relations, since, although it was apparent that Britain's entry into the EEC occupied a key part of the agenda, friendship with France remained central to Germany's interests.[46] Kiesinger claimed that there was considerable support in Germany, and particularly from German industry, for a way to be found which would enable Britain to become a member of the Common Market, although this had little to do with the question of Britain participating in a political union. He regretted that Britain had spurned the opportunity to join the EEC at the outset and at a time when it was better able than any other European country, in terms of the after-effects of the war, to provide the leadership that the rest of Europe needed. Whilst he doubted that Britain was ready for political integration, the German government would find it difficult to be associated with another veto if Britain was prepared to accept all the conditions of entry. Nevertheless, an indication of the extent and depth of the support that the Germans were prepared to give the British initiative was revealed when Kiesinger, confronted by de Gaulle's assertion that there was no possibility of Britain's entry into the EEC at the moment, accepted the position and merely commented that 'he had not come to Paris in order to try to persuade the General of the necessity of British entry into the Common Market', although he did make the point that 'the General could surely not expect him to oppose Britain's wish to join'.[47] Kiesinger's recorded comments in Paris seem at variance with his report to Roberts before Wilson's visit, when he said that he had told de Gaulle 'that for political as well as economic reasons the Federal Government wanted a wider EEC including above all British … membership'.[48] Whereas Roberts believed that Kiesinger 'had said what needed to be said in Paris at this stage',[49] it was evident that under this Chancellor, as Roberts had previously suggested about his predecessor, Germany would 'stop well short of any action which … would be likely to cause the French to leave the Community'.[50]

In his talks with Wilson and Brown, Kiesinger told the British ministers that:

> Germany wanted her support to be effective; she genuinely wanted to help, and to be firm in doing so, but she must manoeuvre with caution. It would be necessary for the German Government to discuss these matters very thoroughly with their French friends … but they must set about this carefully, not weakly but with wisdom and prudence.[51]

Kiesinger asked that the British show understanding if the Germans did not make any solemn public declaration, but said that they could be relied upon to do all in their power in Paris. In response to Brown's complaint that the British press believed that German government had been discouraging towards Britain, and that this would not help to maintain momentum behind the British initiative, Kiesinger said that whilst they could have announced that the French were the real obstacle, or that Britain should be brought into the Common Market at any cost, the only course was the one they were taking, namely that they were impressed by Britain's arguments, would support Britain's endeavours and would talk to the French in this spirit. In reply, Wilson pointed out that whilst German assurances were appreciated, there was a real danger that if Britain were to make a second formal application and were to be rebuffed, this would prove fatal, especially as there was pressure on the British government from both the pro and anti lobbies in the House of Commons. Wilson insisted that it was vital 'to maintain momentum while the German Government and others did what they could to reassure General de Gaulle'.[52]

Although Wilson and Brown left Kiesinger in no doubt about what they were expecting, it is significant that a German government spokesman, in a briefing to British press correspondents, confirmed that efforts would be made objectively to bring Britain into the Common Market but added that the Germans had agreed merely 'to exercise some influence on the French'.[53] This commitment was put into proper context by Brandt, the German Foreign Minister, when, during a press conference in Berlin, he observed that 'The Federal Government could not ... force its views on any other country'.[54] As Wilson later asserted in his memoirs, 'Then, and subsequently, we became increasingly convinced that he [Kiesinger] would never be prepared to press his undoubted conviction that Britain must be admitted to the Six to the point of annoying General de Gaulle'.[55] This was to develop into a point of frustration for the British government, although not to the extent that relations between London and Bonn were ever seriously impaired. As Brandt emphasised in April 1967, in an address to the Foreign Affairs Club in London, 'It would indeed be wrong if we were to let ourselves be misled into regarding occasional problems as a fundamental change in the good relations between our two countries'.[56]

Wilson and Kiesinger held two further bilateral meetings during 1967, either side of the formal decision announced on 2 May by the British government to make an application under Article 237 of the Treaty of Rome for membership of the EEC and parallel application for membership of the European Coal and Steel Community (ECSC) and EURATOM. In the first of their meetings in April, held when the two leaders were in Bonn for Konrad Adenauer's funeral, Wilson indicated that he intended to bring matters to a head by gathering members of his Cabinet for a meeting at Chequers to discuss all aspects of EEC membership. In economic terms, membership would involve a considerable cost, but Wilson believed there would be great benefits in the long run, and that an economically strong Europe would also underpin the political cohesion of Europe and facilitate negotiations with the Soviets. This was not the first time that Wilson pressed upon Kiesinger his opinion that a stronger Europe, meaning an enlarged EEC, would have greater leverage on the Soviet Union in terms of *détente* but his objective was almost certainly to remind the German Chancellor, and his SPD colleagues in the Grand Coalition, that such advantages could not be realised without Britain's membership.

By the time of the meeting at Chequers at the end of April, it had become clear to most if not all members of Wilson's Cabinet that the Prime Minister was anxious to get Britain into the EEC but, as he himself put it, 'To get through the Cabinet a proposal that Britain should apply for entry ... was a formidable task. To succeed and to produce a firm decision without any resignations seemed a near miracle.'[57] At Chequers, Wilson and his colleagues considered alternatives to EEC membership, including going it alone and forming an Atlantic Free Trade Area (AFTA) with the Americans, but it had become obvious even to most of the few members who opposed joining the EEC that neither of these options was viable and the movement in favour had become unstoppable.[58] After a further Cabinet meeting, on 2 May, it was agreed that Wilson would make a statement in the House that afternoon announcing Britain's intention to apply for EEC membership.[59]

There were very few signs during the period between Wilson's announcement and Kiesinger's visit to London in October for their second round of bilateral talks that British pressure would persuade the Germans to take a firm line with the French. On the contrary, it was evident that Kiesinger would not intervene on Britain's behalf, especially in the light of a statement by de Gaulle at a press conference just days after Wilson's announcement in the House, in which the President made it clear that, because of the position of sterling and the effect of Britain's overseas commitments on the development of the Market, the time was not right for British membership of the EEC, and to all intents and purposes indicated that any application by Britain would be vetoed. A dispute with France leading to paralysis within the Common Market and its institutions would be contrary to Germany's interests. But it is difficult to understand what realistically was expected of the Germans. Although there was a widely shared feeling on the British side that Kiesinger's unwillingness to stand up to de Gaulle was simply a rationalisation of his own weakness, and that he would not make the difficult choice that faced him unless he was forced to do so, such feeling was undoubtedly fuelled by frustration and took little account of the difficult position that the German Chancellor faced, caught between two immovable forces. As Palliser was to tell Wilson just days before the Chancellor's visit to London, 'There is, in fact, a good deal of force in Kiesinger's thesis that if we really drive the General into a corner, he will strike out ... then we shall have the categorical veto that it must surely be our objective to avoid'. In recommending patience and a refusal to take no for an answer, Palliser added for good measure that 'it is simply no good our telling Kiesinger that he ought to stand up ... to the General ... we shall not convince him; he will resent having his arm twisted'.[60]

Following two conversations with Kiesinger immediately before his visit to London, Roberts reported that the Germans, and the Chancellor in particular, were most anxious to avoid any show-down which could seriously damage Franco-German relations, and were vulnerable to the kind of pressures from Paris which they refused to exercise there themselves. The problem was that Kiesinger believed his tactics of persuasion were the only ones that were likely to succeed, and that as there was an absolute majority inside Europe and even a majority in France for British membership, he seemed convinced that de Gaulle could be brought round to accept the inevitable, but only if a bridge were built over which he could retreat. Although Roberts considered that there was little choice but to accept and make the best of the support that the German Chancellor was prepared to give, the Ambassador warned Kiesinger that 'while there was understanding and even sympathy for Germany's difficult position, there were sceptics and even critics'. Moreover, the public and informed opinion would be aware only of Kiesinger's public statements, not what might be said to the French in private, and would draw the conclusion that extreme solicitude was being shown for French susceptibilities, and 'this was something he should bear in mind for his public statements in London'.[61]

Wilson's exchanges with Kiesinger followed the lines that each had set out before their meeting. The German Chancellor was upbeat about the prospects for the British application, surprisingly so when de Gaulle had told the Germans a few months earlier that if the British could become real Europeans there would be no grounds for denying them membership of the Community but that 'this process [had] still some way to go'.[62] Kiesinger believed that the President must have realised the strength of the opposition within Europe to his political concepts and was convinced that only by the method he advocated could British membership of the EEC be achieved. Wilson was clearly unimpressed by Kiesinger's assessment of de Gaulle's position, especially since at his last meeting with the President he had derived no impression of any change. As soon became clear, Kiesinger had been too optimistic and, according to *Der Spiegel*, blamed Brandt for not keeping him properly informed.[63] Wilson could not resist hinting at threats, as he was prone to do with the Germans, pointing out that 'if this approach was disappointed there might be a reaction looking towards the search for other solutions'. Wilson emphasised that Britain's application for membership of the Communities was in and that a refusal would not be accepted. If Britain was excluded for some considerable time then '[it] should have to consider how to protect [its] own interests ... not excluding the offset arrangements and British forces in Continental Europe'.[64] Lord Chalfont, the Foreign Office minister with the disarmament portfolio (see Chapter 6), repeated this threat to journalists at the end of the EFTA conference at Lausanne, a few days after Kiesinger's visit. Although the resultant furore caused Chalfont to offer his resignation, Wilson declined to accept it on the basis that his minister had been misunderstood, but the real reason may have been that it was the Prime Minister himself who inspired the remarks.[65] Wilson was also involved in controversy over a report in *The Observer* of remarks he made during a press briefing at the end of Kiesinger's visit. According to that report, the German correspondent of the *Sud-deutsche Zeitung* claimed Wilson had said in effect that:

> Britain had ... a good relationship with the Soviet Union. So the Germans should just reflect for a moment about who could most effectively represent their vital interests ... they should reflect whether ... Moscow would pay more attention to France than to the combined voices of Britain and America.[66]

Reporting on the visit as a whole, *Der Spiegel*, known for its antipathy towards Kiesinger, suggested that 'London was not a really good place for Kiesinger.... In general the impression left by the visit was one of sadness and a certain resentment on Kiesinger's part.'[67]

Within days of Britain's move to devalue sterling, announced on 18 November, de Gaulle repeated his opposition to the British application. This was subsequently confirmed in December by the EEC Council of Ministers, on the basis that the British economy was not strong enough to satisfy the requirements of EEC membership. In the aftermath of this decision, Britain and Germany moved to maintain their consensus on Europe. On 22 December, the Foreign Office instructed Roberts to brief Brandt on British ideas on how to maintain the momentum that had developed behind the British application and to seek greater co-operation with the members of the EEC, other than France. These ideas stemmed from the Official Committee on the Approach to Europe, which had concluded that, on economic grounds, there was no alternative to seeking membership of the EEC as soon as the opportunity presented itself, and that in the meantime it would be advantageous if Britain were able to influence the Community and prevent it from developing in directions contrary to British interests, and therefore Britain should seek as close a consultation with the Five as they would allow.[68] As Brown was to tell the House:

> We, in turn, confirm that our application stands. We do not intend to withdraw it. We now propose to enter into consultations with those five members of the European Community which supported the Commission's view that negotiations should be started at an early stage.[69]

However, the need to move carefully and not to push the Germans too far or too hard quickly became apparent to Roberts after conversations with Brandt and his officials. Roberts emphasised to ministers that:

> it is quite clear that Brandt and the Ministry of Foreign Affairs ... will have great difficulty in persuading the Chancellor who sets great store by his meeting with ... de Gaulle in February ... we should be careful not to lay too heavy a burden on Brandt, who is certainly out to help ... we should hold back.[70]

Although Britain had again been denied membership of the EEC, this was seen in London as a temporary setback. Europe remained a focus of foreign policy and the importance of friendship with Germany had not diminished. Whereas Ponting, for example, suggests that Wilson's approach to membership of the EEC was political, in that 'although the negotiations did fail, he achieved his object of making the EEC a largely bipartisan issue and not a matter of controversy in 1970',[71] this was by no means the main reason why the Labour government remained overtly so committed to entering the Common Market even after the second veto. We have already touched upon the strong commercial reasons that motivated the British application and how these juxtaposed with geopolitical factors.[72] In January 1968, the position was made quite clear to ministers in a paper prepared by the Cabinet Office proposing foreign policy for the next three years.[73] This suggested that British priorities should be: to ensure that the two sides of the Atlantic Alliance remained connected; and, in Europe, to pay particular attention to keeping close to Germany. It also advanced the proposition that Britain's main foreign policy objective should be a continuous movement towards a more cohesive and stronger Europe. These proposals were embraced by a more detailed Foreign Office submission for Cabinet. In commenting on its proposals, Trend suggested to the Prime Minister that Britain could regain influence in world affairs by pressing to a successful conclusion membership of an enlarged EEC, and that it would be unwise, once

Britain had decided not to be a world power in the traditional sense, not to be a European power in the modern sense. For these reasons, Britain had to keep up pressure to join the EEC, and to aim for maximum cooperation with Germany; there was no realistic alternative.[74]

In the months following the second veto, no serious progress was made, although it could hardly be described as a period of inactivity. The British application remained on the table but, despite British anxiety to have German support for its proposals for consultations with the Five, and the German government's willingness to help as far as it could without detriment to its understanding with the French, differences quickly emerged about tactics. The situation was further complicated by an initiative suggested by the Benelux members of the EEC, under which there would be: consultation between the Community and applicant countries so as to facilitate the *rapprochement* and prevent divergence of their respective systems; common action between the European states in fields not covered by the Community Treaties; and progress in the field of political union through closer consultation on important issues.[75] However, as a brief for ministers on the post-veto situation made clear, whilst the Benelux proposals were compatible with British thinking on potential joint action with the Five, anything short of full membership would deny London a full voice in future Community decisions. Moreover, it would be an illusion to suggest that negotiations for associate membership would be any less complicated than those for full membership. In short, Britain could not 'regard anything short of full membership as meeting the urgent political requirements of Europe or the United Kingdom'.[76]

The German position, on the other hand, revealed considerable differences with British thinking and the Benelux proposals. In essence, Bonn considered that the various applications from other members of EFTA remained on the EEC agenda, since France had not opposed the proposed accessions in principle and had indicated that an interim alternative to full membership, with accession in prospect, could be considered. As far as the Germans were concerned, it was only when the question of whether Britain's accession was possible had been officially answered in the negative, and this would depend upon further discussions with Paris, that the German government would consider in what other ways the connection between Britain and EEC countries could be strengthened. What this outline of the respective positions shows is that whilst Britain was determined that it would not be side-tracked into actions that had no prospect of leading to full membership of the EEC, with the aim of ensuring that the EEC did not develop in ways that would make it more difficult for Britain to join later, the Germans remained anxious to move forward in step with the French and to avoid action that might lead to splits within the Six. Although the British Foreign Secretary was sceptical about the German ideas, he was to inform Brandt that he had 'no objections to the German Government exploring them' with the French.[77]

It was against this background of British scepticism and German optimism that, in February 1968, Kiesinger and Brandt travelled to Paris for talks with de Gaulle and his senior ministers. The French President sensed the political pressure on Kiesinger to agree to almost anything which might be interpreted as marking progress towards the future enlargement of the Communities, and which would be acceptable to the other members. He repeated that, although the French considered that Britain was neither politically nor economically ready to join the Communities, France had never been against eventual British accession. But in a situation where Britain, unlike the Six, had not made the sacrifices necessary for entry to the EEC, it was difficult to see what might be done to help. Kiesinger suggested that an agreement between France and Germany that would lead towards negotiations making it possible for Britain and the other countries to join the Common Market was very important. Naturally, much would depend upon Britain's reaction and whether London would maintain its 'all or nothing' attitude, but it should be possible to find a formula that would eventually lead to Britain's entry. Kiesinger emphasised that he was not suggesting something that would commit France to an agreed date for British entry, but his proposal for a formula to be found had been motivated by the recognition that public opinion in Europe wanted specific links with Britain, and on the German side by the wish to prevent institutionalised relations between the Five and Britain that would create a rift in Europe. He sought a way for the Six to remain in contact with Britain whilst the necessary developments could take place, and 'arrangements' which would help Britain put its house in order so that one day it might join the Six.[78]

The declaration that emerged from the Paris talks failed to impress the British.[79] As Lord Chalfont told German ministers:

> Britain ... believed from the start that the German soundings with the French would have no effect and that as the outcome in Paris showed the French had not changed their position ... whilst the French might say one thing to the Germans they were saying something quite different elsewhere.

Chalfont, unwilling as ever to hide his sentiments behind diplomatic niceties, emphasised that there was little time left, since in Britain public opinion had become noticeably disillusioned and the effect of French delaying tactics might force the Foreign Secretary to reassess his position on the EEC. Unless the Germans could come forward with positive proposals based on the Paris declaration that the Five and

Britain would find acceptable, then Britain would have to consider other options. As far as Britain was concerned, 'the Government did not believe that ... full membership would be brought any closer'.[80] The Germans, as Brandt subsequently made clear to Brown, believed that something positive could be made out of the Paris declaration, that the proposal for a customs union in particular could benefit the Six and the other European countries intending to join the Common Market, and that such an 'arrangement' was fully in accord with the conditions that Britain had set out for the interim period before entry (i.e. no association, no inferior status and not be bound by Community policies until entry had been secured).[81]

To some in the Foreign Office, it was Kiesinger who was perceived as the main culprit for Germany's failure to side with the British against the French. As Derek Day, Assistant Private Secretary to the Foreign Secretary, was to put it in a letter to Palliser, 'why don't we start putting the fear of God into Kiesinger? In view of their vulnerable position and early election, we should start playing German politics.' Day went on to argue, in an obvious reference to the offset negotiations, that there would be little point in threatening the Germans with troop withdrawals because 'we keep our troops on the European continent not only to defend Germany, but also to defend ourselves and because it would be very difficult for us to put them anywhere else'. The conclusions that Day drew were that 'we should not disguise from them what the implications would be for a failure on their part to help us into Europe ... but if the stick is wielded, we think that the Prime Minister himself may be the best person to wield it when he goes to Bonn'.[82]

There is little if any evidence to suggest that Wilson acted upon this sort of advice, although it may have been in the back of his mind in November 1968, when he called Herbert Blankenhorn, the German Ambassador, to Downing Street for the infamous late night meeting.[83] Such action, whereby Wilson now linked troop withdrawals with Germany's failure to revalue the mark, was hardly likely to impress Bonn. As Crossman later argued, 'it was one of the most ludicrous pieces of misjudgement ... who are we to threaten the Germans ... if we are seeking to get into Europe, to placate the Germans and win them to our side against the French, why play into the French hands'.[84]

Wilson was more adroit in his handling of the so-called 'Soames affair' in February 1969, just days before his visit to Bonn for talks with Kiesinger. In his account of a conversation between de Gaulle and Christopher Soames, British Ambassador to Paris, Wilson suggested that the former's ideas of a reinstitutionalisation in Europe – in which NATO would disappear and the EEC would be replaced by an enlarged European Association led by a small inner council of Britain, France, West Germany and Italy – were no more than 'a reassertion of the words he had used ... in the Elysée in January 1967 when he had suggested two alternatives ... something entirely new or an agreement – an association'.[85] Uncertainty still surrounds the motives of the French President in his apparent frankness with the British Ambassador. Was it an attempt to get support for his wish to substitute France for the United States as the principal influence in Europe, or was it a rather clever attempt, as Uwe Kitzinger speculates, to 'steer French policy into the curve which finally led to the Treaty of Accession [for Britain]?'[86] Whatever the case, although Wilson claimed that he was reluctant to raise the matter with Kiesinger during their talks, he acknowledged that to fail to do so would allow de Gaulle to 'make capital out of that, and succeed in convincing Dr Kiesinger that we were flirting with anti-EEC moves in Paris while supporting EEC legitimacy in Bonn'.[87] Whilst there is nothing to suggest that Wilson saw benefit in adding to the strains within the Six, the official record of the talks shows that he gave Kiesinger a full account of de Gaulle's remarks and took the opportunity that the situation offered to assert that 'the British Government wanted to strengthen both NATO and the EEC: they wanted to join the European Community not to bury it'. A further example of how Wilson exploited this incident can be seen in his thinly veiled criticisms of the Germans when he suggested that 'on two major issues since the French veto ... Germany stood with France ... not with the four' and when he asserted that 'there was a minority in the United Kingdom which thought in anti-German terms ... [but] the British Government did their best to combat this line of thought'.[88]

Nevertheless, the outcome of the visit did serve to underline positive aspects of the relationship between Britain and Germany. Instead of the usual communiqué, the two leaders issued a joint Anglo-German declaration:

> affirming the two countries' determination to go forward in partnership, challenging the Gaullist position on Europe, reaffirming that the security of Europe depended on the Atlantic Alliance and pledging both governments to further the aims of Britain's joining the European Economic Communities.[89]

After Wilson's visit, an article published in *The Times* (and noted by the German Embassy) suggested that:

> closer relations with Germany were very much in Britain's interests and not just for the short-term aim of membership of the EEC – Wilson had obviously tried hard to ensure that relations

were not impaired and the British Government at last recognised that empty threats to withdraw the Rhine Army achieved nothing and served only to undermine the credibility of Britain's commitment to Europe.[90]

Anglo-German relations and the EEC

By 1970 the political situation in Western Europe had changed. De Gaulle was no longer President of France, Brandt had replaced Kiesinger as German Chancellor and the six members of the EEC had agreed to start negotiations later in the year with the British government about accession.[91] In the context of Labour's policy of seeking German support for its application, it is significant that it was the German Chancellor who, according to British diplomats attending the EEC summit meeting at the Hague on 1 December 1969, 'spoke well ... [and emphasised] that without Britain and other countries desirous of entry, Europe [could] not become what it could and should be'.[92] During his visit to London in March 1970, Brandt commented that 'the Federal Government [had] ... energetically supported the British application for entry and [would] continue to do so'.[93] What this comment left unstated, however, was that German support had always been conditional, in that it would never be at the expense of Germany's relations with France. As Brandt later explained, 'even in retrospect ... it cannot be forgotten how firmly the French leadership intended to keep Britain at a distance ... [and] we wanted to observe the rules and not have one claim to leadership replaced by another'.[94]

Britain's approach to Europe as it developed over the years of the Labour governments is one of the most fascinating aspects of British contemporary history. Wilson has been criticised for his attempts to take Britain into the EEC when, for all the time that de Gaulle remained President of France, there was no prospect of the move succeeding.[95] Even a strategy based on enlisting German support did not persuade the French. The Germans would simply not endanger the Franco-German alliance and would not risk undermining the EEC that a split with France might cause. In that sense, British policy was a failure. On the other hand, there were good reasons for the policy that Britain followed. With the economy in decline, with Britain's armed forces overstretched and with the need to avoid international isolation, the attractions of a deeper involvement in the economic and political development of Europe, which membership of the EEC would bring, were very real. It is also tempting to suggest that the timing of Britain's second application was wrong.[96] However, in 1966, when the Labour government openly stated its commitment to seek membership of the EEC, there was no indication that the main obstacle to Britain's entry, namely President de Gaulle, would have faded from the scene by the end of the decade. In any event, waiting was not a realistic option in circumstances where Britain needed to redefine its role in the world, given the plans to accelerate withdrawal from Empire, given the obvious inadequacies of EFTA as a viable alternative, and with the pressures from business and public opinion for government action.[97] Moreover, if the Labour government failed to give the lead that Britain needed, the opportunity to do so would have been exploited by the Conservative opposition, with consequential electoral benefit. Indeed, as Sir Con O'Neill, Britain's senior diplomat at the negotiations on Britain's application, confirms, 'there was no discontinuity between this application and its success, or between the policy of the successive British administrations which made it, and which converted it through negotiations, into the Accession Treaty signed in Brussels on 22 January 1972'.[98] Thus, the move to establish Britain as a strategic, political and economic force within the EEC, whilst retaining long-standing links with the United States and the Commonwealth, and to do so on the back of a close relationship with Germany, was the obvious and best option at the time; and it is worth noting that the French veto delayed progress towards entry negotiations for only some two years. Despite its failure, Labour's policy did demonstrate Britain's commitment to a future in Europe, however that might be interpreted over the longer term, and it left Britain well placed to move forwards to membership of the EEC once de Gaulle had resigned.

The other element of Britain's European policy, that of cementing relations with Germany, could hardly be construed as a failure. There were strains and frustrations caused by the inability of Germany to force Britain's claim to EEC membership, but Wilson and his ministers were well aware of the limitations on what the Germans could do and, in any event, had little interest in causing a damaging rift between de Gaulle and Germany, or between de Gaulle and other members of the EEC. The EEC as an issue was therefore unlikely to undermine Britain's efforts made both before and after October 1964 to remain close to the Germans. Indeed, as Wilson pointed out in early 1970:

> memories of the past have taken a long time to fade away in the public mind but I believe this has at last happened. More than one of our serious newspapers have commented both at the time of Brandt's visit and since Brandt's departure that Anglo-German relations are at their highest point.[99]

Notes

1 John W. Young, *Britain and European Unity 1945–1999* (2000), p. 82. Other historians support Young's claim. For example, Ponting argues that 'the issue

virtually disappeared from British politics after de Gaulle's veto and Wilson
showed no interest in reviving it before the 1964 election'. See Ponting, *Breach
of Promise*, p. 205. Holland asserts that 'As for Europe, the evidence suggests
that on entering office the Labour Government had no intention whatsoever
of renewing the previous application to join the organisation of the Six'. See
Robert Holland, *The Pursuit of Greatness 1900–1979* (1991), p. 321.

2 Wallace, *Foreign Policy*, p. 86. See also for example Young, *Britain and European
Unity*, p. 88; Ben Pimlott, *Harold Wilson* (1992), p. 397; and Peter Paterson,
Tired and Emotional: The Life of Lord George Brown (1993), p. 234.

3 Vital, *The Making of British Foreign Policy*, p. 109.

4 In his description of British governments' approach to Europe, Wallace
refers to the Conservative government's approach beginning 'shortly after
the 1959 election' and to a 'slow and gradual shift in policy' resulting in 'the
decision to open negotiations ... on 31 July 1961'. He goes on to argue that
'The Labour Party's approach to Europe followed a similarly winding path'.
See Wallace, *Foreign Policy*, p. 85. Similarly, one newspaper reported that in a
meeting with Dr Luns, the Dutch Foreign Minister, the new British Foreign
Secretary, Patrick Gordon Walker, 'closed no doors on British participation
in the talks between the Six of the Common Market on political integration'
and had told him 'that he attached a priority to the principle of continuity'.
See 'Britain May Join Europe Talks', *The Times*, 21 October 1964.

5 Interview material. According to Michael Palliser, Wilson's Private Secretary,
'our key objective of that period ... was to get more active support from
Germany for our membership of the EEC'.

6 John Dickie, *Inside the Foreign Office* (1992), p. 98.

7 Craig, *British General Election Manifestos*, p. 56.

8 Political memoirs of members of Wilson's Cabinet vary in their criticisms of
the Prime Minister. One describes him as 'terribly canny as PM, he never
wants to commit himself unless he has to, and when he must he does it with
great reluctance'. See Crossman, *The Diaries: Volume 3*, diary entry for 13
November 1969, p. 730. Another asserts that 'Harold Wilson, however, failed
to give the Government that sense of direction which only a prime minister
can impart'. See Healey, *Time of My Life*, p. 345. And Crosland, in a more
colourful vein, comments that 'the trouble with Harold is one hasn't the
faintest idea whether the bastard means what he says even at the moment he
speaks it'. Quoted in Ponting, *Breach of Promise*, p. 402.

9 Aufzeichnung über Premierminister Wilson, 25 April 1966, B31/299, PAAA
Berlin. Similarly, Willy Brandt, former German Chancellor, refers to respect-
ing Wilson as 'a man who not only acted on Bismark's dictum that politics
is the art of the possible, but did so with vigorous pragmatism and a well-
developed feeling for the art of the opportune'. See Willy Brandt, *People and
Politics: The Years 1960–1975* (1978), p. 162.

10 Moravcsik, *The Choice for Europe*, p. 175. Cairncross also highlights the effect of
trade patterns when he refers to 'the change in the direction of British trade
helped to move the government to seek entry to the European Community
in 1961 and was an even more powerful influence on the second occasion in
1967'. See Cairncross, *Managing the British Economy*, p. 21.

11 See Young, *The Labour Governments 1964–70: Volume 2*, p. 159.

12 Crossman, *The Diaries: Volume 3*, diary entry for 10 February 1970, p. 812.
Emphasis added.

13 Barbara Castle was clearly becoming concerned about the government's
policy towards the Common Market. Her diary reveals comments in Cabinet
to the effect that 'Every day we read accounts in the press of this or that

development in our policy of which most of us in Cabinet knew nothing. Was it true for instance that we were now making overtures to the Common Market Six?' Castle, *Diaries*, diary entry for 18 March 1965, p. 20.

14 *Ibid.*, p. 33.

15 Gespräch – Schröder mit Gordon Walker, 15 November 1964, *AAPD* (1964), II, p. 1315.

16 See draft steering brief, 26 February 1965, PREM 13/329, PRO.

17 Haftendorn, *Security and Detente*, p. 13.

18 Record of a meeting between the Prime Minister and the Federal Chancellor, 7 March 1965, PREM 13/329, PRO.

19 Comments by Roberts, 2 April 1965, PREM 13/329, PRO.

20 Wilson, *The Labour Government*, p. 218.

21 Labour's manifesto, as admitted, contained 'no clear commitment ... to European entry'. See Crossman, *The Diaries: Volume 1*, diary entry for 4 March 1966, p. 470. The manifesto simply referred to Labour believing that 'Britain, in consultation with her EFTA partners, should be ready to enter the European Economic Community, provided essential British and Commonwealth interests are safeguarded'. See Craig, *British General Election Manifestos*, p. 98. Crossman also confirmed that 'the polls agree that Labour still leads by eight points ... the fact remains that Labour are still in the ascendant, the public think that everything is decided'. See Crossman, *Diaries: Volume 1*, diary entry for 27 March 1966, p. 483.

22 See Gallup, *Gallup International: Volumes 1 and 2*. On the difficulties in assessing public opinion and extrapolating figures from Gallup polls, see Anne Deighton, 'The Labour Party, Public Opinion and the "Second Try" in 1967', in Oliver Daddow (Ed), *Harold Wilson and European Integration: Britain's Second Application to Join the EEC* (2003), pp. 49–51.

23 Wilson's mandate and the strength of public opinion were not the only reasons for a more overt EEC strategy. With the ending of confrontation of Indonesia, the break in the link between American support for sterling in return for a British commitment to retain a military presence east of Suez, and recognition of the limits on British power demonstrated by the Rhodesian crisis, Wilson's government increasingly came to believe that ultimately Britain's interests would be best served by the political and economic advantages of membership of the EEC (see Introduction and Chapter 1). Young supports this line of reasoning when he argues that 'if there is a fundamental reason why Labour turned towards EEC membership it is probably the fact that there seemed no viable alternative. The Commonwealth was bitterly divided over Rhodesia, US President Johnson showed no desire to treat Wilson as a real partner, and in 1967, by agreeing to abandon its bases "East of Suez" the British Government also accepted its demise as a world power.' See Young, *Britain and European Unity*, p. 96.

24 *Hansard*, House of Commons, 735 (10 November 1966), col. 1539.

25 Crossman, *Diaries: Volume 1*, diary entry for Friday 18 February 1966, p. 461.

26 Wilson, *The Labour Government*, pp. 219–220. The Prime Minister's statement drew favourable comment from *The Times*: 'Whatever the Government may now say about some of their unenthusiastic electoral statements a new phase is opening for Britain's relations with Europe ... the Government have been wise to place their cards on the table from the outset and to examine the difficulties before making a formal application.' See 'When and On What Terms?', *The Times*, 12 May 1966, p. 12.

27 Brown's commitment to EEC membership is widely recorded. See for example Paterson, *Tired and Emotional*, p. 234.

28 Telegram number 95, Roberts to the Foreign Office, 2 May 1966, 1051/66
    (Vol. II), FO 1108/4, PRO. In parallel, Roberts' counterpart in London,
    Herbert Blankenhorn, reported the new appointments and suggested that
    there would now be a stronger emphasis on Britain's policy towards Europe.
    Umbildung der britischen Regierung, 6 April 1966, B31/298, PAAA Berlin.

29 It is beyond the scope of this book to dwell on the balance of payments prob-
    lems that forced the government to introduce the package of deflationary
    measures in July 1966, but a relevant account of the crisis and the reac-
    tion of the triumvirate of Wilson, Callaghan and Brown to it can be found
    in Cairncross, *Managing the British Economy*, pp. 150–154. Cairncross also
    observes that 'it is often suggested that devaluation should have accom-
    panied the measures … that might have been preferable to November 1967.
    Alternatively it would have been possible to couple a devaluation with the
    second application for entry to the European Community.' *Ibid.*, p. 274.

30 Wilson, The *Labour Government*, p. 272.

31 Interview material. Palliser also claims that 'I think on reflection that even
    back in 1964 he [i.e. Wilson] was wondering about membership of the EEC.'
    We have already touched upon Brown's pro-European credentials – see note
    27. Although there was a suggestion that the government's decision to take an
    initiative on Europe was Brown's 'price for staying in the Government' – see
    Pimlott, *Harold Wilson*, p. 436 – and Crossman talked about having to 'get Harold
    to capture the European initiative … from George Brown' – see Crossman,
    *The Diaries of a Cabinet Minister: Volume 2: Lord President of the Council and Leader of
    the House of Commons 1966–68* (1976), diary entry for 7 November 1966, p. 113
    – it is hardly credible that such an important economic and geopolitical deci-
    sion could be driven by someone other than the Prime Minister. Support for
    this line of reasoning comes from Cynthia Frey, who asserts that 'Going into
    Europe was 90 per cent the Prime Minister's decision … [although] no minor
    role was played by George Brown' – see Cynthia W. Frey, 'Meaning Business:
    The British Application to Join the Common Market, November 1966–October
    1967', *Journal of Common Market Studies*, 6, 3 (March 1968), p. 199.

32 Crossman claims to have had several conversations with Wilson about Europe
    during November 1966 in which he pressed the Prime Minister to take firm
    action to clarify government policy. See Crossman, *Diaries: Volume 2*, diary
    entries for 3, 7 and 9 November 1966, pp. 105, 113 and 117. For Wilson's
    statement in the House, see *Hansard*, House of Commons, 735 (10 November
    1966), col. 1540.

33 Telegram number 1615, Roberts to the Foreign Office, 10 November 1966,
    ER/421/1966 (Vol. I), EW 5/8, PRO.

34 Ponting, *Breach of Promise*, p. 209. This outcome was predicted by Barbara
    Castle, Wilson's Minister for Transport, who advised the Prime Minister that
    'de Gaulle was determined not to have us in and that the Five would not be
    willing to risk disrupting the Market by defying him'. See *Diaries*, diary entry
    for 19 January 1967, p. 211.

35 See record of meetings held in Paris, 24–25 January 1967, PREM 13/1707,
    PRO. De Gaulle's suggestion of a new arrangement with Britain and the
    dismantling of the EEC was what Wilson had in mind when he mentioned
    the 'Soames affair' to the German Chancellor in February 1969. See Harold
    Wilson's account in *The Labour Government*, p. 610.

36 Crossman, *Diaries: Volume 2*, diary entry for 26 January 1967, p. 212.

37 'Europäische Zusammenarbeit', *Westfalen Zeitung*, 15 November 1967, p. 1.

38 Note to the Prime Minister on 'British Foreign Policy' by Michael Palliser,
    7 July 1967, PREM 13/2636, PRO. Palliser also suggested that the longer

de Gaulle 'can delay our entry the better chance he has of making us fall between the two stools – of Anglo-American–Commonwealth cooperation and Europe – either to kick us while we are down or graciously to help us to our feet – subject of course to swingeing conditions'.

39 Wilson, *The Labour Government*, p. 367.

40 See for example telegram number 1615, Roberts to the Foreign Office, 10 November 1966, ER/421/1966 (Vol. I), EW 5/8, PRO. Also relevant is the result from a Gallup international enquiry simultaneously undertaken for the *Daily Telegraph* among the leaders of commerce, industry and administrative affairs in five of the six EEC states, which showed the Germans (98% of those asked wanted Britain to join) as the most enthusiastic about British entry into the EEC. See *Daily Telegraph*, 24 October 1966, p. 6.

41 Letter from Burke Trend to the Prime Minister, 21 May 1966, C47A/2, CAB 165/151, PRO.

42 *Ibid.* It is relevant to note the advice to Wilson included the suggestion that 'the danger of German predominance on the Continent, whether militarily or economically' was one of the several concerns Britain shared with the French.

43 Willy Brandt, *My Life in Politics* (1992), p. 420.

44 Chancellor's Kiesinger's declaration, 13 December 1966, in Oberländer, *Dokumente zur Deutschlandpolitik*, p. 67.

45 Letter from Roberts to Con O'Neill, 17 November 1966, 1051/66, 1051/66 (Vol. VI), FO 1108/8, PRO.

46 There is little doubt about Kiesinger's point that the main purpose of the visit to Paris was to revive relations with the French – not only had there been the crisis within NATO caused by the withdrawal of the French from the military organisation but problems had also surfaced within the EEC after the so-called 'empty chair crisis', which had only been resolved during 1966 by means of 'the Luxembourg compromise'. In an article entitled 'West Germans Are Reported Not Completely Convinced of London's Readiness', one newspaper claimed that 'West Germany is not ready to press France to admit Britain … the question has now become more closely linked with the question of Franco-German relations. The new Government in Bonn has placed heavy emphasis on rekindling friendship with France.' See *New York Times*, 10 January 1967.

47 Gespräch des Bundeskanzlers Kiesinger mit Staatspräsident de Gaulle, 13 January 1967, *AAPD* (1967), I, pp. 93–94. Doubts about Kiesinger's firmness in dealing with de Gaulle surfaced in the British press. The Bonn correspondent of *The Economist* suggested that whilst 'the Kiesinger–Brandt coalition could plainly count on wide popular backing should it come to a conflict with France about letting Britain into the European community … there is reason for believing that he [Kiesinger] let it be known … that he shared some of the French president's misgivings'. *The Economist*, 21 January 1967.

48 Telegram number 106, Roberts to Foreign Office, 16 January 1967, ER/421/1966, EW 5/8, PRO. Brandt had been very reassuring in advance of the Paris talks when he said that 'I can assure you that the Federal Government stood firmly by the declaration of support for British entry … this would be made clear to the French'. Telegram number 77, Roberts to Foreign Office, 12 January 1967, ER/421/1966, EW 5/8, PRO.

49 Telegram number 106, Roberts to Foreign Office, 16 January 1967, ER/421/1966, EW 5/8, PRO.

50 Letter from Roberts to Sir Con O'Neill, 27 June 1966, ER/421/1966, EW 5/8, PRO.

51 Meeting between the Prime Minister and Foreign Secretary and the Federal German Chancellor and Foreign Minister, 16 February 1967, PREM 13/1708, PRO.
52 *Ibid.*
53 Telegram number 315, Roberts to Foreign Office, 16 February 1967, ER/421/1966, EW 5/8, PRO.
54 Telegram number 92, British Commandant Berlin to Foreign Office, 3 March 1967, ER/421/1966, EW 5/8, PRO.
55 Wilson, *The Labour Government*, p. 368. In a memorandum to the Cabinet summarising the outcome of their visits to the European capitals, Wilson and Brown commented that 'we have never expected that, given the importance which the present German Government attaches to mending Franco-German fences, they would be prepared to exert any intense pressure on the French in favour of British membership'. See 'The Approach to Europe', March 1967, PREM 13/1478, PRO.
56 Address by the German Federal Minister for Foreign Affairs, 12 April 1967, B31/307, PAAA Berlin.
57 Wilson, *The Labour Government*, p. 387.
58 The point about alternatives to the EEC is taken up by Frey, who claims that 'the addresses by Wilson at the Guildhall, Callaghan during the debate in the House of Commons in May, and Brown before the Western European Union in July, all signal recognition that Britain cannot go on resisting Europe and the environment that sustains the European Community'. See Frey, 'Meaning Business', p. 230.
59 In his statement, Wilson was careful to say 'let no one think … that there is no other course for Britain except entry'. But he went on to assert that 'although there will be those who … will urge upon us the acceptance of new economic groupings … the House must recognise that this is not a current alternative. With all the choices open to us … this is the right choice, the right decision to make.' *Hansard*, House of Commons, 746 (8 May 1967), cols 1096–1097.
60 Note from Michael Palliser to the Prime Minister, 21 October 1967, PREM 13/1527, PRO.
61 Telegrams numbers 1397 and 1403, Roberts to Foreign Office, 19 October 1967, PREM 13/1527, PRO.
62 Deutsch–Franzosische Regierungsbesprechung, 13 July 1967, *AAPD* (1967), II, p. 1067.
63 'Sehr Eilig', *Der Spiegel*, 30 October 1967.
64 Record of meetings between the Prime Minister and the Chancellor of the Federal Republic of Germany, 23–25 October 1967, PREM 13/1527, PRO.
65 This assertion is suggested by Crossman, who comments either that Chalfont is an 'incredibly inexperienced journalist turned politician or that someone isn't telling the truth'. See Crossman, *Diaries: Volume 2*, diary entry for 31 October 1967, p. 543. Crossman also claims that at the dinner for Kiesinger there was 'a little bit of vague rumbling by George and Harold that we must have a fallback position, we can't stand for ever here. We must be prepared to let the EEC feel that our being kept out would be very damaging to them.' *Ibid.*, p. 542.
66 Extract from *The Observer* (29 October 1967) referred to in a letter from Derek Day, Assistant Private Secretary to the Secretary of State at the Foreign Office, to Michael Palliser, 8 November 1967, PREM 13/1527, PRO.
67 'Das ist so wichtig, so wichtig', *Der Spiegel*, 30 October 1967.

68 'Consequences of United Kingdom Exclusion from the EEC', 11 December 1967, EC 1/3/1/5, FCO 20/10, PRO.
69 *Hansard*, House of Commons, 756 (20 December 1967), cols 1267–1269.
70 Telegram number 13, Roberts to Foreign Office, 3 January 1968, EC 1/3/1/5, FCO 20/10, PRO.
71 Ponting, *Breach of Promise*, p. 214.
72 See note 10.
73 'British Foreign Policy for the Next Three Years', 14 January 1968, PREM 13/2636, PRO.
74 Burke Trend to Prime Minister, 26 February 1968, PREM 13/2636, PRO.
75 Brief for Minister's visit to the International Green Week Exhibition in Berlin, January 1968, EC 1/3/1/5, FCO 20/10, PRO.
76 Brief: Europe post-veto, January 1968, EC 1/3/1/5, FCO 20/10, PRO.
77 Note for Secretary of State, 24 January 1968, EC 1/3/1/5, FCO 20/10, PRO.
78 Deutsch–franzosische Konsultationsbesprechung, 15 February 1968, *AAPD* (1968), I, p. 195.
79 The Paris declaration, 16 February 1968, *AAPD* (1968), I, pp. 193–196.
80 Discussion involving Duckwitz and Lahr with Lord Chalfont, 22 February 1968, *AAPD* (1968), I, p. 239. Chalfont was also correct in his assessment that British public opinion was swinging against the Common Market. In February 1968, only 33% of those asked in a Gallup poll believed that the government should do its best to keep alive the question of Britain entering the Common Market; in subsequent Gallup polls up until the general election in June 1970 a majority of those asked opposed applying for membership. See Gallup, *Gallup International: Volume 2*, pp. 968–1134.
81 Brandt an Brown, 26 February 1968, *AAPD* (1968), I, pp. 262–267.
82 Letter from Day to Palliser, 11 October 1968, PREM 13/2627, PRO.
83 See Chapter 3, note 92.
84 Crossman, *Diaries: Volume 3*, diary entry for 26 November 1968, p. 273.
85 Wilson, *The Labour Government*, p. 610.
86 Uwe Kitzinger, *Diplomacy and Persuasion: How Britain Joined the Common Market* (1973), p. 37.
87 Wilson, *The Labour Government*, p. 610.
88 Record of a meeting between the Prime Minister and the Federal German Chancellor, 12 February 1969, PREM 13/2675, PRO.
89 *DBPO III I*, p. 119, fn. 11.
90 Telegram number 330, London to Bonn, 17 February 1969, B31/370, PAAA Berlin, and see *The Times*, 15 February 1969, p. 10.
91 Agreement on the principle of enlargement was reached at the Hague summit meeting of EEC leaders in December 1969. As Derek Urwin puts it: 'the Hague summit was the most significant event within the Community since its inception. It opened the way to enlargement of the club, set down pointers for the development of common policies, reaffirmed a faith in ultimate political integration, and was an augury of the new style of decision making that would develop in the 1970s.' See Derek W. Urwin, *The Community of Europe: A History of European Integration since 1945* (1991), p. 138. At a meeting between Wilson and Brandt in London, Wilson paid tribute to 'the decisions taken at The Hague in which Herr Brandt had played such a prominent role'. See record of the first meeting, 2 March 1970, PREM 13/3222, PRO.
92 Telegram number 605, The Hague to FCO, 1 December 1969, PREM 13/2631, PRO.
93 Federal Chancellor's reply to the greetings of the Lord Chancellor, 3 March 1970, 2 March 1970, PREM 13/2631, PRO.

94 Brandt, *My Life,* p. 420.
95 See for example Jeffreys, *The Labour Party*, p. 78.
96 See Katharine Böhmer, '"We Too Mean Business": Germany and the Second British Application to the EEC, 1966–67', in Oliver J. Daddow (ed.), *Harold Wilson and European Integration: Britain's Second Application to Join the EEC* (2003), p. 222.
97 See Tony Judt, *Postwar: A History of Europe since 1945* (2005), p. 307, for supporting comment about the limitations of EFTA as a genuine alternative to the EEC.
98 David Hannay (ed.), *Britain's Entry into the European Community: Report on the Negotiations of 1970–72 by Sir Con O'Neill* (2000), p. 9.
99 Telegram number 544, text of a message from Wilson to President Nixon, 5 March 1970, PREM 13/3222, PRO.

Conclusion

The years between 1964 and 1970 are often considered as a period crucial in British post-war history, as a period when Britain faced the consequences of the loss of Empire and of increasing international economic competition. For the Labour governments under Harold Wilson, the challenges were immense: managing an economy beset by serious balance of payments problems, with all the implications this held for Britain's world position; preserving Britain's nuclear status, after intimating that it should be abandoned and, at the same time, preventing the spread of nuclear weapons; maintaining the viability of the Atlantic Alliance and the coherence of its nuclear strategy; fostering a *détente* with the Soviet Union that would reduce tension without undermining the security of either Britain or its partners in NATO; and, above all, establishing a new role for Britain in the world based on becoming a leading member of the EEC. A common factor in all of these aspects of foreign policy was the priority given to Europe, which, it has been contended here, was facilitated by Britain's relationship with Germany. As Michael Stewart later put it, in the context of Britain's approach to Europe: 'It was, of course, British policy to reach a close understanding with Germany'.[1]

The subject of Britain's relations with Germany has held a certain fascination for historians and political observers, and continues to do so. Historians have often seen the Anglo-German relationship as fundamental in shaping European and world history.[2] Whilst this would be a generalisation too far if applied to the Wilson years, the discussion in this book has shown that both London and Bonn attached considerable importance to their bilateral relationship, specifically worked to ensure that it held good, and that moving towards a common position on European policy was a key factor in their understanding. What has been done here to underpin this assessment is to set the Anglo-German relationship in a multilateral context, involving France, the Soviet Union and the United States, and to make extensive use of official documents covering the entire period, both British and German, released under each country's thirty-year rule. This approach has enabled a more critical view to be formed of the period as a whole, of the bilateral contacts between Britain and Germany across a wide spectrum of foreign policy issues, and of the actions and motivations of the principals involved.

There can be little doubt that by the time the Labour government took office in October 1964, relations between Britain and Germany had recovered after the difficult situation caused by the ill feeling between Harold Macmillan and Konrad Adenauer. There were, after all, good reasons why a sound relationship was in the interest of both countries. Britain was one of the four powers with special responsibility for Germany and Berlin, the British army was deployed in strength on German territory and formed part of the ultimate guarantee for the security of Germany, both were allies in NATO, and Britain was potentially a useful ally in the quest for a solution to the German problem. Seen from a British perspective, it made sense for Britain to have as its partner a Germany that had developed into a major economic and military force within Europe, and it would make even more sense for this partnership to form the bedrock of any second bid by Britain for membership of the EEC, when the time to make it was deemed right. The final seal of approval on the course of Anglo-German relations, and the improvement that had set in after the Macmillan–Adenauer era, can be judged in the context of the visit by the Queen to Germany made in May 1965, barely twenty years after the end of the Second World War. As the Queen herself told the audience at her state reception in Bonn, 'my presence here this evening is proof of the good relations between our peoples'.[3]

Nevertheless, a Wilson-led government was viewed with some apprehension within Germany. The Prime Minister had not endeared himself to the Germans during and immediately after the general election, with his perceived anti-German rhetoric, and by the suspicion that he was Germanophobic. He also led a party that had no natural affinity with the CDU majority party in Germany and had, within its left wing, MPs who were not known for their affection for Germany. Whilst Wilson was forthright in his opposition to German access to nuclear weapons, what he said merely repeated Labour's manifesto commitment and, in any event, had the support of the British public and most, if not all, of the international community. His 'error', as such, was to sound openly hostile at a time when Britain needed German support for sterling and when government assessments indicated that future developments in Europe could best be shaped by Britain and Germany in alliance. In practice, however,

Wilson was too pragmatic a politician to allow either his personal feelings or the extreme views held by some members of his party to dictate British policy towards Germany, as the Germans themselves quickly assessed, and as the controversy over the appointment of Herbert Blankenhorn as German Ambassador in early 1965 demonstrated (see Chapter 1). Wilson was under considerable pressure from the moment he became Prime Minister, not least to ensure electoral survival. With a party deeply divided over membership of the EEC, and with his own lingering attachment to the Commonwealth and Britain's world role, it is hardly surprising that he was also cool towards Germany's aspiration of a united Europe. Despite such differences, the official record suggests that Wilson and his ministers moved to improve institutional contacts with their German opposite numbers, and accepted Stewart's advice on the importance of Germany to Britain's longer-term interests.[4]

An immediate challenge to Labour's approach to Anglo-German relations arose from the requirement to agree nuclear sharing arrangements within NATO. The Party was committed to renegotiate the Nassau agreement and opposed the MLF. Although Britain acknowledged that NATO's non-nuclear members should have a greater say in Alliance nuclear strategy, this was only insofar as it would not lead to German control over nuclear weapons nor impede an agreement with the Soviet Union on non-proliferation. The problem for Wilson and his ministers was how to satisfy these concerns, maintain Britain's nuclear status but convince left-wing critics that the opposite was the case, and retain German goodwill. By the time Britain launched its ANF proposals, however, in what should be seen as a ploy to kill off the MLF, President Lyndon Johnson had already lost interest in the MLF concept and the German government was split on the question. For Bonn, however, an overt commitment to the MLF remained necessary, both to increase the pressure for a solution to NATO's nuclear sharing problem and to serve as a bargaining chip in non-proliferation negotiations. Nevertheless, the change of heart by the American President, confirmed during Wilson's visit to Washington in December 1964, effectively spelled the end of a hardware solution to NATO nuclear sharing.

Britain's ANF proposals therefore served their purpose. In addition, they enabled Wilson to claim the renegotiation of Nassau, demonstrated a commitment to non-proliferation whilst maintaining Britain's nuclear status, and helped ensure that Germany was denied access to nuclear weapons. They also increased pressure on, and bought time for, the United States to come forward with an alternative solution to nuclear sharing. In most ways, the NPG concept was the ideal answer for the non-nuclear members of the Alliance, since it gave them direct participation in the planning of NATO's nuclear strategy. Ultimately, the final word on NATO's nuclear sharing arrangements rested with the United States, but Britain's role was important in supporting the need for Germany and other non-nuclear powers to be involved in nuclear decisions, and in encouraging the United States towards the NPG option. For these reasons, NATO's nuclear sharing problem never had an adverse effect upon Anglo-German relations.

The severest test for bilateral relations between Britain and Germany was posed by the dispute over the exchange costs of the BAOR, particularly in the period up to 1967. To some extent the Labour government talked itself into a corner, by condemning the agreement with the Germans entered into by its Conservative predecessors and then by consistently threatening troop withdrawals unless its demands for more money were met. As the dispute unfolded, Britain's position relied increasingly on bluff, since the costs of moving troops and their support facilities back to Britain would have far exceeded the exchange burden incurred by maintaining the BAOR in Germany. This was also well understood by the Germans. Despite extravagant claims made in Parliament, asserting that exchange costs had been largely offset, ministers and their officials were well aware that certain elements in the agreements, such as civil purchases, would have been made anyhow and in that sense were dubious to say the least. Moreover, Britain was committed by treaty to maintain troops at prescribed levels and was not entirely free to make unilateral reductions to the BAOR.

Nevertheless, threats of troop reductions had a certain potency, especially when linked to comparable action by the United States and, in that context, were a perfectly legitimate tactic in order to squeeze concessions from the Germans. Even though the Germans were sensitive to any weakening of the guarantee about their security, it would have made little sense for either Britain or the United States to engage in troop reductions on any significant scale without reciprocity from the Soviet Union, and at a time when NATO was formally about to adopt a flexible strategy based on strong conventional forces. For Britain, there was an urgent need to reduce pressure on the balance of payments account and this was a primary factor in the tactics adopted during the offset negotiations with the Germans. However, once the declaration had been made during 1967 to seek membership of the EEC, a softening in Britain's approach to the offset negotiations became clearly discernible. From this point, the exchange costs of the BAOR as an issue assumed far less urgency, as Britain sought to demonstrate its European credentials and to cultivate good relations with the Germans. The offset problem was an aspect of the bilateral relationship where differences did emerge between London and Bonn, and where the potential existed for considerable harm. However, agreement was always reached on offset payments and the BAOR remained largely undisturbed throughout the period as an important part of NATO forces in Germany. The German government did not share the view that the bilateral understanding with Britain was somehow damaged. As Kurt Kiesinger's staff commented in 1967, 'the exchange costs negotiations ... have not so far had any significant effect on Anglo-German relations'.[5]

Considerations of EEC entry were a major factor in Britain's attitude towards the Harmel study conducted during 1967 by NATO member states. If the period up to this point had been marked by differences between Britain and Germany over the exchange costs of the BAOR, Harmel turned out to be an opportunity for both governments to co-operate at a crucial point in NATO's existence. It was an opportunity not wasted by either side. For Britain, working closely with Germany to steer the work of the key sub-group dealing with East–West relations and the German problem, Harmel was seen as a chance to earn goodwill and to demonstrate a commitment to Europe having, during the study, made the formal announcement of the intention to seek membership of the EEC. The Germans, on the other hand, came to regard Harmel as crucial to their *Ostpolitik* aspirations, and saw in it the means to harness Alliance diplomacy in the search for a solution to the divisions within Europe. As Helmut Schmidt was to put it, 'the impelling motive of our Eastern operation was the recognition that security through deterrence is only one essential element of stabilizing the framework of international relations and that security through lessening tension is a supplementary one, no less essential'.[6]

The fact that the Harmel report was produced at all can be seen as the successful conclusion of efforts by members of the Alliance to overcome the challenge by France mounted against the viability of NATO as an instrument of *détente*. The outcome of the Harmel study can be considered as rather more than a compromise, in that all NATO members, including France, accepted that the Alliance, in addition to its military role, would play a more active role in the management of East–West relations. Moreover, Harmel showed that Alliance members were receptive, and could respond, to pressure from public opinion and, in so doing, guaranteed that NATO would remain an effective instrument for Alliance solidarity. The principal players in this episode of NATO's political development were the United States and France. Nevertheless, Britain and Germany played important supporting roles and, just as they had done during the trilateral offset negotiations, in creating the NPG as the answer to

NATO's nuclear sharing problem and when agreeing a more flexible approach to NATO nuclear strategy, showed that they could work together to reach mutually acceptable outcomes. Harmel might not have been one of the more eye-catching examples of Alliance politics, but it was another positive factor in the relationship between Britain and Germany during the 1960s.

The agreement on a revised nuclear strategy, reached in December 1967 by NATO members, was the culmination of an attempt by the United States to persuade its European allies to accept that, in an era of nuclear stalemate between the superpowers, a defence strategy based purely on a massive nuclear retaliation in the event of a Soviet attack, of a conventional nature, lacked credibility. On the other hand, there was broad recognition among the European members of NATO that the United States would not risk nuclear devastation in their defence, and that a more realistic balance had to be set between the use of conventional and nuclear forces. In that sense, the NATO strategy of flexible response represented a compromise between the increased conventional capability that the United States wished to see deployed in support of the deterrent, and the level of forces that European members of the Alliance were prepared to countenance.

Britain and Germany shared similar concerns about flexible response. Whilst both governments accepted the need for sufficient conventional forces to deal with minor incursions, both insisted that NATO must continue to rely on nuclear escalation in the event of a large-scale attack, conventional or nuclear. The Germans in particular, given their exposed position, were extremely sensitive about a strategy that envisaged either extended conflict on German soil or ceding territory to an aggressor, and argued that nuclear deterrence was the only viable strategy. In the event, MC 14/3 provided for a range of options should deterrence fail and, although both British and German ministers continued to hold reservations about its viability, the revised strategy was regarded as the best compromise that could be reached. The exchanges within NATO about nuclear strategy, especially the guidelines for the use of tactical nuclear weapons that were agreed by the NPG in November 1969, revealed a high degree of understanding and co-operation between British and German representatives. In that sense, NATO proved to be a fruitful arena for Anglo-German relations. As Ambassador Frank Roberts in his annual report for 1967 put it, 'close agreement on the whole complex of questions associated with NATO ... left broadly no discordant note in Anglo-German relations'.[7]

The Labour government in 1964 brought with it a strong commitment to counter the spread of nuclear weapons. The challenge it faced, however, was how to dispose of the MLF, retain Britain's nuclear capability whilst denying the same prospect to other European states, particularly to the Germans, and convince its left wing that it was serious about non-proliferation. The ANF seemingly fulfilled all these requirements, but must be regarded more as a political fix, designed to fudge Labour's pre-election commitments on nuclear weapons. The reality was that it never could have served as the road map leading to a global NPT. For one thing, the Soviet Union made it abundantly clear that any form of MLF involving Germany would be unacceptable and would bar progress towards an agreement on non-proliferation. For another, the British government's real intentions could be judged by the fact that, soon after it launched the ANF proposal, plans were announced to present at the ENDC a draft global treaty on non-dissemination of nuclear weapons.

In practice, however, although Britain's status as a nuclear power ensured that it would be involved in the crafting of an NPT, the leading roles were played by the United States and the Soviet Union. Two important difficulties had to be overcome: how to close the door to proliferation and allow for a solution to the NATO nuclear sharing problem, especially one acceptable to Germany; and how to implement a safeguard regime that would gain international acceptance, including by the Soviet Union, and incorporate a role for EURATOM. The success of the NPG, and particularly the acceptance of it by Germany, as the answer to NATO nuclear sharing arrangements, and a compromise regime so that the IAEA and EURATOM safeguards could be reconciled, were measures that facilitated final agreement on the NPT. Britain's part in these proceedings was strongly influenced by its intention to join the European Communities, including EURATOM, and its strategy of maintaining a good relationship with Germany. It was a factor that, in 1969, led to the signature of the treaty by Germany, admittedly committed by then to a more dynamic *Ostpolitik*, and it was helpful in fostering Anglo-German relations. As Wilson and his ministers agreed 'we ... played a leading part in negotiating the NPT and in urging others to sign and ratify it'.[8]

There can be little doubt that Europe in its broadest sense had a profound impact upon the bilateral relationship between Britain and Germany. For Labour ministers, the unequivocal message from their advisers was that Europe would become increasingly important to Britain's role in the world; for Germany, an integrated Europe would offer the best prospect of ending the divisions of the past. From the outset, the Labour government adopted a dual approach towards Germany and its *Ostpolitik*, such as it was at the time: firstly, to encourage a more flexible attitude by the Germans towards their neighbours to the east; and secondly, to strengthen a relationship through which it could influence German policy in ways conducive

to Western interests. In these ways, tension in East–West relations would be eased and progress towards a peaceful settlement in
Europe could be realised. Of immediate importance was the need
to persuade the Germans to abandon the Hallstein doctrine and to
accept that reunification could be realised only through a *détente* with
the Soviet Union. Whilst it needed the appearance of the Grand
Coalition, and particularly the involvement of Willy Brandt, to bring
much-needed flexibility, and confidence, in *Ostpolitik*, Germany could
always work on the basis that it had British support. This was an
important consideration for Bonn, in that Britain was well placed to
act as an interlocutor between the superpowers and to advocate its
peaceful intentions in Moscow.

The logic of Britain's approach to *Ostpolitik* came into even sharper
focus once Wilson's government formally announced its intention to
seek membership of the European Communities. German goodwill
would be an important factor if Britain's application were to succeed.
In other words, and this was a point well appreciated by the Germans,
Britain could be relied upon to support its *Ostpolitik* and would expect
in return German support for its bid to join Europe. The linkage
between *Ostpolitik* and Britain's approach towards Europe remained
a continuous thread in British foreign policy, even after the membership bid failed and the Labour government was removed from power.
The conclusion that can be drawn from this assessment is that the
future development of Europe, as a major factor in Britain's foreign
policy objectives and as the focus of *Ostpolitik*, was the essential reason
why, during the period 1964–70, Britain and Germany were increasingly drawn closer together, and why it was in both their interests to
ensure that those differences that did arise were not allowed to mar
their relationship.

In October 1964, in the early days of its new government, Britain's
future relationship with Europe appeared uncertain. In reality,
however, the economic and political advantages that had motivated
Britain's first EEC application were no less compelling, and if there
was to be a realignment of foreign policy priorities in the light of
Britain's dire economic circumstances, and as withdrawal from east
of Suez became increasingly inevitable, then a place at the heart of
Europe would best serve as Britain's new role in the world. Initially,
Wilson offered few clues as to his thinking about Britain's future. He
undoubtedly regretted any diminution of Britain's status as a world
power and any weakening of the Commonwealth, but he appreciated
from an early stage that, by not engaging more fully with Europe,
Britain ran the risk not only of being isolated but also of missing the
opportunity to ensure that the EEC developed in ways conducive to
British interests. The Labour government can be criticised for its late

conversion to Europe, but that would be to ignore the problems faced by its Prime Minister in ensuring electoral survival and of managing a party badly split on the issue.

Once electoral survival had been assured, the decision could be made to seek membership of the European Communities. Labour's tactics were to demonstrate that Britain was committed to Europe and to enlist German support for its application. Whilst the first of these policies would always be difficult to fulfil given Britain's traditional links with the United States, ministers could point to Britain's role within and support for NATO, and to its active part in securing a *détente* with the Soviet Union, as evidence of a strong interest in the future of Europe. As to German support, this would always be on the condition that Germany would do nothing that would undermine its relationship with France or damage the EEC. The validity of Britain's strategy can be judged by the fact that it remained unaltered even after the resignation of President Charles de Gaulle and despite the election defeat in 1970 of Wilson's government. The official record shows that ministers were frustrated by the lack of progress with Britain's EEC application and that, on occasion, this spilled over into relations with Germany, but it was also recognised that, despite de Gaulle's intransigence, pressure for Britain's entry into the EEC had to be maintained. Both London and Bonn had a strong interest in British membership of the EEC and this was of overriding importance in Anglo-German relations at the time.

In an article on Brandt's visit to London in March 1970, *The Times* commented that 'Britain and Germany have often in the past twenty years not known quite how to take one another'.[9] As the chapters in this book have shown, there was considerable scope during the period 1964–70 for misunderstanding and irritation between the two governments, but they have also demonstrated that this was never allowed to undermine or halt their genuine attempt to put the past behind them. This finding has to be put alongside the doubts about the relationship expressed by some scholars, for example that 'those who believe that Anglo-German relations grew "progressively better" from the creation of West Germany in 1949 to the end of the Cold War, simplify reality'.[10] It should also be considered in the light of recent assessments of public opinion in the 1960s and the people-to-people problem still believed to exist.[11] Nevertheless, in circumstances where each government believed it was in its interest to have the support of the other, and worked to ensure cooperation was achieved, it can be reasonably concluded that, during the period 1964–70 at least, and despite their differences of opinion in some areas, at the political level a close relationship existed between Britain and Germany across a range of complex issues. Britain and Germany may not have shared a special relationship, as in the widely accepted sense of the expression, but the understanding that did exist was designed to serve the political and economic interests of both countries. For Britain, the principal objective was a new role in the world, as a prominent European power but one maintaining strong links with the United States and the Commonwealth. For Germany, the ultimate goal was to overcome the divisions in Europe, with a united Germany at its heart. By the end of the 1960s, both countries could look forward with some confidence to the future, with NATO more firmly established as the guarantor of European security, with discernible improvement in East–West *détente* and with Europe on the threshold of an important step towards further political and economic integration.

Notes

1 Michael Stewart, *Life and Labour: An Autobiography* (1980), p. 163.
2 See for example Klaus Larres, 'Introduction' in Klaus Larres (ed.), *Uneasy Allies: British–German Relations and European Integration since 1945* (Oxford, 2000), p. 1.
3 'Glanzvollen Empfang für die britische Königin', *Westfalen Zeitung*, 19 May 1965, p. 1.
4 Memorandum by Michael Stewart, 'Policy Towards Germany', 5 August 1965, C(65) 119, CAB 129/122 (Pt 2), PRO.
5 'Stand der deutsch–britischen Beziehungen', end September 1967, B136/3045, 20, BA Koblenz.
6 Schmidt, 'Germany in the Era of Negotiations', p. 46.
7 Roberts to Secretary of State, 'Germany: Annual Review for 1967', 3 January 1968, RG 1/1, FCO 33/91, PRO.
8 Conclusions of a Cabinet meeting, 11 December 1969, CC (69) 60, CAB 128/44 (Pt 2), PRO.
9 'Herr Brandt in London', *The Times*, 28 February 1970, p. 7.
10 Young, 'West Germany', p. 173.
11 Ramsden, *Don't Mention the War*, p. 417.

Appendix 1

The Future Tasks of the Alliance – Report of the Council

Final communiqué of the North Atlantic Council, Brussels, 13–14 December 1967, at which the Harmel report was approved. Taken with permission from the NATO on-line library, http://www.nato.int/docu/comm/49-95/c671213b.htm (last accessed May 2007).

1. A year ago, on the initiative of the Foreign Minister of Belgium, the governments of the fifteen nations of the Alliance resolved to *'study the future tasks which face the Alliance, and its procedures for fulfilling them in order to strengthen the Alliance as a factor for durable peace'*. The present report sets forth the general tenor and main principles emerging from this examination of the future tasks of the Alliance.

2. Studies were undertaken by Messrs Schutz, Watson, Spaak, Kohler and Patijn. The Council wishes to express its appreciation and thanks to these eminent personalities for their efforts and for the analyses they produced.

3. The exercise has shown that the Alliance is a dynamic and vigorous organization which is constantly adapting itself to changing conditions. It also has shown that its future tasks can be handled within the terms of the Treaty by building on the methods and procedures which have proved their value over many years.

4. Since the North Atlantic Treaty was signed in 1949 the international situation has changed significantly and the political tasks of the Alliance have assumed a new dimension. Amongst other developments, the Alliance has played a major part in stopping Communist expansion in Europe; the USSR has become one of the two world super powers but the Communist world is no longer monolithic; the Soviet doctrine of *'peaceful co-existence'* has changed the nature of the confrontation with the West but not the basic problems. Although the disparity between the power of the United States and that of the European states remains, Europe has recovered and is on its way towards unity. The process of decolonisation has transformed European relations with the rest of the world; at the same time, major problems have arisen in the relations between developed and developing countries.

5. The Atlantic Alliance has two main functions. Its first function is to maintain adequate military strength and political solidarity to deter aggression and other forms of pressure and to defend the territory of member countries if aggression should occur. Since its inception, the Alliance has successfully fulfilled this task. But the possibility of a crisis cannot be excluded as long as the central political issues in Europe, first and foremost the German question, remain unsolved. Moreover, the situation of instability and uncertainty still precludes a balanced reduction of military forces. Under these conditions, the Allies will maintain as necessary, a suitable military capability to assure the balance of forces, thereby creating a climate of stability, security and confidence. In this climate the Alliance can carry out its second function, to pursue the search for progress towards a more stable relationship in which the underlying political issues can be solved. Military security and a policy of détente are not contradictory but complementary. Collective defence is a stabilizing factor in world politics. It is the necessary condition for effective policies directed towards a greater relaxation of tensions. The way to peace and stability in Europe rests in particular on the use of the Alliance constructively in the interest of détente. The participation of the USSR and the USA will be necessary to achieve a settlement of the political problems in Europe.

6. From the beginning the Atlantic Alliance has been a co-operative grouping of states sharing the same ideals and with a high degree of common interest. Their cohesion and solidarity provide an element of stability within the Atlantic area.

7. As sovereign states the Allies are not obliged to subordinate their policies to collective decision. The Alliance affords an effective forum and clearing house for the exchange of information and views; thus, each of the Allies can decide its policy in the light of close knowledge of the problems and objectives of the others. To this end the practice of frank and timely consultations needs to be deepened and improved. Each Ally should play its full part in promoting an improvement in relations with the Soviet Union and the countries of Eastern Europe, bearing in mind that the pursuit of détente must not be allowed to split the Alliance. The chances of success will clearly be greatest if the Allies remain on parallel courses, especially in matters of close concern to them all; their actions will thus be all the more effective.

8. No peaceful order in Europe is possible without a major effort by all concerned. The evolution of Soviet and East European policies gives ground for hope that those governments may eventually come to recognize the advantages to them of collaborating in working towards a peaceful settlement. But no final and stable settlement in Europe is possible without a solution of the German question which lies at the heart of present tensions in Europe. Any such settlement must end the unnatural barriers between Eastern and Western Europe, which are most clearly and cruelly manifested in the division of Germany.

9. Accordingly the Allies are resolved to direct their energies to this purpose by realistic measures designed to further a détente in East–West relations. The relaxation of tensions is not the final goal but is part of a

long-term process to promote better relations and to foster a European settlement. The ultimate political purpose of the Alliance is to achieve a just and lasting peaceful order in Europe accompanied by appropriate security guarantees.

10. Currently, the development of contacts between the countries of Western and Eastern Europe is mainly on a bilateral basis. Certain subjects, of course, require by their very nature a multilateral solution.

11. The problem of German reunification and its relationship to a European settlement has normally been dealt with in exchanges between the Soviet Union and the three Western powers having special responsibilities in this field. In the preparation of such exchanges the Federal Republic of Germany has regularly joined the three Western powers in order to reach a common position. The other Allies will continue to have their views considered in timely discussions among the Allies about Western policy on this subject, without in any way impairing the special responsibilities in question.

12. The Allies will examine and review suitable policies designed to achieve a just and stable order in Europe, to overcome the division of Germany and to foster European security. This will be part of a process of active and constant preparation for the time when fruitful discussions of these complex questions may be possible bilaterally or multilaterally between Eastern and Western nations.

13. The Allies are studying disarmament and practical arm control measures, including the possibility of balanced force reductions. These studies will be intensified. Their active pursuit reflects the will of the Allies to work for an effective détente with the East.

14. The Allies will examine with particular attention the defence problems of the exposed areas e.g. the South-Eastern flank. In this respect the present situation in the Mediterranean presents special problems, bearing in mind that the current crisis in the Middle East falls within the responsibilities of the United Nations.

15. The North Atlantic Treaty area cannot be treated in isolation from the rest of the world. Crises and conflicts arising outside the area may impair its security either directly or by affecting the global balance. Allied countries contribute individually within the United Nations and other international organizations to the maintenance of international peace and security and to the solution of important international problems. In accordance with established usage the Allies or such of them as wish to do so will also continue to consult on such problems without commitment and as the case may demand.

16. In the light of these findings, the Ministers directed the Council in permanent session to carry out, in the years ahead, the detailed follow-up resulting from this study. This will be done either by intensifying work already in hand or by activating highly specialized studies by more systematic use of experts and officials sent from capitals.

17. Ministers found that the study by the Special Group confirmed the importance of the role which the Alliance is called upon to play during the coming years in the promotion of détente and the strengthening of

peace. Since significant problems have not yet been examined in all their aspects, and other problems of no less significance which have arisen from the latest political and strategic developments have still to be examined, the Ministers have directed the Permanent Representatives to put in hand the study of these problems without delay, following such procedures as shall be deemed most appropriate by the Council in permanent session, in order to enable further reports to be subsequently submitted to the Council in Ministerial Session.

Appendix 2

A Declaration on Europe

The British–Czechoslovak Declaration on Europe, below, is taken from file FO 371/188501, PRO.

1. Affairs of Europe must be conducted in accordance with the purposes and principles of the UN Charter. There is a broad tradition which is shared by all and it can only be to the advantage of all to build upon shared experiences and to recognise common interests. There is not least a common interest in survival.

2. The prosperity of Europe and the welfare of its citizens requires bilateral and general co-operation in economic, social and cultural matters. It is clear that there is today a greater popular understanding than ever before of the need to overcome the barriers impeding such co-operation, to avoid wasteful competition and to recognise the necessity of solidarity of mankind as a whole. It is the duty of all the Governments concerned to respond to this.

3. Security in Europe, as elsewhere in the world, requires that the relations between states should be conducted in accordance with the principles and purposes of the United Nations Charter. There must be respect for the sovereign equality and territorial integrity of states of peoples. There must be non-intervention in the internal affairs of others. International agreements must be carried out in good faith. There must be recognition of the duty to refrain from the threat or use of force in any manner inconsistent with the purposes of the UN Charter. Any disputes and difficulties which arise must be settled by peaceful means.

4. The stability of Europe requires a Solution of the situation in Central Europe with due regard to the purposes and principles of the United Nations and in accordance with justice and the wishes of the peoples concerned.

5. In the pursuit of prosperity, security, and stability in Europe the efforts of Governments will be greatly supported by an informed public opinion convinced that the aim of policy is the welfare of the peoples in accordance with justice and equity. Public opinion will be the more convinced if

it is satisfied that in the pursuit of these aims Governments are making progress, even on a limited basis, wherever progress is possible.

6. Therefore in formulating their policies towards each other, the Governments concerned should be guided by the following principles and objectives which are both interconnected and mutually reinforcing, and which are necessary to the peace and prosperity of Europe and to ensuring its proper role in the world community of nations:

    (i)   Agreements on a limited basis should be sought in fields of activity where the common interest is clear, in order to prepare the way for more far-reaching accords;

    (ii) To help raise the living standards throughout Europe and to permit the more efficient use of resources, all the states concerned should seek to improve and extend their economic relationships – should keep constantly in review their trading and economic policies so that these may produce the greatest mutual advantage, they should seek actively to develop international standards and agreed systems of measurement and calibration. It should be their special concern to identify and overcome those obstacles to closer economic co-operation which arise from differences in their various economic systems;

    (iii) In the interest of mutual understanding which depends upon the exchange of experiences and ideas, wider contacts should be encouraged by Governments at all levels;

    (iv) In Europe, as elsewhere, all economically-advanced states whatever their political structure, should recognise a common responsibility to co-operate in helping, to the best of their ability, to solve the economic, social, and technological problems which face the developing countries of the world;

    (v) The resort to force must be renounced as a means of settling any existing disputes or any disputes which may arise in the future;

    (vi) There must be a vigorous search for progress on measures of arms control and disarmament, with general and complete disarmament under effective international control as the final objective.

7. Every Government subscribing to this Declaration declares its intention to be guided by these principles and objectives and affirms its intention to work for the prosperity, security, and stability of Europe. To this end it also declares its willingness to develop scientific, technical, and cultural co-operation, believing that in this fashion it is possible to help realise individually and in partnership each country's human and material potential. It will also seek to promote the best possible commercial and economic relations with the other states subscribing to the Declaration, and in particular to consider arrangements for economic consultation and the exchange of views and information in this and other fields in whatever form seems most convenient in each particular case.

Bibliography

Place of publication is London unless otherwise specified.

Primary sources

Unpublished
The following series of documents at The National Archives, Public Record Office, Kew:

CAB 21 Cabinet Office: Registered Files.
CAB 128 Cabinet: Minutes.
CAB 129 Cabinet: Memoranda.
CAB 130 Cabinet: Miscellaneous Committees, Minutes and Papers.
CAB 133 Cabinet Office: Conferences and Ministerial Visits, Minutes and Papers.
CAB 134 Cabinet Office: Minutes and Papers.
CAB 148 Cabinet Office: Defence and Overseas Policy Committees and Sub-committees, Minutes and Papers.
CAB 151 Cabinet Office: Disarmament Committee, Minutes and Papers.
CAB 165 Cabinet Office: Ministerial Committee on Europe, Minutes and Papers.

DEFE 5 Ministry of Defence: Chiefs of Staff Committee, Memoranda.
DEFE 7 Ministry of Defence: Registered Files.
DEFE 13 Ministry of Defence: Private Office, Registered Files.
DEFE 19 Ministry of Defence: Non-Proliferation, Minutes and Papers.
DEFE 24 Ministry of Defence: Defence Secretariat, Registered Files.
DEFE 25 Ministry of Defence: Chief of Defence Staff, Registered Files.

EW 5 Department of Economic Affairs: External Relations Division, Registered Files.
EW 8 Department of Economic Affairs: Registered Files.

FCO 10 Foreign and Commonwealth Office: Political Departments, General Correspondence.
FCO 20 Foreign and Commonwealth Office: Common Market Department, Registered Files.
FCO 28 Foreign and Commonwealth Office: Political Departments, Registered Files.

FCO 30 Foreign and Commonwealth Office: Political Departments, Registered Files.
FCO 33 Foreign and Commonwealth Office: Political Departments, Registered Files.
FCO 41 Foreign and Commonwealth Office: Political Departments, Registered Files.
FCO 66 Foreign and Commonwealth Office: Political Departments, General Correspondence.

FO 371 Foreign Office: Political Departments: General Correspondence.
FO 800 Foreign Office: Various Ministers' and Officials' Papers.
FO 1108 Foreign Office: United Kingdom Delegation to European Communities, General Correspondence.

PREM 13 Prime Minister's Office: Correspondence and Papers 1964–1970.

T 236 Treasury: Overseas Finance Division, Registered Files.

The following series of documents at the Politisches Archiv des Auswärtigen Amts, Berlin:

B20 EWG, Beitritt Großbritannien:
Band 1496 – January 1968 to October 1968.

B31 Länderreferat IA5, Großbritannien:
Band 272 – January 1964 to December 1964.
Band 285 – January 1965 to December 1965.
Band 288 – January 1965 to December 1965.
Band 298 – January 1966 to December 1966.
Band 299 – January 1966 to December 1966.
Band 306 – January 1966 to December 1966.
Band 307 – January 1967 to December 1967.
Band 369 – January 1968 to December 1971.
Band 370 – January 1968 to December 1971.

The following series of documents at the Bundesarchiv, Koblenz:

B136 Bundeskanzleramt Band 3: Aktengruppe 1.
4762 Band 2: 1966–67 (television and radio interviews).

B136 Bundeskanzleramt Band 5: Aktengruppe 3.
3040 Band 15: 1965–66 (foreign policy).
3044 Band 19: 1967 (foreign policy).
3045 Band 20: 1964–67 (foreign policy).
3068 Band 31: 1967 (foreign policy).
3120 Band 15: 1965–67 (NATO).
3126 Band 4: 1964–70 (NATO).
3133 Band 1: 1962–65 (stationing costs).
3134 Band 2: 1965–69 (stationing costs).
3135 Band 1: 1963–67 (stationing costs).
3136 Band 2: 1967–69 (stationing costs).
3137 Band 3: 1969–70 (stationing costs).
6822 Band 1: 1961–69 (defence policy).
6900 Band 4: 1967–68 (armaments).
6901 Band 5: 1968 (armaments).
6902 Band 6: 1968 (armaments).

6903 Band 7: 1968–69 (armaments).
6904 Band 8: 1969 (armaments).
6915 Band 1: 1962–67 (international armaments).

Nachlässe und Persönliche papiere in Bundesarchiv (Koblenz)
N1351: Personal papers of Herbert Blankenhorn, German Ambassador, London –
(1965–69).
190: 1966.
206: 1966–70.

The following newspapers at the Stadtarchiv, Höxter:

Westfalen Zeitung – various editions between 1965 and 1970.

The following documents at the Churchill College Archive Centre:

Personal papers of Michael Stewart – British Foreign Secretary 1965–66, 1968–70.
STWT 7/1/9 – International briefing: Labour's foreign policy 1964–70.
STWT 14/1/9 – Press cuttings 1–30 July 1965.
STWT 14/1/13 – Press cuttings 1–26 November 1965.
STWT 14/1/22 – Includes Anglo-German relations.
STWT 12/3/8 – Speeches and lectures 1970–78.
STWT 9/7/29 – Labour Policy Coordinating Committee, June 1969–May 1970.

Personal papers of Sir Frank Roberts – British Ambassador, Bonn 1963–68.
Box 2 – Personal file 1963–1968, Bonn.

Published
*Documents on British Policy Overseas, Series III. Volume I: Britain and the Soviet Union,
1968–72* (1997).

Foreign Relations of the United States
1961–63:
Volume VIII: *National Security Policy* (Washington, DC, 1996).
Volume XIII: *West Europe and Canada* (Washington, DC, 1994).

1964–68:
Volume XI: *Arms Control and Disarmament* (Washington, DC, 1997).
Volume XIII: *Western Europe Region* (Washington, DC, 1995).
Volume XV: *Germany and Berlin* (Washington, DC, 1999).

Akten zur Auswärtigen Politik der Bundesrepublik Deutschland
1964–70 (München, 1995, 1996, 1997, 1998, 1999, 2000 and 2001).

Oberländer, Gisela (ed.). *Dokumente zur Deutschlandpolitik*, Bundesministerium für
Innendeutsche Beziehungen (Frankfurt am Main, 1984).

Parliamentary Debates (*Hansard*), House of Commons.
Parliamentary Debates (*Hansard*), House of Lords.

NATO on-line archives (www.nato.int/archives/):
Report of the Committee of Three on Non-Military Cooperation in NATO.
The Future Tasks of the Alliance (Report of the Council/Harmel report).

Government publications
Statement on the Defence Estimates 1965, Cmnd 2592.
Statement on the Defence Estimates 1966, Cmnd 2901.
Statement on the Defence Estimates 1967, Cmnd 3203.
Supplementary Statement on Defence Policy 1967, Cmnd 3357.
Statement on the Defence Estimates 1968, Cmnd 3540.
Statement on the Defence Estimates 1969, Cmnd 3927.

Secondary sources

Autobiographies, memoirs and diaries
Ball, George W. *The Past Has Another Pattern: Memoirs* (1982).
Benn, Tony. *Out of the Wilderness: Diaries 1963–67* (1987).
Benn, Tony. *Office Without Power: Diaries 1968–72* (1989).
Brandt, Willy. *People and Politics: The Years 1960–1975* (1978).
Brandt, Willy. *My Life in Politics* (1992).
Callaghan, James. *Time and Chance* (1987).
Castle, Barbara. *The Castle Diaries 1964–70* (1984).
Crossman, Richard. *The Diaries of a Cabinet Minister: Volume 1: Minister of Housing 1964–66* (1976).
Crossman, Richard. *The Diaries of a Cabinet Minister: Volume 2: Lord President of the Council and Leader of the House of Commons 1966–68* (1976).
Crossman, Richard. *The Diaries of a Cabinet Minister: Volume 3: Secretary of State for Social Services 1968–70* (1977).
Healey, Denis. *The Time of My Life* (1990).
Jenkins, Roy. *A Life at the Centre* (1991).
Macmillan, Harold. *Riding the Storm 1956–1959* (1971).
Macmillan, Harold. *Pointing the Way 1959–1961* (1972).
Macmillan, Harold. *At the End of the Day 1961–1963* (1973).
Pearce, Robert (ed.) *Patrick Gordon Walker: Political Diaries 1932–1971* (1991).
Stewart, Michael. *Life and Labour: An Autobiography* (1980).
Wilson, Harold. *The Labour Government 1964–1970: A Personal Record* (1971).

Books
Aldous, Richard and Lee, Sabine (eds). *Harold Macmillan: Aspects of a Political Life* (1999).
Alford, B. W. E. *British Economic Performance, 1945–1975* (Cambridge, 1993).
Ash, Timothy Garton. *In Europe's Name: Germany and the Divided Continent* (1993).
Balfour, Michael. *Germany: The Tides of Power* (1992).
Beckerman,Wilfred (ed.). *The Labour Government's Economic Record: 1964–1970* (1972).
Bluth, Christoph. *Britain, Germany and Western Nuclear Strategy* (Oxford, 1998).
Brivati, Brian and Jones, Harriet (eds). *From Reconstruction to Integration: Britain and Europe since 1945* (1993).
Brown, Chris. *Understanding International Relations* (1997).
Cairncross, Alec. *Managing the British Economy in the 1960s: A Treasury Perspective* (1996).
Cairncross, Alec and Eichengreen, Barry. *Sterling in Decline: The Devaluations of 1931, 1949 and 1967* (Oxford, 1983).
Cleveland, Harlan. *NATO: The Transatlantic Bargain* (New York, 1970).
Cohen, Warren I. and Bernkopf Tucker, Nancy (eds). *Lyndon Johnson Confronts the World: American Foreign Policy 1963–1968* (Cambridge, 1994).

Craig, F. W. S. (ed.). *Conservative and Labour Party Conference Decisions 1945–1981* (Chichester, 1982).

Craig, F. W. S. (ed.). *British General Election Manifestos 1959–1987* (Aldershot, 1990).

Daddow, Oliver, J. (ed.). *Harold Wilson and European Integration: Britain's Second Application to Join the EEC* (2003).

Darwin, John. *Britain and Decolonisation: The Retreat from Empire in the Post-war World* (1988).

Dewey, Peter. *War and Progress: Britain 1914–1945* (1997).

Dickie, John. *Inside the Foreign Office* (1992).

Dockrill, Saki (ed.). *Controversy and Compromise: Alliance Politics Between Great Britain, the Federal Republic of Germany, and the United States of America, 1945–1967* (Bodenheim, 1998).

Dockrill, Saki. *Britain's Retreat from East of Suez: The Choice Between Europe and the World* (Basingstoke, 2002).

Europe: The Case for Going In, published for the European Movement (British Council) (1971).

Freedman, Lawrence. *The Evolution of Nuclear Strategy* (Basingstoke, 2003).

Freeman, J. P. G. *Britain's Nuclear Arms Control Policy in the Context of Anglo-American Relations, 1957–68* (1986).

Gallup, George, H. (ed.). *The Gallup International Public Opinion Polls, Great Britain 1937–1975: Volume 1 (1937–1964), Volume 2 (1965–1975)* (New York, 1976).

Gordon Walker, Patrick. *The Cabinet* (1972).

Hackett, General Sir John (and others). *The Third World War: A Future History* (1978).

Haftendorn, Helga. *Security and Détente: Conflicting Priorities in German Foreign Policy* (New York, 1985).

Haftendorn, Helga. *NATO and the Nuclear Revolution: A Crisis of Credibility, 1966–1967* (Oxford, 1996).

Hannay, David (ed.). *Britain's Entry into the European Community: Report on the Negotiations of 1970–72 by Sir Con O'Neill* (2000).

Hennessy, Peter. *Having It So Good: Britain in the Fifties* (2006).

Heuser, Beatrice. *NATO, Britain, France and the FRG: Nuclear Strategies and Forces for Europe, 1949–2000* (1997).

Holland, Robert. *The Pursuit of Greatness 1900–1979* (1991).

Jäckel, Eberhard, Longerich, Peter and Schoeps, Julius (eds). *Enzyklopädie des Holocaust. Volume 3* (München, 1998).

Jefferys, Kevin. *The Labour Party since 1945* (1993).

Johnson, Paul (ed.). *20th Century Britain: Economic, Social and Cultural Change* (1996).

Judt, Tony. *Postwar: A History of Europe since 1945* (2005).

Kaiser, Karl and Morgan, Roger (eds). *Britain and West Germany: Changing Societies and the Future of Foreign Policy* (1971).

Kelleher, Catherine McArdle. *Germany and the Politics of Nuclear Weapons* (New York, 1975).

Kettenacker, Lothar. *Germany since 1945* (Oxford, 1997).

Kissinger, Henry. *Diplomacy* (New York, 1994).

Kitzinger, Uwe. *Diplomacy and Persuasion: How Britain Joined the Common Market* (1973).

Krippendorff, Ekkehart and Rittberger, Volker (eds). *The Foreign Policy of West Germany: Formation and Contents* (1980).

Larres, Klaus (ed.). *Uneasy Allies: British–German Relations and European Integration since 1945* (Oxford, 2000).

Le Carré, John. *A Small Town in Germany* (1968).

Lee, Sabine. *Victory in Europe: Britain and Germany since 1945* (Harlow, 2001).

Marquand, David. *The Progressive Dilemma* (1991).

Moravcsik, Andrew. *The Choice for Europe: Social Purpose and State Power from Messina to Maastricht* (1998).

Morgan, Austen. *Harold Wilson* (1992).

Nicholls, A. J. *The Bonn Republic: West German Democracy, 1945–1990* (1997).

Nicholls, A. J. *Fifty Years of Anglo-German Relations: The 2000 Bithell Memorial Lecture* (2000).

Northedge, F. S. *Descent from Power: British Foreign Policy, 1945–1973* (1974).

Orlow, Dietrich. *A History of Modern Germany: 1871 to Present* (1995).

Ovendale, Ritchie (ed.). *The Foreign Policy of the British Labour Governments, 1945–1951* (Leicester, 1984).

Parkin, Frank. *Middle Class Radicalism: The Social Bases of the British Campaign for Nuclear Disarmament* (Manchester, 1968).

Paterson, Peter. *Tired and Emotional: The Life of Lord George Brown* (1993).

Paxman, Jeremy. *The English: A Portrait of a People* (1999).

Pearce, Robert (ed.). *Patrick Gordon Walker: Political Diaries 1932–1971* (1991).

Pierre, Andrew, J. *Nuclear Politics: The British Experience with an Independent Strategic Force 1939–1970* (1972).

Pimlott, Ben. *Harold Wilson* (1992).

Ponting, Clive. *Breach of Promise: Labour in Power 1964–1970* (1989).

Pulzer, Peter. *German Politics, 1945–1995* (Oxford, 1999).

Radice, Giles. *The New Germans* (1995).

Ramsden, John. *Don't Mention the War: The British and the Germans since 1890* (2006).

Reynolds, David. *Britannia Overruled: British Policy and World Power in the Twentieth Century* (1991).

Roberts, Frank. *Dealing with Dictators: The Destruction and Revival of Europe 1930–70* (1991).

Roseman, Mark. *The Villa, the Lake, the Meeting: Wannsee and the Final Solution* (2002).

Sandbrook, Dominic. *White Heat: A History of Britain in the Swinging Sixties* (2006).

Siedentop, Larry. *Democracy in Europe* (2001).

Smith, Eric Owen. *The German Economy* (Abingdon, 1994).

Stewart, Michael. *Britain and Europe* (1969).

Strange, Susan. *Sterling and British Policy: A Political Study of an International Currency in Decline* (1971).

Stromseth, Jane E. *The Origins of Flexible Response: NATO's Debate over Strategy in the 1960s* (1988).

Tomlinson, Jim. *The Labour Governments 1964–1970, Volume 3: Economic Policy* (Manchester, 2004).

Trachtenberg, Marc. *A Constructed Peace: The Making of the European Settlement, 1945–1963* (Chichester, 1999).

Urwin, Derek W. *The Community of Europe: A History of European Integration since 1945* (1991).

Vital, David. *The Making of British Foreign Policy* (1968).

Von Beyme, Klaus (ed.). *Die großen Regierungserklärungen der deutschen Bundeskanzler von Adenauer bis Schmidt* (München, 1979).

Wallace, William. *The Foreign Policy Process in Britain* (1975).

White, Brian. *Britain, Détente and Changing East–West Relations* (1992).

Young, John W. (ed.). *The Foreign Policy of Churchill's Peacetime Administration 1951–1955* (Leicester, 1988).

Young, John W. *Britain: And the World in the Twentieth Century* (1997).

Young, John W. *Britain and European Unity 1945–1999* (2000).

Young, John, W. *The Labour Governments 1964–1970. Volume 2: International Policy* (Manchester, 2003).

Ziegler, Philip. *Mountbatten: The Official Biography* (1985).

Ziegler, Philip. *Wilson: The Authorised Life of Lord Wilson of Rievaulx* (1993).

Zimmermann, Hubert. *Money and Security: Troops, Monetary Policy, and West Germany's Relations with the United States and Britain, 1950–1971* (Cambridge, 2002).

Journal articles

Ahonen, Pertti. 'Franz-Josef Strauss and the German Nuclear Question, 1956–1962', *Journal of Strategic Studies*, 18, 2 (June 1995), pp. 25–51.

Albert, E. H. 'Bonn's Moscow Treaty and Its Implications', *International Affairs*, 47, 2 (April 1971), pp. 316–326.

Barman, Thomas. 'Britain, France and West Germany: The Changing Pattern of Their Relationship', *International Affairs*, 46, 2 (1970), pp. 269–279.

Baylis, John. 'NATO strategy: the case for a new strategic concept', *International Affairs*, 64 (1988), pp. 43–59.

Beaufre, André. 'The Sharing of Nuclear Responsibilities: A Problem in Need of Solution', *International Affairs*, 41, 3 (July 1965), pp. 411–419.

Berger, Stefan and Lilleker, Darren G. 'The British Labour Party and the German Democratic Republic During the Era of Non-recognition, 1949–1973', *Historical Journal*, 45, 2 (June 2002), pp. 433–458.

Blackett, P. M. S. 'Thoughts on British Defence Policy', *New Statesman*, 5 December 1959, pp. 783–790.

Boulton, J. W. 'NATO and the MLF', *Journal of Contemporary History*, 7, 3–4 (July–October 1972), pp. 275–294.

Bozo, Frédéric. 'Détente Versus Alliance: France, the United States and the Politics of the Harmel Report (1964–1968)', *Contemporary European History*, 7, 3 (November 1998), pp. 343–360.

Brandt, Willy. 'Détente Over the Long Haul', *Survival*, 9, 10 (October 1967), pp. 310–312.

Brandt, Willy. 'German Policy Towards the East', *Foreign Affairs*, 46, 3 (April 1968), pp. 476–486.

Buchan, Alastair. 'The Multilateral Force: A Study in Alliance Politics', *International Affairs*, 40, 4 (1964), pp. 619–637.

Bull, Hedley. 'International Theory: The Case for a Classical Approach', *World Politics*, 18 (1966), pp. 361–377.

Cairncross, Alec. 'From the Treasury Diaries of Sir Alec Cairncross: Four Anglo-French Conflicts 1967–8', *Contemporary European History*, 6, 1 (1997), pp. 117–131.

Callenius, Hans Walter. 'Die Deutschlandpolitik der britischen Labour-Regierung', *Deutsche Aussenpolitik*, 10, 2 (1965), pp. 1061–1072.

Craig, Gordon, A. 'Die Chequers Affäre von 1990: Beobachtungen zum Thema Presse und internationale Beziehungen', *Vierteljahreshefte für Zeitgeschichte*, 39 (1991), pp. 611–623.

Dobson, Alan. 'The Years of Transition: Anglo-American Relations 1961–1967', *Review of International Studies*, 16 (1990), pp. 239–258.

Dockrill, Saki. 'Britain's Power and Influence: Dealing with Three Roles and the Wilson Government's Defence Debate at Chequers in November 1964', *Diplomacy and Statecraft*, 11, 1 (March 2000), pp. 211–240.

Dockrill, Saki. 'Forging the Anglo-American Global Defence Partnership: Harold Wilson, Lyndon Johnson and the Washington Summit, December 1964', *Journal of Strategic Studies*, 23, 4 (December 2000), pp. 107–129.

Duckwitz, Georg Ferdinand. 'Truppenstationierung und Devisenausgleich', *Aussen Politik: Zeitschrift für internationale Fragen*, 18 (1967), pp. 471–475.

Dumbrell, John. 'The Johnson Administration and the British Labour Government: Vietnam, the Pound and East of Suez', *Journal of American Studies*, 30 (1996), pp. 211–231.

Epstein, Leon D. 'The Nuclear Deterrent and the British Election of 1964', *Journal of British Studies*, 5, 2 (May 1966), pp. 139–163.

Fielding, Jeremy. 'Coping with Decline: US Policy Towards the British Defense Reviews of 1966', *Diplomatic History*, 13 (1999), pp. 633–656.

Foschepoth, Josef. 'British Interest in the Division of Germany after the Second World War', *Journal of Contemporary History*, 21 (1981), pp. 391–411.

Foster, William C. 'New Directions in Arms Control and Disarmament', *Foreign Affairs*, 43, 4 (July 1965), pp. 587–601.

Frey, Cynthia W. 'Meaning Business: The British Application to Join the Common Market, November 1966–October 1967', *Journal of Common Market Studies*, 6, 3 (March 1968), pp. 197–230.

Gordon Walker, Patrick. 'The Labor Party's Defense and Foreign Policy', *Foreign Affairs*, 42, 3 (April 1964), pp. 391–398.

Greenwood, Sean, 'Frank Roberts and the "Other" Long Telegram: The View from the British Embassy in Moscow, March 1946', *Journal of Contemporary History*, 25 (1990), pp. 103–122.

Healey, Denis. 'British Defence Policy: A Lecture Given at the Royal United Services Institute (RUSI) on 22 October 1969', *Royal United Services Journal*, 656 (1969), pp. 15–22.

Healey, Denis. 'On European Defence', *Survival*, 11, 4 (April 1969), pp. 110–115.

Healey, Denis. 'NATO, Britain and Soviet Military Policy', *Orbis*, 13, 1 (spring 1969), pp. 48–58.

Hitchens, Christopher. 'Say What You Will About Harold', *London Review of Books*, 2 December 1993, pp. 7–9.

Hughes, R. Gerald. '"We Are Not Seeking Strength for Its Own Sake": The British Labour Party, West Germany and the Cold War, 1951–64', *Cold War History*, 3, 1 (October 2002), pp. 67–94.

Jones, Matthew. 'A Decision Delayed: Britain's Withdrawal from South East Asia Reconsidered, 1961–1968', *English Historical Review*, 472 (June 2002), pp. 569–595.

Kiesinger, Kurt. 'German Foreign Policy', *Survival*, 9, 2 (February 1967), pp. 47–49.

Kunz, Diane. 'Lyndon Johnson's Dollar Diplomacy', *History Today*, 42 (1992), pp. 45–51.

Lee, Sabine. 'Perception and Reality: Anglo-German Relations During the Berlin Crisis 1958–1959', *German History*, 13, 1 (1995), pp. 47–69.

Mackintosh, John P. 'Britain in Europe: Historical Perspective and Contemporary Reality', *International Affairs*, 45, 2 (April 1969), pp. 246–258.

Maloney, Sean M. 'Berlin Contingency Planning: Prelude to Flexible Response, 1958–63', *Journal of Strategic Studies*, 25, 1 (March 2002), pp. 99–134.

McNamara, Robert. 'The Western Debate: The American Conclusions', *Survival*, 4, 5 (September–October 1962), pp. 194–200.

Merkl, Peter H. 'The German Janus: From Westpolitik to Ostpolitik', *Political Science Quarterly*, 89 (winter 1974–winter 1975), pp. 893–824.

Morgan, Kenneth O. 'The Labour Party's Record in Office: The Wilson Years 1964–70', *Contemporary Record*, 3, 4 (April 1990), pp. 22–25.

Morgan, Roger. 'Washington and Bonn: A Case Study in Alliance Politics', *International Affairs*, 47, 3 (July 1971), pp. 489–502.

Northedge, F. S. 'Britain as a Second-Rank Power', *International Affairs*, 46 (1970), pp. 37–47.

Ritterhausen, Johannes R. B. 'The Postwar West German Economic Transition from Ordoliberalism to Keynesianism', Institut für Wirtschaftspolitik an der Universität zu Köln discussion paper 2007/1 (January 2007). Available at www.iwp.uni-koeln.de/DE/Publikationen/dp/dp1_07.pdf (last accessed May 2007).

Rosenbach, Harald. 'Die Schattenseiten der "Stillen Allianz": Der deutsch-britische Devisenausgleich 1958–1967', *Vierteljahrschrift für Sozial und Wirtschaftsgeschichte*, 85 (1998), pp. 196–231.

Schmidt, Helmut. 'Germany in the Era of Negotiations', *Foreign Affairs*, 49, 1 (October 1970), pp. 40–50.

Schrafstetter, Susanna and Twigge, Stephen. 'Trick or Truth? The British ANF Proposal, West Germany and US Nonproliferation Policy, 1964–68', *Diplomacy and Statecraft*, 11, 2 (July 2000), pp. 161–184.

Schröder, Gerhard. 'Germany Looks at Eastern Europe', *Foreign Affairs*, 44, 1 (October 1965), pp. 15–25.

Schwarz, Hans-Peter. 'Adenauer und die Kernwaffen', *Vierteljahrshefte für Zeitgeschichte*, 37 (1989), pp. 567–593.

Sommer, Theo. 'Bonn Changes Course', *Foreign Affairs*, 45, 3 (April 1967), pp. 477–491.

Stewart, Michael. 'Britain, Europe and the Alliance', *Foreign Affairs*, 48, 4 (1970), pp. 648–659.

Vital, David. 'Double-Talk or Double-Think? A Comment on the Draft Non-Proliferation Treaty', *International Affairs*, 44, 3 (July 1968), pp. 419–433.

Von Hassel, Kai-Uwe. 'Détente Through Firmness', *Foreign Affairs*, 42, 2 (January 1964), pp. 184–194.

Von Hassel, Kai-Uwe. 'Organizing Western Defense: The Search for Consensus', *Foreign Affairs*, 43, 2 (January 1965), pp. 209–216.

Wright, Jonathan. 'The Role of Britain in West German Foreign Policy since 1949', *German Politics*, 5, 1 (April 1996), pp. 26–42.

Young, John W. 'The Wilson Government and the Davies Peace Mission to North Vietnam, July 1965', *Review of International Studies*, 24 (1998), pp. 545–562.

Zimmermann, Hubert. '… they have got to put something in the family pot!: The Burden-Sharing Problem in German–American Relations 1960–1967', *German History*, 14, 3 (1996), pp. 325–346.

Zimmermann, Hubert. 'The Sour Fruits of Victory: Sterling and Security in Anglo-German Relations During the 1950s and 1960s', *Contemporary European History*, 9, 2 (2000), pp. 225–243.

Book chapters

Böhmer, Katharine. '"We Too Mean Business": Germany and the Second British Application to the EEC, 1966–67', in Oliver J. Daddow (ed.), *Harold Wilson and European Integration: Britain's Second Application to Join the EEC* (2003), pp. 211–226.

Byrne, Paul. 'Pressure Groups and Popular Campaigns', in Paul Johnson (ed.), *20th Century Britain: Economic, Social and Cultural Change* (1996), pp. 442–459.

Costagliola, Frank. 'Lyndon B. Johnson, Germany, and "the End of the Cold War"', in Warren I. Cohen and Nancy Bernkopf Tucker (eds), *Lyndon Johnson Confronts the World: American Foreign Policy 1963–1968* (Cambridge, 1994), pp. 173–210.

Deighton, Anne. 'British–West German Relations, 1945–1972', in Klaus Larres (ed.), *Uneasy Allies: British–German Relations and European Integration since 1945* (Oxford, 2000), pp. 27–44.

Deighton, Anne. 'The Labour Party, Public Opinion and the "Second Try" in 1967', in Oliver J. Daddow (ed.), *Harold Wilson and European Integration: Britain's Second Application to Join the EEC* (2003), pp. 39–55.

Frankel, Joseph. 'The Intellectual Framework of British Foreign Policy', in Karl
    Kaiser and Roger Morgan (eds), *Britain and West Germany: Changing Societies
    and the Future of Foreign Policy* (1971), pp. 81–103.
Howlett, Peter. 'The Golden Age 1955–1973', in Paul Johnson (ed.), *20th Century
    Britain: Economic, Social and Cultural Change* (1996), pp. 320–339.
Lee, Sabine. 'Pragmatism Versus Principle? Macmillan and Germany', in Richard
    Aldous and Sabine Lee (eds), *Harold Macmillan: Aspects of a Political Life* (1999),
    pp. 113–130.
Young, John W. 'West Germany in the Foreign Policy of the Wilson Government,
    1964–67', in Saki Dockrill (ed.), *Controversy and Compromise: Alliance Politics
    between Great Britain, Federal Republic of Germany, and the United States of America,
    1945–1967* (Bodenheim, 1998), pp. 173–195.

Newspaper articles
Ash, Timothy Garton. 'The Chequers Affair', *New York Review of Books*, 27
    September 1990, p. 65.
Ivory, William. 'My Father the Hero', *Times Magazine*, 2 February 2002, pp. 51–52.
McKinstry, Leo. 'Which Decade Really Swung?', in 'Times Books' supplement to
    The Times, 5 August 2006, p. 10.
Riddell, Peter. 'Not Quite a Poodle, Not Quite a Bulldog', *The Times*, 4 February
    2002, p. 12.
Sandbrook, Dominic. 'Put Him in His Place', in 'The Blair Years 1997–2007' sup-
    plement to *The Observer*, 8 April 2007, p. 49.
Wavell, Stuart. 'Apartheid in the UK? They're Having a Genetic Joke', *Sunday
    Times News Review*, 23 July 2006, p. 7.

Unpublished material
Easter, David. Unpublished thesis, 'British Defence Policy in South East Asia and
    the Confrontation 1960–66', University of London (1998).

Lecture notes
Lecture by Sir Michael Quinlan (Permanent Under-Secretary of State, Ministry
    of Defence), 'NATO Nuclear Philosophy', at the Royal College of Defence
    Studies, 26 October 1982.

Correspondence
Rt Hon Lord Callaghan of Cardiff, KG (Chancellor of the Exchequer 1964–67;
    Home Secretary 1967–70).

Interviews
Sir Roger Jackling, son of Sir Roger Jackling (deceased), British Ambassador
    (1968–72) to the Federal Republic of Germany, on 21 June 2002.
Sir Michael Palliser, former Private Secretary (1966–68) to Harold Wilson, on
    6 August 2001.
Sir Andrew Stark, former Head of Chancery, British Embassy, Bonn (1964–68),
    on 10 December 2001.
Mr J. H. Adam Watson, Assistant Under-Secretary at the Foreign Office, and co-
    rapporteur for sub-group1 of the Harmel study, on 29 May 2001.
Sir Oliver Wright, former Private Secretary (1964–66) to Harold Wilson, on
    8 January 2002.

Index